D0937032

WITHDRAWN

The Roman City of
LONDON

The Roman City of
LONDON

RALPH MERRIFIELD

LONDON
ERNEST BENN LIMITED

FIRST PUBLISHED 1965 BY ERNEST BENN LIMITED
BOUVERIE HOUSE · FLEET STREET · LONDON · EC4
© RALPH MERRIFIELD 1965

PRINTED IN GREAT BRITAIN

Foreword

THE PURPOSE OF the present volume is to provide an account of Roman London for the general reader, including a guide for the visitor, and also to summarise what is known of this subject for those with a more specialised interest in the history and topography of the City of London. This summary is necessarily brief, but a reference is given to the source of information, published or unpublished, in the case of each find, so that the student will know where to look for further details. Its scope is limited to the walled city of Londinium and its immediate environs, and does not include Roman remains to the south of the Thames or west of the Fleet.

The story of the gradual accumulation of this information over many years is told in Chapter I, and the author is indebted to all the workers mentioned therein, each of whom has made his contribution to the sum total of our knowledge, usually in difficult and frustrating conditions. He owes a special debt, however, to those who have generously made available to him information in advance of their own publication of it: to Professor W. F. Grimes for certain measurements and other details not yet published: to Messrs. G. C. Dunning and F. Cottrill for kindly lending plans and excavation notes of their pre-war investigations, and to the Society of Antiquaries of London for permitting the use of this material: to the Corporation of London for the use of the archives of Guildhall Museum: to Messrs. Adrian Oswald, I. Noel Hume and the author's present colleagues at the Museum for supplementing these records with additional information from their personal knowledge and recollections. He is also very grateful to Mr. Norman Cook, Keeper of Guildhall Museum, for his encouragement and valuable advice, to Mr. Peter Marsden for his constant help and co-operation, and to Dr. J. P. C. Kent of the British Museum for his kind assistance in numismatic and historical matters.

The author is particularly indebted to Mr. E. A. Chambers, the cartographer, for his highly skilled and patient work on the map.

In addition, acknowledgement is gratefully made to the following for help in various special fields: Professor J. M. C. Toynbee, Professor Sir Ian Richmond, Dr. D. J. Smith, Dr. G. A. Webster and Messrs. V. Bicknell, F. J. Collins, B. R. Hartley, K. Marshall and D. J. Turner.

The author would also like to express his gratitude to the following institutions for kindly supplying photographs, or for permitting him to photograph and use their copyright material: the British Museum, the London Museum, the Ashmolean Museum, Guildhall Museum, Guildhall Library, the Soprintendenza alle Antichità in Rome, the National Geographic Magazine, the Revue Archéologique, the Bank of England, the National Provincial Bank, the Roman and Mediaeval London Excavation Council, the Worshipful Company of Goldsmiths and the Warburg Institute.

Finally, thanks are due to the author's wife for her invaluable assistance as secretary, indexer and critic, and for her tolerance during the preparation of this book.

Contents

MAP

Plates

FOLLOWING PAGE 164

1 London in the second century, *reconstruction by A. Sorrell.*
2 London in the third century, *reconstruction by A. Sorrell.*
3 London in the third century, *reconstruction by R. W. Nicholson.*
4 Portion of tombstone of Classicianus, as found in 1852.
5 Portion of tombstone of Classicianus, as found in 1935.
6 Tombstone of Classicianus, the Procurator, reconstructed.
7 Writing-tablet with procuratorial stamp, and label, Walbrook.
8 Roof-tile with stamp P P BR LON, Leadenhall Street.
9 Memorial to the wife of a slave of the province, Ludgate Hill.
10 Stamped silver ingot, early fifth century, Tower of London.
11 Corroded mass of coins of the late third century, Newgate Street.
12 Barbarous coins of late third-century hoard, Newgate Street, after cleaning.
13 Gold medallion commemorating the arrival of Constantius Chlorus at London in A.D. 296.
14 Coins of the London Mint, A.D. 288–325 (1–15) and 383–8 (16). 1, 2, Carausius: 3, 4, Allectus: 5, Diocletian: 6, Constantine I as Caesar: 7, 8, Constantine I as Augustus: 9, Licinius I: 10, Crispus as Caesar: 11, Constantine I: 12, Constantine II as Caesar: 13, Constantine I: 14, Constantine II as Caesar: 15, Helena: 16, Magnus Maximus (gold solidus).
15 Section, St. Swithin's House, Walbrook, showing Roman tessellated floor, mediaeval chalk floor and seventeenth-century tiled floor.
16 Roman foundations supporting mediaeval walls and eighteenth-century walls, Minster House, Martin Lane.
17 Roman building revealed by the mechanical grab, Newgate Street.
18 Ancient stream-bed, Newgate Street.
19 Roman planking attached to piles, probably the revetment of a stream-bank, St. Mary-le-Bow church.

74 Marble sculptures and stone vessel in temple of Mithras, Walbrook (as found.)
75 Marble hand of Mithras, holding sacrificial knife, from temple of Mithras, Walbrook.
76 Marble head of Serapis, from temple of Mithras, Walbrook.
77 Marble figure of Mercury, from temple of Mithras, Walbrook.
78 Marble head of Mithras, from temple of Mithras, Walbrook.
79 Dioscurus in oolite, found near temple of Mithras, Walbrook.
80 Bacchus with Silenus, satyr, maenad and panther, in marble, from temple of Mithras, Walbrook.
81 Silver strainer or infuser and container, from temple of Mithras, Walbrook.
82 Lid of silver container of infuser, from temple of Mithras, Walbrook.
83 Decoration round wall of silver container from temple of Mithras, Walbrook. (*Periphotograph.*)
84 Marble relief of Mithras killing the bull, found in Walbrook in 1889.
85 Marble figure of river god, found in Walbrook in 1889.
86 Altar of Diana from Goldsmiths' Hall.
87 Figure of Atys (?) from Bevis Marks.
88 Mother-Goddesses found near St. Olave Hart Street.
89 Silver plaque representing mother-Goddesses, found in Moorgate.
90 Bronze head of Hadrian, from the Thames near London Bridge.
91 Bronze fore-arm from well, Seething Lane.
92 Bronze figure of archer, found in Queen Street.
93 Capital with sculptured faces, found re-used as building material in Camomile Street bastion.
94 Sculpture of lion attacking a deer, found re-used as building material in Camomile Street bastion.
95 Figure of soldier, found re-used as building material in Camomile Street bastion.
96 Tombstone of soldier of Second Augustan Legion, from Ludgate Hill.
97 Bronze helmet of legionary soldier, found in London, probably in the Thames.
98 Spearhead with centurial inscription, found in well, Bucklersbury House, Walbrook.

Line Drawings in Text

Note:
Numbers in bold type (e.g. **123**) refer to entries in
the Gazetteer (pp. 189–325) and the large map at
the back.

TO THE MEMORY OF

ALBERT THOMAS MERRIFIELD

WHO LOVED THE CITY OF LONDON

★

CHAPTER ONE

Archaeology in the City of London

THE SITE OF an ancient city is often marked by a hillock or
mound, in the Middle East called a *tell*, that is of purely artificial origin. Its development is due mainly to the following
causes: life in cities is dependent on material brought from
outside, and much of this is of a durable character – especially,
of course, building material; moreover, since human beings
avoid unnecessary work, once it has been brought into the city,
it is seldom taken out again, even when it becomes useless, for
the disposal of refuse by removal is a very recent development.
The ruins of a building destroyed by fire or natural decay are
therefore hardly ever cleared away completely, but are merely
levelled to provide a new surface on which its successor can be
built. This process continued over many centuries produces a
sizeable mound, in which the successive levels of occupation
lie one above the other in order of age, with the oldest at the
bottom. The City of London stands on such a *tell*, but as it has
been in existence for less than two thousand years, its vertical
growth can hardly be compared with, for example, that of
Jericho, where five and a half millennia of occupation have
left a mound nearly fifty feet high. Nevertheless, in London
the earliest Roman ground level lies in places eighteen
feet beneath the modern street level, and the mound on which
the modern City stands would be more obvious if it had not
been partially submerged by the waters of the Thames, which
at high tide are about fourteen feet higher in relation to the land
than they were in early Roman times. This change in water level
has also contributed to the burial of the earlier surfaces, for the
flooding of low-lying areas as the land sank made it necessary
to dump on them great quantities of material in order to raise
the ground level above the water, and so maintain occupation.

The fact that the Londons of the past lie buried beneath the modern streets of the City was realised as early as the time of Stow, who records the discovery in 1595 of a 'fair pavement like unto that above ground' fifteen feet deep at the corner of Bread Street and Cheapside. He also noted that all was made ground to a depth of more than seventeen feet, and commented 'thus much hath the ground of this City in that place been raised from the main'.[1]

The antiquaries of the seventeenth and eighteenth centuries, however, were for the most part more interested in the finds of Roman burials in the outlying parts of the City than in the remains of the Roman town itself, which were less easily understood, and usually provided few relics that were complete enough to grace a collector's cabinet. A unique opportunity for investigation came when the mediaeval city was swept away by fire in 1666, and a great deal of Roman London must have come to light in the subsequent rebuilding. Sir Christopher Wren, however, as 'Surveyor-General and principal Architect for rebuilding the whole city', had more important things to think about, though fortunately a few of his observations concerning finds of Roman remains have been recorded.[2] These include not only the burials and kilns found on the site of St. Paul's, but also the Roman street on which the foundations of the tower of St. Mary-le-Bow were laid – the earliest record of the discovery of a Roman street in London – and the great building in Bush Lane, which was then believed to be the governor's palace and the basilica, and is in fact almost certainly a public building of some kind. Occasionally ancient topographical features were noted, especially when they caused difficulties in building, like the stream-bed under St. Lawrence Jewry.

Roman remains of many kinds came to light between the late eighteenth and mid-nineteenth centuries during excavations for sewers. These were normally laid along the middle of the modern streets, and the discovery of Roman buildings in the lines of Lombard Street, Leadenhall Street, Lothbury and Gresham Street showed that the modern street plan had no obvious relationship with that of the Roman city.[3] Some of the walls encountered presented formidable obstacles to the excavators, and occasional notes were made on sewer plans which have since proved useful to archaeologists. There was, however, also a considerable amount of genuine antiquarian interest by various 'curious gentlemen' of the time, such as A. J. Kempe, W. Herbert and others, whose accounts, published mostly in *Archaeologia* and the *Gentleman's Magazine*, have proved of lasting value, although the precise positions of the Roman structures which they observed are seldom recorded.

The outstanding personality among the nineteenth century antiquaries was Charles Roach Smith, a City pharmacist, who pursued his researches into Roman London with a single-minded devotion which made him the great pioneer of this subject. A youthful interest in Roman coins and other antiquities acquired during his apprenticeship at Chichester was revived by the exciting discoveries which were being made in the sewer excavations of London, although his working hours, from 6 a.m. to 8 p.m., in the service of a wholesale druggist in Snow Hill, for several years gave him little opportunity to pursue his hobby. Fortunately, in 1834 he was able to buy his own business in Lothbury, and this flourished to the extent that he could afford an assistant. From this time he was an assiduous watcher of sewer and building excavations in the City, and an enthusiastic collector of antiquities found by the workmen. Another fruitful source of material for his collection was the gravel and silt dredged from the bed of the Thames when the channel was deepened on the site of Old London Bridge between 1834 and 1841. This was spread on the river bank further upstream, and many coins, bronze figurines and other objects were found in the gravel which had been dumped along the towing path between Hammersmith and Barnes.

Roach Smith was constantly at loggerheads with the City authorities, who disapproved of his intrusions at excavations and resented his reiterated demands that the City itself should do something about its antiquities. In particular, he urged that a City museum should be established for their preservation. A proposal to this effect had been considered by the Court of Common Council in 1824, but nothing came of it, although some antiquities from the site of the Old General Post Office were acquired. Two of the four or five large private collections from sewer excavations were offered to the Corporation, but without success, and were subsequently broken up and sold by auction. It was not until the rebuilding of the Royal Exchange in 1841 that an important group of antiquities was acquired by the Corporation.[4] An ante-room of Guildhall Library was then fitted up as a museum to house the Roman objects from this site. In the meantime, Roach Smith, in despair of persuading the Corporation to accept its responsibilities, determined to form his own Museum of London Antiquities. He was compelled to move from Lothbury in 1840, because his house was due to be demolished – the occasion of another row with the Corporation, who were his ground landlords. He then went to much larger premises in Liverpool Street, and here was able to display his collection and make it available to scholars. When he published his catalogue in 1854, the Museum contained more than a thousand specimens, half of which were Roman.[5] Soon afterwards it was sold to the British Museum for £2000, and Roach Smith himself retired to Strood in Kent, where he found a new interest in fruit-growing. His great work on Roman London, *Illustrations of Roman London*, was written in the early years of his retirement and published in 1859. The material in this and in his contributions to periodicals such as *Archaeologia* provided a firm base for subsequent studies in the subject.

Several leading British archaeologists have served their apprenticeship in London, and among these is the man who has been appropriately described as the father of scientific archaeology. Colonel Lane-Fox, later known as General Pitt-Rivers, recorded the excavation of pile structures in the valley of the Walbrook in 1866, without fully understanding them.[6] After his inheritance in 1880 of estates rich in archaeological remains in Dorset and Wiltshire, he was to evolve a technique of excavation with meticulous recording and careful attention to stratification. These methods have formed the basis of modern scientific archaeology, but there was no opportunity to apply them in London until eighty years after Pitt-Rivers' investigations in Copthall Avenue.

A few years later we find the City Corporation taking a much more creditable part in the preservation and recording of its antiquities. When Queen Victoria Street was being constructed in 1869, a fine mosaic pavement was found between Bucklersbury and Poultry, and was reported to the London and Middlesex Archaeological Society. J. E. Price, an officer of the Society, took steps to secure accurate measurements and plans, and the pavement was visited by the Council of the Society, the Lord Mayor, who was one of its Vice-Presidents, and various members of the Library Committee. The Lord Mayor expressed a wish that the pavement should be acquired for the City

Museum, and with the permission of the Metropolitan Board of Works it was in due course removed by the City Architect. Before this was done, however, elaborate drawings were made by order of the Library Committee and subsequently used to illustrate Price's monograph on the subject,[7] which also contained a chromo-lithograph based on a water-colour drawing of the pavement provided by a member of the Court of Common Council (*Plate 65*). The discovery seems to have aroused exceptional interest, comparable only with that caused by the temple of Mithras in recent times, and during the three days on which the pavement was made accessible to the public before it was lifted, it was visited by more than 50,000 people (*Plate 63*). Soon after this, Guildhall Library was rebuilt with a large exhibition room for the Museum in its basement, and the mosaic pavement was set in the wall of the new Museum room.[8]

The London and Middlesex Archaeological Society continued to take an active interest in City excavations, as a result of Price's energy and enthusiasm; and the Museum at Guildhall was greatly enriched by a characteristic collection of Roman personal ornaments, shoes, tools, coins and pottery, found in or near the Walbrook stream on the site of the National Safe Deposit Company in 1872–3, and by an important group of Roman sculptured stones and architectural fragments which had been re-used as building material in the Camomile Street bastion, found in 1876. Valuable, if discursive, papers by J. E. Price on both of these sites were published as separate monographs.[9]

The excavation and publication of the Camomile Street bastion was a happy example of co-operation between the London and Middlesex Archaeological Society, the Corporation of London and the architect responsible for the development of the site. The Librarian to the Corporation was informed of the discovery of architectural fragments during the clearance of the site, and reported this to Price, who went at once to Camomile Street and found that no further excavation was intended on the site of the bastion itself, of which a considerable part of the foundation remained below the surface. The architect, W. G. Banks, agreed to continue the excavation at the expense of the London and Middlesex Archaeological Society, and allocated two or three labourers to the task, under the personal superintendence of his assistant, whose name was

Henry Hodge. The structure proved to be of great interest[10] and contained sculptures of major importance, including a figure of a Roman soldier[11] and a large head, which may be that of the Emperor Philip I.[12] The investigation continued for nearly a month, and Hodge drew detailed plans and a section of the bastion. Drawings based on these and illustrations of the finds were later prepared for publication with financial assistance from the Corporation, which also took charge of the finds. These were presented to Guildhall Museum by the free-holder through the good offices of the architect. As is nearly always the case, however, this fortunate co-operation between the several parties concerned in the affair was due mainly to the zeal of an individual. Unlike Roach Smith, John Edward Price seems to have had the useful ability to engage the interest of men whose duties might otherwise have led them to discourage his activities.

The interest in Roman London which he aroused in the architect, Henry Hodge, was to bear valuable fruit a few years later. In 1880, the old Leadenhall Market was demolished, and excavations for the new building commenced. The existence of a large Roman structure on this site was known from the discovery of a massive wall near Half Moon Passage in 1848, and observations of the new excavations were made by E. P. Loftus Brock, who reported his finds to the British Archaeological Association and exhibited a series of plans, which he never published, and which are now lost.[13] Fortunately, a plan, a perspective drawing, showing both Roman and mediaeval remains on the site, and a number of beautifully executed scale drawings of details of the Roman structures by Henry Hodge have survived, and are now in Guildhall Library. (See *Plates* 48–50.) This valuable series of archaeological documents forms the basis of our knowledge of London's great basilica.[14] The most astonishing fact of all is that this London architect, at a date when scientific archaeology was scarcely in its Wessex cradle, should have carefully recorded in neat water-colour drawings the ancient strata which were sealed beneath the mediaeval foundation arches. A study of these in conjunction with subsequent observations, and perhaps with other finds yet to come, may one day give us the key to the sequence of events in the history of the basilica, which is of the greatest importance for research into the development of Roman London.[15]

The last fifteen years or so of the nineteenth century seem to have been a bad period for the archaeology of the City. There are relatively few records of finds of Roman remains, and of these only two or three are recorded with any precision. The barrenness of this period is a reminder of the dependence of our studies on a few enthusiastic individuals, who made it their business to keep a watch on building sites and to follow up any rumour of an interesting discovery. It is a sobering thought that an excavation took place in Walbrook in 1889, almost certainly on the site of the temple of Mithras, and from it came a rich haul of antique marble sculptures. These were acquired by James Smith, an East End dealer, who eventually sold three of them (which may or may not be the whole of the group) to W. Ransom, a private collector, without of course imparting precise, and therefore incriminating, information about their provenance.[16] As a result, strong doubts were felt concerning their genuineness as antiquities of Roman Britain, and it was suspected that they belonged to the large series of classical sculptures imported to this country in the last three hundred years. Only the discovery of similar imported works of art in Italian marble in a scientifically dated context in the Temple of Mithras in 1954, immediately adjacent to a foundation laid about 1889, has finally cleared them of this suspicion. (See *Plates* 84–5.) It is difficult to imagine that a find of such importance would have escaped the notice of Roach Smith or Price, if either had been active at this period.

Soon after the turn of the century, however, a new and better era began, thanks to the partnership of two antiquaries, Dr. Philip Norman and Francis W. Reader, who now took a keen interest in London finds and maintained a constant watch on building excavations in the City until the First World War. Their full and admirably illustrated reports appeared mainly in *Archaeologia*[17] and set an example of prompt and detailed publication which few of their successors have been able to follow. Much of our knowledge of the Roman city wall is derived from these important papers. Philip Norman, already well known for his topographical books and water-colours, does not seem to have been drawn to the study of Roman London until he was nearly sixty, and his active work in the physically difficult conditions which prevail on building sites continued until he was seventy-three, when the war brought most building operations in the City to an end. Thirteen years later, as a very old man, he was to serve with Francis Reader on the committee appointed by the Royal Commission on Historical Monuments to make an inventory of Roman monuments found in London.

Reader had already contributed an important section on the Roman city wall to an earlier publication which is a landmark in the study of Roman London. This was Volume I of the *Victoria County History of London*, published in 1909. It also contained contributions by two officials of the British Museum – Reginald A. Smith of the Department of British and Mediaeval Antiquities, on the subject of burials and roads, with conclusions that are no longer acceptable; and a topographical index, with plans, and notes on Roman pottery found in London, by H. B. Walters of the Department of Greek and Roman Antiquities.

Philip Norman seems to have been directly responsible for the adoption of a more active policy towards the investigation of building sites by the Corporation of London, through the instrumentality of the staff of Guildhall Museum – a policy which has since been followed as consistently as circumstances would allow. The last site with which Norman was personally concerned was apparently that of the old General Post Office on the east side of St. Martin's-le-Grand. Early in 1914 the contractors had excavated a great quadrilateral cavity twenty-two feet deep, in the bottom of which could be seen the lower portions of numerous rubbish pits, with their fillings intact. Norman obtained the permission of the General Post Office for the excavation of these, and successfully applied to the Court of Common Council and to the Goldsmiths' Company, whose Hall adjoins the site, for funds to carry out the work. Guildhall Museum, which had always been administered by the Librarian and his staff as a side-line, at last had a full-time official, who, although designated only by the somewhat undignified title of Museum Clerk, was responsible under the Librarian for the curatorial work of the Museum. Frank Lambert, the holder of this post, was to become Director of the Liverpool Art Gallery and in due course President of the Museums Association, but for a number of years his talents were at the service of City archaeology. He was now permitted by the Guildhall Library Committee to supervise the excavation of the Roman rubbish pits in St. Martin's-le-Grand, and the following year produced a useful report on their contents and those of similar pits on another site in King William Street.[18] His study of the pottery from these excavations led him to investigate the distribution throughout the City of various closely datable types of pottery, in an attempt to throw light on the development of Londinium[19] – a line of research which was later pursued by T. Davies Pryce.[20] When building was resumed in 1919 after the break of the war years, Lambert again found time amid his other duties to observe building sites in the neighbourhoods of London Wall and King William Street, and published his finds in 1921 in considerable detail, in the best tradition of Norman and Reader.[21]

Another museum with an interest in Roman London had appeared, however, and two of its Keepers were later to dominate the archaeological scene in London and to make outstanding contributions to the study of the Roman city. In 1911, through the initiative and generosity of the late Viscount Esher and the late Viscount Harcourt, a collection of objects representing the life and history of London from the earliest times to the present day was brought together at Kensington Palace to form the nucleus of the London Museum. Two years later, Stafford House, formerly the town house of the Dukes of Sutherland, was presented by Viscount Leverhulme to the nation for the purpose of housing this collection, and was renamed Lancaster House. The London Museum was concerned with the whole of Greater London, whereas the interest of Guildhall Museum was limited to the City. Since the City was practically the whole of London – apart from Westminster and Southwark – until Tudor times, the two museums were inevitably in competition for Roman and mediaeval antiquities, and in the early days of the London Museum the rivalry was not always very friendly.

A dealer named G. F. Lawrence, long remembered as 'Stony Jack' by London workmen, was active in the City in this period, and collected a great many important antiquities by the time-honoured but questionable method of visiting building sites and purchasing them from the labourers who found them. This is not strictly legal, since all antiquities found on a site are the property of the owner of the freehold, unless they happen to be treasure trove, when they are normally the property of the Crown. In the City of London, however, treasure trove can be claimed by the Corporation under the terms of a Charter granted by Charles I, which confirms earlier rights of the City to treasure trove in the City or Southwark. By established custom the finder is rewarded the full market value of gold or silver which, after an inquest by the Coroner, is declared to be treasure trove,[22] but he has no claim at all on any other antiquities he may find on somebody else's land. Human nature being what it is, however, in order to collect casual finds on building sites at all, it is usually necessary to come to terms with the finder. This is now done by the legal fiction that the money given is merely a reward, but its payment gives the collector no title to the object recovered, which remains the property of the ground landlord, unless he is willing to relinquish it. Fortunately the freeholds of most City properties are owned by Livery Companies or by banks and insurance companies, who are usually sufficiently public-spirited to present their antiquities to museums where they will always be accessible to the public and to scholars. In some instances, as at the Bank of England, a private site museum has been established to house some of the finds, but these also are available for purposes of research. Freelance collecting is to be deprecated, not so much because it deprives wealthy institutions of possessions which are theirs by accident, and which they do not know they own, but because it must be done in secrecy; and the objects secured are therefore lost to science, until in due course they appear in the sale-room or in a private collection without any record of the circumstances in which they were found, and often without any provenance at all. The marbles found in Walbrook in 1889, to which reference has already been made, are a typical example of this. It is, however, impossible to prevent such activities entirely, especially when the collector has an established network of useful contacts, and it may be argued that in some circumstances it is in the better interests of archaeology to make a friend of him, to ensure that his more notable acquisitions do not disappear without trace. This was evidently the view taken by the early authorities of the London Museum, and G. F. Lawrence soon became their agent, performing valuable services in helping to build up the archaeological side of the new collection. As a result important antiquities, which would otherwise have been lost, passed into public ownership with records of the circumstances of their discovery. As may be imagined, however, these activities were viewed with a somewhat jaundiced eye from the City. In more recent years the relationship between the two museums has been completely friendly, and few objects of importance from the City have been acquired by the London Museum without prior consultation with Guildhall

Museum. It was entirely through the good offices of W. F. Grimes, then Keeper of the London Museum, that Guildhall Museum acquired the magnificent collection of antiquities found on the site of Bucklersbury House, Walbrook, in 1954–5, including the valuable sculptures from the Temple of Mithras which he had himself excavated, and could easily have secured for the London Museum. The present good relations between the two museums are about to lead to actual union, for it has been decided to establish a new Museum of London which will absorb them both.[23]

The first two Keepers of the London Museum did not themselves take an active part in archaeological work in London, apart from a dramatic scene in which the first, Sir Guy Laking, escorted on horseback the Roman boat found on the site of the new County Hall on its journey from Westminster to the museum. The third Keeper, however, appointed in 1926, was one who was determined to restore to British archaeology the standards evolved by General Pitt-Rivers, and who had already demonstrated his ability to get things done by bringing to life the new National Museum of Wales at Cardiff. His name, later to become almost synonymous with archaeology in the minds of the televiewing public, was Mortimer Wheeler. He was at once plunged deeply into the study of Roman London, for the Royal Commission on Historical Monuments intended to devote a volume of their Inventory of Monuments in London to this subject, and appointed him as Honorary Secretary of the Committee that was set up for the purpose. The resulting Report,[24] published in 1928, for which Sir (then Dr.) Mortimer Wheeler was primarily responsible, brought together all the known facts relating to Roman London in a volume which has since been our standard reference work on this subject. Wheeler's Introduction was a brilliant survey which dealt with all aspects of the matter on the basis of the evidence then available. Hypotheses were boldly formulated, and although some details of these are no longer acceptable, much of the overall picture, drawn with imagination as well as scholarship, has never been superseded. Another publication by Mortimer Wheeler on Roman London, which appeared two years later, also contains a great deal that is of lasting value. This was the London Museum handbook, *London in Roman Times*, one of the admirable series of catalogues and guides which was produced for the Museum under Wheeler's Keepership.

In the meantime building operations in the City still continued, and the preparation of the Royal Commission's Report
showed how important it was to maintain constant observation
on them, and to record any ancient structures that were brought
to light. Lambert had left Guildhall Museum in 1924, and his
successor, Quintin Waddington, desperately needed some assistance. It was clearly impossible for one man to carry out the
entire curatorial work of a growing museum, and also to be
available at all times to visit building sites. Under the influence
of Lord Crawford, the Chairman of the Royal Commission on
Ancient Monuments, and Mortimer Wheeler, an attempt was
made to persuade the City Corporation to undertake definite
responsibilities for this work and to make an additional appointment for the purpose. The City Librarian compromised by
appointing a young architect named Anthony Lowther, who
was an enthusiastic amateur archaeologist, as a part-time,
unpaid volunteer observer of building sites. As the latter was at
this time in practice near the British Museum, a considerable
journey from the sites he was intended to visit, and as much of
his spare time was already devoted to the archaeology of Surrey
– a subject with which he has since always been closely associated – the arrangement fell far short of what was required; but
Lowther continued for a time to give valuable help to Waddington, purely as a voluntary service, at considerable personal
inconvenience.

Fortunately, another institution now intervened. The Society
of Antiquaries of London has world-wide interests, but to some
extent it has always had a special concern with local antiquities.
Individual Fellows of the Society had played a leading part in
the investigation of Roman London for a hundred years, and
their reports had always been welcomed for publication in the
Society's periodicals. Now, however, it was becoming clear that
amateur endeavour in the post-war world could no longer keep
pace with the work that was required, and the Society of
Antiquaries took a momentous and unprecedented step. This
was the appointment of a professional investigator of excavations in the City of London. The first holder of this office was
E. B. Birley, now Professor of Romano-British History and
Archaeology in the University of Durham. He was appointed in
1928, but his tenure was brief and he was concerned with only
one site – that of the Midland Bank in Prince's Street.[25] The
following year he was succeeded by G. C. Dunning, later to

become an Inspector of Ancient Monuments and our leading authority on mediaeval pottery. He did valuable work as the Society's investigator for five years, obtaining important evidence concerning the basilica,[26] and recording many other Roman structures in all parts of the City. He also investigated the evidence for the two great fires of Roman London, which had considerable significance in relation to the early development of the city, and later published an important paper on this subject.[27] Dunning was succeeded in 1934 by Frank Cottrill, now Curator of the Winchester Museum, who was the last investigator employed by the Society of Antiquaries. During his three years of office he recorded some interesting early Roman buildings in the area to the south of the basilica, and made notable additions to our knowledge of the city wall. As co-author with Walter Bell and Charles Spon, he helped to write a useful book on this subject, in which he was responsible for the section dealing with the Roman wall.[28] Perhaps his most valuable work, however, was the observation of a number of patches of gravel metalling which indicate the presence of Roman roadways. Evidence of this kind is easily overlooked, and great credit is due to Frank Cottrill for making a major contribution towards our scanty knowledge of the street-plan of Roman London.

Cottrill was not replaced when he left in 1937, and responsibility for the observation of building sites reverted to Guildhall Museum, still an adjunct of Guildhall Library with a single officer. In 1939, however, Waddington was given an assistant, Adrian Oswald, who was later to succeed him, and eventually became Keeper of the Department of Archaeology of the Birmingham Museum. Before the Army claimed him, when the Second World War brought archaeological investigation in the City to a close, Oswald observed an excavation for a subway in Aldersgate Street, which revealed the existence of a late Roman gate in the city wall, and also worked on the site of All Hallows Church, Lombard Street, where a complex sequence of Roman buildings came to light.

Between 1940 and 1945, a third of the City of London was destroyed by enemy action, and archaeologists were thereby presented with their greatest opportunity. The square mile of Britain that is of the greatest historical importance had hitherto revealed its archaeological secrets only in tantalising glimpses. Because its importance has endured, it has remained fully occupied, and the least possible delay has been allowed to

elapse between the destruction of a building and the erection
of its successor. There had consequently never been any opportunity to excavate for the sole purpose of gaining knowledge.
The remains of the past had come to light only when holes were
dug for new foundations or for sewers, and the most that was
ever permitted to the archaeologist was a hurried extension of
one of these holes. Even this was rare enough, and much more
frequently he was only allowed to make a brief examination of
what had been revealed by the workmen's excavation. In these
circumstances, it had never been possible fully to apply the
methods of scientific excavation which had been evolved by
General Pitt-Rivers. The German bombs had now cleared
many acres of the City, and these were likely to remain unoccupied for a number of years, so that there was at last time and
opportunity for painstaking investigation.

The most extensive area of damage lay in the western part of
the City, stretching from the Barbican to Cheapside and thence
to the river, surrounding St. Paul's with devastation except to
the south-west, and extending along the river from Blackfriars
railway bridge almost to London Bridge. Further west still,
was another bombed area between Ludgate and Holborn – of
less archaeological significance, as it lay beyond the walled city.
In the eastern part of the City, an area of devastation lay to the
west of the Tower, between Lower Thames Street and Leadenhall Street, but not extending to the west of Great Tower Street
or the northern part of Lime Street into the district that is
archaeologically the most important of all – at least to the
student of Roman London – the nucleus of early settlement
east of the Walbrook, which contained the Roman basilica.
Another extensive bombed area lay to the north of the Tower
of London, and this contained a considerable stretch of the
Roman city wall. The central part of the City to the west
of the Walbrook, like that to the east, had on the whole escaped,
except for a comparatively small area to the south and south-
west of the Mansion House, which was to prove of great
archaeological interest.

In these areas of devastation, there was now no insuperable
barrier to the unhurried, methodical excavation which was
necessary to disentangle the complex evidence left by nearly
two thousand years of occupation. This does not mean that the
task was now easy, however, for the rubble of bombed buildings
lay thickly over the ground, and beneath this were cellars,

usually with thick concrete floors. Only when a clearance had been made below these would archaeological excavation be possible.

The essential requirements were a highly skilled and experienced Director of Excavations, labour and money, and to obtain these it was necessary that some kind of organisation should be set up. The first initiative came from the Council for British Archaeology, a body which had been founded in 1943-4, with a view to co-ordinating archaeological activities, so that full advantage might be taken of the opportunities for investigation which would occur when the war ended. A letter was sent on 25 May 1944, by the C.B.A., inviting the Society of Antiquaries to undertake archaeological work in the City. No immediate action was taken, but on 26 April 1945 the Council of the Society appointed a nucleus Committee of Seven, which invited the co-operation of the City authorities. This request was at first received without enthusiasm, but after Professor (now Sir Ian) Richmond and W. F. Grimes, then Keeper of the London Museum, had been given the opportunity to put the Society of Antiquaries' case before the Improvements and Town Planning Committee, it was agreed that the Corporation should allow their Librarian to serve on the Committee. The co-operation of the Ministry of Works was similarly enlisted, and it was agreed that the Chief Inspector of Ancient Monuments should also serve on the Committee. On 21 November Mr. Grimes was appointed to supervise the initial work, but the acute shortage of labour made it impossible for him to start until the following spring.

It had been decided that some preliminary work must be undertaken with a view to defining the problems to be solved, before any public appeal could be made, and that in the meantime the work would be controlled entirely by the Society of Antiquaries, under the supervision of W. F. Grimes. The latter accordingly commenced his first excavation in the City on 25 March 1946, on a site in Billiter Avenue, financed mainly by the Society.

Two months later the interim Committee recommended that the controlling body should be enlarged, by inviting various persons to serve and institutions to send representatives, and that it should be called the *Roman London Excavation Committee*. It was also recommended that Mr. Grimes should be invited to act as its Director of Excavations. The enlarged body which was thus established held its first Annual General Meeting on 14 July 1947, when its rules were drawn up and its name established. The original name was not considered satisfactory, on the grounds that the interests of the Committee should not be limited to the Roman period, and the rather cumbersome title of *Roman and Mediaeval London Excavation Council* was adopted instead. Appeals for funds were circulated, with rather disappointing results, but various Livery Companies and other City institutions contributed, and a generous annual grant was made by the Ministry of Works. The actual excavations were carried out mainly by a small group of workmen employed for the purpose, under the direction of Mr. W. F. Grimes, later to be appointed a Professor of the University of London and Director of its Institute of Archaeology. The work continued unremittingly in all seasons and almost all weathers, with hardly a break for more than fifteen years, although Professor Grimes was able to devote only part of his time to it. This was found to be a satisfactory arrangement, as much of the work was not archaeological at all. Many laborious hours of clearance and concrete breaking were required on nearly all sites before excavation could begin, and for this only the supervision of a reliable foreman was necessary. Nevertheless, the demands of his other work soon made it necessary that Professor Grimes should have an assistant with a full knowledge of his methods and requirements, and in due course he was able to obtain one – first, the late Dr. Charles Bellerby, a trained scientist though without previous archaeological experience; and after the latter's untimely death, Mrs. Audrey Williams – now Mrs. Grimes – an experienced archaeologist who had been Curator of the Verulamium Museum. It was not considered practicable to make an extensive use of volunteer labour, although a useful group of volunteer diggers operated at week-ends for a considerable time under the leadership of Mr. George Rybot.

The most striking accomplishment of the Roman and Mediaeval London Excavation Council was the elucidation of the problem of the fortifications in the Cripplegate area. Here Professor Grimes was able to show, by a brilliant series of excavations and deductions, that an earlier fort had determined the line taken by the Roman city wall, whose curious re-entrant had always puzzled archaeologists and topographers. Once the initial clue had been given, a skilful campaign of excavation was carried out, with cuttings at points where identifiable features might be expected if the basic hypothesis were correct. In planning this, advantage was taken of the standardisation of Roman military practices, whereby a fort normally conformed to a regular pattern. As a result the hypothesis was proved beyond any possible doubt, and various details of the fort were recovered.

Other excavations yielded less definite results, and their value will probably not be fully realised until much more work has been done. The aim was to make at least one cutting on all sites that were available, and although this purpose could not be completely achieved, future archaeologists will possess a series of precisely recorded sections in many parts of the City. Ideally this work would have been followed up by area excavations, carried out by the same scientific methods, but this was quite beyond the resources of the Excavation Council. More money, time and labour would have been needed, but even if these had been available, investigation on this scale would have required a number of full-time supervisors whose skill approached that of Professor Grimes himself. The latter's work has shown very clearly the great complexity of archaeological deposits in the City, through continued use and re-use of the same ground. Earlier pits are intersected by later ones, and these in their turn may be cut by even later intrusions. The absence of good building stone in the immediate neighbourhood of London led to the extensive robbing of stone walls, which may be indicated only by robbers' trenches containing no trace of the original stone. For the same reason, many structures were wooden, and traces of these are not easily detected, except where the wood has survived in water-logged conditions. A great part of the value of the work of the Excavation Council has been the correction of false impressions received in the unfavourable conditions of building excavations, where subtle details of this kind can seldom be observed.

In the minds of the general public, however, all other achievements were overshadowed by the spectacular discovery in 1954 of the temple of Mithras with its buried works of art. This find, which brought fame and even a little fortune[29] to the Council, was one of pure chance, but this in no way diminishes the credit due to the excavator for the skill and pertinacity with which he exploited the unexpected opportunity, in circumstances made more difficult by the tremendous public interest which was aroused. The purpose of the excavation was to obtain a section across the ancient stream-bed of the Walbrook and its banks, and the place selected because it was the most free from encumbrances happened to coincide with the only important Roman building on the stream banks in this area. Moreover, there had been remarkably little disturbance in post-Roman times, so that most of the plan of the building could be recovered and its history, as revealed by the stratification, could be fully worked out. Characteristically, Professor Grimes was not diverted from his primary purpose by the discovery of this building at an early stage of the excavation, but completed the difficult task of taking his section across the deep, water-logged deposits of stream silt, before he made any further examination of the intriguing building with the rounded apse. A portion of this lay clearly visible for many weeks to passers-by in Walbrook, without attracting any particular attention. Even when the building had been identified by Professor Grimes as a basilican temple, and a report to this effect had been published in the Press, only a mild interest was taken. Then the marble head of Mithras was found, identifying with certainty the mystery cult which had been practised in the temple; *The Times* quoted Kipling, and the fat was in the fire. It soon became clear that to the long-established hazards of archaeological work in central London must be added another – that of overwhelming public interest in an age of mass communication. If you wish to see building contractors cower and property developers turn pale, you need only whisper the words 'Temple of Mithras'. To understand this it is necessary to appreciate the circumstances in which the find was made, as well as its immediate conse-quences. Professor Grimes had learnt that this large bombed site to the west of Walbrook was shortly to be developed, and had therefore selected it for his next excavation. He had excavated with permission of the site-owners, which had been given on the usual understanding that no delay would be caused to the builders, who were shortly to erect a fourteen-storey block of offices there. The deadline had almost been reached, and Professor Grimes was preparing to abandon the excavation, when the head of Mithras was found, and suddenly the full light of publicity blazed on the site. Archaeology was becoming increasingly popular under the stimulus of television and other mass-media of information, but the unveiling of an ancient mystery cult in the workaday world of the City seemed to touch a chord of imagination and romanticism in many who had never before fallen under its spell. There was immediately an overwhelming public demand for an opportunity to visit the excavation, and the site was opened for inspection each evening for nearly a week. The numbers who arrived exceeded all expectation, and the crowds were marshalled into a queue which eventually extended from Cannon Street to the Bank Station. It is estimated that 10,000 people passed through the site on the first day; on the second the number had grown to 15,000, and between 300 and 400 disappointed people had to be turned away when the site was closed at dusk. During the final week-end, the hours were extended and the site was opened from 2.30 to 6.30 p.m. On the last day, Sunday, 26 September, the queue was at one time nearly a mile long, and it is estimated that about 35,000 people were admitted, many of them after waiting for an hour and a half. Again hundreds had to be turned away when the site was finally closed.

All this was bad enough, from the point of view of the contractors and site-owners, but even more alarming, with its threat of unpredictable cost and indefinite delay, was the strong public demand that somehow the temple should be preserved. Questions were asked in the House of Commons, and the site was hurriedly inspected by Sir David Eccles, then Minister of Works. The demand was a natural one, but to those who knew the full circumstances it seemed unreasonable to hope that the temple could remain where it was. The architect's plans for the new building had of course cost a great deal to produce, and now all the complex apparatus of labour, material and machinery was assembled – also at great cost – to carry them out. The temple could not have been incorporated without such a radical alteration of the plans as would virtually have required the redesigning of the building. The unstable nature of the subsoil made it necessary to drive piles every few feet to support the structure, so that the survival of the temple intact in the middle of the building would have left a serious gap in its foundations. If all the weight had been transferred to the outside piles, the load would have been greater than the ground could carry, so that it would almost certainly have been necessary to replan the whole building to make it considerably lighter. The estimate of the cost of all this was not less than £300,000. It could hardly be expected that the owners of the site, a subsidiary company of the Legal and General Assurance Company, should bear a cost of this magnitude without compensation, and it was equally unreasonable to expect the Ministry of Works to allocate half of its total annual expenditure on the preservation of ancient monuments to this one building. The idea that the money required could be raised by public subscription was merely wishful thinking. The impossibility of obtaining such a sum in this way, in spite of the interest shown, was clearly demonstrated by the lack of response to the collecting boxes which were placed in prominent positions on the site for the benefit of the excavation fund. After more than 80,000 people had visited the temple, a total of only £250 had been raised – less than a penny per head.

To everyone's relief, Mr. A. V. Bridgland, Chairman of the Legenland Property Company, the owners of the site, suggested a sensible compromise; the Company would have the remains of the temple removed and subsequently reconstructed, at its own expense, on a neighbouring site in Queen Victoria Street. In due course this was done, and the ground-plan of the temple of Mithras, rebuilt from its original material, now lies almost unheeded on a terrace outside Temple Court (11 Queen Victoria Street) – a rather pathetic monument to a nine days' wonder. The excavation itself was, of course, of the greatest importance and interest, and from the point of view of an archaeologist the agitation had one very valuable result; it won a respite of a fortnight in which Professor Grimes was able to complete his investigation, and during which more marble sculptures were found.[30] Moreover, the decision to preserve the remains of the temple led to the removal of a nineteenth-century foundation from the north wall, revealing a unique silver box which had evidently been hidden in a secret recess there.[31] All this treasure and a great deal of additional information would have been lost, if the owners of the site had not generously permitted the fortnight's delay, at an estimated cost of about £4000. The additional cost of the removal, storage and reconstruction of the fabric of the temple was at the time estimated to be about £10,000. The owners were equally generous with the valuable finds from the site, which were presented to Guildhall Museum.

The harmful aspect of the affair was the development of the myth that a temple of Mithras or its equivalent lurked on every building site, and that archaeological investigation threatened ruin to contractors and site owners. There was even talk of insurance against the peril of encountering antiquities,[32] and the estimated losses of the Legenland Company were usually multiplied several times when the story was repeated in the City. It was useless to point to the long history of archaeological work in London, in which public interest had been aroused to an embarrassing degree on only two occasions, separated by eighty-five years: the discoveries of the Bucklersbury pavement and of the temple of Mithras, both of which were complete enough to be readily understood – a very rare occurrence in the much disturbed soil of the City of London. These fears are now, it is hoped, gradually dwindling, but in one very recent instance it proved impossible to obtain permission to excavate a promising site, which lay cleared and derelict for months, because the owner wished to sell the land, and evidently thought that archaeological discoveries might prejudice his chances. Fortunately the purchaser was more reasonable, and there was still time for a rather hurried excavation before the contractors commenced work.

Rebuilding in the City began shortly after the war, and it was clear that the Roman and Mediaeval London Excavation Council, with its very limited resources, would have no opportunity to carry out area excavations in addition to its vital work of sampling with scientific precision in as many places as possible. The builders, however, now began to clear large areas for the foundations of the new office blocks, and antiquities of many kinds were revealed. It was therefore necessary to fall back on the old opportunism of rescue archaeology, somewhat discredited by contrast with the scientific work of the Excavation Council, which clearly demonstrated the possibilities of error inherent in less precise methods. Nevertheless, identifiable portions of ancient structures were being revealed by the builders, and it was clearly necessary that they should be recorded, since they at least gave some indication of the nature of the occupation of the site, at a time which could usually be defined within broad limits. Moreover, pieces of pottery and other durable relics of the past were coming to light in great quantities, and these were not only intrinsically interesting and very occasionally beautiful, but also potentially of scientific value, especially when they were found in associated contemporary groups, as in the fillings of refuse pits or wells. It was desirable that these finds should be collected and preserved for future study.

Responsibility for this rescue work was undertaken by the staff of Guildhall Museum, which was gradually increased after

the war. When Adrian Oswald left for Birmingham at the end
of 1949, and was succeeded by Norman Cook as Keeper of the
Museum, it was increased to five, and one of the new appoint-
ments was that of a full-time excavation assistant. The first
holder of this post was I. Noel Hume, a young man who at that
time had had no formal training in archaeology but had shown
great enthusiasm and promise as a volunteer assistant. He made
good use of his opportunity, and quickly acquired a reputation
as a pioneer in post-mediaeval archaeology. This led to his
appointment in 1957 as Chief Archaeologist at Colonial
Williamsburg, the eighteenth century museum town of Vir-
ginia, U.S.A. He was equally interested in the Roman period,
however, and made a considerable contribution to our knowledge of Roman London, including the reconstruction of the
plan of a bath-house in Cheapside from the fragmentary
remains observed during the builders' excavation. His successor,
Miss Eve Rutter, located the ancient stream-bed of the Walbrook in two places, and recorded various Roman finds, but by
chance was concerned more with mediaeval structures than
Roman during her tenure of office as excavation assistant.
When she left after marriage, she was succeeded by Peter
Marsden, a young man who had caused some sensation by dis-
covering a Roman ship in Southwark at the age of eighteen.
Later, in the service of the Museum, he was to find another at
Blackfriars and, as a result, has developed a particular interest
in naval archaeology. He has recorded a number of important
Roman buildings, including a bath-house in Upper Thames
Street and a portion of the great Roman building on the site of
Cannon Street Station, and has done especially useful work in
observing the inconspicuous traces of Roman road metalling
which will help to reconstruct the street-plan of Londinium.

If our knowledge of Roman London still resembles a jigsaw
puzzle with most of the pieces missing, a number of the pieces
which we now have fit together, giving us some idea at least
of the general character of the whole picture. What possibilities
of filling the gaps does the future hold? The areas which were
destroyed by bombing within the walls of Londinium have for
the most part been rebuilt, and the excavations of the Roman
and Mediaeval London Excavation Council have come to an
end. Much more information will come from the close study of
its past work, and the correlation of its firmly based and detailed
information with the sketchy observations, hastily made over

a much wider area during building excavations, will no doubt yield valuable results. For this we must await the full reports by Professor Grimes. Opportunities for careful excavation under controlled conditions will in future be very rare indeed, if the rebuilding of the City proceeds as in the past; and the use of mechanical excavators now makes observation during building operations difficult and often dangerous. It must of course be continued, for recent work has shown that even in these circumstances useful scraps of information can be gleaned. It is necessary, however, that every opportunity should be taken – and if possible opportunities should be created – for archaeological excavations, even if this can only be a small extension of a builders' excavation carried out during a week-end or public holiday. A recent example of this was the clearance and identification of part of a Roman bath-house, which fortunately came to light just before the builders' work stopped for August Bank Holiday week-end, 1964. This important task was carried out with great speed by two groups of amateur diggers, who recovered a substantial portion of the plan of the building and obtained evidence of the approximate date when its heating system had ceased to be used.[33]

The archaeological purist will object that hurried work of this kind cannot be perfectly accurate, and that misconceptions may therefore arise from it. To some extent this is true – as it is true of all discoveries of Roman London before the excavations of the Roman and Mediaeval London Excavation Council – and the possibility of error and misinterpretation must always be recognised in any archaeological work which falls short of perfection. It may also be true, in general terms, as a well-known archaeologist has recently pronounced, that even in the case of rescue work a bad excavation is worse than no excavation, as it may mislead. In a city of historic importance, however, where the buried remains of the past are normally quite inaccessible until they are destroyed, it would be very wrong to neglect any opportunity to examine them before destruction because circumstances did not permit an investigation of the highest standard. In fact, of course, speed and a considerable degree of care and accuracy can, with training, be combined, and a cadre of skilled diggers who were available at short notice for emergencies in the City could play a vital part in future work.[34] What *is* important is that the validity of all evidence should be carefully scrutinised, giving due consideration to the circumstances in which it was collected. Here a clear distinction must be drawn between facts and their interpretation. Unorthodox methods of investigation, including observation of builders' excavations, can reveal some of the facts but not all of them, and therefore the *interpretation* of any evidence obtained in this way must remain suspect until it is corroborated by further finds – as it often is. Even in the worst conditions, however, certain undoubted *facts* are revealed – and we cannot afford to ignore any of these, however they may come to light. Archaeologists in London must therefore be prepared to adapt their methods to whatever circumstances they find, and in extreme cases might even make good use of a bull-dozer themselves – if they can ever afford to do so. It is a clumsy implement compared with the trowel, but it could reveal very rapidly the existence – and probably the shape – of a Roman building before it disappeared for ever.

Nevertheless, Professor Grimes has clearly demonstrated that the careful methods of scientific excavation are essential for a full understanding of the complexities that are to be found on City sites, and it is most desirable that further investigations of this kind should take place, especially in those areas which escaped serious damage in the last war, and in which no scientific excavation has therefore yet been possible. The most important of these to the student of Roman London is the area between the eastern part of Cornhill and the western part of Leadenhall Street in the north, and the eastern part of Lombard Street and western part of Fenchurch Street in the south. This contained the Roman basilica and forum, and also two early phases of building which apparently antedated the latter. Sufficient has been observed in builders' excavations to show the complexity and great interest of this area, which holds the key to the early history of Londinium. A careful scientific examination here would be of the greatest value, and more than one important problem could probably be solved by a single cutting methodically excavated in the right place.

Rebuilding in the City of London has now entered a new phase, in which old properties will be demolished and their sites developed in order to make more efficient use of valuable land. The only opportunity for controlled excavation will occur in the interval between demolition and rebuilding, but for this to be carried out satisfactorily, a period of several weeks would be required. It is, of course, in the interests of the owners to rebuild with the least possible delay, so that the prospects of the archaeologists are not very bright. Nevertheless it is hoped that some compromise may be reached, and that the more enlightened owners, bearing in mind the increase of revenue which will result from redevelopment, will be prepared to make a comparatively small financial sacrifice in order that this last opportunity may be taken. The present generation of archaeologists, administrators, City Fathers and site owners bears a heavy responsibility, and will certainly be blamed by posterity if it allows important evidence for London's early history to be destroyed without making a very determined effort to record it. Unlike its predecessors, it can hardly plead ignorance as an excuse.

Will anything remain to be examined by future investigators, with improved techniques – and perhaps with better opportunities, if they live in a more enlightened age – when the steel and concrete office-blocks of today in their turn become obsolete and are demolished? (Their other possible fate need not be considered, as it is unlikely to be followed by archaeological investigation.) In the case of some buildings – as for example Bucklersbury House, Walbrook, and Elizabeth House, Bush Lane – there will be nothing at all, since all traces of earlier occupation have been destroyed by excavations to a great depth over their whole area. Others, however, such as Mitre House, Cheapside, and the Salvation Army International Headquarters in Queen Victoria Street, are built on pile foundations and a considerable part of their area is not deeply excavated. Some scope will therefore remain for future generations, but it will be severely circumscribed, and archaeologists who are to come will survey the great chasms made by our builders, and will bitterly regret the lost opportunities of the mid-twentieth century. In many respects the history of archaeology in the City of London recalls the story of the Sibylline Books. Knowledge is offered to each generation at a price – and is destroyed when the price is not paid. The price rises for each generation – in terms of actual cost and also of difficulties to be overcome – and the remaining store of information diminishes. None has yet been prepared to pay in full – and only a very small part of the exceptional bargain offer made by the Sibyl in 1946 was accepted. If ever a generation arises that is prepared to pay the full price of a total scientific excavation over whatever area is then available, complete pages of the Book will be won. But by that time very few pages indeed will remain.

REFERENCES

1. John Stow, *A Survey of London*, 1603, Kingsford ed., Vol. I, p. 345.

2. Christopher Wren, *Parentalia*, p. 265.

3. We now know that there is a relationship between certain modern streets and their Roman predecessors, and suspect that other instances of this will be found, but it is clear that most of the main thoroughfares of the modern City have diverged considerably from the lines of the Roman streets.

4. A report by the architect, Sir William Tite, on the finds from this site was published as a monograph, *A Descriptive Catalogue of the Antiquities found in the Excavations at the New Royal Exchange*.

5. C. Roach Smith, *Catalogue of the Museum of London Antiquities*, printed by subscription, 1854.

6. *Anthropological Review*, V, pp. LXXI ff.

7. J. E. Price, *A Description of the Roman Tessellated Pavement found in Bucklersbury; with Observations on Analogous Discoveries*, 1870.

8. It remains there at the present time, and since this basement room is now used as the Library book-store, the pavement will unfortunately remain inaccessible to the public until it is removed for exhibition in the new Museum of London.

9. J. H. Puleston and J. E. Price, *Roman Antiquities Recently Discovered on the Site of the National Safe Deposit Company's Premises, Mansion House, London*, 1873: and J. E. Price, *On a Bastion of London Wall, or Excavations in Camomile Street, Bishopsgate*, 1880.

10. See **B10**, and *Fig.* 7, p. 69.

11. *Plate* 95.

12. J. M. C. Toynbee, *Art in Britain under the Romans*, 1964, p. 55.

13. *J.B.A.A.*, XXXVII, pp. 90–1.

14. See *Arch.*, LXVI, pp. 225–35: *R.C.H.M.*, pp. 35–42: also pp. 132–6 of the present volume.

15. The present usefulness of Hodge's sections is limited by the fact that the strata, although carefully described, are not dated, and are not directly related to the Roman structures which he recorded.

16. *Arch.*, LX, pp. 43–8.

17. *Arch.*, LIX, pp. 125–42: LX, pp. 169–250: LXIII, pp. 257–344.

18. *Arch.*, LXVI, pp. 235–69.

19. Ibid., pp. 269–74.

20. *Arch.*, LXXVIII, pp. 73–110.

21. *Arch.*, LXXI, pp. 55–112.

22. Treasure trove is gold or silver, whether bullion, coin or plate, of which the original owner is unknown, and which has been deliberately concealed with a view to subsequent recovery. Thus gold or silver which has been accidentally lost, or buried without any intention of recovery, as in the case of ornaments buried with the dead, is not treasure trove. In recent years the City Corporation has successfully claimed two items of treasure trove: a small hoard of Roman silver denarii found in Budge Row in 1958, and the silver box and infuser found in the Temple of Mithras in 1954. In both cases the full reward was paid to the finder.

23. A Bill to establish the new Museum received the Royal Assent on 2 June 1965. The new institution will be of unique character, since it will be financed in equal parts by the Treasury (now responsible for the London Museum), the City Corporation (responsible for Guildhall Museum), and the Greater London Council. It will be administered by a Board of Trustees representing these three authorities. The Guildhall and London Museum collections are to a great extent complementary – the former being the stronger in its Roman and Mediaeval sections, and the latter in Prehistory and Post-Mediaeval antiquities. Both are at present housed in temporary and unsatisfactory accommodation: Guildhall Museum with its exhibition and offices in the Royal Exchange, and its stores and laboratory at Guildhall: the London Museum with its exhibition and offices at Kensington Palace, and many stores remaining at Lancaster House, its former home, and elsewhere. It is proposed to build a new and well equipped museum building near Aldersgate Street, within the City of London, but just outside the City wall – an appropriate site for a museum which will be concerned both with the historic walled city and with the immense development of London beyond the walls.

24. *Royal Commission on Historical Monuments (England), An Inventory of the Historical Monuments in London, Vol. III, Roman London,* 1928 – now unfortunately long out of print.

25. *Ant. Journ.,* IX (1929), pp. 219 ff.

26. *J.R.S.* XXI (1931), pp. 236–8.

27. 'Two Fires of Roman London,' *Ant. Journ.,* XXV (1945), pp. 48–77.

28. W. G. Bell, F. Cottrill and Charles Spon, *London Wall through Eighteen Centuries,* 1937.

29. A reward of £3000 when the silver box and strainer found in the temple were declared Treasure Trove and claimed by the Corporation of London in accordance with its Charter rights. The reward was paid to Professor Grimes personally, but was allocated by him to the work of the Council.

30. *Plate* 74.

31. *Plates* 81–3.

32. Building contractors have in fact occasionally taken out insurance with Lloyd's, to cover themselves against the cost of any delay resulting from the discovery of antiquities, since they operate under a penalty clause which makes them responsible for this. The risk, however, seems to be negligible, since nobody has any legal power to stop their work in the name of archaeology. The only possible cause of delay would be moral pressure brought to bear by public opinion, or overwhelming and embarrassing public interest – as in the case of the Temple of Mithras. Neither is likely to be aroused by fragmentary walls and scraps of barely distinguishable floors, which are all that normally survive even on sites of the greatest archaeological importance.

33. See p. 142.

34. A team of volunteer diggers known as the City of London Excavation Group has now been formed, sponsored by the London and Middlesex Archaeological Society and Guildhall Museum. Working at week-ends, under the supervision of Mr. N. Farrant, it has already carried out several useful excavations.

CHAPTER TWO

★

Historical Outline

THROUGHOUT PREHISTORY the Thames served as a highway into Britain, and small settlements were made in suitable places on its banks. Very slight traces of the presence of Bronze Age and other prehistoric people have been found from time to time in the City area, but there is no indication that it was ever a site of importance before the Roman conquest. There was in fact nothing to make it in any way preferable to the many other gravel areas beside the Thames in the eyes of early settlers. The clay hinterland of London was covered by thick forest and presented a considerable barrier, while the Lea valley four miles downstream offered much more ready access to the interior. Further upstream, where the river could be more easily crossed, there were extensive gravel areas which were favourable to occupation, and it was in this region – between Battersea and Mortlake, and farther west in the neighbourhood of the Brent and the Crane – that the more important prehistoric settlements developed, while the site of London itself remained neglected.

The legend of a pre-Roman London dies hard, although Sir Mortimer Wheeler in the Royal Commission's Report of 1928 finally disposed of the alleged evidence in its favour, allowing only the possibility that a few pieces (less than a score) of pre-Claudian imported Italian pottery found in the City and Southwark might indicate that 'a few prospectors from the Roman world . . . may have built a wharf and a warehouse somewhere near the site of London Bridge a decade or so before the legions arrived'.[1] The import of this ware from Arezzo seems to have ceased at the time of the Roman conquest, when it was replaced by the South Gaulish Samian ware which had supplanted it in the Roman armies some years before. The London

29

finds are therefore likely to have arrived in Britain before
A.D. 43,[2] though not necessarily in the London area. At Camulodunum (Colchester), however, most of the Arretine ware – in
a proportion of 5 to 1 – was found in post-conquest deposits.[3]
Fine wares of this kind were valued and were therefore likely to
survive for several decades, if not for a generation or two, and
in the case of the fine Gaulish ware it was also observed at
Camulodunum that 'the Claudian troops and their immediate
civilian following had on an average two old Decorated Sigillata bowls in use for every three new ones'.[4] Since, however,
there was good reason to believe that the Italian wares, in
whatever context they were found, were pre-conquest imports
acquired by the Belgic aristocracy of Camulodunum, Professor
Hawkes concluded that 'Pryce and Oswald's view (*Arch.*
LXXVIII, 74 ff.) that the remarkable Arretine series from
London probably implies a pre-conquest settlement of continental traders is hereby in no way upset, but rather confirmed'.[5] As was pointed out in the Royal Commission's Report,
however, the Arretine pottery found in London has a wide
distribution, ranging from Southwark to north of Bishopsgate.
This is difficult to reconcile with the idea of a small pre-Claudian
trading post, but does correspond with the distribution of
pottery of the time of Claudius and Nero, and is therefore
readily explained in a post-conquest setting.[6] Even if we accept
the proposition that it is unlikely to have been brought to
Britain either by the invading forces or by traders at any subsequent date, its presence can be readily explained by the
hypothesis that one ingredient of the early population of
London was derived from the native aristocracy which had
provided the principal market in Britain for this ware. Trade
or official business probably induced some well-to-do tribesmen
from Camulodunum, Verulamium and Calleva, where Arretine pottery is known to have been in use, to take up residence
in London soon after the founding of that city, and the household equipment which they brought with them is likely to have
included their best crockery. The pre-conquest merchants who
brought this ware to Britain, on the other hand, would not
have found the site of London a particularly convenient base
for trading with the tribal centres before the arrival of the
Roman road-builders. Sir Mortimer Wheeler's conclusion in
1928 was that 'there is at present no valid reason for supposing
that London existed prior to A.D. 43'.[7] The extensive excava-

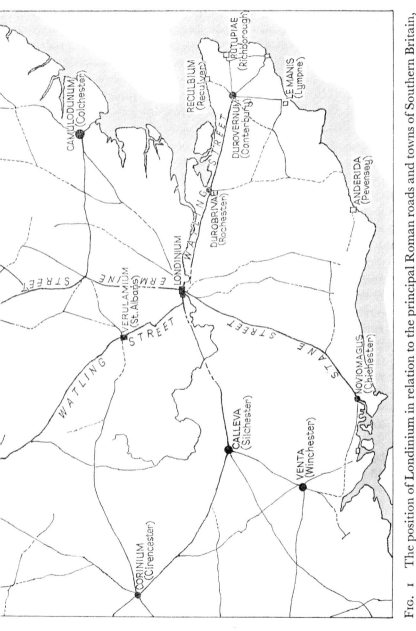

FIG. 1   The position of Londinium in relation to the principal Roman roads and towns of Southern Britain, based on the Ordnance Survey Map of Roman Britain.

31

tions which have since taken place have produced no evidence
to contradict this view, and against the enormous quantities of
post-conquest material which have now been found, the few
earlier pieces dwindle to almost complete insignificance. In
default of any confirmatory evidence, therefore, and in view of
its geographical improbability, it is suggested that the pre-
Claudian trading-post should now join the pile city of Cassivel-
launus in the limbo of abandoned theories of the origin of
London.

★   ★   ★

The potentialities of the site of London could only be realised
under an authority which was not only vitally concerned with
the access of sea-going ships, but was also capable of establish-
ing and maintaining a system of landward communications on
both sides of the river. The requisite condition for the development of this city, therefore, was the existence of a government
with strong continental interests, political control of a large
area north and south of the Thames, and considerable engin-
eering skill at its command. Such a government was first
established in Britain by the Romans, who seem to have
appreciated the possibilities of the site of London almost from
the beginning. At an early stage in their conquest of the country
they must have constructed a bridge across the Thames, very
near the tidal limits of the river at that period, and their subsequent road system was necessarily centred upon it. The position
was chosen where firm gravels gave good access to both banks,
and at the lowest point which was unaffected by the ebb and
flow of tides. It was also a place which could easily be reached
by ships from the Continent, so that inevitably there developed
an important centre for the collection and distribution of goods
by land and water. Its earliest use is likely to have been as a
military supply base, but the development of all kinds of
commerce quickly followed. The bridge was therefore the
parent of the city, but the birth of the latter was probably not
long delayed; certain features of the street plan suggest, in fact,
that its nucleus may even have been created before the permanent roads to the interior were laid out. (See pp. 114–20, 130).

The exact circumstances in which London began remain
conjectural since, although it can be assumed that the bridge
must have been built soon after the invasion, we do not know
in what phase of the conquest this took place. It is clear that

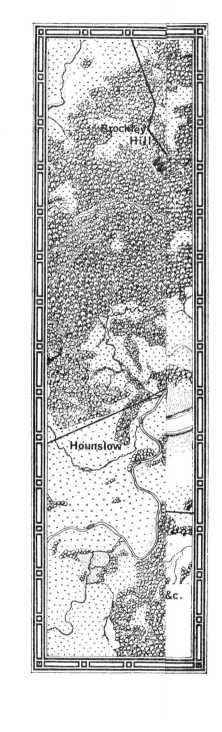

the Roman army was divided into three parts, of which the central column, consisting of the Fourteenth and Twentieth Legions, advanced to the north-west through the Midlands. The right wing, consisting of the Ninth Legion, marched to the north, skirting the Fens; while the Second Legion, under the future Emperor Vespasian, was on the left wing and proceeded to conquer the west of England. Since Watling Street and Ermine Street were presumably military roads laid out to supply the forward areas, probably quite soon after the initial conquests, it is likely that they mark respectively the lines of advance of the central force and the right wing. As Watling Street lies beneath the Edgware Road and therefore points, not to the City, but to Westminster, it has sometimes been suggested that the initial crossing of the Thames took place in this area, and that the Roman forces diverged somewhere in West London. Since a base camp must have been established, this hypothesis implies an early Roman occupation to the west of Londinium, at least for a short time, and no trace of this has ever been found. There is, on the other hand, a strong concentration of finds of early Roman pottery in the City, especially to the east of the Walbrook,[8] and Ermine Street (on the line of the Kingsland Road) points directly to this area. It is therefore more likely that the Roman base was on the site of the City almost from the beginning, and that the line of Watling Street was determined by the existence of an earlier trackway to Verulamium, the tribal centre of the Catuvellauni (as Mr. Margary has suggested[9]) rather than by the starting point of the Roman army.

If the account given by Cassius Dio is to be trusted – and he was writing more than 150 years after the event – the Romans first crossed the Thames in their initial campaign of A.D. 43 somewhere very near the site of the City. After their defeat on the Medway, the Britons are said to have retreated to the Thames 'at a point near where it empties into the ocean and at flood-tide forms a lake'. This was evidently in the tidal part of the river below the site of London Bridge – possibly in the Pool of London. It is unlikely that it was very much further downstream, for the Britons were able to cross the river by fords. The pursuing Romans did not know these, and found it difficult to follow, although the German auxiliaries swam across. Some others 'got over by a bridge a little way upstream, after which they assailed the barbarians from several sides at once and cut

down many of them'.[10] The reference to the bridge has been
quoted as evidence for a pre-conquest London Bridge, but if
there was no settlement of importance in the City area, as now
seems reasonably certain, it is hardly conceivable that there
would have been a bridge there. If the Britons had bridged the
Thames, it would probably have been several miles upstream
where there had long been considerable prehistoric settlements,
and this could hardly be described as 'a little way'. It is of
course much more likely that they used only fords, which
provided quite easy crossings of the river upstream from Westminster. It has been suggested that Julius Caesar had built a
temporary bridge at London during his campaign of 55 B.C.[11],
but this seems unlikely. In any case it is hardly credible that
such a bridge had remained in good order, maintained by the
Britons although they had no particular interest in a crossing
at this point, and that it had survived to assist another invader
when it was obviously in the interests of the defenders that it
should be destroyed. It is much more likely that the bridge
mentioned by Dio was a temporary military structure, probably
made of rafts, built by the invading army itself, whose engineers
were aware of the river obstacle and must have come prepared
to deal with it. It is doubtful, however, whether such a bridge
could have been built quickly enough to have allowed the van-
guard of the Romans to overtake the retreating enemy, as described by Dio, and it seems possible that in this account a later
transit by a bridge has been confused with the initial crossing.

It is, however, very probable that the construction of a fairly
substantial bridge was commenced almost immediately, for at
this point there came a curious pause in the campaign, during
which the Roman commander, Aulus Plautius, waited by the
banks of the Thames until the arrival of the Emperor Claudius
with reinforcements. The Romans had had some losses through
incautiously pursuing the enemy, but it is likely that the real
reason for the delay was a pre-arranged plan, by which the
Emperor was to have the honour of leading the army into
Camulodunum, the capital of the ruling Belgic dynasty. For
political reasons, therefore, the natural inclination of the troops
to follow up their initial victory had to be checked, and the
campaign brought to a temporary halt. In these circumstances
the maintenance of morale and discipline among thousands of
men must have been a serious problem, and any experienced
commander would have looked for a considerable task to

occupy them. The building of a substantial bridge, so that the Emperor – and perhaps even the corps of elephants which accompanied him – could cross the Thames with dignity, would have served this purpose admirably. The provision of such a bridge must in any case have been planned as a necessary preliminary to the conquest of Britain, and it seems unlikely that the opportunity at least to commence work on it would have been missed. The suggestion that London Bridge was built in this phase of the conquest cannot, of course, be easily reconciled either with Dio's reference to an earlier bridge or with his statement that Claudius had to fight a battle to cross the Thames. The reliability of Dio's account is doubtful, however, and it is contradicted by Suetonius, who says that the Emperor fought no battles in Britain and suffered no casualties.[12] The last statement is confirmed by the inscription[13] from Claudius' own triumphal arch, which also claims that he had no losses; and it is hardly credible that none would have been suffered in a contested river-crossing. Nevertheless – again according to the inscription – he received the submission of eleven kings during his sixteen days in Britain, so that the foundation for the conquest of the country had been securely laid before his departure. It may therefore be suspected that a bridgehead supply base on the site of London had already been established, but definite historical or archaeological evidence of this is lacking.

That Londinium was a military base in an early phase of the conquest can be deduced from its position, especially in relation to the Roman road system, but cannot easily be proved. Dr. Graham Webster has listed a considerable quantity of finds of Roman military equipment in London, mostly from the Walbrook,[14] but although some of these are demonstrably early, they cannot for the most part be dated very closely, and many may be as late as the period of occupation of the Roman fort at London – after about A.D. 100 – when military activities in the town were of quite a different kind and for a different purpose. There is little doubt of the military importance of London in its early days, however, but it was soon overshadowed by the rapid commercial development of the city, and it is this which is emphasised when the name of Londinium first appears in the pages of history seventeen years after the invasion.

In A.D. 60, southern and eastern Britain had long been pacified, and the Roman governor, Suetonius Paulinus, was prosecuting a vigorous campaign in the west. He had just struck a decisive blow against native resistance by invading Anglesey, the stronghold of Druidism, when the news reached him that East Anglia was in revolt. Prasutagus, King of the Iceni, who had recently died, had tried to ensure part of his inheritance for his children by making the Emperor a co-heir. The servants of the Procurator moved in and began to seize the property, at the same time alienating the tribal notables by revoking grants made to them by Claudius after the peaceful submission by the Iceni. The mounting arrogance of these Treasury officials culminated in the sacking of the palace, the flogging of Boudicca, widow of Prasutagus, and the rape of her daughters. The insulted queen raised her tribesmen in revolt, and they were joined by the Trinovantes to the south, whose grievance was the confiscation of their tribal lands for the settlement of army veterans at Camulodunum. Here, on the site of the old capital of Cunobelinus, Claudius had established a *colonia*, which was to be the capital of the new province and the centre of the state cult of Emperor-worship. The retired soldiers who had been settled there had made no attempt to organise their defences, and their garrison was small. They appealed for help to the Procurator, who sent them barely two hundred poorly armed men. Only the temple held out for two days; the rest of the town fell at once to the native horde, and was put to fire and the sword. An attempt at rescue by the commander of the Ninth Legion (stationed at Lincoln) ended in disaster and the loss of two thousand infantrymen.

The way to London was now open to the rebels, and it is significant that Suetonius' first thought was to save it. Tacitus tells us that Londinium was not dignified by the title of *colonia*, but was a great centre of commerce, crowded with traders.[15] The military importance of London is not mentioned, but there is little doubt that it was still an important supply base, and its position at the centre of communications made it of vital strategic importance. Paulinus pressed on to London as quickly as possible with his cavalry alone, having sent a messenger for reinforcements from the Second Legion in the south-west. These troops did not move, owing to a failure of nerve by the officer in command, and Paulinus realised that he had insufficient men to hold London. In spite of the entreaties of the inhabitants, he gave the order to march, allowing those civilians who were able and willing to do so to accompany him. Many women, old people, and others who did not wish to leave their homes remained behind. Verulamium (St. Albans) was similarly abandoned as Suetonius withdrew westward to make contact with his troops. Both towns met a terrible fate when the hordes of tribesmen arrived. In the laconic words of Tacitus, they did not take or sell prisoners, as was customary in war, but rushed to avenge their own future punishment with butchery, hanging, fire and crucifixion. In the three towns destroyed by the rebels – Camulodunum, Londinium and Verulamium – 70,000 people lost their lives.

It is not impossible, as suggested by the Royal Commission's Report, that the skulls found in various parts of the stream-bed and banks of the Walbrook may be the decapitated heads of some of these unhappy victims.[16] A more certain witness to the tragic end of the first London is a layer of burnt debris, including great quantities of clay daub, often with impressions of wattle, red in colour and hardened by fire. It contains pottery of the mid-first century, and lies immediately above the first occupation level which rests on the natural surface of the ground. The burnt daub is of course the remains of houses of simple construction, but not necessarily native in style, since the method is described by the Roman architect Vitruvius,[17] and fragments of painted wall-plaster have been found mingled with the daub on at least one site.[18] This early burnt level is not infrequently exposed during builders' excavations, especially on the east side of the Walbrook, in the area to the south of Cornhill. It also occurs on the west side of the Walbrook, however, and has been recognised as far west as King Street (**50**), and more doubtfully even in Watling Street (**80**). The distribution of burnt Samian pottery of the period Claudius-Nero has also been studied by Mr. G. C. Dunning, and gives an indication of the extent of the town destroyed by Boudicca (*Fig.* 9).

The tragic events of A.D. 60–1 seemed very near in 1950, when the builders were excavating for the foundations of St. Swithin's House, Walbrook. The characteristic burnt layer was found overlying the old ground level to a thickness of one to two feet, covering Samian ware and other pottery of the period before A.D. 60. In one place it filled and covered a pit which had been dug for the disposal of rubbish, but which had been only partly filled with refuse when the fire came. At the bottom of the hole was the usual accumulation of broken pottery, but on the top of this was a great amphora of the kind used for importing and storing wine, and this was quite undamaged.

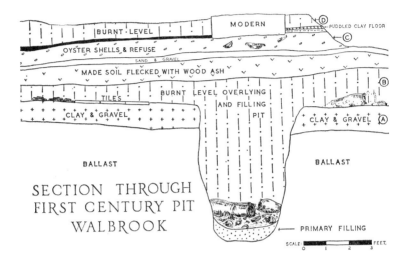

FIG. 3   Section through the Boudiccan fire deposit and an earlier pit, site of St. Swithin's House, Walbrook. *Drawn by I. Noel Hume (Guildhall Museum).*

Beside it lay a large double-handled wine-jar which was broken cleanly across the neck, probably by the fall of the amphora, but was otherwise perfect and seemed to have been unbroken when it was thrown away. Covering the wine-vessels and filling the rest of the pit were the ashes of the fire (*Fig.* 3 and *Plate* 120). Since complete pots are seldom thrown away under ordinary conditions, it seems likely that someone rapidly disposed of a considerable quantity of wine just before the house went up in flames. There is nothing to show whether the wine jars were emptied by looting tribesmen, or by the householders, determined to empty their cellar before they marched with Suetonius, or to gain courage while they awaited the arrival of Boudicca.

What little we know of the London before Boudicca is based on scraps of archaeological information, mostly obtained under conditions which precluded scientific accuracy, and a few sentences of Tacitus, who should be reliable, since his informant was his father-in-law, Agricola, who had served in Britain as a staff officer under Suetonius Paulinus at the time of the revolt. Unfortunately Tacitus merely mentions London in passing, and it is tempting to read too much by implication into his terse phrases on a subject which concerned him very little. He tells us that the rebels, avoiding forts and garrisons, made for those places which were most worth looting and were unguarded by defenders.[19] The three principal places to which he refers were of course Camulodunum, Londinium and Verulamium. Camulodunum, as he tells us elsewhere, had no rampart or trench, so the implication is that London likewise had no fortification. In view of the strategic importance of the northern bridgehead and the vital part which it must have played as a supply base, however, it seems hardly credible that it had never been defended. It is true that no fortifications of an early date have yet been found in London, but as they would have consisted of ditch and palisaded rampart only, any surviving traces would not easily be recognised in a builders' excavation. There is, however, one positive piece of evidence which suggests that the first London was laid out according to an official plan, which in this context is likely to have been military. The only Roman street we know which is almost certainly pre-Boudiccan is the east-west road beneath Lombard Street. (See **290**; also pp. 118–20.) This is parallel with the river, and presumably at a right-angle with the line of the bridge, so that it looks very much like the main road (*decumanus maximus*) of a planned area, whether fort or town. It can hardly be reconciled with the idea that the first London was the haphazard settlement of traders at the bridge-head and along the trunk roads leading from the bridge – a casual ribbon development of the kind which seems to have taken place at a later date on the southern side of the river.[20] In fact, no indication of main roads diverging directly from the bridge itself has been found, and it seems likely that London was at the beginning a planned centre from which these roads departed, rather than a natural growth at their junction. It might be expected that it would have been fortified in the early days of the conquest, but its defences had probably been allowed to fall into disrepair in the seventeen years before the revolt, since London seemed to be far behind any possible danger zone. Nevertheless, Suetonius' original intention was to defend London, and it seems to have been the lack of troops which determined his withdrawal rather than the indefensibility of the site itself.

There is some indication that not all of the buildings of the first London were jerry-built structures of wattle and daub, the

burnt remains of which form the bulk of the Boudiccan fire
level. Immediately north of Lombard Street, very early foundations of ragstone and tiles have been found aligned on the east-
west road (**243** and *Fig.* 23 walls *C*). These antedate a ragstone
building which was occupied in the Flavian period and
in all probability are pre-Boudiccan.[21] A building with stone
foundations at such an early date is more likely to have
been constructed for some official purpose than to have
been the private house of a merchant, however prosperous.
Like the east-west road itself, it can hardly be reconciled with
the conception of the origin of London as a mushroom town of
private enterprise which grew up almost accidentally in a
favourable position.

It may be suspected that London, almost from the first, was
found to be a much more convenient centre for the financial
administration of the province than the official capital at
Colchester. This side of the provincial government was under
the control of the *procurator*, who was responsible, not to the
military governor (*legatus*), but directly to the Emperor himself.
Decianus Catus, the procurator whose oppression was the cause
of Boudicca's revolt, was evidently not himself at Camulodunum,
as he sent two hundred men there when the settlers appealed for
help. He was subsequently able to escape by ship to Gaul, so it
seems more likely that he was in London than anywhere else.

His successor, Julius Classicianus, died in office and was
buried in London, so it is a reasonable assumption that his
headquarters were there. The evidence for this is the discovery
of his tomb-stone re-used as building material in the filling of
one of the bastions of the city wall (**B2**) – one of the most
important historical documents of Roman Britain (*Plates* 4–6).

Classicianus found a province which was being devastated by
punitive warfare. Suetonius had finally defeated Boudicca
somewhere north-west of Verulamium, and had massacred her
armies, trapped in their own wagon-lines. Not content with this,
but determined to teach a lesson that would never be forgotten,
he proceeded to ravage the territory of the rebels and other
tribes whose allegiance was doubtful. Classicianus strongly disapproved, perhaps partly on humanitarian grounds, but also
because he realised that the economy of an important part of
the province was being wrecked. He therefore complained to
Nero, who sent a special investigator to Britain. As a result of
the latter's report, Suetonius was ordered to suspend operations,

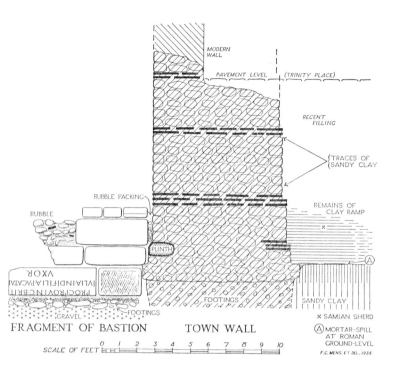

Fig. 4   Section through the Roman city wall and bastion, Trinity Place, showing part of inscription from the tomb of Classicianus *in situ* in the bastion (**B2**). *Reproduced by permission of F. Cottrill and the Society of Antiquaries of London.*

and soon afterwards was recalled. His successor, Petronius Turpilianus, adopted a policy of conciliation and gradually the province recovered its prosperity. Roman Britain therefore owed much to the procurator Classicianus, who had the courage to oppose the angry Suetonius in his hour of revenge, and the political skill to persuade an unbalanced and tyrannical Emperor to follow in this instance the path of statesmanship and moderation.

In 1852 a portion of an inscription and a bolster-like ornament, evidently from a large tomb, was found re-used as building material in a bastion of the city wall in Trinity Place, Tower Hill (**B2**). This bore the name 'FAB(I) ALPINI CLASSICIANI', and Roach Smith suggested that it was quite within the bounds of probability that it was from the tomb of the procurator, Julius Classicianus, mentioned by Tacitus – especially since Classicianus was a very uncommon name.[22] Archaeologists of a later generation would have none of this, for they had the correct scholarly scepticism of attempts to connect casual archaeological finds with the personages of history. They therefore preferred to think that this imposing tomb belonged to some unknown Fabius Alpinus Classicianus – or even to 'Fabius Alpinus, formerly of the navy,' regarding *Classicianus* as an adjective derived from *classis* (fleet).[23]

More than eighty years later, however, when an electricity sub-station was being constructed for the London Passenger Transport Board in 1935, what remained of the bastion was uncovered, and in the lowest course was found a slab of stone with another portion of the inscription, set upside down (*Plate* 5 and *Fig.* 4). This made it quite clear that Roach Smith was right after all, for there was the title of the procurator – 'PROC. PROVINC. BRIT'... (PROCURATOR PROVINCIAE BRITANNIAE) – Procurator of the Province of Britain. The second portion of the inscription also gave the name of Classicianus' wife, Julia Pacata, the daughter of Indus, who had the tomb set up. This is of considerable interest, as Julius Indus, the procurator's father-in-law, was a Gallic cavalry commander who had remained loyal to the Romans in a revolt of his own tribe, the Treveri, forty years earlier, and had played the principal part in pacifying the rebels.[24] It has been suggested that his daughter, who may well have been born about this time, was named Pacata in memory of these events.[25] If so, Classicianus had a constant reminder of his father-in-law's success in preventing bloodshed, and of the advantages of a liberal policy in dealing with rebellious provincials.

The burial of the procurator in London is not the only indication that the offices of the financial administration were to be found there. A wooden writing-tablet, found in or near the Walbrook and now in the British Museum, is branded with the inscription 'PROC AVG DEDERVNT/BRIT PROV' ('Issued by the Imperial Procurators of the Province of Britain') (*Plate* 7). This type of tablet, with a wax surface on which a short letter or memorandum could be written with the *stilus*, was commonly used in Roman Britain for business purposes. There is no doubt that this example was an official issue for use by the

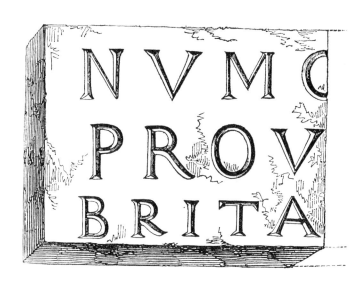

F
IG
. 5   Portion of the dedicatory inscription of a temple for the
state cult of the Emperor, found in Nicholas Lane (284). From
C. Roach Smith: Illustrations of Roman London.

procurator's clerks, whose office was presumably not very far
away.

The presence in London of public buildings constructed by
the Roman authorities is indicated by the use of bricks made at
a local brickworks which was apparently controlled by some
branch of the provincial administration. These are stamped
with the letters 'P. PR. BR'., 'P. P. BR'., or some variant of this,
often followed by the abbreviation 'LON' for Londinium (*Plate*
8). The second and third abbreviations probably stand for
Provinciae Britanniae, but we do not know the significance of the
first *P*. Various suggestions have been made – none of them
very convincing. It is unlikely that either the *Publicani*, tax-
collectors, or *Portitores*, customs officers, would have been concerned with building operations in various parts of the city to
the extent suggested by these bricks. *Procurator* or *Procuratores*
would be more satisfactory, since the procurator was concerned
with the financial affairs of the province on a much wider basis

than either of these relatively minor officials, but such a harsh contraction is considered to be unlikely. All that can really be said is that the bricks were produced under an official but presumably civilian authority, evidently concerned with building, which has been compared with the Ministry of Public Building and Works.[26] If the usual interpretation of *PR. BR.* is correct, it was not a local authority, but one concerned with the whole province. The fact that these bricks have only been found in London is therefore indicative of the city's close links with the provincial administration.

Can we go further, and claim that London did eventually supplant Camulodunum as the official capital of the province? There are several pieces of evidence which suggest this. The most important symbol of the status of Camulodunum was the great temple to the divinity of the Emperor, which served as the last refuge of its defenders against Boudicca, and provided strong foundations for the Norman castle more than a thousand years later. Before A.D. 60 this was the centre of the state cult in Britain and the meeting place of the provincial council, but we do not know whether it continued to function as such after that date. No comparable building has ever been found in London, but a fragment of an inscription, found apparently re-used as building material in a later wall in Nicholas Lane (284), indicates the presence of a temple of the state cult probably set up by the provincial council, at a date which, from the style of lettering, can hardly be later than the early second century (*Fig.* 5).[27] Since the letters were six inches high, the inscription evidently came from a building of considerable size and importance.[28] Such a temple was not necessarily the meeting-place of the provincial council, but its existence suggests a new status for London in the ceremonial and religious life of the province, with which the council was primarily concerned. There is moreover an indication that some at least of the work of the provincial council was probably carried on in London at a fairly early date, for the young wife of one of its slaves was buried on Ludgate Hill in the late first or early second century.[29]

That London had in effect achieved the status of provincial capital by the early years of the second century is also suggested by the construction of a large stone fort at about that time to the north-west of the city. This was a period of military re-organisation and consolidation on the frontiers, and there was certainly trouble in the north early in the reign of Hadrian, but as far as we know there was no threat in the south-east which demanded the permanent stationing of a large body of troops in London. No doubt accommodation was required there from time to time for soldiers passing through the city, but a stone fort of standard pattern is more likely to have been intended as the home of a permanent garrison than as a mere transit camp. Even the selection of the site, on the outskirts of the town and away from the main roads, seems to have been made principally with a view to the maintenance of discipline among resident troops. A large permanent garrison might certainly be expected in a provincial capital, where it would be required for cere-monial purposes and to provide the Governor with a body-guard, orderlies and despatch-riders.[30] It could not easily be explained, at this period, in a London which had remained merely a commercial and financial centre of indeterminate status.

The prestige of Londinium in the late first and early second century is also reflected in the grandiose town-planning scheme which re-shaped its centre during this period, and provided it with a great basilica of exceptional size – apparently more than 500 feet long, a length without parallel in this country, and in Rome itself surpassed only by the great Basilica Ulpia (570 feet). Further details of this vast structure and the problems surrounding it will be discussed in a later chapter. Here it is sufficient to say that it served as law-court, exchange, town hall and community centre, and its ambitious scale indicates more clearly than anything else that public life in Roman London was truly metropolitan. There is evidence that the western part of the basilica was built, and the north-south skirting roads were laid out, in mid-Flavian times or later,[31] but the piers and cement floor which apparently formed part of the western side of the forum were not earlier than the reign of Hadrian.[32] It is possible that the great bronze statue of that Emperor, the head of which was found near London Bridge (*Plate* 90), was set up in the forum as part of this scheme.

At the height of its pride and prosperity, however, disaster again struck Roman London. On many sites in the central part of the City, both east and west of the Walbrook, a thick layer of burnt material has been found, very much like that which marks Boudicca's destruction of London in A.D. 60. This layer, however, contains pottery of the early second century, and has

been found overlying deposits containing datable material of
the late first or early second century. Its distribution has been
studied by Mr. G. C. Dunning, together with that of the mid-
first century fire.[33] Of particular value in the study of both fires
has been the closely datable Samian pottery which was imported in large quantities from Gaul for use as table-ware.
Normally of sealing-wax red, it is frequently found in the burnt
levels transformed to a glossy black, often with a bubbly
texture. Experiment has shown that this occurs when ordinary
red Samian is heated to a temperature of more than 1,100° C. in
the absence of oxygen, so that the red ferric oxide of iron which
gives it its colour is changed to black ferrous oxide. It was
therefore possible for Mr. Dunning to fill in many gaps in his
distribution maps by showing the provenance of burnt Samian
of the appropriate dates in museum collections (*Figs.* 9–10). These
maps show that the second century fire, which devastated at
least sixty-five acres, was much more extensive than the
Boudiccan fire, for London had grown considerably during the
interval between them. It has also been suggested that the distribution of the sites of the later fire indicates that it began in the
western part of the city and then spread eastward, fanned by a
westerly wind.

The date when this disaster occurred can be fairly closely
defined by the great quantity of datable Samian ware which is
associated with it. It took place in the reign of Hadrian,
probably between A.D. 125 and 130.[34] No political disturbance
at this time is known, and it seems likely that its origin was
purely accidental. Its rapid spread was evidently due to the
fact that the central part of the city was now fairly closely
built-up, with many houses of timber and clay.

Other troubles, which in some areas must have been almost
as disastrous, seem to have afflicted London during the second
century. These were the result of natural changes which were
taking place in the relative water-level, and were probably due
to a gradual sinking of the land in south-eastern Britain rather
than to an actual rise in the water-level. We know that the
present level of high tide in the London area is more than
thirteen feet higher in relation to the land than it was in early
Roman times.[35] These changes were already well advanced before the end of the Roman period, and were having an appreciable
effect in the low-lying districts of Londinium as early as the second
century. The part most affected was the valley of the Walbrook,

where the stream silted and wide areas on its banks were subject to flooding. Occupation was maintained only by dumping earth on the marshy flood-deposits and so raising the ground level artificially. Moreover this process had to be repeated periodically, as the waters continued to rise, and the latest dry level was itself swamped. The banks of the Walbrook had been the scene of intense commercial activity in the late first and early second century, and a great variety of manufactured goods was handled there (*Plates* 125–40). There seem to have been few permanent structures near the stream at this period, and it is likely that temporary booths, stalls and possibly small boats were used by the merchants. The stream-bed was only twelve to fourteen feet wide, so that traffic on the river must have been very limited, and the Walbrook cannot have been part of the docks of the Roman port, as was once believed. It seems, however, to have been the scene of a great market, which no doubt made some use of the narrow water-way. The evidence of coin-finds from the stream and adjoining banks suggests that this phase of intense activity came to an abrupt end soon after A.D. 155, when the revetted banks collapsed.[36] This seems to have been directly attributable to the silting of the stream and the swamping of the valley, resulting from the relative rise in the water level.

Similar difficulties seem to have been encountered in the area of Cheapside, where a very rapid build-up of successive occupation levels suggests that rising water may have been an annoyance even in the late first and early second centuries. (See **50**, **52**.) Trouble of this kind certainly came to the small bath-house on the site of the Sun Life Assurance Society (**55**) at a later date, probably towards the end of the second century, when the spring which fed its water tank overflowed and submerged the latter completely beneath a thick deposit of silt (**53**).

The vitality of London was too strong, however, to be checked by fire or flood, and vigorous efforts were made to overcome the deteriorating conditions in the wetter parts of the city. With all its drawbacks, the middle part of the Walbrook valley eventually became a smart residential quarter, where rich merchants or officials raised luxurious town houses high above the banks of the earlier stream on wooden piles and dumped material. The fine mosaics found in Bucklersbury and on the site of the Bank of England (**194**, **171**) belonged to houses of this kind, and are a testimony to the wealth and taste of the more fortunate Londoners of the late second and early third centuries. (*Plates* 65, 68–9.)

Then, at a date which is still uncertain, but cannot be earlier than the last ten years or so of the second century, the most enduring monument of Roman London was built. This was the great city wall, which was to determine the shape of London for more than a thousand years, and was to serve as the foundation of its defences for an even longer period (*Plates* 39–45).

It was constructed mainly of ragstone with courses of bonding-tiles and a sandstone plinth, above which it was about eight feet thick, gradually reducing to about seven feet at a height six feet or so above the plinth.[37] The total height is of course unknown; the highest piece of the Roman wall recorded survived to a height of about fourteen-and-a-half feet above the plinth. The new wall enclosed the whole of the landward side of the city from the Tower to Ludgate, and no doubt extended southward to the river bank at each end, but there is no evidence that it continued along the river-front. Such riverside walls as have been found are of quite a different character, and do not seem to have been continuous or homogeneous. They were probably river embankments rather than defensive walls, though they may have served both purposes to some extent. The great landward wall, on the other hand, was evidently planned and built as a single structure. The only important variation in its construction occurred when the walls of the fort were reached. The lay-out of the new city wall had been planned so that the north and west walls of the fort could be incorporated with it, thereby saving a great deal of labour and material. Since, however, the wall of the fort was only about half the thickness of the new city wall, a thickening had to be added to the inner face of the fort wall to bring it to the standard thickness of the city wall. This portion is therefore a double structure, consisting of an outer wall which was part of the fort built early in the second century, and an inner which was added when the city wall was built (*Plates* 35–6, 38).

The city wall is just over two miles long, and if it stood to a height of twenty feet above the plinth, making due allowance for a further reduction in thickness at a higher level, such as occurred in the mediaeval rebuilding of the wall, and for the walls of the fort which were already standing, it can be estimated that well over one million cubic feet of ragstone were required. This had to be brought from quarries near Maidstone, the nearest source of good building stone, which had been supplying material for the more important buildings of Roman London as early as the first century.

The best means of transport for bulk of this kind was by boat, and the Medway and Thames provided a water-way from quarry to city. In 1962 a small portion of an ancient wooden vessel came to light in the Thames mud at Blackfriars, when work was being carried out for the new under-pass, and in the following year another portion near the bow of the ship was fortunately enclosed by a coffer-dam. This made excavation possible in reasonably dry conditions in the area which was enclosed, and it was found that the vessel was in a fact a keel-less flat-bottomed barge, evidently of local type, and in some respects remarkably like the Thames sailing barges of recent times (**26**). Although carvel-built, like all Roman ships, there was nothing classical about it, and in many ways it was extra-ordinarily crude, evidently relying on the massive strength of its timbers, to which the planks of the bottom and sides were secured with huge clench nails, rather than on skill in construction (*Plates* 30–1). Its age was at first uncertain, but clear evidence of a Roman date soon appeared. After it sank there was a lapse of time during which gravel was washed into it, and then the sides collapsed. The starboard side overlay and effectively sealed the earlier gravel filling, from which came a quantity of Roman pottery, and nothing of a later date. The pottery was pre-dominantly of the second century, but with one or two pieces of the late third century, so the side cannot have collapsed before that date, which may have been a long time after the vessel was wrecked. In the mast-step, which had been cut into one of the massive transverse ribs, was a worn copper coin (*as*) of the Emperor Domitian, which has been struck in A.D. 88–9. This had evidently been put there for luck, as was the custom when wooden ships were constructed in this country in recent times.[38] The coin must have been in circulation for quite a long time before it was put into the mast-step, and it seems to have been selected mainly for its reverse type, which lay uppermost. This represents the goddess of luck, Fortuna, holding a ship's rudder (*Plates* 33–4). The date of the coin, therefore, merely gives us a date *after* which the mast must have been fitted, and from the condition of the coin, it must have been years after.[39] The evidence in fact suggests that the boat was built in the second century and wrecked towards the end of that century or a little later. Many of the timbers had been attacked by the Teredo worm, and this species cannot live long in fresh water alone, so that the vessel, which was evidently not intended for the open sea, must have made repeated journeys to the Thames estuary. Lying on the bottom of the barge aft of the mast-step was a considerable quantity of Kentish ragstone, extending as far aft as could be examined. There seems little doubt, therefore, that this was one of the carriers of building material from the Medway, and it is by no means unlikely that it was carrying a load for the building of the city wall itself when it met disaster near the mouth of the Fleet.

Clearly there must have been impelling reasons for this great and costly undertaking, but an evaluation of these depends entirely on the precise dating of the work, which so far escapes us. The most definite piece of evidence which we now have is a worn coin of Commodus, of A.D. 183–4, found during one of Professor Grimes's excavations in a deposit which clearly ante-dated the city wall.[40] Since the coin had evidently been in circulation for some time before it was dropped, the city wall can hardly be earlier than the last years of the second century. Another piece of evidence suggesting a similar date may be cited. A section across the internal earth rampart which is known to be contemporary with the wall, cut by Mr. R. Gilyard Beer just east of the White Tower in 1954, dated the bank on pottery evidence to the late second century.[41] Philip Corder showed that similar dating evidence exists for the walls of a number of Romano-British towns, and suggested that they were built on the orders of Clodius Albinus, governor of Britain and a claimant for the Empire in the period of anarchy which followed the death of Commodus.[42] Septimius Severus, who eventually gained the supremacy over his rivals, offered Albinus the rank and title of Caesar in 193, thereby virtually appointing him as his successor. This, however, was merely to keep the west quiet while Severus dealt with Pescennius Niger, his rival in the east. As soon as Italy and the east were under control, in 195, he declared Albinus a public enemy. The latter, in reply, had himself proclaimed Emperor by his army, and crossed over into Gaul with all the troops he could muster, denuding Britain of its frontier garrisons. He was decisively defeated and killed in 197, and the armies of Severus brought order again to Britain, where the north had been over-run by tribesmen from beyond Hadrian's Wall.

Corder's suggestion was that most of the city walls of the province were built on the orders of Albinus between 193 and 197, in preparation for the civil war with Septimius Severus which he knew was inevitable, and which he knew could only be fought by diverting all the military resources of Britain from their proper purpose of frontier defence. It did not require great foresight to realise that the cities of the province, which were the principal repositories of Roman civilisation, might survive only through the strength of their own defences. This theory has one great merit; it allows adequate time – about three years – for these tremendous tasks to be carried out, and the walls of London, as of other cities, were evidently not built in haste to meet a sudden danger.

It is unlikely that city walls would have been built in the reign of Severus, for his resources were strained to the utmost in the restoration of the essential defences of northern Britain, but one theory would attribute them to his successor, Caracalla. It was suggested that the cities were allowed to build walls as a privilege in the reign of the latter, as a corollary of his grant of Roman citizenship in A.D. 212 to all free inhabitants of the Empire.[43] It is now known that some at least of the town walls of Roman Britain are of a considerably later date in the third century; but the problem is complicated by the fact that in some cases they replaced earlier earthwork fortifications, apparently constructed late in the second century. These have not been detected in London, and it is conceivable that the most important town in Britain was given priority for its stone defences, which may therefore be more nearly contemporary with the earlier phases elsewhere.

It must be remembered, however, that the archaeological dating of the city wall of London – and of most other cities of Roman Britain – at present only gives us the terminal date *after* which the wall was built. It does not tell us how long after, and evidence may yet come to light which will compel us to advance the actual date of building further into the third century. It is salutary to recall the views which have been successively held on this subject by leading scholars during the last fifty years.

One contributor to the Victoria County History believed that it was Constantinian, another that it was not later than the middle of the second century. Haverfield, while emphasising that no definite conclusion could be reached, favoured the late third century. Wheeler, in the Report of the Royal Commission, published in 1928, concluded that 'it was built in the half-century following the Boudiccan rebellion.'[44] All these views were based on general considerations of topography, analogies with the Continent, and a supposed association between the silting of the Walbrook and the building of the wall. No archaeological dating evidence for the actual structure of the wall itself had then been found, but in the years which followed this gradually accumulated. Fragments of early second century pottery were found at the original ground level near the wall, and in the ramp which was piled against it.[45] It was then concluded that the wall was built in the reign of Hadrian, probably between about A.D. 120 and 130. In 1950, however, Professor Grimes found embedded in the mortar of the wall a coin of Aelius, Hadrian's adopted heir, struck in A.D. 137, and drew the conclusion that the city wall was built 'after, if not much after, A.D. 140.'[46] As we have seen, his subsequent discovery of a worn coin of A.D. 183-4, antedating the wall, led him to add another half-century to this date, and this has been confirmed by pottery evidence elsewhere. It would clearly be rash, however, to assume that finality has now been reached, and that further evidence will not compel us to advance the date again.

After Severus' defeat of Albinus in A.D. 197, he took drastic political action which must have had a very considerable effect on the status and functions of London as an administrative centre. This was the division of Britain into two provinces, Upper and Lower Britain, each with its own army and military governor. The purpose was of course to prevent some future governor with a large army at his disposal from following the example of Albinus and laying claim to the Empire. The dividing line is uncertain, but Lincoln and York are known by inscriptions to have been in Lower Britain, while Chester and Caerleon were in Upper Britain. York, where there was at this time a *domus palatina*, the residence of Severus during his campaign in the north, undoubtedly became the capital of Lower Britain, and it seems equally certain that London continued to be the capital of Upper Britain.[47] This would evidently have resulted in a considerable diminution of its status, even though the Upper Province was the more important, with two Legions against the one in Lower Britain. Another view, however, was expressed in the Report of the Royal Commission. On the assumption that the Watling Street formed the boundary – and there are objections to this, on the ground that it would have divided the tribal territories of both the Catuvellauni and Cornovii – it was suggested that London may have belonged to neither province, but served as a centralising authority between the two local administrations and the Emperor. This, however, was admittedly mere speculation.[48]

Whatever its political fortune may have been, London cannot have remained unaffected by the general economic troubles which developed as the third century advanced. The decay of Romano-British cities in this period has in the past been exaggerated, and city life certainly continued even if civic development came to an end. In the case of London, however, with its vital interest in overseas trade, the effects must surely have been greater than in the tribal capitals which merely served as markets for the surrounding countryside. The civil wars and barbarian invasions which brought disaster to so many prosperous communities in Gaul in the third quarter of the century must have destroyed a large part of London's trade; while the relative isolation of Britain following the usurpation of Postumus in A.D. 259, which severed the three western provinces from the rest of the Empire for fourteen years, must have resulted in an economic stagnation from which London would have been one of the worst sufferers. The wretched makeshift coins produced in London as elsewhere in crude imitation of the already degenerate coins of the Gallic usurpers are symptomatic of these unhappy times. A hoard of five hundred of these was found just north of Paternoster Row in 1961, concealed in a hole or gully dug in what had once been the good gravel surface of a roadway or courtyard (**17**. *Plates* 11–2). Public amenities were no doubt neglected, but of this there is little direct evidence. The small bath-house in Cheapside apparently did not survive long into the third century, but we do not know the circumstances of its decay and final destruction (**55**). It was probably in this period also that refuse was allowed to accumulate on a white cement floor which is likely to have formed part of the forum (**230**). The picture is not one of unrelieved gloom, however, and some of the citizens of Roman London seem to have continued to live in comfort and even luxury. The building of fine town houses seems to have continued at least into the early third century, to which some of the best London mosaics are tentatively attributed on stylistic grounds[49] (*Plate* 65). One house at least that is of considerable pretensions was apparently built at a date well advanced in the third century. This was the building with a patterned mosaic pavement found on the site of No. 11, Ironmonger Lane, in 1949 (**151**, *Plate* 67). Here the earliest floor overlay a pit which was not filled in before about A.D. 220, and it seems likely that the mosaic was laid at a considerably later date.[50]

Even more striking is the major reconstruction of an earlier building which took place on Lloyd's site in Lime Street, at a date which must be later than A.D. 270 (**331**, *Fig.* 6). After the demolition of the earlier walls and before the new floors were laid, a handful of thirty-two little copper coins, barbarous copies of the issues of Gallienus, Tetricus and other Emperors of about A.D. 260–275, similar to those found in Paternoster Row, were dropped into a small hole made with a pointed stick within the corner of the building, beside the new foundations.[51] The evidence strongly suggests that this was done at the time of reconstruction, probably as a foundation deposit to ensure good fortune for the new building. A striking feature of this little hoard was the high proportion of die identities – coins struck from the same dies. Two obverse dies and two reverse dies in the same workshop had produced sixteen of the coins, and four other dies had been used twice, accounting altogether for twenty coins, which are likely all to have come from the same unofficial mint in London – if it can be dignified by that title. This is in marked contrast to the Paternoster Row hoard, where only three identical obverse dies and two reverse dies were found in more than 500 coins. Most of the Lime Street coins showed little wear and had obviously come straight from the workshop which made them – and this cannot have been far away. We therefore have a curious paradox – the replacement of a building by a considerably more substantial one at a time when these miserable little coins, indicative of economic squalor and political chaos, were being produced in the premier city of Britain. A possible explanation is that they continued to be made, for a time at least, for use as small change, in a period of greater stability which followed.[52] Britain was then even more isolated, but was under a resolute and able ruler, who seems to have grappled firmly with the country's military and economic problems, and may well have provided the stimulus for reconstruction in London.

In A.D. 286 or 287, a commander of the Channel Fleet, the *Classis Britannica*, found himself in serious trouble with the authorities. He was a Menapian – a member of a sea-faring

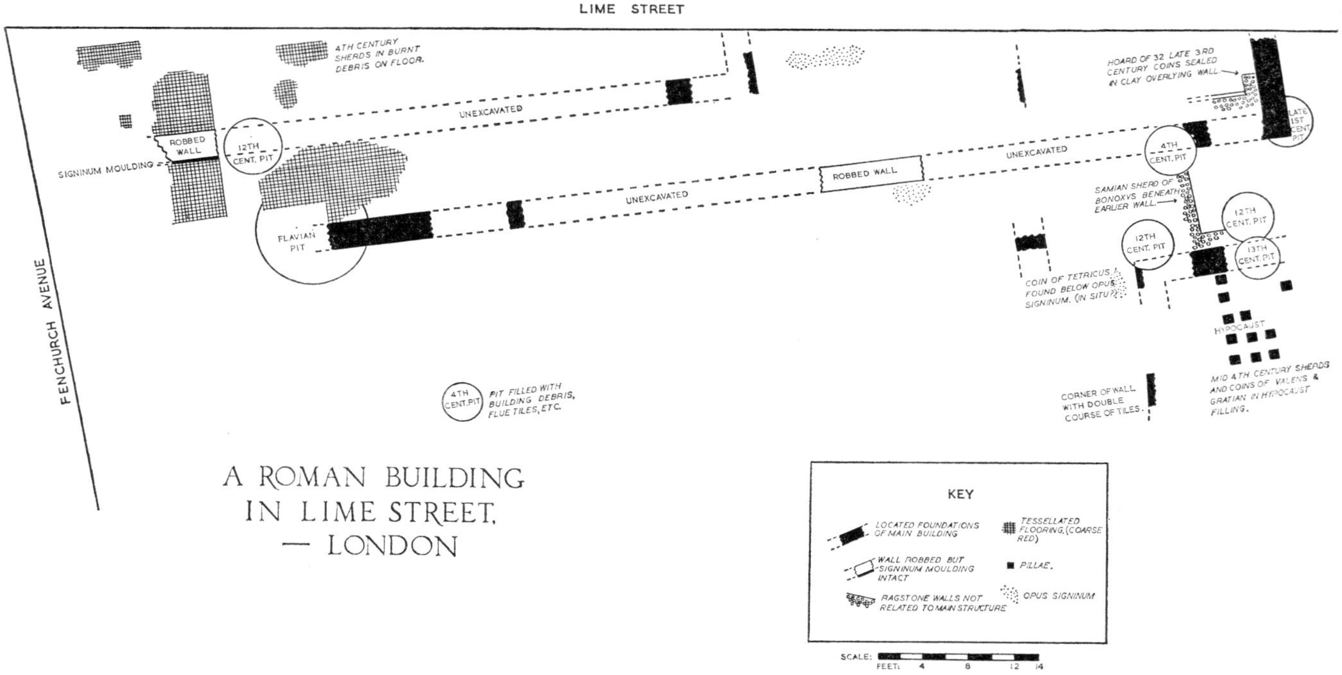

Fig. 6 Plan of a late Roman building and earlier remains in Lime Street (331). *Drawn by I. Noel Hume (Guildhall Museum)*.

55

tribe in what is now Holland – named Marcus Aurelius
Mausaeus Carausius, a man of humble origin who had rapidly
risen to a position of high command under Maximian by his
undoubted ability. His task was to suppress the Frankish and
Saxon pirates whose raids were harassing the coastal towns and
villages. His operations were highly successful but were planned, it was suspected, so that the pirates were caught *after* their
depredations, when they were loaded with loot. This was not
returned to the rightful owners or handed over to Maximian,
but was kept by Carausius for himself. There is even a suspicion
that he was at times in league with the pirates, and shared their
booty with them. Eventually his misbehaviour was reported to
Maximian, who ordered his arrest, which would no doubt have
been shortly followed by his execution. Carausius, however,
crossed immediately with his fleet to Britain and declared himself Emperor. Maximian of course attacked him as soon as he
could build himself ships, but was defeated, and Carausius was
reluctantly recognised as an equal by Diocletian and Maximian,
who now shared the Empire. Britain and the Channel, including its southern side apparently as far inland as Rouen, were
acknowledged as the territory of Carausius, although his so-
called partners in the Empire clearly did not intend that this
arrangement should continue for longer than was absolutely
necessary, and in practice the isolation of Britain must have
been almost complete. Nevertheless, Carausius ruled his
island-empire for six years, and ruled well, so that even his
enemies' flatterers, who are our only source of information,
have nothing to say against him. His portrait suggests a certain
geniality combined with the roguery, and this, with his very
real abilities, may well have secured the loyalty and even
affection of his subjects.

It was Carausius who established the first official mint in
London, using the mint-mark ML (*Plate* 14 (1-2)). This was not
his only British mint, for he also issued coins with the mint-
mark C, which have usually been attributed to Camulodunum.
If this is correct, it must reflect the revival of Colchester to
something more nearly approaching its early glories, with some
corresponding diminution of the importance of London. It is
quite possible, however, that the C does not stand for Camulodunum at all, and an alternative suggestion is Clausentum
(Bitterne). The important role of the navy in preserving the
empire of Carausius may have made it expedient to have a

special mint to provide the sailors' pay. A variant CL of this mint-mark, used by Carausius' successor, Allectus, seems as likely to be an abbreviation of Clausentum as of Camulodunum.

The reign of Carausius came to an end in 293, when he was assassinated by Allectus, his financial minister, who declared himself Emperor, possibly under circumstances similar to Carausius' own revolt, to save himself from the consequences of his own misdeeds. He seems to have lacked the redeeming qualities of Carausius, and is said to have been a hard master during his reign of three years.

In 296, Constantius Chlorus as Caesar (a junior colleague of the Emperor) ruling in the west, collected together a fleet for the reconquest of Britain. His forces were divided into two parts, one of which, under his prefect Asclepiodotus, slipped past Allectus' fleet in the fog and landed on the Hampshire coast. Allectus, who had collected a large army by draining all the northern defences of troops, marched to intercept the invaders, but was defeated and killed. The remains of his army straggled back to London, and proceeded to plunder it. The timely arrival of Constantius Chlorus, however, put a stop to the looting. He seems to have been delayed by the fog, but eventually made his way round the coast of Kent and up the Thames, making short work of the surviving rabble of Allectus' army in the streets of London.[53] This event is commemorated by a magnificent gold medallion, found in 1922 in a great hoard of coins and jewellery at Beaurains, near Arras (*Plate* 13). The reverse shows Constantine riding along what is evidently intended to be the bank of the Thames, with the galley which brought him lying alongside in the river. In front of him is a fortified city gate, before which is a kneeling female figure, clearly a personification of London, since beneath her are the letters LON. Here then is our earliest view of London, and it would be pleasant to think that the gate with its twin towers was an accurate representation of one of the city gates of Londinium. Unfortunately there is little doubt that it is purely conventional, and since the medallion was struck at Trier in Gaul it is quite likely that the designer had never even seen London.

Constantius Chlorus is described on the Arras medallion as REDDITOR LUCIS AETERNAE, 'the restorer of the eternal light' – the light of civilisation which came from Rome. It seems likely that the ending of Britain's period of independence and isolation was in fact welcomed by most of its inhabitants in the sentiment expressed by the medallion. To London in particular, both as a stronghold of Roman civilisation and as a port with outward-looking interests, it gave promise of better times, so that the arrival of Constantius not only rescued the Londoners from immediate danger but held obvious advantages for their future. Any loyalty which may have been felt for Carausius would hardly have been transferred to his murderer, Allectus, who was in any case now dead, and in these circumstances it might be expected that the Londoners would have received Constantius with enthusiasm.

The point is emphasised, as a contrary suggestion has been made to account for the curious treatment of the London mint which followed under the rule of the Tetrarchy. After an early issue of the reformed coinage of Diocletian marked LON (*Plate* 14 (5)) soon after the arrival of Constantius Chlorus, the London mint issued coins for ten years without a mint-signature, contrary to the usual practice of the time. It has been suggested that this was a mark of disgrace, perhaps accompanied by some loss of status for the city, either because the welcome accorded to Constantius – for which the medallion may have been prepared in advance – did not come up to expectation, or because London had become too closely identified with the rule of the usurpers.[54] It seems likely, however, that such a punishment would have been inflicted at once, and not after a marked issue had already been produced.

Nevertheless a radical change in the organisation of Britain now took place, and this must have had a drastic effect on the political status of London. For civil administration the Empire was divided into twelve parts, called dioceses, of which Britain formed one, with an official called a *vicarius* at its head. There was, however, a rigid hierarchical system in which the *vicarius* was responsible not directly to the Emperor, but to the prae-torian prefect of Gaul, who ruled Transalpine Gaul, Britain and Spain from his headquarters at Trier. The diocese itself was divided into a number of small provinces. In Britain there were four: Britannia Prima, Britannia Secunda, Maxima Caesariensis (named after Galerius Maximianus) and Flavia Caesariensis (named after Flavius Constantius Chlorus). Unfortunately we know very little about these divisions – not even where they were. A writer of the early thirteenth century, Giraldus Cambrensis, says that London was the capital of Flavia Caesariensis and York the capital of Maxima Caesariensis, while Prima was in the west, and Secunda in Kent. Evidence from an inscription indicates that Cirencester was in Britannia Prima, and so gives confirmation to one of these attributions.[55] London at this time is therefore likely to have been the capital of one of the small provinces and also the head-quarters of the *vicarius* of the diocese. In the latter capacity it would have served as a link between the provincial governments and higher authority, but could not be regarded in any sense as the working capital of all Britain. Civil administration was now divorced from military command, and the principal head-quarters of the latter was at York. From this northern base Constantius carried out the task of rebuilding the fortifications of the northern frontier, and eventually undertook a punitive war against the tribes which lived beyond it. York was un-doubtedly the centre of power in Britain at this period, and it was here that Constantius died and his son Constantine was proclaimed. London, however, remained the principal nerve centre of Britain, and possessed the only mint, with the mint signature (now PLN) reappearing towards the end of 306. It continued to issue coins in the name of Constantine I, his colleagues and sons, until about A.D. 326, when it was closed down (*Plate* 14(6–15)). Thereafter Britain drew its coinage from the mints of Gaul, especially Trier, and the London mint did not function again until its probable revival in the reign of the usurper Magnus Maximus.

The emergence of Constantine I as the supreme ruler of the Empire brought one change of the greatest importance to London as to the rest of the Roman world. Although he was baptised only on his death-bed, he strongly favoured Christi-anity throughout his reign, and worked to establish a powerful and united Church which would be the spiritual counterpart of his own unified earthly Empire. There is no doubt that Christianity existed in London before the time of Constantine as a clandestine religious movement, subject at times to savage persecution, although we have no direct evidence of it. There are, however, numerous finds which illustrate the diverse paganism of the city, showing that the cults both of classical deities, such as Diana and Mercury, and of the Celtic Mother-Goddesses flourished equally (*Plates* 86, 88–9). The distinction is more apparent than real, since Celtic deities were often identi-fied with their Roman counterparts and were represented in classical form. A particular favourite in London seems to have

been Venus – or a Gaulish deity of similar attributes and functions who was equated with the Italian goddess. Her figurines in
pipe-clay were imported in considerable quantity from Central
Gaul, for use both in household shrines and as votive offerings
in temples. Such cults had the appeal of popular superstition,
and provided the conservative-minded with the comfort of
traditional rites sanctioned by ancestral custom. They gave
little satisfaction, however, to the genuinely religious, who
turned more and more to the oriental mystery cults. These
offered their initiates emotional warmth, which could lead to
mystical ecstasy, and the promise of a happy life after death.

Like all great ports, London was wide open to these exotic
influences, and some archaeological evidence of their presence
has been found. The inscription 'LONDINI AD FANVM
ISIDIS,' scratched on a wine-jug in the London Museum,
bears witness to the presence in London of a shrine to the
Egyptian goddess Isis, not necessarily in Southwark where the
jug was found. A bronze pair of forceps, decorated with the
heads of Attis, Cybele, and the eight planetary deities of the
Roman week, found in the Thames near London Bridge and
now in the British Museum, may well have been an instrument
used in ritual self-mutilation by the priests of the Asiatic goddess Cybele, as was suggested by Mr. A. G. Francis.[56] The
greatest of all the oriental mystery cults, however, was that of
Mithras, which satisfied the same emotional needs as the rest,
but also upheld the ideal of a noble life. Its insistence on purity,
honesty and courage had a strong appeal in a world where
these qualities were so often conspicuously and disastrously
lacking. It was this, rather than the favour of Emperors, which
made Mithraism the strongest rival to Christianity. Men of
action were especially drawn to it, and it was the Roman
soldier who brought the cult of the Persian god of light from
Asia Minor, and carried it to the furthest outposts of the
Empire. Merchants also found it congenial – perhaps because
honesty really is the best policy in the world of commerce –
and Mithraism flourished in ports such as Ostia, where at least
fifteen temples of the cult have been identified. In London we
know of only one, found by Professor W. F. Grimes on the site
of Bucklersbury House, Walbrook, in 1954, but it is likely that
there were others which have remained undiscovered or have
been destroyed piecemeal in building excavations without
being recognised. The Walbrook Mithraeum was richly fur-

nished with expensive marble sculptures imported from Italy, and although we know that one of its congregation was a retired soldier,[57] most were probably well-to-do merchants, who found that the probity enjoined on the followers of Mithras was by no means incompatible with success in business. The Persian god was the guarantor of faith and the protector of contracts, however informally undertaken. 'My word is my bond' is a phrase with a Mithraic ring which has become part of the tradition of the City of London, expressing a principle which is both admirable and in the long run seldom unprofitable.

The nobility of Mithraism, however, should not blind us to its failings and weaknesses. It is true that the fundamental idea of its theology – that there is a universal struggle between the forces of good and evil, in which men must take their part – represents a notable advance in the religious thought of the Roman world. The basic monotheism, or rather dualism, of the Persian religion was masked, however, by the absorption of pagan deities into an elaborate cosmology, which helped to make it acceptable to the pagan world, but also enmeshed it in a web of superstition and abstruse symbolism, in which elements of barbaric savagery were preserved. There was little room for the gentler virtues in the harsh Mithraic code, while the organisation of the cult as a society for male initiates only excluded half of the human race from participation. Above all, its central figure, the divine mediator between God and men, was himself as mythical and dehumanised as any other personification of a natural phenomenon. These were the weaknesses which undermined Mithraism and ensured the eventual triumph of Christianity.

We have little archaeological evidence in London of the historical fact of Roman Christianity, mostly, no doubt, because of the comparative rarity of finds of any kind of the late Empire, due to the removal of the higher occupation levels by mediaeval and later builders. A Chi-Rho symbol scratched on the base of a pewter bowl from Copthall Court, now in the London Museum, is the only example of the monogram of Christ – the commonest of all emblems of Christianity in the Roman Empire – found in Londinium itself, although several ingots of pewter stamped with this sign were found three and a half miles away in the Thames at Battersea.[58] The two lamps with the Chi-Rho monogram in the Guildhall Museum are of Eastern Mediterranean type and of unknown provenance. If they were found in London, it is likely that they were post-Roman imports. In the case of other finds which have been quoted as examples of Christian symbolism or iconography, such as the silver disc from Lothbury bearing a helmeted bust and an apparent cross which has been thought to represent Constantine's vision of the Cross, the interpretation must be regarded as extremely doubtful.[59] We do not yet know any Christian church of Roman London, and the tradition that St. Peter's upon Cornhill is of Roman origin remains unproved.[60]

It is perhaps fitting that the clearest archaeological testimony to the triumph of Christianity in London should come from the defeated pagan gods themselves. The marble sculptures of Mithras, Minerva, Serapis and Mercury, with the colossal hand of Mithras, excavated by Professor Grimes in 1954, were sealed beneath a floor of the temple which seems to have been laid quite early in the fourth century – although we must await Professor Grimes's detailed assessment of the evidence in his forthcoming report, before the dates of the various phases of the temple can be given with any confidence. From their condition these sculptures had evidently been very carefully buried, no doubt by the followers of Mithras or their priests to save them from some danger which threatened them. It is unlikely that this came from any transitory event, such as the disorders which followed the defeat of Allectus, for the sculptures remained buried and were eventually forgotten. It is likely, therefore, that the danger continued, and its most likely source was the implacable enemy of Mithraism. In the latter part of the third century and the beginning of the fourth, Christianity and Mithraism were locked in a struggle for survival and supremacy, which was made all the more bitter by the fact that they had certain features in common. To the Christians the Mithraic analogies to their own beliefs and practices seemed a blasphemous parody, which had to be suppressed when they achieved political power. According to Cumont, Christian persecution of Mithraism did not get into full swing until after the reign of Constantine I,[61] but the burial of the sculptures in the Walbrook temple evidently took place at a much earlier date, and it may be significant that the Mithraea on Hadrian's Wall also seem to have been wrecked quite early in the fourth century.[62] Christianity may therefore have been politically dominant in Britain even at the beginning of the reign of Constantine.

The London Mithraeum was not destroyed after the burial of the pagan sculptures, and while it is possible that it was converted into a Christian church, there is no evidence at all that this was the case. All that can be said is that the building continued in use, and a further floor was laid above the one which sealed the pit containing the sculptures. That it was used again for a religious purpose of some kind is indicated by the laying of a stone block for an altar base in the centre of the apse, not earlier than the middle of the reign of Constantine.[63] Paganism was not yet dead, however, and one of the most intriguing finds of 1954 was a marble group representing Bacchus with his usual companions, found (unfortunately by workmen) above the level of the latest floor of the temple (*Plate* 80). This was presumably brought to the temple after the dangers which led to the burial of the Mithraic sculptures had passed, and inevitably one thinks of the reign of Julian the Apostate (A.D. 360–3). This Emperor, who was himself a pagan philosopher and an initiate of Mithraism, alone among the successors of Constantine was hostile to Christianity and gave official favour to a revival of paganism. Again, we must await Professor Grimes's detailed study of the dating evidence, and it may be that this will indicate a somewhat earlier date for the final phase of the Walbrook temple.[64] If so, the latest use of the temple may have been for a clandestine paganism which escaped discovery. No sign was found of any deliberate destruction, and the Bacchic group seems to have remained, unburied and virtually unharmed, in the north-east corner of the building until it was overwhelmed by debris as the temple fell into ruins.[65]

Some hint of the cosmopolitan character of late Roman London is given by the finds from the Walbrook temple. Marble sculptures imported from Italy may merely indicate a congregation that could afford the best, though it evidently had overseas connections through which its requirements could be met. There is, however, more than one suggestion of an influence from eastern Europe, which can best be explained by the presence of worshippers from Danubian lands. Thus the bull-slaying relief found in Walbrook in 1889, which almost certainly came from the temple of Mithras (*Plate* 84), has close affinities in its composition with a relief from Siscia, and Professor J. M. C. Toynbee has suggested that it may have been carved from Italian marble by a Danubian sculptor in Britain.[66] Similarly, the closest parallels to the Bacchus group come from

Rumania and Bulgaria, and Professor Toynbee is of the opinion that, although this is likewise of Italian marble, 'a Balkan origin may with some reason be ascribed to it.'[67] There is also a portion of a marble medallion representing in low relief the Danubian rider-gods with the central figure of a goddess and various symbols, in a group which relates to a Thracian mystery cult. Similar medallions, usually in lead, are not uncommon in eastern Europe, with a concentration on the middle Danube, and are extremely rare in the west.[68] Even the mysterious silver box (*Plates* 81–3), which came to light in circumstances suggesting that it had been concealed in the north wall of the temple, seems to have eastern affinities in its decoration,[69] and the only close parallel to the strainer which it contained comes from Czecho-Slovakia – much further west, but still within the Danubian area.[70]

If we have little archaeological evidence of Christianity in fourth century London, apart from the reflection of its triumph in the vicissitudes of a pagan temple, we know from an historical record that London had a bishop named Restitutus, who attended the Council of Arles in 314 with two other British bishops – the bishop of York, and another who is described as Adelfius, bishop of *Colonia Londinensium*. The last is clearly an error, since London was not a *colonia* and would not have had two bishops. Lincoln, Colchester, and even Caerleon have been variously suggested as the *colonia* which possessed the third bishopric.[71]

There are several references to London in the second half of the fourth century by the historian Ammianus Marcellinus, all concerning military operations against barbarian invasions. In A.D. 360, Julian, then Caesar in command of the Gallic provinces under Constantius II, sent his general Lupicinus to drive out the Picts and Scots who were ravaging the frontier districts. This was the first large-scale barbarian invasion suffered by Britain, although some similar trouble of this kind had induced Constans to make a personal visit in 342–3. We are told that Lupicinus, a good soldier, but conceited, avaricious and cruel, came in the middle of winter to Boulogne and crossed the Channel to Richborough. Thence he marched to London as a convenient base for his campaign.[72]

Seven years later, in 367–8, a much more serious crisis of the same kind occurred, in which Saxons, Picts and Scots made a concerted attack. The Picts, aided by the treachery of the frontier garrisons, overran Hadrian's Wall and the rest of the northern defences; the Scots, who came from Ireland, swept over the lowlands from the west coast; while the Saxons and Franks invaded the south-east. The Count of the Saxon Shore, who was the commander of the coastal defences, and the Duke of Britain, as the commander-in-chief of the inland forces was called, were both defeated and killed. London was protected by its great defensive wall, but was in a state of siege and faced disaster, while the neighbouring countryside was ravaged by the barbarians. An able general, named Theodosius (father of Theodosius the Great), was sent by Valentinian to deal with the situation, and, like Lupicinus before him, he crossed to Richborough with a large force and made his way to London, clearing Kent of the marauding bands as he came. The barbarians, who were loaded with booty and were driving prisoners in chains and cattle before them, seem to have offered little resistance, and Theodosius freed the wretched captives and restored their property, retaining only a small portion of the plunder for his own soldiers. Great was the rejoicing in London when Theodosius entered the beleaguered city, where he was received with enthusiasm by the inhabitants. He made it his base and after marshalling all the forces that were available, marched out the following year to destroy the barbarians and to bring back order to the country. In this he was successful, and the cities and fortresses which had fallen were all in due course restored.

It was perhaps for its services in the preparation of this campaign that London was honoured with the new name 'Augusta'. We only know definitely that this high-sounding name was bestowed after 326, when the London mint of Constantine was closed, and before the last quarter of the fourth century, when Ammianus was writing his history. He seems to imply that Augusta is a fairly recent name, and perhaps significantly calls London 'Lundinium, an old town since named Augusta' in his account of the arrival of Theodosius, and 'Augusta, which the ancients named Lundinium,' in his reference to the general's departure from the city for his successful campaign the following year.[73] This cannot of course be taken as evidence that the new name was given in 369, and it is as unlikely that Theodosius would have had authority to take such a step on his own initiative as that he would have given thought to such a matter at that particular time. It does, however, suggest

that Ammianus may have associated the change with Theodosius' stay in London, and the subsequent victory celebrations
would have provided a fitting occasion for the Emperor to
bestow the honour. The new name survived the rulers' gratitude
to Theodosius himself, but it was *Londinium* that was destined to
endure into post-Roman times. *Augusta* was used for official
purposes, but the old name evidently remained in general use
in the daily life of the citizens.

One of the officers of Theodosius was a Spaniard named
Magnus Clemens Maximus, who remained in Britain and rose
to high command. Like Albinus nearly two hundred years
earlier, he decided to make a bid for the Empire, and with the
same disastrous results. In 383 he made himself Emperor of
Britain, and proceeded to withdraw troops from the frontier
defences, including Hadrian's Wall, in order to do battle with
Gratian on the Continent. Money to pay his army was an early
requirement, which he seems to have met by reviving the
London mint, to issue gold *solidi* and silver *siliquae*, but no
bronze. These coins have the mint signature AVG, which most
numismatists accept as an abbreviation for Augusta (*Plate* 14,
No. 16). This attribution has been challenged by a minority,
and Augustodunum (Autun) in Gaul has been suggested as an
alternative, principally on the grounds that the issue of gold
and silver coins is usually an indication of the presence of the
Emperor.[74] We know that Maximus crossed the Channel and
soon became master of Gaul and Spain as well as Britain.
Thereafter he must have spent a great deal of time in Gaul,
especially as the Rhine frontier seems to have received more of
his attention than the frontiers of Britain, which were inevitably
overrun by the barbarians when their garrisons were withdrawn. Since he had the large and important mint of Trier,
however, there seems no good reason why he should have
needed a new mint at Autun, and we know very little either
about his movements during the five years of his reign, or about
the observance of the rule that gold and silver coins should be
issued only when the Emperor was in the neighbourhood. There
were apparently two issues from the mint with the signature
AVG; the first presumably dates from the time when Maximus
first raised his standard, and the second after his agreement with
Theodosius, the son of his old commander, who was ruling in
the east. This took place in 384, when Maximus was threatening
to invade Italy, where the boy Valentinian II was the nominal

ruler, and it was necessary to buy him off with some kind of recognition. In the second issue of coins (*Plate* 14, No. 16), the inscription VICTORIA AVGG shows that Maximus was claiming to be one of the two Augusti, the other evidently being Theodosius. The young Valentinian is scornfully ignored by this mint. The second issue may therefore have been struck any time after 384 and before the final clash with Theodosius in 388, when Maximus was defeated at Aquileia and put to death. London is clearly the most likely place for the first issue of Maximus, and the second issue may well have been produced during a return visit to Britain which history has not recorded.

The revival of the London mint was brief, however, and we have only one further indication of the status of London in the last years of Roman Britain. It is clear that it remained the financial capital, for in the *Notitia Dignitatum*, a late Roman official document which contains the civil and military estab- lishment of Britain (probably representing conditions towards the end of the fourth century but with some later additions), one of the posts listed is that of the 'Officer in charge of the Treasury at Augusta.'[75]

In the last few years of the fourth century, a serious and apparently successful attempt was made, on the instructions of Stilicho, the Vandal general who was acting as Regent for the youthful Honorius, to restore order in Britain and to drive out the barbarians. The defences were reorganised, and for the last time the dying Roman Empire briefly held Britain under its protection. Rome herself was now in danger, however, and troops were withdrawn from Britain for the Gothic war in A.D. 401 or 402. In 406, the remaining forces, resenting the neglect of the central government and hoping to provide a more effic- ient defence for Britain, set up in rapid succession two short- lived usurpers, named Marcus and Gratian, both of whom were murdered. Their choice then fell on one Constantine, later known as Constantine III, who sent a message to Honorius, the ruler of the Western Empire,[76] explaining that he had acted under compulsion. Honorius at once acknowledged him as a colleague, and Constantine, like Maximus before him, crossed over to Gaul and devoted his attention to the Rhine frontier, so that Britain was in worse case than before, and once more revolted. The governors appointed by Constantine were expelled, and an appeal for help was sent to Honorius. The latter, how- ever, had trouble enough of his own, for the Goths were masters of Italy, and Rome itself was soon to fall. Accordingly he sent a reply – the well-known Rescript of 410 – which gives the traditional date for the ending of Roman rule in Britain. In this he bade the local British authorities look to their own defences, and in effect granted them – at least temporarily – their independence.

London was well fitted to defend itself, with its great defensive wall to which had been added projecting towers or bastions, semi-circular or horseshoe-shaped in plan, from which the approaches to the wall could be covered by the fire of the defenders. The bastions are of two kinds, possibly serving a rather different purpose and built at different times. With the exception of the Wardrobe Tower bastion (Bastion 1) and the bastion beneath the vestry of All Hallows Church (Bastion 11), those in the eastern part of the city wall whose method of construction is known were solid, at least in the lower part, the core being packed with re-used stone, some from buildings and some evidently obtained from the tomb-stones and other monuments of the cemeteries just outside the town. (See *Fig.* 7 and *Plates* 93–5.) This suggests that they were built in an emergency, when defence requirements were sufficiently urgent to override any reluctance to show disrespect to the dead. It is true that the tombs robbed were pagan, but even these would no doubt have remained undisturbed under normal conditions. The purpose of this type of bastion was evidently to provide a firm platform which would carry a heavy catapult or spring-gun (*ballista*), used by the Romans as artillery.

The western group of bastions are hollow at the base – with one exception (Bastion 17) – and contain no re-used material. Their mediaeval successors had arrow-slits, still to be seen in Bastion 14, and it may be that these hollow bastions were always intended for the use of lighter weapons, although they could have been covered with timber platforms which would have supported light artillery of the *ballista* type, as seems to have been the case with the hollow bastions at Caerwent.

There is evidence of a general re-organisation of the defences of Romano-British towns in the late Roman period, involving the addition of bastions, sometimes accompanied by the widening of the defensive ditch beyond them to serve as a death trap for the attacking forces as they came under fire from the *ballistae*. At Caerwent and Great Casterton the bastions were dated by coins as not earlier than about the middle of the fourth

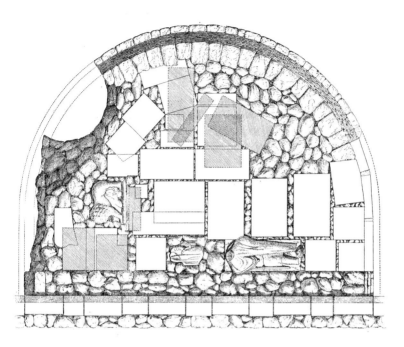

FIG. 7 Plan of the bastion in Camomile Street, showing Roman
sculptures *in situ* in the core of the bastion (**B10**). From *J. E. Price:
On a Bastion of London Wall.*

century, and at Aldborough pottery evidence pointed to a
similar date.[77] In London the dating is at present inconclusive,
and we also have to account for the completely different construction of the two groups of bastions. It has usually been
assumed that these are of different dates, and that the solid
bastions are likely to be earlier, since the eastern side of the city
would probably have had priority in matters of defence, as it
was nearer to the danger of attack from the sea. Even if this
argument is valid, very little time need have elapsed between
the building of the two groups, and it has been suggested that
the difference between them may have resulted from the adoption of a more economical method of construction after the
supply of stone from tombs and disused buildings had been
exhausted.[78] One piece of evidence, however, suggests that the
hollow bastions may even be of post-Roman date. When Pro-

fessor Grimes excavated Bastion 14 in 1948, a hard gravelly layer which appeared to be the floor was found at the level of the off-set of the city wall – very near Roman ground level – and in this was a coin of Constans, (issued 346–50). This is gratifyingly consistent with the coin evidence from the bastions of Great Casterton and Caerwent, and provided that the gravel layer was in fact the original floor of the bastion, as it appeared to be, it would indicate that the latter was built about the middle of the fourth century or later. The cumulative evidence from Great Casterton, Caerwent and London would further suggest that the defences of Romano-British towns were strengthened in this way as an act of imperial policy not very much later than the middle of the century, perhaps as a result of the visit of Constans in 343. Unfortunately for our peace of mind, very near the coin in Bastion 14 was found a little bronze pendant with a highly stylised animal ornament, which has been dated to about the ninth century.[79] This appears to have been found just above the surface of the gravel floor. If it had been embedded in the gravel, it would suggest very strongly that the bastion was not built until the Anglo-Saxon period, and might reasonably be attributed to the year 883 when King Alfred refortified London against the Danes. Its presence above the floor might only mean that the bastion was thoroughly cleaned out at this period, the accumulated rubbish being cleared to the original Roman floor surface. It should also be mentioned that the bastion was built in a style of masonry very similar to the refacing of the city wall against which it was built, and that this refacing has been observed elsewhere. We have as yet no indication whether it should be attributed to Anglo-Saxon or late Roman builders, but a major repair of this kind suggests a longer period of dilapidation than a century or two. More evidence is clearly required before any conclusion can be drawn, but the excavation of Bastion 14 has thrown doubt on the Roman date of the whole group of hollow bastions.

There seems, however, no reason to suppose that the solid bastions of the eastern part of the wall are anything but late Roman. They contained nothing but Roman material, and two of them (Bastions 6 and 7) possibly had the typically Roman courses of bonding-tiles. Moreover, one of the two hollow bastions of the eastern group (Bastion 11) was evidently built while the Roman city ditch was still open. The portion of the ditch immediately in front of the bastion had been filled with

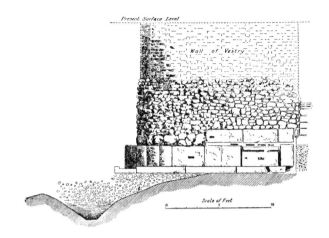

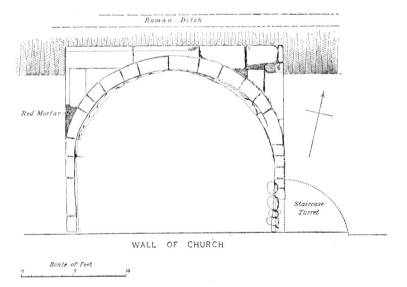

F IG. 8 West elevation and plan of the bastion at All Hallows, London Wall, showing the footings of the bastion overlying the filling of the Roman city ditch (**B 11**). From *Archaeologia LXIII*, *by permission.*

chalk, flint and stones to support the foundations which overlay
it (*Fig.* 8), but on either side it had 'clearly remained open
for some time after the building of the bastion, accumulating
mud and rubbish against the obstruction of the bastion footings.'[80] As for the hollow bastions of the western group, the
balance of probability perhaps still inclines slightly towards a
late Roman date, as the coin of Constans found in the floor of
Bastion 14 would suggest. It would be surprising if no attempt
were made to complete the series for the whole circuit of the
defences before the end of the Roman period, even if the initial
project were unaccountably left unfinished for a period. Until
this was done, the improved defences could easily be outflanked
and would therefore be of little value. Moreover, each bastion
needed the support of its neighbours, since a *ballista* could not
be declined sufficiently to cover the ground immediately around
its own bastion.[81] There was therefore a strong incentive for the
completion of the series once it had been begun, although the
gap of eight hundred yards between the two groups of bastions
seems never to have been filled. Since the use of bastions, both
solid and hollow, is so characteristic of late Roman defence, and
is so closely linked with a typically Roman weapon, we should
perhaps remain reluctant to accept a post-Roman origin for
either eastern or western group in London *as a whole* until more
definite evidence emerges.

St. Germanus, Bishop of Auxerre, visited Britain in 429 to
combat the Pelagian heresy,[82] and found a country harassed by
barbarian inroads. The Roman cities of the south were still
intact and ruled by their own magistrates, but their defence was
entirely in their own hands and was apparently purely local.
The account given is of Verulamium, but London must have
been in very much the same position. It is said that Germanus,
who had been a distinguished soldier in his youth, helped to
organise the local militia and led them out to victory against the
invaders, after teaching them the war-cry 'Alleluia' and, no
doubt, also the rudiments of military tactics.[83]

Roman rule had gone, but some at least of the cities of
southern Britain survived and retained the vestiges of Roman
civilisation at least until the middle of the fifth century. There
can be no doubt that London was one of these. They were hard-
pressed, however, and in 446 sent to the Roman authorities a
final appeal for help, which was refused. In the midst of their
other troubles, they were still concerned with spiritual prob-

lems, and once more Pelagianism was laying siege to the British conscience. An appeal to the Pope in 447 was more successful than the appeal to the Emperor, and the indefatigable, but now aged, Germanus appeared once more in Britain, this time to do combat only with his spiritual opponents.

It is hardly likely that in London, where the foundations of mediaeval and later buildings have destroyed most of the late Roman levels, any archaeological evidence of fifth century occupation should come to light, but in Verulamium the historical records of the visits of St. Germanus have recently been supplemented by finds which show clearly not only that the occupation of the city continued well into the fifth century, but that all the amenities of Roman civilisation had not been lost at a date which cannot fall far short of the middle of the century. A large house found in the 1959 excavations had evidently been built after about A.D. 370, as a coin of Valens was found in the make-up beneath its floor. It was subsequently rebuilt and elaborate mosaic pavements were laid, one of which was later repaired, no doubt after a considerable period of use. The house was again rebuilt, and a corn-drying furnace was inserted – a significant indication of the abandonment of the countryside for the greater security of the town, and of the preoccupation of town-dwellers with rural matters early in the fifth century, for this phase can hardly be of earlier date. After the collapse or demolition of this building, it was replaced by a large buttressed hall of unknown use, but clearly fifth century in date. Finally, cutting through the wall and buttress of this structure, evidently after its destruction, a wooden water-pipe of Roman type was laid, the iron collars of which have survived.[84] (See *Plate* 109 for a similar wooden water-pipe with iron collars.) It is difficult to see how this could possibly be earlier than A.D. 450, a date well into the Dark Age, when the survival of such an amenity as a piped water supply is, to say the least, surprising. It is a testimony to the strength of the urban tradition in Roman Britain, and this cannot have been less persistent in London.

The only definite reference to London in the history of this period is found in the Anglo-Saxon Chronicle, but this is an account compiled centuries later and no reliance can be placed on it. It is said that after the battle of Crecganford (possibly Crayford in Kent) between the Britons and the Saxons under Hengist, attributed to the year 457, the defeated Britons took refuge in London. Whether this is true or not, in the light of the evidence from Verulamium the survival of Roman London, or rather sub-Roman London, until the middle of the fifth century can hardly be questioned. Can we go further, and claim a continued existence for the city throughout the Dark Ages until it re-emerged triumphantly, after the reintroduction of Christianity and the revival of trade in the seventh century, as once more the see of a Bishop, the home of a mint and the 'mart of many nations resorting to it by sea and land'?[85] This has been the subject of much inconclusive debate, but the two extreme views – that London lay derelict and deserted for more than a hundred years, and that it maintained a continuity of fully organised civic life all through the disturbance of the Anglo-Saxon settlement – have both been generally abandoned. It now seems unlikely that the city was ever unoccupied, since its fortifications, even in a state of decay, made it a place of relative safety, which must have attracted refugees from the surrounding countryside. For the same reason, its own inhabitants must have been reluctant to leave, and in any case had nowhere to go. There may therefore even have been an increase in the population at first, but this would have been rapidly checked by economic necessity. With the removal of the machinery of central government, the dislocation of communications and the collapse of foreign trade, the livelihoods of most Londoners must have disappeared. If the economic basis for survival were subsistence farming on the land around, this could have supported only a small population, whose efforts to scratch a living can have left little leisure to maintain the amenities of civilisation, and are unlikely to have produced the surplus necessary to feed the craftsmen and other specialists who are an essential part of urban life. A less gloomy picture has however been drawn by some scholars. Teutonic settlers were already familiar in the later years of Roman rule, when they received land in return for service as mercenaries, and the invaders were likewise looking for land rather than loot, so that their impact was felt in the countryside rather than the cities. The departure of the Romans and arrival of the Anglo-Saxons therefore probably brought no sudden and catastrophic change in the life of Romano-British townsmen, however much they may have been affected in the long term by the disappearance of central government and the decline of trade. It has been suggested that their industries did not die completely, but that London in particular continued to produce the cheap jewellery, combs, tweezers and other articles of modest luxury that are commonly found in early Anglo-Saxon cemeteries in eastern England.[86] Some exotic goods, such as rings of elephant ivory and glass from the Rhineland, also found their way to these pagan graves, so that a certain amount of overseas trade must have continued, and it might be expected that a share of this would have passed through London.[87] Nevertheless, even allowing that the life of the Dark Age farmers was sufficiently above subsistence level for some townsmen to make a living as craftsmen or merchants, it can hardly be denied that the fortunes of London were now at their lowest ebb. The sub-Roman city of the fifth and sixth centuries must have been a slum of decaying buildings in which past greatness could be more readily discerned than any future promise.

REFERENCES

1. *R.C.H.M.*, pp. 19–27. See also Appendix III, pp. 179 ff.

2. The possibility that some are much more recent imports cannot be entirely ruled out. One example is from the Chaffers' collection, which also contains three Greek lamps of the third or fourth century B.C., likewise said to have been found in London. Chaffers seems to have been a somewhat indiscriminate purchaser from workmen, who sometimes sold antiquities 'planted' by dealers.

3. C. F. C. Hawkes and M. R. Hull, *Camulodunum*, 1947, p. 190.

4. Ibid., p. 179.

5. Ibid., p. 190, footnote.

6. *R.C.H.M.*, p. 27.

7. Ibid.

8. *Arch.*, LXXVIII, pp. 73 ff.

9. I. D. Margary, *Roman Roads in Britain*, I, p. 47.

10. Cassius Dio, Ῥωμαικὴ Ἱστορία LX, 20. Loeb Series Trans., VII, 419.

11. Gordon Home, *Roman London*, 1948, p. 42.

12. G. Suetonius Tranquillus, *De Vita Caesarum – Divus Claudius*, 17.

13. Now in the Palazzo dei Conservatori in Rome.

14. *Arch. Journ.*, CXV, pp. 84 ff.

15. Cornelius Tacitus, *Annals*, XIV, Cap. 33. A *colonia* was a settlement of Roman citizens, and was the highest grade of civic dignity.

16. *R.C.H.M.*, pp. 15 f. A curious story told by Geoffrey of Monmouth of a massacre by decapitation on the banks of a brook within the city may, it is suggested, be a remote traditional echo of an actual event transferred to the wrong period and circumstances. It is more likely, however, that similar discoveries of skulls in the Walbrook had been made in the Middle Ages, and that the story was invented to account for them.

17. Vitruvius Pollio, *De Architectura*, Bk. II, Ch. VIII, 20. Vitruvius condemns the method of building with wattle and daub, principally on account of inflammability.

18. Nos. 30–2, Lombard Street.

19. . . . barbari omissis castellis praesidiisque militarium, quod uberrimum spolianti et defendentibus intutum laeti praeda et laborum segnes petebant. (*Annals*, XIV, Cap. 33.)

20. K. M. Kenyon, *Excavations in Southwark*, pp. 11 f.

21. *Trans. London and Middlesex Arch. Soc.*, Vol. 21, Pt. I, pp. 72 ff.

22. Roach Smith, *Illustrations of Roman London*, p. 28.

23. *R.C.H.M.*, p. 171.

24. Tacitus, *Annals*, III, 42.

25. *Ant. Journ.*, XVI (1936), p. 6.

26. R. E. M. Wheeler, *London in Roman Times* (London Mus. Cat. No. 3), p. 50.

27. It has been variously interpreted: 'To the Divinity of Caesar' (*or of* Claudius) . . . 'and of the Province of Britain', or . . . 'set up by the Province of Britain.'

28. The letters are larger than those of the important Forum inscription from Verulamium (four inches) but smaller than those of the comparable inscription from Wroxeter (nine inches).

29. An inscription in memory of the nineteen-year-old Claudia Martina, wife of Anencletus, slave of the province, from Ludgate Hill, is in Guildhall Museum (*Plate* 9).

30. A tomb-stone of a military policeman known as a *speculator* was found in Playhouse Yard (*R.C.H.M.*, p. 173, No. 14). Dr. J. C. Mann has pointed out that these officials always served at provincial capitals. (*Antiquity*, XXXV, p. 318.)

31. See **214, 225, 232** and pp. 134–5.

32. See **239** and pp. 136–7.

33. *Ant. Journ.*, XXV (1945), pp. 48–77.

34. The writer is indebted to Mr. Brian Hartley for a re-assessment of the dating of the fire in the light of new knowledge of Samian ware.

35. See R. E. M. Wheeler, *Antiquity*, III (1929), pp. 28–9.

36. *Ant. Journ.*, XLII, pp. 38–52.

37. These are average measurements only. There was a considerable variation in the thickness of the wall.

38. A recent example, reported in *The Times* in 1963, was the placing of a sovereign in the mast step of the racing yacht *Royal Sovereign*, the challenger for the America's Cup.

39. No trace of the mast itself remained, and it had evidently been salvaged after the wreck.

40. The coin was found in an accumulated deposit into which had been inserted the thickening added to the fort wall when the city wall was built. *J.R.S.*, XLVII (1957), p. 220.

41. *Arch. Journ.*, CXII (1956), p. 23, footnote 3.

42. Ibid., pp. 22–4.

43. A. L. F. Rivet, *Town and Country in Roman Britain*, p. 93.

44. *R.C.H.M.*, pp. 73–9.

45. F. Cottrill, *London Wall through eighteen centuries*, 1937, p 19.

46. *J.R.S.*, XLI (1951), p. 134.

47. R. G. Collingwood and J. N. L. Myres, *Roman Britain and the English Settlements*, 2nd ed., p. 173.

48. *R.C.H.M.*, pp. 60–1.

49. The writer is indebted to Dr. David Smith for his cautiously expressed views on this difficult subject.

50. D. Dawe and A. H. Oswald, *11 Ironmonger Lane*, 1952, p. 117.

51. *Numismatic Chronicle*, 6th Series, XV (1955), pp. 113 ff.

52. Another explanation might be that coins which had become obsolete and valueless were considered good enough for a luck-offering.

53. It has been suggested that the carvel-built ship found in the mud of the Thames when the foundations of County Hall were excavated in 1910, and now in the London Museum, may have been a unit of the fleet of Allectus sunk by the ships of Constantius. Coins of Tetricus and Carausius are said to have been found beneath a rib, and coins of Carausius and Allectus were found lying directly on the bottom of the vessel. A large stone was embedded in a strake, and the suggestion has been made that this was a warlike missile. The evidence is inconclusive, however, and the ship seems to have been a merchant ship rather than a warship. (For a detailed description, see W. E. Riley and L. Gomme, *Ship of the Roman Period discovered on the Site of the New County Hall*, L.C.C. publication, 1912. There is also an account in *London in Roman Times*, London Mus. Cat. No. 3, 1930, pp. 151–4.)

54. R. A. G. Carson and J. P. C. Kent, 'Constantinian Hoards and Other Studies in the Later Roman Bronze Coinage,' *Numismatic Chronicle*, Sixth Series, XVI (1956), p. 88.

55. Dr. J. C. Mann, however, has pointed out that Maxima Caesariensis alone was given a governor of consular rank in the fourth century, and is therefore more likely to have contained London. (*Antiquity*, XXXV, pp. 318 f.)

56. *Proceedings of the Royal Society of Medicine*, XIX (1926), p. 95.

57. See Note to *Plate 84*, p. 179.

58. In the British Museum.

59. Now in the British Museum. See Roach Smith, *Catalogue of London Antiquities*, p. 63, and W. R. Lethaby, *Londinium: Architecture and the Crafts*, p. 220.

60. Precedence for St. Peter's as the oldest church in London was claimed in the Middle Ages, and in Stow's time there was a tablet in the church stating that it had been founded by a (legendary) King Lucius about A.D. 179 as an Archbishop's see, which was removed to Canterbury in the time of St. Augustine. The church stands within the site of the Roman basilica, where there may well have been a Christian chapel in late Roman times.

61. F. Cumont, *The Mysteries of Mithra*, 1910, p. 200.

62. J. P. Gillam and I. MacIvor, 'The Temple of Mithras at

Rudchester,' *Archaeologia Aeliana*, Fourth Series, Vol. XXXII, p. 218.

63. Professor W. F. Grimes in *Recent Archaeological Excavations in Britain*, edited by R. L. S. Bruce-Mitford, 1956, p. 141.

64. The coin evidence alone seems to suggest (but not prove) an earlier date.

65. The worst damage seems to have occurred after the group was discovered, for the upper part of the faun, the heads of the satyr, maenad and snake, and the left hand of Bacchus all appeared to have been broken off quite recently. The most careful search revealed no trace of them on or near the find-spot, and it is suspected that they were removed by souvenir hunters.

66. J. M. C. Toynbee, *Art in Roman Britain*, 1962, p. 154.

67. Ibid., p. 130.

68. *Jahrbuch des Römisch-Germanischen Zentralmuseums*, Mainz, V. (1958), pp. 259 ff.

69. J. M. C. Toynbee, *loc. cit.*, pp. 173–4.

70. From a third-century grave at Stráže. See J. M. C. Toynbee, *A Silver Casket and Strainer from the Walbrook Mithraeum in the City of London*, Leiden, 1963, p. 8 and *Plate* XII.

71. *R.C.H.M.*, p. 5.

72. Ammianus Marcellinus, *Rerum Gestarum*, XX, i (ed. C. U. Clark, 1910).

73. Ibid., XXVII, viii; XXVIII, iii.

74. *Numismatic Chronicle*, Sixth Series, Vol. VII, pp. 122–5.

75. *Praepositus thesaurorum Augustensium.*

76. Theodosius left the Empire to be divided between his two sons, Honorius and Arcadius, in 395.

77. *Arch. Journ.*, CXII, pp. 27 and 33.

78. Gordon Home, *Roman London*, 1948, p. 147.

79. W. F. Grimes, in *Recent Excavations in Britain*, edited by R. L. S. Bruce-Mitford, 1956, p. 133; and *J.R.S.*, XXXIX (1949), p. 107.

80. *Arch.*, LXIII (1912), p. 274.

81. See *Arch Journ.*, CXII, pp. 35–6.

82. A philosophy of free-will, taught by Pelagius in opposition to Augustine's doctrine of grace. Pelagius was a Briton, although he did not himself teach in this country, and his ideas evidently had a strong appeal for his compatriots – an appeal which is still felt by some today.

83. This story has been doubted by some modern writers, reluctant to believe that a good theologian could also be a successful soldier, and it is suggested that the spiritual victory of Germanus was confused with a military one. It seems unlikely, however, that his biographer, writing in the same century, should have fallen

into this error, or could have confused Pelagians with Picts and Saxons.

84. *Antiquaries' Journal*, XL (1960), pp. 19–21.

85. Bede's description of London early in the eighth century.

86. T. C. Lethbridge, in *Dark Age Britain*, edited by D. B. Harden 1956, pp. 120 ff.

87. Ibid., pp. 121 ff.

★

CHAPTER THREE

The Topography of Roman London

Introduction and Notes on Map

THIS CHAPTER will best be understood by reference to the map in the pocket. Here an attempt has been made to plot finds of structures and topographical features of Roman London recorded from the time of Queen Elizabeth I to July 1964, when the map was completed. This was last done in 1927, on behalf of the Royal Commission on Historical Monuments for the *Inventory of the Historical Monuments in London, vol. III, Roman London*, published the following year, and the Royal Commission's map and inventory, though long out of print, have remained the standard reference work on Roman London ever since. The present map and gazetteer are not only based on the content of this admirable and comprehensive survey, but have been to a considerable extent modelled on its form. In the thirty-seven years which have elapsed since the publication of the Royal Commission's map, it has inevitably become out of date and also practically unobtainable, so that it seemed worth while again to attempt to summarise in this way the recorded finds of Roman London.

In the present work, an attempt has been made to re-plot or to check the plotting of features recorded in the 1927 map, and in a number of cases slight alterations have been made. It is often by no means easy to transfer a structure from a site plan to its correct position on a map of the City. The former is usually derived from a builders' plan, and this may show considerable variation from the shape of the site as it appears in the Ordnance Survey. In the case of old plans, adjustments may since have been made to the boundaries of the site; not infrequently only a part of the outline of the site is indicated, and it is sometimes difficult to ascertain whether a particular edge represents the building-line or kerb-line. While every care has been taken to avoid error, it can hardly be hoped that complete success has been achieved in a task of this complexity. Moreover no structure can be more accurately placed than it is in the original site-plan, and in most cases measurements for these were taken under great difficulties in the middle of building operations. It follows that absolute accuracy cannot be guaranteed, although it is hoped that errors will seldom exceed a few feet. Where there is considerable doubt concerning the position of any structure, this has been indicated by a ring.

To keep the map to a manageable size and a convenient scale, only the walled city of Londinium and its immediate surroundings have been included. Southwark, with its important Roman remains, and the City west of the Fleet River, where interesting finds have been made in the Church of St. Bride's, have reluctantly been excluded from the map and gazetteer, and from the scope of the present volume. The scattered Roman remains in London which lie beyond these two areas are of course considerably less relevant to a study of the Roman city, and can hardly be regarded even as suburban.

Finds made since 1927, and a few earlier items which had been missed, have been added to the map and one or two structures, mostly chalk walls suspected of being mediaeval, have been omitted. The years since the war have of course been especially productive of archaeological discoveries in the City of London, owing to the bombing and rebuilding of large areas within the Roman city. The result has been that there are twice as many entries in the new map as the old, excluding those relating to the city wall, in which the increase is 50 per cent. It has therefore been necessary to limit the description given in the gazetteer to a brief summary of each find, but references have been given where possible to fuller accounts, and in the case of unpublished material there is an indication of the source of information. Records of finds on building sites between 1928 and 1938 have been generously supplied by Messrs. G. C. Dunning and F. Cottrill, who successively served as archaeological observers on behalf of the Society of Antiquaries of London; those from 1939 onwards are mostly the work of the staff of Guildhall Museum, past and present. The years since the war, however, have also seen the first series of excavations to be undertaken for purely archaeological purposes in the City of London. These have been carried out with great skill by Professor W. F. Grimes, who, as Director of Excavations for the Roman and Mediaeval London Excavation Council, has brilliantly exploited the unique opportunity offered by the clearance of so much of the site of Londinium. The full report of these excavations is eagerly awaited by all students of the history of London, for the sifting and interpretation of the great mass of fully documented facts which Professor Grimes has accumulated will surely eventually solve many outstanding problems. The summaries of these finds which have been published annually have already added immensely to our knowledge of the topography of Roman London.[1] They have been used with gratitude in the preparation of the present work. Since, however, many of the plans have not yet been published, it has not been possible to plot on the map all of the structures found in these excavations. In such cases, the finds have been included in the gazetteer, and reference numbers alone have been placed on the map near the position where they occurred.[2]

The structures and features shown on the map are all believed to be Roman, although in some cases the dating evidence is inconclusive. It is therefore by no means unlikely that a few items of a later period have been erroneously included. Where any serious doubt existed, the entry was made if the balance of probability inclined towards a Roman date, and the basis of this judgment is usually indicated in the gazetteer or elsewhere. An exception to this rule will be found in the section dealing with the city gates, where for convenience the example of the Royal Commission's map has been followed, and an entry has been made for each of the later city gates, including the mediaeval Moorgate, in order that the question of its Roman or non-Roman origin may be discussed. For the same reason, all the bastions have been included, although, in the case of some of the hollow bastions of the western group, the balance of probability of a Roman as against a post-Roman date is now very nearly even. (See pp. 69-72.)

It must be emphasised, however, that this is only a map showing where traces of Roman London have been found. *It is not a map of Roman London at any one period, but includes structures which are known not to have co-existed.* To give a true picture of the Roman city as it really was, only the structures which were in existence at a given time should be represented, and ideally a series of such maps for different periods should be compiled. Unfortunately our knowledge does not permit this to be done, for the closely dated structures of Roman London are in a very small minority, and in even fewer cases do we also know with certainty the duration of a building's existence. There is little hope, therefore, that a detailed map or maps of Roman London on these lines will ever be produced.

Physical Geography

Roman London first developed on the east side of the tributary of the Thames later called the Walbrook, and it is here that the earliest structures have been found, as well as most of the traces of the mid-first century burnt level, which probably represents the extent of the city burnt by Queen Boudicca in A.D. 60 (*Fig.* 9). Here there was a gravel hill, or rather a plateau, which was eminently suitable for settlement, and was no doubt one of the reasons why the Romans chose to bridge the Thames at this point, which also lay very near the tidal limits of the river in Roman times. Unfortunately the contours of the site of Londinium before the Romans have yet to be worked out – a piece of basic research for which there is ample material in the many records of bore-hole and sewer sections. These will undoubtedly be of great value to the historical geographer of early London, since they will inform him not only of the contours of the original surface, but also of the nature of the sub-soil in every area. Their interpretation is not always easy, however, and requires some knowledge of Pleistocene and Holocene geology. To these may be added those archaeological sections, published and unpublished, which extend to natural soil and are sufficiently precise in their relationship to Ordnance Datum levels. The subject is of great importance and interest, and is recommended to physical geographers as a research project. Until this work is done in detail, we can have no clear picture of the primitive site of London – the geographical setting in which Roman London developed. The present contours of the City give only an approximate indication of this, and in some respects are very misleading. For nearly two thousand years men have been at work changing the face of London to their requirements, partly in response to the inexorable rise of the water level, partly in

the course of necessary rebuilding, and partly in the deliberate
creation of artificial features, as in the terracing of a slope or
the building up of a road level above the surrounding ground.
The original (pre-Roman) natural surface may lie anywhere
between about ten and twenty feet below the modern pavement
level, the variation being due mainly to the activities of man,
ancient and modern.

The Thames was somewhat wider in Roman times and
extended approximately to the southern side of the modern
Thames Street. To the north of this the gravel bank seems to
have risen steeply to a height of more than twenty-five feet in
the region of Cannon Street. Near London Bridge it was apparently terraced in the late first and early second centuries, by
means of wharf-like structures of timber, forming an embankment in which the ground was levelled by dumping earth and
other material behind wooden retaining walls. (See **304, 306,
308**.) Further north the rise was more gradual – another eleven
or twelve feet to the eastern part of Lombard Street. To the
north and east the surface seems to have been uneven, but
relatively level, probably with the top of Cornhill as the highest
point. To the west it dropped steeply into the valley of the
Walbrook, a small tributary of the Thames which survived
above ground until the end of the Middle Ages, and remains a
force to be reckoned with beneath the surface, where, in spite
of modern drainage, its hidden springs are still an embarrass-
ment to builders. To the west the land level rose again, apparently to a few feet higher than the high ground east of the
Walbrook, the highest natural level within the Roman city
being in the area between Newgate Street and Cripplegate.
Further west, the ground dropped steeply to the valley of the
Fleet, a much larger tributary than the Walbrook. Like the
eastern hill, the western seems to have been fairly level on the
top, with a steep slope towards the Thames. In the region of
Lambeth Hill, and probably elsewhere as well, this steep bank
was artificially terraced in Roman times, with chalk platforms
laid on wooden piles and held by retaining walls. (See **110** and
Plate 29.)

It has been said that Roman London was built on two gravel
hills, but this statement, though perfectly correct, gives a somewhat false impression unless two qualifications are added. The
hills are practically plateaus, with a wide stretch of uneven but
more or less level ground on the top; and the gravel is capped

with a layer of brick-earth in many places. This yellowish-brown clay has some disadvantages as a sub-soil for settlement in a wet climate, although these can be reduced by careful drainage. It provides a most useful material for building, however, for it can be baked into bricks, or used more easily and cheaply – though less satisfactorily – for walls of wattle and daub. It was utilised in both these ways in Roman London, and was also frequently dumped when it was necessary to raise the surface of the ground. An additional use was for pot-making – an industry which was evidently carried on within the City, for Roman pottery kilns were found by Wren on the site of St. Paul's (22), and pottery 'wasters' – spoilt pots presumably from a nearby kiln – were found in Copthall Close (137). For all these purposes holes were dug in the clay, and these were often subsequently filled with refuse. The gravel was also quarried to provide metalling for roads and courtyards, and make-up material to raise the level of floors. One of these Roman gravel-pits was found in 1841 on the site of the Royal Exchange (180), and others have recently been discovered to the south of Carter Lane (83). The natural contours have therefore been artificially modified not only by building up but also by cutting away, so that the top of natural soil in an excavation is not necessarily the original ground surface. A series of observations over a considerable area may be required to determine the true level of this. Our present information suggests that the eastern hill rose to a height of about forty feet above Ordnance Datum, and the western about three feet higher.

Between them lay the valley of the small stream later known as the Walbrook[3] – a valley which still exists, although the modern contour is considerably less pronounced than it was at the time of the first settlement, when there was a drop of more than thirty feet from the eastern hill to the edge of the stream. Our knowledge of the Roman Walbrook has been greatly increased by an excavation carried out by Professor Grimes in 1953 on the site of Bucklersbury House (247). Previously deposits of black mud containing much organic material had been observed during building excavations over a wide area in the Walbrook valley, and these were believed to be part of the actual bed of the stream itself, which was thought to be about 120 feet wide. The extent of the black mud in the region of Cloak Lane suggested that the width might be even as much as 248 feet near the mouth. The stream was therefore believed to be navigable by large ships as far as the site of the Bank of England, and it seemed possible that it might have been one of the docks of the Roman port. Professor Grimes found that in fact the actual channel was not wider than twelve to fourteen feet, and was quite shallow, so that its use for water traffic, even by the smallest boats, must have been very limited. It was, however, subject to flooding, and deposits of silt were found alternating with layers of peaty clay for a considerable distance from the stream-bed on the eastern bank. There is no doubt that the black 'peat' so often observed in the Walbrook valley consisted of similar flood deposits, so that its extent marked, not the bed of the stream, but its flood-plain. Both are shown on the map, since in some areas the flood deposits are the only indication of the proximity of a stream, but the edge of the flood plain is an approximation only, and is not based on precise information. It was not in any case fixed, but probably moved outwards as the Roman period advanced. Within its limits occupation could be maintained by raising the level of the ground artificially, and so far from being a useless morass, the middle Walbrook valley eventually came to be regarded as a desirable place of residence, attractive for its central position, and perhaps also for its abundant water-supply. Throughout the Roman period, however, the level of the water in south-east Britain was steadily rising in relation to the land, probably due to the gradual sinking of the latter, although geographers are not yet certain of the exact nature of the change which was taking place. As a result, the Walbrook, which was becoming more and more sluggish, repeatedly silted and flooded, each time cutting a new bed at a slightly higher level. Continued efforts were therefore necessary to maintain the occupation of its banks. In the early stages these were revetted, the dumped material which was used to raise the level being held back from the stream-bed by planking fixed to vertical posts. Eventually, however – probably during the second century – the revetments collapsed as the waters rose higher, and thereafter the stream seems to have been a mere runnel, cutting its way through accumulated layers of silt at ever higher levels.

The Walbrook had a number of 'feeders,' two of which seem to have been scarcely smaller than the main stream itself, and there were several other rivulets in the western part of the City. There is clear evidence for the existence of each of these, but until we have a more detailed knowledge of the natural contours of London, the exact course of any stream must remain partly conjectural. Where a reasonable conjecture could be made, however, it has been indicated on the map, since it was considered that a truer picture of the geography of London would be given if known portions of the same stream were linked by a probable course, than if they were shown in isolation. In some instances – especially for the main stream of the Walbrook – the line of a ward boundary gives a useful clue, since these divisions of the City probably date from Anglo-Saxon times, and are likely to have been demarcated by physical features. A good example of this occurs in the western part of the City, where the boundary between the Wards of Castle Baynard and Farringdon Within follows a small stream closely for nearly two hundred yards (12). The streams in Anglo-Saxon times did not necessarily exactly follow their Roman predecessors, and the line of the ward boundaries on and near the bed of the Walbrook suggests a more meandering course than that taken by the Roman stream.

Not all these streams and streamlets survived into Anglo-Saxon times, however; some of them were probably covered quite early in the Roman period, and should not therefore be regarded as open streams after the development of the Roman city, but as lines of subterranean drainage like the Walbrook itself today. In some instances the rising water-table apparently caused the re-emergence of these buried springs. On the site of the Sun Life Assurance Society in Cheapside, for example, there seems to have been a stream which was covered by dumped clay, apparently early in the second century. Its subterranean waters presumably supplied the water-tank of the small bath-house on this site until they eventually rose and flooded the whole tank, forming a pool or open stream above it. (See 53.)

It is likely that there was a connection between the early water-course seen in the south-eastern corner of this site and the revetted stream found beneath the church of St. Mary-le-Bow on the opposite side of Cheapside (63). The direction of this was southerly, but it is not impossible that it turned sharply to the east and flowed into the Walbrook by way of a water-course near Well Court (89), joining the tributary observed near Pancras Lane (65 and 192). If so, its post-Roman successor may have determined the southern boundary of the Ward of Cheap. Since, however, on the present evidence it is as likely to have continued directly southward to the Thames, in this instance no conjectural course has been indicated.

In the case of the main stream of the Walbrook and its two principal feeders, the points of entry into the city are marked by brick-lined culverts, constructed to allow them to pass through the city wall when the latter was built across their courses. These have been recorded immediately west of All Hallows Church, at the southern end of Blomfield Street, and west of Copthall Avenue (**W29, W30** and **W33**). A second culvert seems to have been constructed five feet higher than the first to admit the central stream at the bottom of Blomfield Street, evidently after the lower channel had been blocked and the water was flowing at a higher level. These three main streams must have united to the west of Throgmorton Avenue, and thereafter the Walbrook continued in a single channel through the site of the Bank of England, across the middle of Prince's Street and the eastern end of Poultry, and thence west of the modern street of Walbrook, reaching the Thames about fifty yards west of Cannon Street Station. Between Prince's Street and Cannon Street it was fed by at least three streamlets flowing from the north-west, but the exact courses of these and their relationship with one another remain obscure. It is clear, however, that the area between Aldermanbury and Milk Street in the west and Moorgate in the east was originally traversed by small streams, and was naturally wet in Roman times. Geographically it seems to be a western extension of the Walbrook valley, and similar conditions to those near the main stream prevailed, though to a lesser degree. As the water-table rose with the gradual sinking of the land, there seems to have been an increasing tendency towards flooding in the neighbourhood of the small streams, and this was countered by raising the land level artificially. There was consequently a rapid build-up of made ground in some places, even quite early in the Roman period. (See **50**.)

The Growth of Roman London

A study of the distribution of early pottery in London – especially of the fine imported red Gaulish wares, often stamped with the names of potters who can be closely dated – has shown concentrations of finds of the earliest period of the Roman occupation on the eastern hill, in Southwark near London

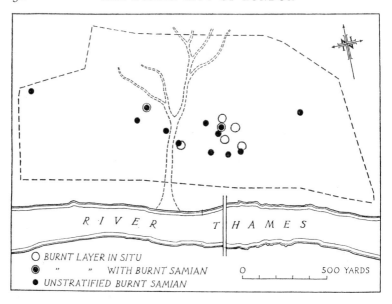

FIG. 9   Distribution map of mid-first century burnt layers and burnt Samian ware. *Based by permission on the map by G. C. Dunning, with additions for the following sites:* St. Swithin's House, Walbrook: 30–2 Lombard Street: All Hallows, Lombard Street: 59–60 Gracechurch Street.

Bridge, in the valley of the Walbrook, and in some areas on the western hill. The main concentration, however, lies on the eastern side of the Walbrook.[4] A clearer picture of the extent of the earliest town, however, was obtained by Mr. G. C. Dunning, who plotted the distribution of the evidence for the mid-first century fire which destroyed it, almost certainly in A.D. 60 when London was abandoned to the fury of Queen Boudicca.[5] This evidence consists of deposits of burnt daub and other material dated by pottery to the middle of the first century, and also of burnt pottery of the same date in museum collections, which is likely to have come from similar deposits that have not been recorded. (See *Fig.* 9.) The principal concentration lies on the southern and western slopes of the eastern hill, between Cannon Street and Cornhill, and extending just to the east of Gracechurch Street. There is little doubt that this represents the

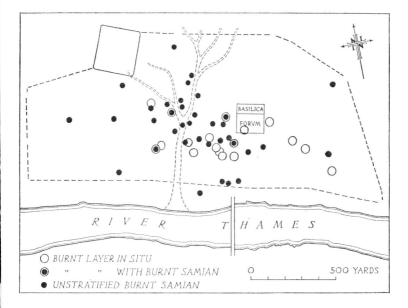

FIG. 10 Distribution map of early second century burnt layers and burnt Samian ware. *Based by permission on the map by G. C. Dunning, with additions for the following sites:* St. Swithin's House, Walbrook: St. Swithin's Church, Cannon Street: Plough Court: All Hallows, Lombard Street.

nucleus of the first City. Outside this area, the fire extended to the west into the Walbrook valley, but seems to have been confined to the middle part of the valley where the stream was bridged. Further west it occurred in the Cheapside area in the neighbourhood of the road from the bridge.

By A.D. 60, therefore, the small town on the eastern hill had already begun to expand to the west; and its further growth in the next sixty or seventy years was also demonstrated by Mr. Dunning in a similar way, by mapping the traces of the second great fire of Roman London, which occurred about A.D. 125–30 (*Fig.* 10).[6] This shows a considerable development in an easterly direction, where the early second century burnt level has been recorded on a number of sites. An apparent extension to the northern part of the Walbrook valley is suggested by the distribution of burnt pottery of this period, but the validity of this is more doubtful, since quantities of material were dumped in this area during the second century and later, to raise the ground level above the Walbrook floods, and burnt pottery from elsewhere in the City might well have been included. Traces of the fire are scattered in the western half of the City, suggesting a less intensive occupation, and in the eastern half they are entirely absent from the Bishopsgate area. We know very little about this district in Roman times, although a number of mosaic pavements were found there many years ago. These were almost certainly of late date, and it is possible that the area was still undeveloped in the early second century. This would be rather surprising, however, since the main road to the north must have passed through the district, and it is more probable that the empty space in the distribution map is merely indicative of the gap in our knowledge. Even if no fire occurred there, it does not necessarily mean any lack of occupation, any more than it did in the Great Fire of 1666 when the same region escaped damage. The area south of Cripplegate is also a blank on the map, and we now know that it was occupied by a fort when the Hadrianic fire took place. On the other hand, the suggestion of a sparse occupation of the western end of the City has on the whole been confirmed by other investigations. In the neighbourhood of St. Paul's and St. Martin's-le-Grand the cremation urns of a cemetery of the first century have been found – a certain indication that this district then lay outside the town, since it was the Roman custom to bury the dead outside the inhabited area. There seems to have been some occupation of an industrial character in these parts at a fairly early date, however. Wren found four pottery kilns on the site of St. Paul's (22), and the area between the two branches of the stream north of Newgate Street seems to have been used as a brick-field (1). Both of these industries are more likely to be found on the outskirts of the town than in a residential quarter. The region to the south-east of St. Paul's Cathedral, between the western end of Cannon Street and Knightrider Street, was quarried for gravel in Roman times (83, 84) and has produced few Roman structures apart from the mysterious long wall on the line of Knightrider Street, which seems more likely to have been a boundary or precinct wall than part of a building (93–99). (See also p. 146.)

The valley of the Walbrook remained relatively undeveloped, though apparently much frequented, until the second century was well advanced. There seem to have been few buildings of any size or importance near the stream until the Antonine period, although paradoxically an abundance of small manu-factured articles, including ornaments, tools and coins, were lost during the first century of the Roman occupation in the stream-bed and in the floods which frequently covered its banks (*Plates* 125-40). More than 100 *stili*, for example, used for writing on wax-covered tablets, were collected by the staff of Guildhall Museum on the site of Bucklersbury House alone. Personal ornaments and small tools of many crafts were hardly less common, and more than 160 coins were recorded from this site in a continuous sequence, commencing in the reign of Claudius and coming to an abrupt end with the 'Britannia' issues of Antoninus Pius in A.D. 154–5.[7] An equal abundance of finds, associated with a similar range of coins, was found where the Walbrook crossed the site of the National Safe Deposit Company (**195**) and the Bank of England (**168**). The likeliest explanation seems to be that the banks of the stream remained for the most part open ground during the first century and the first half of the second, but were intensively used for commercial purposes by traders and craftsmen who contented themselves with temporary booths or stalls, and so left little structural evidence of their presence. Their losses of stock and tools may be partly accounted for by casual accidents and the periodic flooding of the Walbrook, but it is by no means unlikely that some of these objects were deliberately dropped into the stream as votive offerings to propitiate a local deity. The end of this phase of activity seems to coincide with a collapse of the revetted banks soon after the middle of the second century – the effect of the continued sink-ing of the land and relative rise of the water-level. This must have ended the use of the stream even by the smallest boats, for it now became a shallow runnel, but it is doubtful if trade in the Walbrook valley was ever dependent on the small amount of water traffic which the narrow channel would admit. The flooding of the banks is likely to have become increasingly severe, however, and although occupation was certainly main-tained in some areas by a continued dumping of material to raise the ground-level, the casual occupants of the streamside are likely to have been driven away. The diminishing quantity of coins found in the Walbrook dating from the first half of the second century may indicate that business in this area, which was apparently at its peak in Flavian times, was already in decline before it apparently came to a sudden end soon after the middle of the century.[8]

It is not unlikely that there was a complete break in occupation in some parts of the Walbrook valley while marshy conditions prevailed in the middle of the second century, but gradually the land was reclaimed by the dumping of clay and other materials to a height of several feet. The ground so laboriously recovered was now used for building. Timber structures on pile foundations began to appear, with an occasional stone building, of which the temple of Mithras is the most notable example (**248**). To the north of this, houses with fine mosaic pavements were built at the very edge of the stream (**194, 171**). The date of these is still uncertain, but it is likely that they are Antonine or later, rather than early second century as was formerly thought. The pavements on the site of the Bank of England overlay deposits containing pottery of the early second century, as also did a mosaic pavement north of Lothbury (**157**), but this merely shows they are later than that date, and if there were a break in occupation they might be considerably later. The Bank of England mosaics have been tentatively attributed by Dr. David Smith on stylistic grounds to the late second or early third century, and the Bucklersbury pavement to the early third century.

Cemeteries

As we have seen, the extent of Londinium at any period is reflected by the distribution of contemporary burials, since it was the Roman custom, enforced by law, to dispose of the dead outside the inhabited area, often near a road. The earlier burials are cremations, and can usually be approximately dated by the type of pot used as an urn for the burnt remains. In the third century, however, the practice of burying the unburnt body in a coffin of wood, lead or stone, gradually replaced cremation, and burials of the latter part of the third century and later are almost always inhumations of this kind. These are not invariably accompanied by pottery, coins and other datable material buried with the corpse.

Apart from a few isolated examples scattered through the town, which must have contravened the usual rule of segregation from the living, the Roman burials are grouped in three main areas: an eastern cemetery to the south of Aldgate High Street, in the neighbourhood of the Minories and extending eastward to Alie Street: a northern cemetery around Bishops-gate with a westward extension to Moorgate: and a western group of burial grounds between St. Martin's-le-Grand and the River Fleet, with an extension to the north into Smithfield.

The last group was divided by the stream in the western part of the city, and was interspersed with brickfields and pottery kilns. Its earlier cremation burials were mostly concentrated in three areas: in the southern portion of St. Martin's-le-Grand: in the north-eastern part of St. Paul's Cathedral: and in the neighbourhood of Warwick Square. The St. Martin's-le-Grand urns were of the first century, as also were those from Warwick Square, with one exception which carries the use of the latter burial ground into the second century. Little is known about the cremations from St. Paul's, which were found during the excavations for the foundations of Wren's Cathedral. They were accompanied by lamps, flasks and other grave goods, and were overlaid with inhumations which may well be post-Roman. Outside the city wall in the Smithfield area have been found cremation urns of the Antonine period and early third century, as well as inhumation burials which are presumably third or fourth century. Cremations of the first century and late inhumations have also been recorded to the south of the Roman road from Newgate, between the city wall and the River Fleet. On the far side of the Fleet, cremation urns ranging in date from the first to the third century have been found near the bottom of Shoe Lane.

Most of the northern cemetery at Bishopsgate lay outside the city wall, although several cremation urns and one inhumation have been found just inside it. (See **317**.) Other cremations recorded from London Wall and Broad Street are as likely to have been found outside the line of the wall as inside it. Dated burials outside the wall in this area range from the beginning of the Roman occupation to the late third century.

The eastern cemetery south of Aldgate seems to have been wholly outside the city wall, apart from two isolated crema-tions in Mark Lane and Fenchurch Street, which may be unconnected with it. The range of dates in this cemetery is from the first century to the fourth (*Plate* 124).

The distribution of the burials therefore bears out the

undeveloped character of the western end of the city in the early
period. It would perhaps be rash, however, to draw the converse
conclusion from the apparent paucity of burials in those parts
of the northern and eastern outskirts which were later enclosed
by the city wall, for comparatively few Roman remains of any
kind have been found there. Nevertheless, it is probable that
these districts were from an early date in a much closer proximity to the daily activities of the living, and were therefore
considered unsuitable for burials, even though they may not
have been fully occupied.

(Full details of all burials known in 1927 can be found in
Appendix I of the Report of the Royal Commission on Roman
London.)

The Cripplegate Fort

The outstanding discovery of post-war investigation in London has been the Roman fort in the north-west corner of the
Roman city. The curious re-entrant angle of the line of the city
wall between Cripplegate and Newgate had never been satisfactorily explained, although Sir Mortimer (then Dr.) Wheeler
had seen its principal significance when he suggested in the
Report of the Royal Commission that 'this salient represents a
skirting, by the wall, of a quarter already definitely laid out
before the wall was built'.[9] The nature of this quarter and its
relationship to the later city defences was conclusively demonstrated by Professor W. F. Grimes, who carried out a series of
excavations in this area, extending over a number of years since
the war, on behalf of the Roman and Mediaeval London
Excavation Council. This was one of the most devastated parts
of the City, where many acres of bombed buildings were long
abandoned to the invasion of nature. In these derelict cellars,
overgrown with elder and willow-herb, the archaeologist could
choose his areas for investigation with a view to the specific
problems he wished to solve, and, for the first time in the City of
London, could work at the pace required for meticulous
observation, without feeling the breath of the impatient building contractor on his neck. The difficulties inherent in any city
site remained – in particular the complexities resulting from
human activity over a long period in the same area – but these

could be overcome by the skilful and methodical technique of an experienced excavator.

Since in this area interest centred on the defences, a series of trenches were excavated on the line of the city wall, and it soon became apparent that here it did not conform with the normal structure of the Roman wall as it was known elsewhere. Instead of a single wall, eight to eleven feet thick, with courses of bonding-tiles running through it, and an internal bank which rested against the inner face and was clearly contemporary with it, the wall was found to be double, with a longitudinal fissure dividing it into two not quite equal parts; there were no bonding-tiles or sandstone plinth in the outer wall, and the inner wall was evidently later than the internal bank, into which it had been inserted with its foundations above the original ground level. The solution to the mystery was found when Professor Grimes excavated at the inner angle of the Aldersgate re-entrant. Here the outer wall curved unexpectedly eastwards through ninety degrees while the inner wall came to an end (**W47**). The foundations of a small, not quite rectangular building were found attached to the inner face of the outer wall near the centre of its curving angle (**31**). This gave the clue to the interpretation of the whole complex, for it was clearly recognisable as the corner turret of a typical rectangular Roman fort, set according to the standard pattern within the curve of its corner (*Plate 35*).

It now became clear that the inner wall, already known to be later than the outer, was in fact merely a thickening added to the north and west walls of the fort when the city wall was built. A considerable saving in labour and material was effected by incorporating these two fort walls in the new defences, by joining the new town wall to the north-east and south-west corners of the already existing fort. The new wall, however, was twice as thick as the fort walls, which were only four feet wide, so the inner wall was added to bring them to the standard thickness of eight to nine feet.

The prior existence of the fort explained not only the curious Aldersgate re-entrant but also several other features of the city wall in this area. About 235 yards east of the right-angled corner made by the wall near St. Giles Cripplegate, which evidently marked the north-west corner of the fort, the city wall made a slight angle near Aldermanbury in its otherwise straight northern face. It seemed likely that this would indicate the junction between the north wall of the fort and the city wall, and so would mark the north-east corner of the former.[10] Midway between these two points – i.e. in the centre of the presumed north wall of the fort – is Cripplegate, a city gateway known to have been in existence before the Norman Conquest, and long regarded as a Roman gate, although it did not give access to a known Roman road.[11] Since Roman forts are normally symmetrical, this is exactly where the north gateway of the London fort should be.

Even without any further excavation, therefore, a clear picture had already emerged of a typical rectangular stone fort, more than 250 yards long and about 235 yards wide, enclosing an area of about twelve acres – much smaller than the great legionary fortress headquarters of Caerleon (fifty acres), Chester (fifty-six acres), and York (forty acres), but equalled only by the largest of the auxiliary forts, such as Newstead (ten to thirteen acres). It could have housed a garrison of 1,500–2,000 men.

Professor Grimes then planned a series of excavations to locate and identify various features of the structure, and in this he was considerably helped by the standardisation of Roman military design. The line of the south wall was traced from the south-west corner of the fort to a point east of Wood Street. There was a great deal of later disturbance, and the wall itself had disappeared in many places, but fortunately the outer ditch proved to be a more enduring feature. This was a V-shaped cutting, shallow but penetrating to a sufficient depth into the natural brick-earth to escape subsequent disturbance in many places. The position of the south gate (32) was found just to the west of Wood Street, which further north coincides with the central street of the fort, and is evidently its direct descendant. Traces of the hard gravel metalling of the roadway through the gate remained, and in the ditch, which was con-tinuous across its line to the south, were found holes for the posts which supported a bridge. Near the south-east corner of the fort the wall had almost completely disappeared, but the beginning of the curve of the ditch could be seen before it passed beneath the street of Aldermanbury to turn northwards through ninety degrees (34). On this side at least the ditch seems to have served as a drain, since a brick culvert was built into the city wall immediately above it, when it was blocked by the new wall at the south-west corner of the fort (W48).

Since Wood Street evidently represents the central roadway (*via praetoria*) of the fort, although in subsequent ages it has diverged slightly to the east, it seemed likely that the two small streets, Silver Street and Addle Street, which intersected it at right angles, might have a similar relationship to the main transverse roadway (*via principalis*). This was found to be the case, for the foundations of the western gateway were dis-covered at the western end of Silver Street, on the north side of Falcon Square (**G7**). It was a double gate, with a rectangular turret containing a guardroom on each side, and two central piers of masonry dividing the roadway. These had evidently supported double archways at the front and back, and in general form the gateway must have closely resembled Roman Newgate. (See reconstruction of Newgate, *Plate* 43.) It was mainly built of ragstone like the rest of the fort, but the turret walls had plinths of sandstone. The northern turret and central piers, with a surviving portion of the gravel metalling of the northern carriage-way, were first excavated (*Plate* 37), and subsequently Professor Grimes was able to observe and record a portion of the north-west corner of the southern turret. Unlike the northern and central portion, this unfortunately could not be preserved.

Between the west gate and the south-west corner of the fort, the foundations of a small internal turret were found (**W45**). Small towers of this kind probably gave shelter in bad weather to the guards on the ramparts and also provided a raised plat-form at a higher level for a look-out. In battle this would also serve as a vantage point for discharging missiles. The corner turrets had a similar function, but were probably also used to mount heavy *ballistae*, like the later bastions. Such features would no doubt have been included, even in a garrison fort, to conform with regulations, although the possibility of an enemy attack must have seemed very remote in the London of Trajan and Hadrian. A careful search was made for a corresponding intermediate turret to the north of the fort gate, but it was found that no such turret had ever existed. (*See Plate* 36.)

Traces of the western perimeter roadway were found near the south-west corner of the fort, and also to the north of the west gate, where fragmentary walls of a Roman stone building fronting it were also discovered (**27** and **28**). This was evidently one of the military buildings, but in this area there were also traces of an earlier occupation, consisting of small pits, gullies and possible hut sites. Similar early features were found in the northern angle between Silver Street and Wood Street (**29**), where the headquarters (*praetorium*) of the fort should have stood but, disappointingly, all traces of its foundations had been removed by later building excavations. The only extensive remains of any of the internal buildings of the fort which have yet been found were on the site of St. Alban's Church, Wood Street (**33**). Here were the foundations of two buildings, parallel with the central road of the fort, and facing each other across another north-south gravel roadway, also parallel with the central road. The western building consisted of a single row of rooms with a corridor on the west side and a narrow verandah on the east. The eastern building was similar, but the verandah was on the west, so that the two barrack-blocks – as they almost certainly were – faced each other across the gravelled street.[12]

On this site again, earlier pits, post-holes and gullies were also found, and these had been filled with clay, presumably to level the ground when the fort was built. They contained pottery at least as late as the late first century, and it now seems likely that the fort itself was not constructed until the early second century.

A date in the latter part of the first century was originally suggested, based on the dating of a limited quantity of pottery, which, from the position in which it was found, must have been earlier than the building of the fort. The first evidence of this kind by its very nature usually indicates a date which is too early, and if further finds compel a revision of the original conclusion, it is almost always in the direction of a later date. A coin of Vespasian struck in A.D. 71, and considerably worn by circulation before it was lost, was found in a pit underlying the bank of the fort wall, showing that the latter could hardly have been constructed before A.D. 80,[13] and several pieces of closely datable Samian pottery found in similar circumstances point to a considerably later date – certainly after the turn of the century. The evidence for the dating of the fort has not yet been fully evaluated, but it now seems more likely to have been built in the reign of Trajan than any of his predecessors.

We do not know whether it continued in existence as a separate entity after the building of the city wall, but it is by no means unlikely that it did. The survival of its main streets as modern thoroughfares certainly suggests that no major changes were made in its internal lay-out, but this does not necessarily mean that it continued to be a fortified enclosure.

Pottery from the filling of the ditch near the south-east corner of the fort (34) ranged in date from the late first century at the bottom to the late second or early third at the top, so the ditch at least is unlikely to have survived the building of the city wall. The drainage gully which replaced it and was associated with the culvert through the wall contained material ranging in date to the late third century (W48). The western gateway (G7) evidently continued in use as one of the gates of the city wall, but it was eventually blocked by a ragstone wall, and had no mediaeval successor – unlike the other known gates of the Roman city. The date of the blocking is unknown, but it is more likely to have taken place in late Roman times or in the Dark Ages (using the term in its broadest sense) than in the Middle Ages. It may possibly have been consequent on the construction of the gate at Aldersgate (G8), which was apparently inserted after the building of the wall.

The City Wall

The line of the Roman city wall from the Tower of London to Ludgate has long been known – in fact it would be more accurate to say that it has never been forgotten, since it survived throughout the Middle Ages and forms the framework of the topography of the modern City. This can best be appreciated by following its line as closely as possible on foot, with a map. For much of its length the line is closely followed by some modern feature – a street, alley or building-line – and at intervals it will be found necessary to cross busy thoroughfares – at Tower Hill, Aldgate, Bishopsgate, Moorgate, Aldersgate, Newgate and Ludgate – which give access to traffic in and out of the City now as in the Middle Ages, when they passed through gateways in the city wall. With the exception of Moorgate (G4) and (less certainly) the Postern on Tower Hill (G1), these gateways were already in existence in Roman times. Apart from Aldersgate (G8) which seems to have been inserted after the building of the city wall, they probably accommodated earlier Roman roadways. It will be noticed that the city wall changes direction perceptibly at Aldgate and Bishopsgate, as might be expected if the roadway was an existing landmark when the line of the wall was laid out. Cripplegate, as we have seen, is a special case, being a fort gate earlier than the city wall, and today, as in Roman and mediaeval times, is less used by traffic and gives access only to minor roads.

Only at Newgate (**G9**) have sufficient remains of the Roman gate been found for its plan to be reconstructed with some confidence (*Fig.* 11). It was very similar to the west gate of the fort, already described, with a rectangular guardroom on each side, and sufficient width between them (thirty-five feet) to indicate that there was a double entrance. (See *Plate* 43.) It has been noted that the plinth of the gate-towers was four and a half feet higher than that of the city wall, but this does not necessarily mean that the gate was much later than the wall, as has been suggested, since the road surface may have been considerably higher than the general ground-level in the neighbourhood – although it must be admitted that the difference in level seems excessive. There is, however, no reason to doubt the Roman date of the structure, which is typically Roman in plan and fabric, and retained at the north-west angle a characteristic double course of bonding-tiles. It was incorporated in a later (mediaeval) gate, which projected further west.

At Aldersgate we seem to have the remains of a gate of a different type, with boldly projecting, bastion-like flanking towers, but again with a double entrance (**G8**). This is deduced from two piers at the centre of the gateway, and a mass of masonry projecting from the north face of the city wall immediately to the west of it, observed by Mr. A. H. Oswald in 1939 during the excavation of a subway beneath Aldersgate, connecting the General Post Office and Alder House. The gate had apparently been inserted after the building of the city wall, for the foundations of the northern pier cut through the flint and clay footings of the wall, which presumably continued originally right across Aldersgate. The projecting mass of ragstone rubble masonry overlay the wall footings and was clearly later than the wall, but in places it seemed to have been roughly keyed into the north face of the latter. A date in the Roman period rather than later is probable, since a course of bonding-tiles was seen on the east side of the projection, just above the level of the plinth of the city wall, and the foundations of the piers consisted of ragstone blocks set in courses in characteristic 'herring-bone' fashion. Above the latter were offsets consisting of massive blocks of ragstone cemented with a hard pink mortar, which also seemed to be typically Roman. Large fragments of Roman building-tiles which had been set

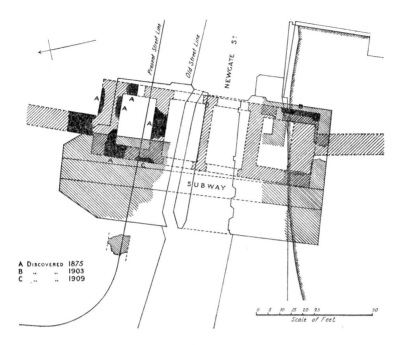

FIG. 11   Plan of Roman Newgate with mediaeval reconstructions.
From *Archaeologia LXIII, by permission.*

in a similar pink cement were found incorporated in the footings of the seventeenth-century gate, which were also revealed,
suggesting that there had been a considerable Roman structure
at this point. The site had earlier been occupied by a silt-filled
marshy hollow, which had made it necessary to widen and
deepen the footings of the city wall, and to reinforce them with
large blocks of ragstone and, in places, with piles. The silt,
which contained pottery of the early second century, was
covered with a layer of clean yellow sand, and in some places
the footings of the wall rested on this, while in others they cut
right through to the natural gravel beneath the silt. The footings of the piers of the ancient gate were carried right through
the marsh to the firm gravel beneath, but the projection on the
north of the wall rested on black silt, unfortunately containing

nothing datable, which had apparently accumulated above the layer of yellow sand after the building of the wall.[14]

Of the other Roman gates practically nothing is known. Portions of a probable flanking tower of two periods were found in 1907 when excavating for a sewer in the roadway at Aldgate, and it is possible that the earlier was Roman. It was built of ragstone and very hard white mortar, and contained a few fragments of Roman tile (**G2**). Similarly at Bishopsgate, a mass of ragstone rubble masonry containing portions of Roman tile was found in 1905 near the north angle of Wormwood Street and Bishopsgate Street. It had been carefully faced on the southern side, and probably formed part of a western gate-house projecting about twenty feet on the inside of the wall. A fragment of Roman wall at right angles with the city wall on the other side of Bishopsgate may have formed part of the eastern flanking tower, projecting outside the wall (**G3**). These features are too indefinite, however, to give any indication of the shape of the gate.

As may be seen from the map, many portions of the Roman city wall have been recorded between the Tower and Ludgate, and outside the Fort area these conform to a standard pattern of construction, except in minor details. The footings are of clay and flint or clay and ragstone, with ragstone rubble concrete some ten feet thick above. Above this foundation is a plinth of sandstone – of Kentish origin like the ragstone – on the outside of the wall just above the Roman ground-level, with a triple facing-course of bricks at the same level on the inner face of the wall. There is usually an offset between the top and second brick, level with the chamfered plinth on the outer face. This course of bricks is a facing only, and is not carried through the wall, which is composed of ragstone rubble concrete – i.e. of irregularly shaped pieces of ragstone set in extremely hard white cement. Above the plinth and facing-course the wall is faced with squared blocks of ragstone in four or five regular courses. Then comes a triple course of bonding-bricks which is carried right through the wall – at this level about seven and a half or eight feet thick. There is, however, again an offset on the inner face between the top and second brick, reducing the thickness of the wall by a few inches. This again consists of rubble concrete with a facing of five or six courses of squared ragstone before the next brick bonding-course is reached. Usually this is only a double course, with its top set back another few inches

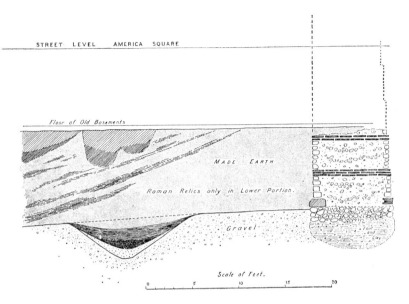

STREET LEVEL   AMERICA   SQUARE

Floor of Old Basements

MADE   EARTH

Roman   Relics   only   in   Lower   Portion.

Gravel

Flint and Clay

Scale of Feet.

0   5   10   15   20

FIG. 12   Section of the Roman city wall and ditch, 15–16 America
Square (**W13**). From *Archaeologia LXIII, by permission.*

about six feet above the level of the plinth (*Plate* 41). In a
number of places the Roman wall has survived into recent
times with a third similar bonding-course, about ten feet above
the plinth. In two places it has been recorded surviving to
a height of fourteen and a half feet with a fourth bonding-course
(**W25** and **W51**). Above this level only mediaeval rebuildings
of the wall have been found, and we have no knowledge of the
original height of the Roman wall.

The bricks used throughout are the standard Roman building
tiles, about seventeen and a half inches by twelve inches, and
one and a half to two inches thick. No re-used stone or brick
seems to have been employed.

In several places traces of a V-shaped Roman ditch, ten to
sixteen feet wide and four and a half to six and a half feet deep,
have been found outside the city wall, about ten to fifteen feet from
its base (*Fig.* 12, **W13, W16, W28, W53**). No doubt this originally
existed outside most other stretches of the wall, where it has

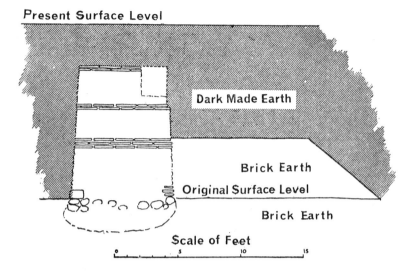

FIG. 13   Section of the Roman city wall and inner bank, G.P.O. site, King Edward Street (formerly site of Christ's Hospital) (**W52**). From *Archaeologia LXIII, by permission.*

since been destroyed either by the cutting of the mediaeval city ditch or by subsequent building excavations. On the site of the General Post Office the Roman ditch had been recut and enlarged to a width of twenty-five feet and a depth of fourteen feet (**W54**). A more indefinite indication of the cutting of a second ditch was also noted in one section near New Broad Street (**W28**).[15]

Traces of an internal bank of earth piled against the inner face of the city wall have been found in several places, and it is likely that this was a constant feature of the defences, in London as in other Roman towns, although it has seldom been noticed (**W10, W52**). The material would no doubt have been derived from the ditch and foundation trenches, and the purpose was to give additional strength to the base of the wall (*Fig.* 13).

In three places small internal turrets have been found built against the inside of the Roman city wall (**W3, W5, W10**). (*Fig.* 14. *Plate* 45.) They were apparently constructed at the same time as the wall, and it seems likely that their purpose was to give protected access to the ramparts above. The three known turrets are all attached to the eastern wall, and are spaced at irregular intervals.

The extreme hardness of the rubble concrete of the Roman wall ensured its survival below the modern ground-level long after the dismantling of the city defences, and in many places even to the present day, since it was so much easier to leave it alone or to incorporate it in a new foundation than to get rid of it. Moreover, since its line – or rather that of its mediaeval successor – inevitably formed the boundary between adjoining properties, it has left a lasting mark on the topography of the City. Only south of Ludgate is there any doubt as to its position within a few feet – but here the uncertainty is considerable. No indisputable trace of the Roman wall has yet been found in this area, presumably because it was removed at an early date. According to Stow, permission was given to the Archbishop of Canterbury by Edward I to take down a part of the city wall, from Ludgate to the Thames, for the enlargement of the new church of the Black Friars.[16] This Dominican community, which had been established in Holborn in 1221, was given the site of Castle Baynard in 1278 for the erection of a church, cloister and other buildings. It seems to have included both of the Norman castles which defended the western corner of the city – Baynard's Castle itself[17] and the Tower of Mountfiquit. These were now destroyed and their stones no doubt re-used in the building of the priory. The city wall was then rebuilt by orders of the King in 1283–4 to enclose the Dominican precinct. Its new course from Ludgate was westward along the line of Pilgrim Street, and then southward along the east bank of the Fleet. The earlier wall had presumably continued in a southerly direction from Ludgate, though it seems unlikely that it was exactly in line with the wall north of the gate, as indicated by earlier maps of Roman London. If it existed at all on this site when the priory was built, it can hardly have failed to influence the lay-out of the latter. It therefore seems likely that its line was perpetuated by some part of the priory. Whether it was completely demolished, or – as seems more likely – partly incorporated in the new buildings is unknown, but Roach Smith describes a wall, unfortunately not precisely located, of three distinct constructions (**W61**). The first he believed to be the Roman city wall, the second a Norman or early mediaeval reconstruction, and the third, which contained the remains of a passage or window, a portion of the Blackfriars priory. There is no certainty that the wall ten feet thick which had been seen at an earlier date in Playhouse Yard was either the city wall or of Roman construction, especially as one account says that three similar walls were found (**W60**). Roach Smith's observation on the site of the *Times* office cannot, however, be disregarded, and due weight must be given to the opinion of such an experienced antiquary. If he was right, the Friars did not demolish the city wall completely, but used the lower part for the foundations of a building-line in their new priory. It seems likely that this was the western wall of the choir and the eastern wall of the cloister – a line subsequently followed by the eastern side of the alley called Church Entry.

Nevertheless, the possibility remains that a considerable part of the city wall south of Ludgate had been destroyed before the Friars acquired the site, in the construction of Baynard's Castle and the Tower of Montfiquit. This may account for the absence of any evidence for the Roman wall in Blackfriars when a careful watch was kept for it in 1925 – except for the discovery of pieces of rubble and of bonding-bricks cemented in later walls.[18] It has even been suggested that the Roman city wall did not continue in a southerly direction from Ludgate, but turned towards the south-east, being represented by the fragment eight feet thick found in Carter Lane (**24**).[19] No confirmation of this has ever been found, and it remains more likely that the wall continued in the shortest line to the river.

Equally uncertain is the existence of a riverside defensive wall, although there was a tradition, recorded by Fitzstephen in the twelfth century, that there had been a wall with bastions on the south side of the city, which had been destroyed by the Thames long before that date.[20] Traces of massive walls, apparently of the Roman period, have been observed in various places in Upper and Lower Thames Street, and have been thought to be part of this riverside city wall (**114, 123, 124, 261, 279** and **311**). None of these is of the same construction as the landward wall, and they differ considerably from one another. River walls of some kind they probably were, but they give no support to the idea that a continuous river wall was constructed as part of a single scheme for the defence of London, like the landward wall. The longest stretch of apparently continuous wall was observed by Roach Smith during sewer

8-10 COOPER'S ROW

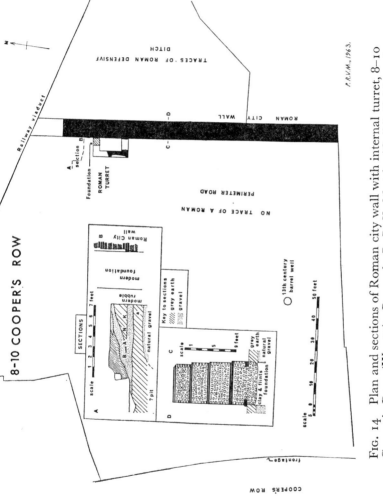

FIG. 14   Plan and sections of Roman city wall with internal turret, 8–10 Cooper's Row (W9–10). *Drawn by P. R. V. Marsden (Guildhall Museum).*

9—TRCOL

excavations in Upper Thames Street in 1841 (**114**). No obstruction was met between Blackfriars and Lambeth Hill, but at the
foot of the latter a great wall was encountered, 'which formed
an angle at Lambeth Hill and Thames Street.'[21] It was eight to
ten feet thick, and was built upon oak piles, over which was a
layer of chalk and stones. Upon this was a course of large sandstone blocks, each three to four feet by two by two-and-a-half
feet, forming the substructure of the wall, above which its body
was of ragstone and flint with courses of tiles. In the lower
part were many re-used architectural fragments. This wall continued, with occasional breaks due to earlier demolition, as far
as Queenhithe.[22] Roach Smith had previously observed a wall
of precisely similar character at the junction of Queen Street
and Thames Street (**124**), and he had no doubt that the stretch
of wall beneath Lambeth Hill and Queen Street was continuous
and formed part of the riverside city wall. Since then, however,
other massive walls of similar character have been found to the
north of this line near Lambeth Hill (**113**, **115**), and it seems
likely that the 'angle' observed by Roach Smith was in fact the
junction between his supposed city wall and a north-south
wall seen near the bottom of Lambeth Hill in 1961. It is now
clear that a complex structure with very thick walls was built on
this site over a chalk platform supported by piles, constructed
in Roman times after the demolition of earlier buildings (Cf.
116). Roach Smith's east-west wall seems to have formed part
of this, and therefore can hardly have been a portion of the city
wall. It must, however, have been very near the river's edge,
and it is quite possible that it was a river wall or quayside
associated with the structure behind.

There is therefore no clear archaeological evidence for a
homogeneous southern wall in any way comparable with the
landward city wall, although there were no doubt not only the
river walls of embankments and quays, but also defensive fortifications, both in Roman and later times. These, with the river
itself, may have been considered adequate protection for the
southern side of the city, but presumably special measures must
have been taken to prevent the outflanking of the two ends of
the landward wall, and here at least a return of the city wall
along the banks of the Thames might be expected. Investigations were carried out at the eastern end of the wall within the
Tower of London by the Ministry of Works in 1955, before the
building of the new Jewel House (**W1**). Unfortunately it was

found that the city wall had been broken away to the south as a result of subsidence due to river action – and this was probably also the fate of many stretches of river wall (or walls) as Fitz-stephen stated. In this area all evidence for any junction with a river wall had been lost, since the ground had been cleared to a depth below the level of the footings of the city wall, and made up with rubble when the Ordnance Offices were built. A massive wall which ran from west to east and then turned south was found between the Lanthorn and Wakefield Towers, but this was believed to be mediaeval from the character of the masonry, and therefore has not been marked on the map. It may be noted, however, that a fill of earth which post-dated it contained only late Roman pottery, so its post-Roman date may be open to question.[23]

If a riverside city wall was in existence in this area in the early Middle Ages, it seems likely that its line would have been followed by the southern part of the inner curtain wall of the Tower of London, built in the late twelfth and early thirteenth century. There is, however, no evidence that any earlier work was incorporated in the latter, although it has been noted that the spacing of the Lanthorn, Wakefield and Bell Towers is approximately the same as the distance (about 180 feet) between the Wardrobe Tower – built on a bastion of the city wall – and the Lanthorn Tower. This might indicate that the Lanthorn, Wakefield and Bell Towers – and perhaps also the Middle Tower, 170 feet west of the Bell Tower – were also built on the sites of earlier bastions which were spaced at regular intervals along the riverside wall.[24] Again, there is no archaeological evidence to support this, and if the inner curtain of the Tower had in fact been preceded by an earlier river wall with bastions, it cannot be assumed that it was necessarily Roman.

The Bastions

The bastions of the landward wall are in any case not regularly spaced, but vary in distance from one another from 115 to 385 feet. They were built against the face of the city wall and do not generally seem to have been bonded into it.[25] They were evidently added at a later date – or more probably at two later dates – and there is a distinct possibility that the second group is post-Roman. Such evidence as we have for dating them has been discussed in another chapter (pp. 69–72). Topographically, they fall into two groups – an eastern group of ten between the Tower and Bishopsgate (**B1–10**), with a single bastion to the west of Bishopsgate (**B11**); and a western group of ten between Cripplegate and Ludgate (**B12–21**). It is possible that there were once additional bastions, of which no trace or record has been found, in both groups, so that there may originally have been a more even spacing, but it can never have been completely regular. Between the two groups is a remarkable gap of eight hundred yards along the northern side of the wall in which no bastion is known.

In size the bastions whose measurements are known varied from nineteen to twenty-eight feet in diameter and from fifteen to twenty-six feet in projection, some being semi-circular and others horseshoe-shaped. They were of two distinct methods of construction, corresponding approximately with the two geographical groups. The eastern bastions which have been adequately recorded were, with the exception of the Wardrobe Tower, solid at the base, and they contained many architectural fragments and sculptured stones re-used as building material. Most of the latter seem to have come from monuments in the Roman cemetery just outside the city, and these include some of the most important finds of Roman London. (See *Plates* 4–6, 95.) In several instances (**B6, B7** and **B9**) courses of bonding or facing tiles have been recorded, and it is possible that this was a feature common to the whole group. Bastion 11 was exceptional in that it rested on a plinth of large re-used blocks which in turn rested on a rectangular platform of re-used flat slabs overlying a filling of the Roman ditch (*Fig. 8*).

The western group of bastions were built hollow from the base, like the Wardrobe Tower in the eastern group, but here again there is one exception (**B17**), which is solid. As far as is known, they contained no re-used stones of Roman date,[26] and it is doubtful if they had courses of tiles.[27] It is usually assumed that the western group is later, since the eastern half of the city, more important in Roman times and nearer to attack from the sea, is likely to have been given priority in any strengthening of the defences. As we have seen, it is not unlikely that the eastern bastions are late Roman and the western post-Roman in origin, but more evidence is required before the problem of their date can be definitely solved. (See pp. 69–72.) It should be noted, however, that the masonry (of small random rubble set in cement) found in the western bastions is very similar to that of a refacing of the city wall at St. Alphage churchyard and a patch behind Bastion 14 (**W40** and **W42**), which must have taken place when the Roman wall was in an advanced state of disrepair and had lost its original facing of squared blocks of ragstone.[28] Most, if not all, of the bastions probably continued in use throughout the Middle Ages and, like the city wall itself, were partially rebuilt.

The Streets

A Roman road in London was made from the local gravel, put down in closely rammed layers, generally with the addition of cement to make an intensely hard surface of gravel concrete. This was usually cambered so that there was adequate drainage from the crown of the road to a gully at its edge. Repairs were made by the addition of more gravel and a new surface, and if the road was in use for a long period this process was repeated many times, so that eventually a considerable thickness of gravel was accumulated. In section (as it is usually seen) this has a characteristically layered appearance, and a number of successive cambered surfaces can often be detected. (Cf. *Plate* 26.)

Unfortunately, a complete section of a Roman road is very rarely seen in London. If it lies beneath a modern road, it will probably already have been cut by nineteenth century sewers and other later intrusions, and in any case is hardly ever accessible. If it lies beneath modern buildings, it is likely to have been cut by excavations for foundations or refuse-pits of post-Roman date. Only small portions of metalling will usually have remained undisturbed here and there, and these are not only inconspicuous but individually may be impossible to identify with certainty. Gravel courtyards were made in very much the same way as roads, and although they required less frequent repair, and therefore did not usually accumulate such a great thickness of gravel, a small piece of a Roman courtyard is quite indistinguishable from a small piece of Roman road, most of the thickness of which may have been removed in later building excavations. Even compacted gravel make-up, intended only to raise or level the surface of the ground, can be deceptively like road material. A portion of apparent road metalling cannot therefore be taken as an indication of a Roman roadway *by itself*, but a series of similar finds may amount to an acceptable body of evidence. It is therefore important that all possible traces of Roman gravel metalling should be carefully recorded, although many of these may eventually prove to be unconnected with any Roman street. All artificial gravel deposits known to the author, that are apparently of Roman date and are of a kind indistinguishable from Roman road metalling, have been shown on the map (brown stipple), in the hope that future discoveries may fall in line with some of these to indicate the position of roadways. A proportion of them are undoubtedly merely the remains of courtyards, but as they are of similar character to road material, for convenience they have all been described as 'gravel metalling'.

In addition to traces of actual road metalling, we have a few other clues to the position and direction of Roman streets. We know that roads must have led to each of the gates, and also that the Romans usually favoured a regular rectangular street-plan, although there are nearly always irregularities in points of detail, and the rectangular blocks may be intersected by a road set at a different angle (generally indicating that the street-plan was superimposed on a pre-existing road). Buildings were not always aligned on the nearest road, but a consistent alignment of buildings in any area usually indicates that there was a road parallel, or at a right angle, with this somewhere in the vicinity. The remains of buildings will not of course be found on the line of a *contemporary* roadway, but where the replanning of streets has taken place (as is known to have happened in the centre of Roman London) traces of earlier buildings may well lie in the line of a later Roman street, which would have passed over them. The absence of Roman buildings in the line of a street which continued in existence from the earliest times until the end of the Roman period, however, may provide important confirmatory evidence for its position and direction. One other clue may possibly be of value when we know more about the minor streets of Roman London; in some continental cities (e.g. at Trier) there is a tendency for bastions to be placed opposite or near the ends of Roman streets, presumably to facilitate access to the bastion, but perhaps also reflecting a division of civic responsibility for defence in late Roman times.

In recent attempts to reconstruct the lay-out of Roman London, it has been assumed that the city first developed

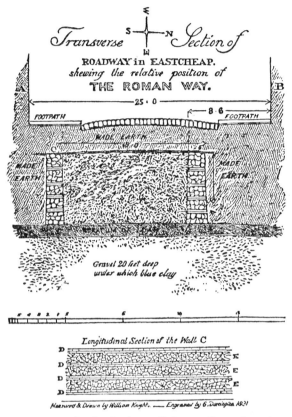

A, B, Frontage line of modern houses; C, Roman wall supporting road;
D, D, Layers of Roman tile; E, E, Kentish ragstone

FIG. 15   Section of Roman roadway in Great Eastcheap (296).
From *Gentleman's Magazine*, 1833.

around main roads diverging directly from the bridgehead, which might be expected to survive as a permanent feature of the street plan after the usual regular grid of streets had been superimposed.[29] (Cf. *Plates* 1 and 2.) This is a perfectly reasonable – and indeed likely – hypothesis, since London undoubtedly developed because of its importance as a centre of communications by water and land, and it was the river crossing which determined the concentration of the latter on the site of Londinium. Unfortunately there is as yet not a single scrap of evidence for the existence of any trunk roads diverging straight from the bridgehead. The one find which has been cited as a probable indication of a diagonal road, leading in a north-easterly direction from the bridge towards Aldgate,[30] can hardly, from its position, have formed part of such a road. This was the apparent roadway of gravel concrete between two ragstone walls found in Great Eastcheap in 1831 (**296.** *Fig.* 15).[31] One observer thought that this 'tended from Cannon Street in the direction of Little Eastcheap,'[32] and another that it was 'inclining N.E. of Little Eastcheap towards Aldgate.'[33] It is the second view, coupled with an unfortunate misplacement of the find to the top of Fish Street Hill – an error based on a confusion between Great Eastcheap and the present East-cheap, which first appears in the Victoria County History[34] – that has led to the belief that it was part of a direct road from the bridgehead to Aldgate. This would be impossible if, as is generally supposed, the Roman bridge lay to the east of the present London Bridge.

Although we do not know the exact position of the Roman bridge, it is unlikely that it lay to the west of the site of Old London Bridge – the stone bridge completed in 1209 about 100 feet east of the present structure. Great quantities of Roman coins and other objects were found on the site of the old bridge during dredging operations in the river bed to deepen the channel, and these apparently extended across the Thames. Roach Smith suggested that they may have been votive offerings, deliberately deposited in the river on the occasions of the building and repairing of the bridge.[35] However this may be, the occurrence of Roman antiquities right across the river in this area – as Roach Smith implies was the case – would suggest that there was a river crossing of some kind in the vicinity. During excavations in Southwark in 1945–7, Dr. K. M. Kenyon found gravel metalling at two points – No. 199, Borough High

Street, and Swan Street – apparently forming part of Stane Street. If this interpretation was correct, the line of the Roman road pointed to a position very near Old London Bridge.[36] The writer is indebted to Miss M. B. Honeybourne for the information that there is considerable evidence, both topographical and documentary – as yet unpublished – that the wooden bridge which preceded the mediaeval stone bridge lay about ninety feet east of the latter, to the east of the church of St. Magnus the Martyr, and about 250 feet east of the present London Bridge. Unfortunately there is no reason to believe that the late Saxon wooden bridge was precisely on the site of the Roman bridge. It could hardly have stood on wooden foundations which had been constructed soon after the Roman conquest; if so they had endured for more than a thousand years, more than half as long again as the life of the mediaeval stone bridge. This seems quite impossible, and it is reasonable to assume that several successive bridges were built between the first century and the eleventh. These are unlikely to have been in exactly the same place – in fact a new substructure could only have been built in a new position. A possible site for one of the earlier bridges – not necessarily the first – is at the bottom of Botolph Lane, where it was noted that the wooden piles, which had been seen along most of the sewer line of Lower Thames Street, were larger and much more closely set than elsewhere (**315**).

The Roman bridge (or bridges)[37] cannot, therefore, be located with any certainty, but presumably lay between the bottom of Fish Street Hill (the site of Old London Bridge) and Botolph Lane, well to the east of the Great Eastcheap road-metalling, which, as we shall see, is likely to have formed part of an east-west road. If a road ever ran directly from this area to Aldgate, no trace of it – or of any building aligned on it – has yet been found.

The road leading from the bridgehead to the north by way of Bishopsgate is also elusive.[38] Gravel metalling was observed by Mr. F. Cottrill in 1932 on the site of Nos. 15–18, Lime Street (*Plate* 27), and the line of this road seemed to be indicated by the footings of a wall which ran in a northerly direction on the western edge of the site (**232**). This line continued to the north would reach Bishopsgate, and continued to the south would arrive at the bottom of Botolph Lane, which has been suggested as the possible position for a Roman bridge. The road-metalling, however, overlay an occupation level containing pottery of about A.D. 50–80, including a potter's stamp that is unlikely to be earlier than A.D. 70.[39] Moreover, in the supposed line of the road to the north a Roman wall and tiled pavement have been found (222 and 223). These may be contemporary with the occupation level beneath the metalling of the road, which could have passed over the remains of the building to the north at a higher level. It is clear, however, that this could not have been the original road to the north from the bridge-head, but was constructed not earlier than Flavian times as part of a major scheme for the replanning of the centre of the City. This also presumably included the building of the great basilica and forum, which are skirted by the road. The corresponding road on the west side of the basilica/forum block seems to be represented by gravel metalling found west of Birchin Lane in 1935 (225). This also overlay earlier occupation levels and refuse deposits, and is likely to be Flavian or later.[40] The original north-south road presumably lay somewhere between these two later roads, and was blocked when the basilica was built. Our only clue to its position are the siting and alignment of a group of early buildings to the north of Lombard Street (228, 229, 229A, 235, 236, 240). These are on the same alignment as Gracechurch Street, but as one of them (229, 229A) evidently extends right across the modern street, the early road cannot lie beneath the latter. A possible position might be to the east of Gracechurch Street (between the building 229 and the later road 232). A road in this area on the same alignment as the group of early buildings to the west would lead in the direction of Bishopsgate to the north and Old London Bridge to the south. There is, however, no positive evidence of its existence, which could not in any case have continued after the building of the eastern end of the basilica, for which an early date has been postulated.[41]

The one road for which we have a considerable amount of evidence, and which seems to have remained a constant feature of Roman London from the earliest times until the full develop-ment of the city, is not a road from the bridge, but an east-west road at right angles with it and about 300 yards to the north of the river. This lies beneath the eastern end of Lombard Street, where fifty yards of the modern roadway have probably been part of a city street since before the revolt of Boudicca. It also partly underlies the western end of Fenchurch Street; but unlike the modern streets, both of which curve away from it in a

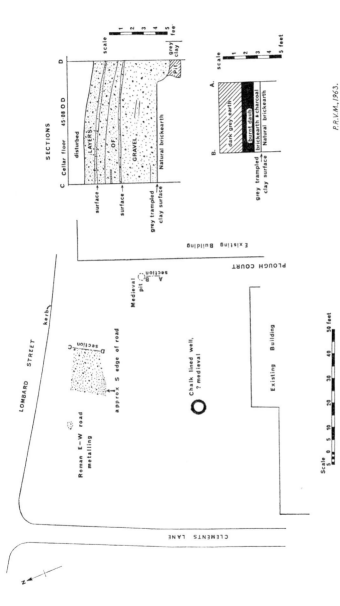

FIG. 16 Plan and sections, 30–2 Lombard Street, showing Roman roadway (**290**). *Drawn by P. R. V. Marsden (Guildhall Museum).*

P.R.V.M., 1963.

119

northerly direction, the Roman roadway evidently continued in a straight line for at least 370 yards. Its gravel metalling has been observed in four places during building excavations to the south of the present streets (**343, 344, 344A** and **290**). It does not appear to have been more than about twenty feet wide, but the thickness of the metalling (up to six-and-a-quarter feet) suggests that it was a road of importance which continued in use for a long time. Two distinct road surfaces have been observed at depths of about eleven-and-a-half and fourteen-and-a-half feet below the pavement of Lombard Street. A very early date for the road was indicated by sections seen on the site of Nos 30–32, Lombard Street in 1962 (**290**). The bottom of the gravel metalling rested directly on the trampled surface of the natural brick-earth, which to the south of the road was overlaid by a thin man-made layer of brick-earth and charcoal covered by a deposit of burnt daub (*Fig.* 16). The latter corresponds in level with similar layers containing pottery of the mid-first century found on other sites in this part of the City, and generally attributed to the destruction of the first settlement by Boudicca in A.D. 60. It seems likely, therefore, that the road was in existence before that date, and it may well be one of the earliest features of Roman London.

Continued to the west, with a very slight deflection to the north, it would have passed by way of George Street, where it may be represented by artificial deposits of gravel on the site of Nos. 13–14 (**197**), and thence beneath the Mansion House to the suggested crossing of the Walbrook at Bucklersbury, where traces of what was described as a 'macadamized roadway'[42] were seen on both sides of the stream on the site of the National Safe Deposit Company in 1872–3 (**196**).

To the west of the Walbrook, gravel metalling has been recorded on four sites in a continuation of this line, which gradually converges at an oblique angle on the line of Cheapside (**192, 64, 62, 61**). The earliest of these finds was made nearly 300 years ago when Sir Christopher Wren was rebuilding the church of St. Mary-le-Bow (**62**), the latest in 1963 during building excavations on the site of Nos. 76–80, Cheapside (**192**). Wren correctly identified his discovery, which he at first thought was natural gravel, as a 'Roman Causeway of rough Stone, close and well rammed, with Roman Brick and Rubbish at the Bottom for a Foundation, and all firmly

76-80 CHEAPSIDE

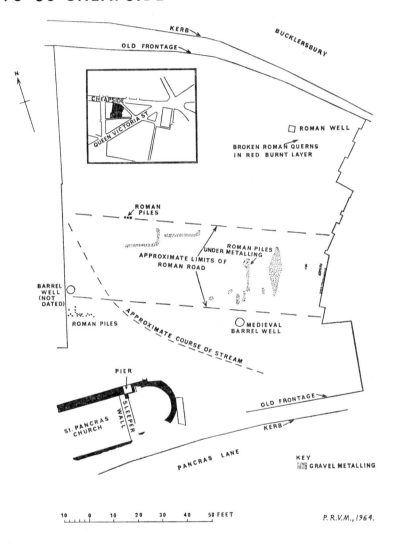

FIG. 17   Plan of site of 76–80 Cheapside, showing Roman and mediaeval remains, including the gravel metalling of the Roman road (**192**). *Drawn by P. R. V. Marsden (Guildhall Museum).*

cemented.'[43] This is a clear description by a careful observer of a typical Roman roadway in the City. The site was evidently not an easy one, since it partly overlay the silt of an ancient stream (63), and Wren decided to 'lay the foundation of the Tower upon the very Roman Causeway, as most proper to bear what he had designed, a weighty and lofty structure.'[43] The position of the Roman road therefore determined the placing of the tower well to the north of the church, and since the gravel metalling would have been useless as a foundation if it was too narrow to support all four walls of the tower, it is clear that the road was of considerable width. This is confirmed by the other finds (64 and 192), which show that it was considerably wider on the west of the Walbrook than on the east. (See *Fig.* 17.) A width between thirty and thirty-five feet seems to be indicated, and in most places the thickness of metalling was about four feet. The southern edge of the roadway was located in an excavation carried out by Mr. George Rybot under the direction of Professor Grimes to the west of St. Mary-le-Bow (61), and here it was parallel with the modern street, giving the impression that the road followed the line of Cheapside. This was evidently not the case to the east of this point,[44] and there is reason to believe that an oblique course across Cheapside was followed to the west of it. The road must eventually have reached Newgate, and a careful watch on the large site north of Paternoster Row revealed no trace of it crossing this area in a line with Cheapside. The only possible evidence of its presence lay near the northern edge of the site (14, 15), and there seemed no doubt that the main part of the road lay beneath Newgate Street, as would be expected if it crossed to the northern side of Cheapside before the latter curves northward to meet Newgate Street. Traces of gravel metalling observed to the north of Cheapside near its western end (36, 37) give further confirmation of this, leaving little doubt that the oblique course of the Roman road continued to the west, and was even accentuated, somewhere along the line, by a distinct kink towards the north. It seems likely, therefore, that the direction of the road edge west of St. Mary-le-Bow was merely a local irregularity, which did not affect the general line of the road. The alternative possibility that a branch road diverged to the south-west at this point must be borne in mind, but is as yet unsupported by any other evidence.

Another Roman east-west street of only slightly less impor-

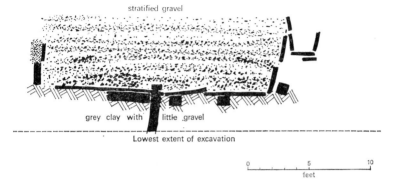

FIG. 18   Section of Roman road, site of Bucklersbury House,
Walbrook (**251**). *Drawn by Miss W. Mumford (Guildhall Museum).*

tance evidently underlies the northern side of Cannon Street
east of the railway station. The edge of this roadway, with a
drainage gully to the north of it, was found on the site of St.
Swithin's Church in an excavation by Professor Grimes, and
again further west in the builders' excavation (**267**). On its
southern side stood – and perhaps in part still stands, deeply
embedded beneath the middle of the modern road – the
mysterious London Stone, made of Clipsham Limestone, of
which the top alone, shaped rather like a tea-cosy, is still
preserved in a niche on the site of St. Swithin's (now the Bank
of China). (**268**, see also *Plate* 28.) Camden believed that it was
a Roman milestone, and he may even have been right, although
there is no certainty of its Roman date. All that we know is that
it was a venerated antiquity in the Middle Ages, when it seems
to have taken on something of the character of a fetish stone.
Its original purpose had evidently been forgotten as early as
the twelfth century, when it was simply called 'Londenstane.'[45]
If it had been an Anglo-Saxon wayside or market cross, as is
sometimes suggested, some memory of this origin would surely
have been preserved in its name at this early date. It is also
unlikely that it was a sacred stone of the pagan Saxon period,

like the one overthrown by St. Augustine at Canterbury (and since set up again by the Ministry of Works),[46] for it was a stone shaped by masons and not a natural monolith. It is therefore feasible that it was a roadside monument of some kind, set up in the Roman period, although the use of Clipsham Limestone might suggest a later date.

A continuation of this road to the east would meet the gravel 'causeway' found in 1831 (**296**), making a line very nearly parallel with the main east-west road to the north, at a distance from it of 420 Roman feet or three and a half *actus*, the unit commonly used by Roman surveyors.[47] It may be suspected that these two roads as originally laid out were quite parallel, with the edge a few feet to the south of the position where it was found by Professor Grimes, but that it moved very slightly to the north with subsequent re-making of the road. It can hardly be doubted that these two roads were created as a deliberate piece of town-planning, the lower one being placed at the top of the steep slope above the river.

The course of the lower road to the west is less regular. A gravel roadway resting on timber foundations was seen near the south-east corner of the Bucklersbury House site, and this must be either a continuation of the main Cannon Street road or a branch-road from it to the north-west (**251**, *Fig.* 18, *Plate* 25). The continuation of a line of wooden posts beneath its northern edge strongly suggested that this was its direction as it approached the Walbrook stream, although the actual metalling was seen in too small an area for its course to be determined (*Plate* 23). If it continued in the same direction after crossing the stream, it would have followed the line of Budge Row to Watling Street. Some indication of possible Roman road metalling beneath Budge Row was in fact observed (**255**), so it seems likely that this mediaeval street had a Roman forbear.

There is no doubt, however, that there was another Roman street in a more westerly direction to the south of Budge Row, also linked with the lower east-west road east of the Walbrook, but of this we know virtually nothing. It is said that the sill of a bridge which crossed the Walbrook was seen during excavations for the District Railway in Cloak Lane (**258**), but no description is given, and it is impossible to judge whether this identification of the structure found is likely to have been correct. A Roman roadway may have followed approximately on the line of Cloak Lane, Great St. Thomas Apostle, Great

Trinity Lane and the eastern part of Knightrider Street, skirting the southern side of the long Roman wall found in the latter; it may equally well have followed the western part of Cannon Street, which is the successor of a line of mediaeval streets, in a direct course to Ludgate; or there may have been two Roman streets following both of these lines. All that can be said is that the lower east-west road on the east of the Walbrook may well have forked somewhere to the west of London Stone, to give access to a third crossing of the stream south of Bucklersbury House, and it now seems unlikely that there was a regular grid of parallel streets in the south-western part of the city.

There is a possible indication of a more regular lay-out immediately to the west of the Bucklersbury crossing, to the north and south of the upper east-west road. A cambered gravel roadway fourteen feet wide, containing Roman pottery, was found during excavations for Queen Victoria Street, between St. Mary Aldermary and St. Antholin Budge Row, and is said to have been nearly in line with modern Watling Street (**92**). This may be merely a continuation of the Budge Row road, which must in any case adjoin it nearby. It may be noted, however, that the eastern part of Watling Street is parallel with the main Roman east-west road to the north, and it is possible that it overlies a secondary Roman road, of which this find formed part. This would lie about 300 Roman feet (two and a half *actus*) to the south of the main road. At about the same distance (280 English feet) to the north of the latter, a layered accumulation of gravel of Roman date, closely resembling road-metal, has been observed on several sites (**46, 47, 49**). If this does represent a roadway, its direction is approximately east-west and, although its precise alignment cannot yet be defined, it *could* be parallel with the main road to the south. On the other hand it may be a continuation of an apparent east-west road seen in Old Jewry (**154**), in which case its course would have converged on the main road. The lowest levels seem to have been deposited immediately above natural soil at the time of the earliest occupation of this area, and the thickness of the accumulation (up to six feet) indicates that the surface was repeatedly renewed. Nine successive surfaces were in fact counted on the site of Nos. 34–35, King Street. This suggests a street rather than a courtyard, but an element of doubt remains, as there is considerable evidence of a rapid build-up of occupation levels in this area, probably in response to the rising water-table (Cf. 50, 52). If, however, this does prove to be a Roman street, parallel with the main road and 300 Roman feet to the north of it, it will show that there was a planned lay-out immediately to the west of the Walbrook in this area, and we might reasonably expect to find a corresponding street the same distance to the south beneath Watling Street, where, as we have seen, its presence is already suspected on other grounds.

Nevertheless it is doubtful if a regular grid of streets extended far to the west, for the Roman buildings found on the sites of Gateway House and Watling House (70–79) were on quite a different alignment. It will be noted, however, that they are nevertheless still parallel with Watling Street, which changes direction so that its eastern, central and western portions are on different alignments. Since the eastern part is parallel with a Roman main road and the central with a complex of Roman buildings, while the western end points almost directly to Ludgate,[48] one is left with the suspicion that this may be yet another mediaeval road which follows the line of a Roman precursor. It is most unlikely, however, that it has any con-nection with the great Roman highway of the same name, which is linked more directly with Newgate than Ludgate.[49] Although it is connected with the bridgehead by the somewhat devious route via Budge Row and Cannon Street, there is no reason to believe that this represents one of the original trunk roads of London. If Watling Street does in fact follow a Roman street along the whole curve of its course – and this remains to be proved[50] – it seems more likely that the latter grew in a somewhat haphazard fashion from a minor street of early date, changing its direction slightly as it developed towards the west.

As we have seen, the Roman fort in the north-west corner of the city had internal roads set at right angles, following the standard form (see pp. 98–9). Since the fort itself was evidently aligned on the main road to the south, it might be expected that a regular lay-out of external streets on a rectangular pat-tern would have been planned in its immediate neighbourhood when it was constructed. There was presumably an external continuation of the via praetoria which gave access to the main road to the south, and there may have been another road-way leading eastward from the via principalis, but no definite archaeological evidence for either has yet been found. The topographical evidence is equally negative, for the southern

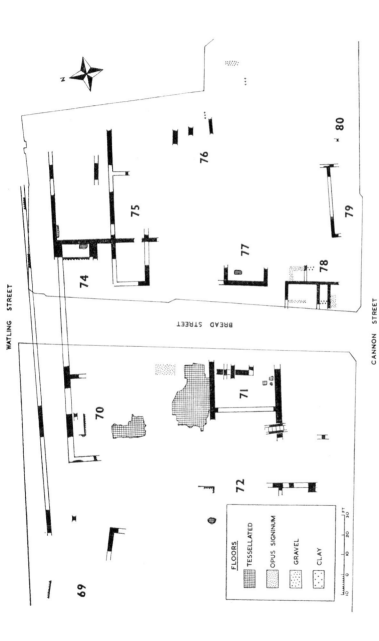

WATLING STREET

BREAD STREET

CANNON STREET

FLOORS
TESSELLATED
OPUS SIGNINUM
GRAVEL
CLAY

69 70 71 72 74 75 76 77 78 79 80

FIG. 19 Plan of Roman buildings aligned on Watling Street, sites of Gateway House and Watling House (69–80). *Drawn from records by I. Noel Hume (Guildhall Museum)*.

part of Wood Street swings well to the east of the hypothetical line of the former roadway, and the latter seems to have left no mark on the more recent street-plan of the City. Similarly, an external road skirting the eastern side of the fort might be expected, but although Milk Street and Aldermanbury lie on or near the line it would follow, no trace of Roman road metalling has yet been detected there, and a section studied recently beneath the northern part of Aldermanbury showed that this part of the street at least did not exist before the thirteenth century. The former existence of a Roman roadway, since destroyed by deep cellars, to the side of the modern street in this area remains a possibility, however.

Two probable north-south streets are known in the western part of the city (*Fig.* 20). The more doubtful of these is represented by a mass of gravel resembling road material found a little to the west of St. Paul's Underground Station (**16, 17,** and possibly **15**). The general trend of its alignment is in the direction of Aldersgate, parallel with the east and west walls of the fort and presumably at right angles with the main road to Newgate. This is just where a Roman roadway might be expected, but it can hardly have continued south of Paternoster Row, for a pavement of red tesserae seen under the north frontage of this street indicated that a Roman building lay in its path (**20**). Moreover, the gravel mass is excessively wide for a minor road (forty feet). It may therefore represent a close or courtyard rather than a street, although it is by no means unlikely that a street leading to Aldersgate lay opposite it on the north side of the road to Newgate. A hoard of late third century coins was found in a gully or pit cut into the gravel near its eastern edge (*Plates* 11–12).

The other find lay further west in Paternoster Square, and this looked much more like a typical Roman roadway. It was seen in section in two places, and had a succession of cambered surfaces with a drainage gully adjoining its eastern side (**9, 10,** *Plate* 26). Roman pottery was found associated with it, including a Samian cup of the first century (*Drag.* form 27), which was embedded in the lip of the gully adjacent to the earliest surface. Although the direction was approximately north-south, it was unfortunately impossible to determine the exact alignment. If a small portion of gravel metalling observed further north (**11**) belonged to this roadway, as seems likely, it did not meet the main road to Newgate at right angles, but

PATERNOSTER DEVELOPMENT

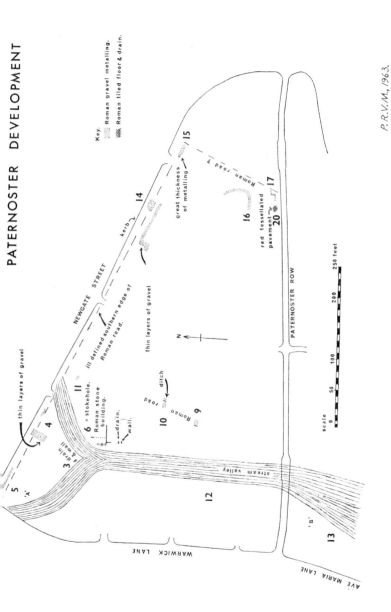

Key:
▨ Roman gravel metalling.
▩ Roman tiled floor & drain.

P.R.V.M., 1963.

Fig. 20 Plan of Roman remains, Paternoster Development site, including gravel metalling of supposed roads. *Drawn by P. R. V. Marsden (Guildhall Museum).*

129

skirted the two curves of the stream nearby tangentially, and if continued in the same line to the north of the main road would have led directly to Bastion 17. For what it is worth, however, it may be noted that the eastern edge of this roadway at the point where it is defined (10) is almost exactly three *actus* (360 Roman feet or 350 English feet)[51] from the line of the western edge of the mass of gravel to the east (16). There is therefore a distinct possibility that we have after all two parallel roads laid out by Roman surveyors at right angles with the main road.

Although we have much to learn about the streets of Roman London, a few tentative conclusions based on our present very imperfect knowledge may perhaps be drawn. The city seems to have been neither a casual growth at an important road junction nor the product of a unified plan, but shows signs of piece-meal development, planned and otherwise. The absence of any clear evidence of through roads is at first surprising in a city which was primarily a centre of communications. The main east-west street leads to Newgate in the west, but not to Aldgate in the east, with which it was presumably linked by a branch road; a direct road from the bridgehead to the east by way of Aldgate is still a possibility, but one which must now be regarded as doubtful; and the basilica seems to have been built without regard for any pre-existing road to the north from the bridgehead. The need for through roads was however hardly felt before the development of modern road transport, for in earlier times London was never merely an incident on the journey, but a place where travel ended and began, and a clearing-house rather than a mere junction. The Roman roads, therefore, seem either to have started from London like the nineteenth century railways, or (in the case of Watling Street and a possible northern by-pass) to have by-passed it closely without actually going through the town (*Fig.* 2). If this was so from the beginning – and there is no real evidence to the contrary – it follows that the nucleus of London existed in some form, possibly merely as a fortified bridgehead, but probably also as a port and military supply base, before the development of the road system of which it became the focal point.

Structures in Roman London

Owing to the fragmentary character of Roman remains found in London, buildings can seldom be identified with certainty. Often only portions of the foundations remain, and these are usually interrupted by later intrusions in so many places that it is impossible to recover a complete ground-plan, even if there is an opportunity to investigate the whole extent of a building. Generally, of course, only tantalising glimpses are obtained in a limited area of excavation. The walls most commonly recorded are of Kentish ragstone, usually in the form of rubble concrete – i.e. irregular lumps of ragstone set in hard mortar – not infrequently with courses of tiles in the superstructure. Many more buildings, however, must have been built of wattle and daub with a timber frame, and the remains of these can rarely be detected in the normal conditions of a builders' excavation. The timber foundations may survive on a water-logged site, but usually traces of the walls are only recognisable when the daub has been transformed by fire into an almost indestructible substance resembling terra-cotta. They are then, of course, no longer *in situ*, since the walls collapse when the building is burnt, and the remains merely form part of one of the featureless 'burnt levels' of Roman London. In at least one instance clay was used for the superstructure of a wall which had a ragstone base (**80**), so that not all Roman 'ragstone buildings' were necessarily as substantial as their foundations would suggest. Conversely, buildings of wattle and daub were not necessarily 'huts' of native type. This was a recognised Roman method of construction, described by Vitruvius, though with disapproval.[52] The presence of painted wall-plaster, mingled with the burnt daub, shows that some buildings of this type, even in the earliest period, were not without pretensions (Cf. **290**). Plaster rendering of this kind is of course quite commonly found on the internal face of ragstone walls. Brick superstructures, built of the flat tile-like Roman building-bricks (usually one-and-a-half by one Roman foot) on rubble concrete foundations as piers and walling are by no means unusual, although the commonest use of these bricks is in bonding-courses interspersed with ragstone. Bricks of other form are more rarely used; they include broken roofing-tiles laid in regular courses with their upturned flanges forming the face of a wall (235, 236) – an unusual method of building which is evidently of early date. Roofing-tiles used for their proper purpose – i.e. with the upturned flanges of the *tegulae* overlaid with curved *imbrices* to form the kind of tiled roof that is still found in Mediterranean countries – seem to have been by no means as common in London as might be expected, and thatched roofs were probably more frequent. Window-glass also, rather surprisingly, is rarely found; although it undoubtedly existed, fragments of broken panes seldom found their way into the household rubbish pits. The better floors are of cement: of the characteristic concrete containing broken tile called *opus signinum*: and of tesserae (small cubes of tile or stone) set in cement. In the humbler dwellings – and sometimes in more important buildings – the floors are of clay, gravel or wood. Evidence of central heating is not infrequent, usually consisting of the remains of the brick pillars which supported a floor above a hypocaust.

THE BASILICA

Of the few public buildings which have been identified, the largest and most important is the great basilica, a vast hall which cannot be less than 500 feet long – about the same length as St. Paul's Cathedral – if the whole of the structure which has been recorded on both sides of Gracechurch Street is in fact a single building, as it appears to be. It combined the functions of law-courts and town hall, and no doubt also served as a meeting-place for the senate of Londinium. Although the parallel is not close, it may be compared with the Guildhall of the City of London, if we include the whole complex of the Guildhall precinct, with its great hall for public gatherings, its rooms for the Court of Aldermen and Court of Common Council, its courts of justice and its administrative offices. In addition, it probably also served the now obsolete function of the Royal Exchange as a convenient meeting-place for business-men.

In view of the importance of Londinium, it is perhaps not surprising that its basilica was very much larger than that of any other Romano-British town, the next in size being that of Cirencester (Corinium) with a length of 333 feet. It is, however, astonishing to find that it is apparently nearly twice as long as the basilica of the great Romano-Gaulish city of Trier (273 feet long).

The usual pattern of a provincial basilica was a great hall with a nave and side aisles separated by colonnades or arcades, and with an apse at one or both ends containing a raised floor or tribune for the magistrate and assessors. On one side of the hall was a row of offices and courtrooms, and the other side generally faced the forum, an open space which was the centre of the life of the city, serving both as market square and meeting-place. This was usually a rectangular courtyard enclosed on three sides by colonnades with rows of shops or offices.

The London building seems to have conformed approximately to the standard pattern, but with a number of puzzling irregularities. The nave lay between two east-west walls which were evidently sleeper walls, carrying the brick piers of a colonnade, or more probably an arcade of arches, which supported the roof (*Fig.* 24, walls *A, A1, B* and *B1.* See also **213, 214, 219, 220**, and *Plates* 48–51). According to a note made by Henry Hodge on the excavations in Leadenhall Market in 1888, 'blocks of oversailing bricks like an arch in red mortar or concrete' were found in the northern part of the building, and it seems likely that these had fallen from the superstructure of the northern arcade. To the north of this was an aisle, which divided the nave from a double row of almost square offices (*C*) in the western half of the building, and apparently from a room or rooms of a different kind, possibly with curved walls, in the eastern half (*D*) (see **211, 214, 217, 218**). No certain trace of a southern aisle and an external southern wall has been found, and it now seems likely that the east-west wall beneath the northern edge of Corbet Court, which was thought to be the external wall, in fact belonged to a different building (*R.* See also **221, 229**). A curious feature is the double wall of the eastern part of the basilica, where a shorter wall (*E*) adjoins the south side of the southern arcade, and is overlaid by the southern edge of one of its piers.[53] (See **220** and *Plate* 50.) The eastern apse (*F*) is adjacent to a continuation of this wall, and as the latter is evidently earlier than the arcade, it has been suggested that it was the side wall of an earlier basilica, which would have been rather less than two hundred and forty feet long.[54] According to this theory, the basilica was subsequently extended to the west, and Mr. G. C.

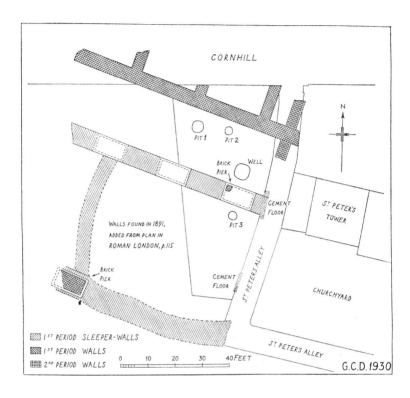

FIG. 21   Plan of portion of Basilica, with earlier well and pits,
Nos. 50 and 52 Cornhill (Map **213, 214**). *By permission of G. C.
Dunning and the Society of Antiquaries of London.*

Dunning has shown that the fragmentary walls east of St.
Michael's Alley (*G*) can be made to fit exactly into a scheme of
apse and cross-walls at the western end of the building closely
comparable with that of the eastern end.[55] He also found that
the original *opus signinum* floor of the northern aisle of the
western part of the basilica overlay pottery of the Flavian
period, so that the western extension cannot have been built before
about A.D. 80–90. (See *Fig.* 22 and **214.**) This is also consistent
with the apparent date of the two north-south flanking roads
(*X* and *Y*) immediately to the east and west of the extended

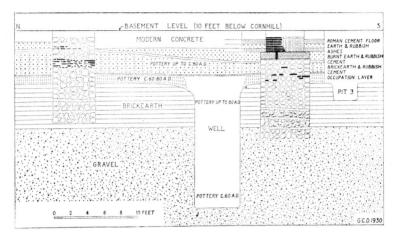

FIG. 22   Section through north sleeper wall with brick pier (right) and northern wall (left) of Basilica, with earlier well and occupation level, No. 52 Cornhill (Map **214**). *By permission of G. C. Dunning and Society of Antiquaries of London.*

basilica. (See **225, 232.**) There is, therefore, a strong suggestion that the centre of Roman London was replanned to provide a much enlarged basilica in Flavian times, and it may be suspected that this was yet another of Agricola's schemes for introducing the splendours of civilisation into Britain.[56] It should be noted, however, that there are difficulties in fitting the remains of the two halves of the basilica into the unified plan of a single building, for the walls of the western half seem to lie a few feet to the north of the corresponding walls of the eastern half. (Cf. walls *B* and *B1*.) There is still, therefore, an element of doubt whether the two halves co-existed to form a single long building. It is even more difficult, however, to fit two successive structures into any reasonable chronology, in view of the early date of the western building and its apparent contemporaneity with both eastern and western flanking roads; and the discrepancies in the plan might easily be accounted for by a small error in plotting or alignment.

   During the excavations of 1881 on the site of Leadenhall Market, two distinct floors were observed. The lower, found over a large part of the site, was of plain brick tesserae, and was covered with the ashes of a great fire; above this was a later pavement of concrete, and there were also traces of white and coloured tessellated pavements whose position in the stratigraphy is unknown. Fragments of wall-plaster decorated with fresco paintings of green foliage on a red ground, also found in Leadenhall Market, give a tantalising glimpse of the interior decoration of the building (*Plate* 54).

THE FORUM

It was usual to have an open area called the forum immediately adjacent to the basilica, and this served both as principal market place and as the civic centre of the town. In Britain, the basilica generally formed one side of a rectangular enclosure around the large open courtyard of the forum, the other three sides consisting of porticos containing rows of shops and offices. Traces of structures which probably formed part of such a forum building have been found in London to the south of the basilica. On the eastern side it seems to be represented by an inner buttressed wall (*H*) on the site of No. 83, Gracechurch Street (**231**), and possibly by an outer wall (*I*) to the east of Lime Street Passage (**232**); on the western side by three walls south of Castle Court (*J, K, L*) and by an outer (robbed) wall in George Yard (*M*) (**227** and **225**). The clearest indications of forum buildings, however, have been seen on the southern side, in the corner between Gracechurch Street and Lombard Street. Here traces have been recorded of a rectangular structure (*N*) approximately parallel with the basilica, and containing brick piers (*P, P1*) which presumably carried an arcade or (in the case of the smaller piers) columns and an entablature (**239, 241,** *Plates* 52–3). One such column base and core was found standing on a cement floor, and it is likely that it rested on a similar pier below floor-level. This structure, which was presumably the southern portico of the forum, cannot be earlier than the second century, for a small copper coin (*quadrans*) of Hadrian was found embedded in the yellow mortar of one of the piers, and a piece of Samian pottery of second century type (*Drag.* form 38) was found beneath its north wall.[57] If, therefore, the replanning of the centre of the town, which apparently took place in Flavian times, also included the provision of a forum to the south of the extended basilica,

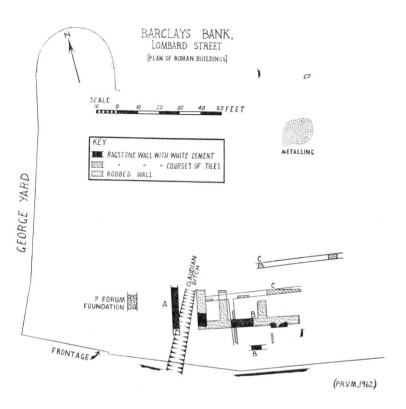

FIG. 23   Plan of successive early Roman buildings on the site of Barclays Bank, Lombard Street (**243**). *Drawn by P. R. V. Marsden (Guildhall Museum).*

as seems likely, this was not actually built until many years later, perhaps in the reign of Hadrian, when a fresh impulse seems to have been given to public works of this kind.[58] A date of this period is in fact indicated for the piers ($P1$) and associated floor, but the wall (N) is considerably later. (See **239**).

The immediate predecessor of the supposed forum building of the second century, in the western corner of Gracechurch Street and Lombard Street, was a building on a different alignment (U), approximately parallel with Gracechurch Street. (See also **240**.) This seems to form part of a fairly large building, which also includes the structures to the north (*Fig.* 24, *S*, and **236**). Other buildings on the same alignment are apparently contemporary (*Fig.* 24, *T*, *R*, *Q*; **235, 229A, 229**), as also probably is a building to the west (*Fig.* 24, *V*; **243,** second building), though this is aligned on the Roman east-west road to the south. There were indications of the deliberate demolition of some of these buildings (*S*, *T*) and a subsequent artificial raising of the ground with building debris, sand or brick-earth, on which a white cement floor has been observed in several places. On the site of All Hallows, Lombard Street, the floor overlay make-up of sand and builder's rubbish containing fragments of two decorated Samian bowls in the style of potters of the late first century, and a dish with the stamp of a potter who is believed not to have commenced work before the reign of Hadrian.[59] The floor was evidently associated with the supposed forum building, since although it overlay the original bases of the piers, it was flush with pink mortar additions which had been placed on two of them. The buildings beneath clearly belong to an earlier town centre which was demolished when the later forum was built. Pottery evidence indicates that they were occupied about A.D. 60–80,[60] so they are likely to have been built in the period of reconstruction after the Boudiccan fire, although there is a suggestion that one of them[61] might be a survivor of the destruction of A.D. 60, while another[62] was apparently not built before the Flavian period. They were all substantial buildings, variously constructed of ragstone and bricks, mostly with foundations of flint rubble. The date of their demolition is uncertain, but it is not unlikely that some of them, at least, survived into the second century. (See **240**.)

There are traces of even earlier buildings which were destroyed before these were built and, although there is no clear evidence of their date, it seems likely that they belong to the first London which was destroyed by Boudicca (*Fig.* 24, *Z*, *Z1*: *Fig.* 23, c: **243, 240, 229A**). Rather surprisingly, they had foundations of ragstone, and at such an early period, when most of the buildings of Roman London seem to have been constructed of wattle and daub alone, this suggests that they were built for some official purpose.

The early history of the centre of Londinium therefore appears to fall into four phases. First, a small public building of some kind with ragstone foundations was built on the northern

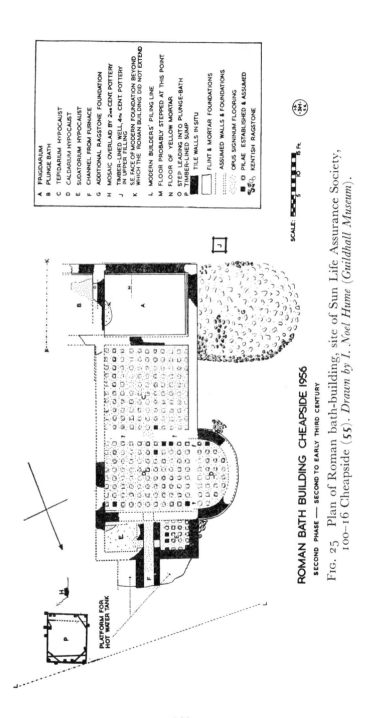

A FRIGIDARIUM
B PLUNGE BATH
C TEPIDARIUM HYPOCAUST
D CALDARIUM HYPOCAUST
E SUDATORIUM HYPOCAUST
F CHANNEL FROM FURNACE
G ADDITIONAL RAGSTONE FOUNDATION
H MOSAIC OVERLAID BY 2ND CENT. POTTERY
J TIMBER-LINED WELL, 4TH CENT. POTTERY
    IN UPPER FILLING
K S.E. FACE OF MODERN FOUNDATION BEYOND
    WHICH THE ROMAN BUILDING DID NOT EXTEND
L MODERN BUILDERS' PILING LINE
M FLOOR PROBABLY STEPPED AT THIS POINT
N FLOOR OF YELLOW MORTAR
O STEP LEADING INTO PLUNGE-BATH
P TIMBER-LINED SUMP

■ TILE WALLS IN SITU

▨ FLINT & MORTAR FOUNDATIONS

⋯⋯ ASSUMED WALLS & FOUNDATIONS

⋰⋰ OPUS SIGNINUM FLOORING

■ ◘ PILAE ESTABLISHED & ASSUMED
ᏏᏏ KENTISH RAGSTONE

SCALE: ▭▭▭▭▭▭▭ 5 10 15 FT

ROMAN BATH BUILDING CHEAPSIDE 1956

SECOND PHASE — SECOND TO EARLY THIRD CENTURY

PLATFORM FOR
HOT WATER TANK

FIG. 25 Plan of Roman bath-building, site of Sun Life Assurance Society,
100–16 Cheapside (55). *Drawn by I. Noel Hume (Guildhall Museum)*.

side of the main east-west street, on which it was aligned. This was succeeded by a group of buildings, almost certainly also public, on a slightly different alignment (parallel with Gracechurch Street) probably when the city was rebuilt after its destruction by Boudicca. Then, not earlier than the mid-Flavian period, perhaps under the influence of Agricola, a new town centre was planned with an exceptionally large basilica and (probably) a forum to the south of it. The basilica was built (or extended) before the end of the first century, but the forum scheme was not completed before the reign of Hadrian. This is a tentative and almost certainly over-simplified summary of what appears at the time of writing to have been the sequence of Roman buildings in this area. It takes no account of the supposed earlier and shorter basilica, the date of which is unknown, since this does not fall obviously either into the first or second phase described above.

BATH BUILDINGS

Several buildings have been identified with varying degrees of probability as public baths, and these, as might be expected, are sited where natural springs are likely to have given an abundant water-supply. The most certain bath-house is a fairly small building found in 1955 to the north of the main Roman east-west road, opposite St. Mary-le-Bow Church (55). Here it was possible to identify the various heated rooms (*tepidarium*, *caldarium* and *sudatorium*), the cool room (*frigidarium*) and even the cold plunge bath (*Fig. 25*). The bather usually first exercised or played games in the *palaestra* (exercise yard), and then undressed in the *apodyterium* (undressing-room), which were not found. He next proceeded through the increasing heat of the *tepidarium* (warm room), *caldarium* (hot room) and *sudatorium* (sweating chamber), and so induced perspiration, which was scraped off together with the dirt by means of a curved implement called a strigil. He often took a hot plunge in the *caldarium*, and then cooled off in the *frigidarium* where he finally took a cold plunge to close the pores of the skin. The heating was by means of hot air which passed through a flue channel into a hollow space beneath the floor, which was supported on pillars of tiles. This bath-house seems to have been built in the late first or early second century, and was rebuilt and enlarged

ROMAN BUILDING, HUGGIN HILL

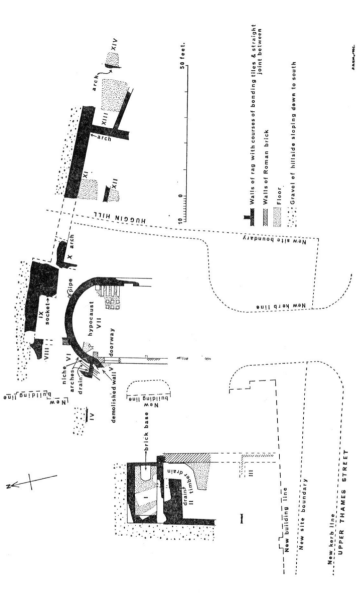

FIG. 26   Plan of Roman bath-building, Huggin Hill, Upper Thames Street. Only the eastern portion (XI–XIV) is included in the map and gazetteer (121). Compartment I appears to be a cold plunge bath, with the base of brick steps at the eastern end. VII is a chamber heated by a hypocaust. The building is set in the slope of the hill-side, with IX serving as the northern retaining wall. *Drawn by P. R. V. Marsden (Guildhall Museum).*

141

in the second century. Its heating system seems to have been abandoned early in the third century, and the building itself was apparently demolished soon afterwards. (See *Plate* 60.)

Another probable bath-house is the building in Lower Thames Street (**353**). This contained a double chamber, similarly heated by a hypocaust, with the apsidal walls that are commonly found in the hot rooms of Roman baths. The presence of a brick seat, forming part of the partition between the two heated chambers, also suggests that the building may have been a public bath-house, rather than a dwelling with central heating. (See *Plate* 61.) An undisturbed Roman deposit, which was evidently part of the original filling of the hypocaust, was found in 1951 during the cleaning of the portion of the building preserved beneath the Coal Exchange. This contained pottery of the third century, which probably indicates the date when the heating system ceased to be used.

A more certain bath-house has recently been discovered in a similar position near the river in Upper Thames Street – unfortunately too late for inclusion in the map. This was found to the west of Huggin Hill in August 1964, and it was obviously a continuation of the building found in 1929 on the east side of this street (**121**, *Fig.* 26, XI–XIV). The walls recorded in sewer excavations (**119, 120**) also probably formed part of the same building. The structures recently found included a westward continuation of the walls found in 1929, with a large apsidal chamber twenty-six feet wide, which had been heated by means of flue passages and a hypocaust (*Fig.* 26, VI–VII; *Plate* 58). A doorway on the western side gave access to the apsidal room. Further west was a compartment with a thick concrete foundation, which may possibly have been the cold plunge (I). The steep slope of the hill had evidently been cut back to accommodate the building, and to the north was a thick ragstone retaining wall. Water passed through the wall of the apsidal chamber by means of a terra-cotta pipe. The hypocaust was eventually filled with dumped material containing a considerable quantity of pottery, none of it later than the early second century, so it seems likely that the heating system went out of use soon after that date, and the building itself may have been demolished and rebuilt.

Small plunge baths have also been recorded in Threadneedle Street (**182**, *Plate* 59) and Cannon Street (**86**). In addition, there were tank-like structures, which may have belonged to bath-buildings, in Lime Street (233) and Mark Lane (348); and a culvert in Monument Street was connected with a brick tank or bath covered on the inside with tesserae on plaster (312).

TEMPLES

Structural evidence alone might suggest that the Roman Londoners put cleanliness a long way before godliness, for we know only one building which is certainly a temple. Other finds, however, clearly show that there must have been shrines to a variety of deities in Londinium. The state cult of Emperor worship is represented by the fragment of a large inscription re-used as building material in Nicholas Lane (284, *Fig.* 5). This presumably came from an imposing temple of classical type, which is likely to have stood somewhere in the neighbour-hood, though it is by no means impossible that it came from quite a different part of the city. The large group of the Mother Goddesses found in Seething Lane (350, *Plate* 88) is unlikely to have been moved far from its original site, and therefore suggests that there was a shrine to these Celtic deities in the neighbourhood of St. Olave's Church. Similarly, the altar with the relief of Diana which was found on the site of Goldsmiths' Hall (38, *Plate* 86) may indicate the presence of a shrine there, although, as this is a more easily portable object and one likely to attract attention, there is in this case a distinct possibility that it was brought from elsewhere.

Two of the early buildings in Gracechurch Street have been regarded as possible temples. The rectangular building with external buttresses and an inner compartment, found on the site of No. 85 (229), had in plan the appearance of a square temple with a central *cella*, until finds on the opposite side of the street in 1964 (229A) showed that the outer compartment on the north side was almost certainly the corridor of an oblong building which extended right across the street (*Fig.* 27). The curious building with two compartments and an angular apse, on the site of Nos. 17–19, Gracechurch Street (235, *Fig.* 24, *T*), has also been thought to be a temple, though one of unusual form. Its purpose will remain doubtful, however, until a close parallel, the use of which is known, is found elsewhere.

The only building which we are certain was used for religious purposes is the temple of Mithras found by Professor Grimes on the east bank of the Walbrook (248) where it was no doubt placed because of the need for water in the ritual of the sect.[63] This was a temple of a special form called a *basilica* – not to be confused with the civic buildings of the same name, but, like them, serving as a place of assembly, rather than a mere shrine for a cult statue, like the ordinary pagan temple. A basilican temple was usually, therefore, associated with a mystery cult, in which a congregation of initiates met to carry out their rites in private. Both architecturally and functionally it had close affinities with the early Christian churches, also called basilicas, and the Walbrook temple, in particular, might easily have been mistaken for a church. It was entered from the east through a vestibule or *narthex*, from which a double door gave access to wooden steps leading down to the central nave, nearly two and a half feet below the floor level of the vestibule. On either side was an aisle, separated from the central nave by a colonnade of seven pillars which supported the roof, and at the western end was a raised sanctuary within a rounded apse.[64] It differed from a church, however, in that the aisles were originally at a higher level than the nave, and served as benches on which the Mithraic congregation sat or reclined. The floor level was gradually raised, in response to the steadily rising water level, and eventually the colonnades were removed, so that the building became an open hall. It continued in use after the burial of the pagan sculptures (see pp. 62 f.), and there is no evidence that it was ever deliberately destroyed.

It is uncertain whether the Mithraeum stood alone as a building in its own right, or whether it was attached to the rear of a private house. It was probably built towards the end of the second century; and a substantial building immediately to the east, on the other side of the modern street of Walbrook, was built not earlier than the Antonine period. (See **264**.) The two buildings are therefore likely to have been contemporary and may well have been connected, but even if they were, it remains an open question whether the temple was an appendage of the house, or the latter merely living quarters attached to the temple.

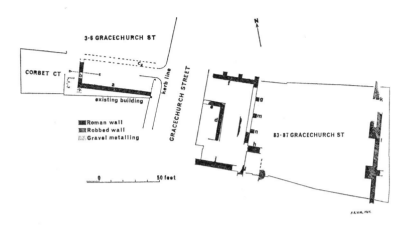

Fig. 27   Plan of Roman building, Gracechurch Street (229. 229A).
Drawn by P. R. V. Marsden (Guildhall Museum).

SOME ENIGMAS

A great structure which, from its size and the massive
character of its walls, must have been an important public
building, stood on the site of Cannon Street Station and Bush
Lane, but we have as yet no evidence of its nature (269–276).
The discovery of numbers of tiles stamped *PP. BR. LON* on the
site in 1868 suggests that some branch of the provincial government was concerned with its construction. Several wooden
drains were found running beneath the foundations towards the
river (276), and it is possible that this building also was a public
bath-house, on a grander scale than is known elsewhere in
London. It was set into the gravel slope of the river bank with
its floors at different levels, and evidently had considerable
architectural pretensions. A striking feature was the massive
platform of ragstone and flint concrete, parallel with the river
(273, *Fig.* 28, *A*). The building was evidently not constructed
before the Flavian period, for the cement floor of the large compartment to the north overlay a rubbish pit of that date. In
1964–5, too late for inclusion in the map, the plan of an east
wing of quite a different character was recovered west of Suffolk

Lane. This contained a series of small and uniform rooms between two corridors. It overlay pottery of the Flavian period, but apparently continued in use until late in the fourth century.

Equally puzzling is the mysterious long wall of Knightrider Street, which extended for at least 400 feet, and probably for more than 580 feet, cutting through the filled-in gravel quarries of an area which seems to have contained few buildings in Roman times (**93–98**, and probably also **99**). The foundations had in places been laid in a boarded trench, for impressions of the vertical timbers have been observed. The wall was of ragstone with some courses of tiles, and was pierced in two places by brick culverts for the passage of water (**94, 97**, *Plate* 56). No trace of any transverse wall adjoining it has ever been seen, so it seems more likely to have been a boundary or precinct wall than part of a large building. There is, however, evidence of a similar wall, approximately parallel with it, thirty to thirty-two feet to the south (**100–102**), and other walls lie immediately to the north-west (**81, 82**).

Here then are two structures, obviously of importance, which cannot yet be identified; but an unsolved problem of quite a different kind must also be briefly mentioned. It might be expected that somewhere in, or more probably just outside, the Roman city would be a theatre or an amphitheatre – or both – and so far no trace of either has ever been found. It has been conjectured that Southwark may have been the quarter for entertainments in Roman as in later times,[65] but this idea is as yet unsupported by any archaeological evidence.

WATER SUPPLY AND DRAINAGE

No elaborate arrangements to supply Roman London with a water supply brought from a distance by aqueducts were necessary, for the city abounded in natural springs, and water could be obtained quite easily in most places by digging fairly shallow wells. These were invariably timber-framed, and were of two kinds: square with a box-like frame of mortised oak planks, and round with a frame of superimposed pinewood barrels (*Plates* 108, 112). Sometimes both kinds of frame were used in the same well, and in most cases the framework did not extend to the bottom, where the well became a simple hole with unsup-

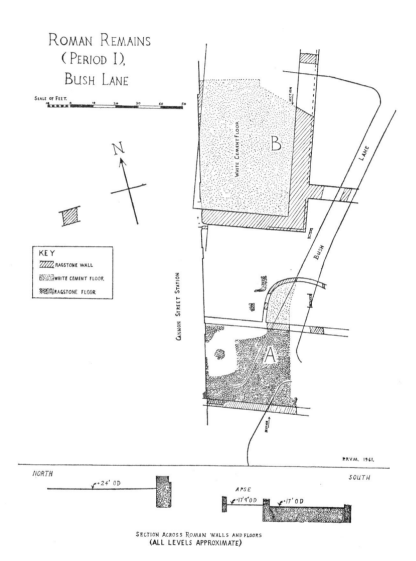

ROMAN REMAINS
(PERIOD I),
BUSH LANE

SCALE OF FEET.

N

KEY

RAGSTONE WALL
WHITE CEMENT FLOOR
RAGSTONE FLOOR

WHITE CEMENT FLOOR

B

BUSH LANE

CANNON STREET STATION

A

P.R.V.M. 1961.

NORTH   SOUTH

+24' OD

APSE

+17'9"OD   +17' OD

SECTION ACROSS ROMAN WALLS AND FLOORS
(ALL LEVELS APPROXIMATE)

FIG. 28 Plan of massive Roman building, Bush Lane (273).
Drawn by P. R. V. Marsden (Guildhall Museum).

ported sides. The discovery in two instances of a large Roman coin at the bottom of a well – in one case embedded in the chalk puddling which was put in when it was constructed – suggests that a luck offering was sometimes made when a new well was dug. (See **177, 264.**)

One area in Queen Street deserves special mention, as the great number of Roman wells suggests that it may have been a source of public supply. On the site of the Bank of London and South America were found fourteen wells of Roman date (**91**), and seven more were recorded on the site of Aldermary House, on the opposite side of the road (**89**). Conditions here must have been particularly favourable, for wells continued to be dug on both these sites in mediaeval and later times, and the small court to the north of Aldermary House is significantly named Well Court.[66] The lack of hygiene in Roman London is clearly demonstrated by the finds on the site of the Bank of London and South America. Here wells which had become useless through silting were used intermittently as cess-pits or for the dumping of refuse, which in one instance included a human head.[67] Nevertheless, new wells continued to be dug for water only a few yards away. In this respect, however, London was no more squalid in Roman than in later times, for wells continued to be placed in close proximity to cess-pits as recently as the late eighteenth century.[68]

The primitive method of drawing water by bucket from a well seems to have been the way in which most Roman Londoners obtained their water supply, for metal handles which are probably from wooden buckets are not infrequently found in the wells. Nevertheless, more sophisticated methods were also in use, and Roman wooden water-pipes joined by iron collars have been found on the site of the Bank of England (**170**, *Plate* 109).

Drainage was arranged with some care, as was necessary in a town where low-lying sites became increasingly water-logged. Open gullies, often lined with planks, are commonly found, and a more substantial brick structure resembling a storm drain was found near the main east-west roadway where the latter approached the stream of the Walbrook (**193**, *Fig.* 29). The natural streams no doubt served as open sewers, as in later times, but this probably did not prevent their use as a conveni-ent water supply for domestic and industrial purposes. House-hold refuse of all kinds, however, was most commonly disposed of by burial, and filled-in rubbish pits and cess-pits have

FIG. 29 A Roman brick drain on a chalk platform resting on wooden piles, found near Bucklersbury (**193**). A similar structure was observed near Lambeth Hill, Upper Thames Street, in 1964. From *J. E. Price: A Roman Tessellated Pavement found in Bucklersbury.*

produced some of our most interesting finds. (See *Plates* 118, 120–3.)

★ ★ ★

In all respects, Roman London seems to have been a city of contrasts, a curious mingling of civilisation and barbarism, of the exotic and the native, in which luxury and squalor went hand-in-hand, and where imposing stone buildings stood in close proximity to wooden shacks. The density of occupation varied greatly, and undeveloped waste-land might lie within a stone's throw of a busy street – at least in the earlier period to which our evidence mostly relates. In these circumstances, any estimate of the size of the population, based on the area of the city and a conjectured density, would be a futile exercise. It would certainly not have been large, however, so that the Roman Londoners were at least spared the horrors of overcrowding, and may well have found their city a pleasant place, in which the splendour was evident and the squalor no more obtrusive than in many towns of modern Europe.

REFERENCES

1. In the *Journal of Roman Studies*.

2. It will be possible to mark the appropriate symbol in its correct place on a copy of the map, if its owner wishes, after Professor Grimes's report has appeared. The Professor is in no way responsible for these omissions, since he has generously given any information for which he has been asked. In the view of the writer, however, it was unreasonable to expect all the details of a forthcoming report to be supplied in advance of publication, especially as this would have imposed an additional burden on a very busy man, and could only have hindered the progress of the report itself.

3. Its name is believed to mean 'Brook of the strangers (*or* Britons).'

4. The evidence is discussed in detail in two pioneer papers – by Frank Lambert in 1915 (*Archaeologia*, LXVI, pp. 269 ff.) and by T. Davies Pryce and Felix Oswald in 1928 (*Archaeologia*, LXXVIII, pp. 73 ff.).

5. G. C. Dunning, 'Two Fires of Roman London', *Antiquaries' Journal*, XXV (1945), pp. 48–52.

6. Ibid., pp. 52–61.

7. *Antiquaries' Journal*, XLII (1962), pp. 38–52.

8. The statistics for the site of Bucklersbury House were as follows: A.D. 50–75, 44 coins; A.D. 75–100, 50 coins; A.D. 100–125, 2 7 coins; A.D. 125–150, 15 coins; A.D. 150–175, 6 coins (only one later than A.D. 155).

9. *R.C.H.M.*, p. 79.

10. The Roman wall and its mediaeval successor have long disappeared in this place, but until the construction of the new road a few years ago, the slight change in the direction of the city wall was perpetuated by a distinct kink in the line of the modern street of London Wall – a remarkable instance of topographical survival. In this case it can be demonstrated that an irregularity in the street plan of the modern City was indirectly derived from the construction of a Roman fort more than 1,800 years ago. It is an intriguing thought that some other topographical oddities may have an equally ancient origin.

11. The existence of a minor Roman road from Cripplegate to Stevenage has recently been postulated (The Viatores, *Roman Roads in the South-East Midlands*, 1964, pp. 185 ff.). There was an ancient bridle-way from Cripplegate through Finsbury, but even if this were of Roman origin – as is not yet proved – it is almost certainly

later than the fort. There is little doubt that Professor Grimes was correct in suggesting that the fort was provided with a north gate merely to conform to the standard pattern. It is unlikely that it led anywhere in particular at the time it was built.

12. No plan has yet been published, so the buildings could not be shown on the map.

13. *J.R.S.*, XLVII (1957), p. 220.

14. Information kindly supplied by Mr. A. H. Oswald.

15. *Archaeologia*, LXIII, pp. 279 ff.

16. Stow, *Survey of London* (Kingsford ed.), I, p. 9.

17. A later building of the same name occupied a site on the water-front further east.

18. *Trans. London and Middlesex Arch. Soc.*, N.S., V, p. 378.

19. *Archaeologia*, LXIII, pp. 305 ff.

20. William Fitzstephen, introductory portion of *Vita Sancti Thomae*, written before 1183.

21. C. Roach Smith, *Illustrations of Roman London*, p. 18.

22. Ibid., p. 19.

23. *J.R.S.*, XLVI (1956), pp. 139 ff.

24. Gordon Home, *Roman London* (1948), p. 145.

25. Bastions 10 and 15 did show traces of an attempt at bonding into the wall.

26. Re-used stones found in **B16** were apparently early mediaeval, and presumably belonged to a later reconstruction of the bastion.

27. None have been found in any of these bastions, but a drawing of **B14** before 1865 seems to show one double course in its upper part.

28. Professor W. F. Grimes in *Recent Archaeological Excavations in Britain*, edited by R. L. S. Bruce-Mitford, 1956, pp. 132, 134.

29. See also I. D. Margary, *Roman Roads in Britain*, I, p. 48.

30. Ibid., p. 50.

31. The ragstone walls are a puzzling feature, and the section cannot be correct as drawn since the walls have no foundations.

32. W. Herbert, *History of St. Michael, Crooked Lane*, p. 20.

33. *Gentleman's Magazine*, 1833 (2), p. 422.

34. *V.C.H. London*, Vol. I, Plan C, opposite p. 43, and p. 100. Elsewhere in the text (p. 37) the find is correctly located 'below Great Eastcheap (now the eastern end of Cannon Street),' and it is stated that the road has not been traced east of Gracechurch Street.

35. C. Roach Smith, *Illustrations of Roman London*, pp. 20–1.

36. K. M. Kenyon, *Excavations in Southwark*, p. 12 and fig. 2. A more recent excavation on this line, however, failed to locate the Roman road with any certainty.

37. It is quite possible that the first bridge was a temporary military structure, such as a pontoon bridge, later replaced by a

permanent bridge built on wooden piles – in a different position, since the first bridge must have continued in use until the completion of the second.

38. The early existence of the road from Bishopsgate is attested by the first century burials found in the neighbourhood (*R.C.H.M.*, pp. 159–61).

39. A stamp on Samian ware of *Pontus* of La Graufesenque.

40. For dating evidence see **225**.

41. It has been suggested that the double southern wall on the eastern half of this building might be accounted for by the existence of an earlier and shorter basilica which did not extend west of Gracechurch Street (*R.C.H.M.*, pp. 40–2).

42. A macadamised roadway is built up of successive layers of broken stone, each subjected to pressure before the next is laid. It is therefore not dissimilar in structure to a Roman road in London, with its layers of compacted gravel.

43. Wren, *Parentalia*, p. 265.

44. Apart from the weight of positive evidence for a straight road running obliquely to a crossing of the Walbrook at Bucklersbury, it seems impossible to find a course uninterrupted by Roman buildings east of the stream for a road which crossed at a more northerly point.

45. The first Mayor of London was named Henricus Filius Eylwini de Londenestane (1188) as his house was situated near the Stone.

46. Found beneath the Saxon crypt of St. Augustine's Abbey.

47. The English equivalent is 408 feet, the exact distance between the southern edge of the northern road at Nos. 30–2, Lombard Street (**290**) and the projected northern edge of the southern road.

48. It may be coincidence that the long Roman wall of Knightrider Street (**93–98**), some 400 feet to the south, is parallel with the western end of Watling Street.

49. An early form of the name of Watling Street in the City is Athelyngestrate (thirteenth century), either meaning 'Noble Street' or derived from the common personal name 'Aethel.'

50. The alleged roadway of flint on a foundation of chalk, said to have been seen at a depth of about twenty feet in 1833 (**73**), is a very dubious piece of evidence.

51. The exact distance on the map is 356 English feet, a discrepancy of less than two per cent which could be accounted for by an error in plotting, or by the possibility that the Roman surveyors measured from the outer edge of the drainage gully rather than the edge of the metalling.

52. Vitruvius Pollio, *De Architectura*, Bk. II, viii, 20.

53. Still preserved in the cellar of Blurton's shop, beneath the

pavement of Gracechurch Street at the corner of Grand Avenue, Leadenhall Market.

54. *R.C.H.M.*, p. 40.

55. *J.R.S.*, XXI (1931), pp. 236–8.

56. An inscription found at St. Albans shows that Agricola was responsible for the building of the forum of Verulamium. *Ant. Journ.*, XXXVI (1956), pp. 7–10.

57. Information from unpublished notes kindly given by Mr. Adrian Oswald.

58. E.g. at Viroconium (Wroxeter), the forum was built under Hadrian, as is shown by an inscription, and here also the Flavian public buildings (a large bath-building) had remained unfinished.

59. *Drag.* Form 37 in the style of Frontinus (Nero-Trajan); *Drag.* Form 29 in the style of Medetus (*c.* A.D. 90–100), and *Drag.* Form 18 with stamp AVENT (Hadrian-Antonine). Information kindly given by Mr. A. H. Oswald.

60. See **229A, 243**.

61. See **243**.

62. See **229**.

63. Cf. G. C. Boon, 'A Temple of Mithras at Caernarvon-Segontium', *Archaeologia Cambrensis*, 1960, p. 140.

64. Christian churches built in Rome in the Imperial period usually have the sanctuary at the western end, so this in itself gave no indication that the building was not a church.

65. Gordon Home, *Roman London* (1948), p. 122.

66. The name is first mentioned on Ogilby and Morgan's Map of London, 1677. (H. A. Harben, *A Dictionary of London*, 1918, p. 618.)

67. The skull, which was without its lower jaw, was partly crushed by a heavy timber which rested on it (Guildhall Museum Excavation Register 81B). From the same well came a pair of leather 'bikini' trunks and a wooden ladder (*Plates* 113–16).

68. A striking example of this was found in Provident Passage, King Street, in 1963.

★

CHAPTER FOUR

Visiting Roman London

IT IS PERHAPS NOT generally known that a number of the remains of Roman London have been preserved *in situ*. Some of these are on private premises, and cannot be visited except by permission of the owners, which is normally granted only by prior arrangement, and then only for visits during ordinary hours of business.[1] Sufficient can be seen without any difficulty, however, to make excursions to the City for this purpose well worth while. These accessible remains are mainly in two areas – in the neighbourhood of the Tower of London and near Aldersgate.

The former group is reached most easily by the District or Circle Line to Tower Hill Station. Almost immediately opposite is All Hallows Barking Church, where a Roman floor of red tesserae (**358**), of the Antonine period or later, can be seen in the crypt, to which admittance can be obtained on application to the Verger. The gully which divides the pavement probably marks the position of a wooden partition wall. The red tesserae laid in the floor of the crypt passage further east are not *in situ*, and no pavement was found in this position. The crypt of All Hallows also contains Roman pottery and other finds from the site, including fragments of important Anglo-Saxon crosses. A cast of the sculptured group of Mother-Goddesses from Seething Lane is also shown.[2]

In the Tower of London itself a short stretch of the Roman city wall (**W2**), has been preserved behind the ruin of the Wardrobe Tower, the lower part of which is formed by the original bastion of the city wall (**B1**, *Plate* 47). This portion of the wall shows clearly its lower structure, with a triple course of tiles forming an off-set on the internal face, corresponding in level with the sandstone plinth on the outside of the wall. Above this is a facing of squared ragstone, and then a triple course of bonding-tiles. The masonry of the bastion stands at one point to a height of about seven feet; the rest of the Wardrobe Tower is believed to be of the twelfth century.

To the north of the Tower, on the opposite side of Tower Hill, an impressive piece of the city wall can be seen (**W6**). Almost the whole of the wall which stands above the modern street level was rebuilt in the Middle Ages, but a fine piece of the original Roman wall has been revealed by the clearance of the cellars of bombed buildings to form a sunken garden. In one place a considerable part of the original inner face remains, consisting of a triple bonding-course of tiles, six courses of squared ragstone, a double bonding-course and five more courses of squared ragstone. The core of the Roman wall stands to a height of about one foot above the modern pavement level. The northern part of the foundations of the small internal turret (**W5**) has been exposed in the sunken garden.

Set in the modern wall which is on the line of the city wall to the north, in the car park behind Tower House, may be seen a cast reproduction of the inscription from the tomb of the Procurator, Classicianus, which was found re-used as building material in the neighbouring bastion (**B2**, see pp. 41–2, *Plates* 4–6). Another cast of this inscription may be seen in Wakefield Gardens, Tower Hill, a few yards to the south. The statue of a Roman emperor in the same garden is a nineteenth century reproduction and has no connection with Roman London.

Further north a particularly fine piece of city wall, standing to a height of about thirty-five feet above the original ground level, may be seen in the courtyard behind Midland House, 8-10, Cooper's Row (**W9**). The mediaeval parapet survives at the top of the wall, and there are round-headed embrasures which may be of Norman date below it. Several rebuildings can be detected above the original Roman wall, which survives to a height of about two-and-a-half feet above the modern court-yard floor, and can be seen below it extending to basement level, which is very near the original ground level. At the bottom, part of the tile offset can be seen with a facing of three courses of squared ragstone above it. Then comes a triple course of bonding-tiles, above which the facing has been removed. Next there are a double course of bonding-tiles, a facing of squared ragstone, a second double course of tiles, a facing of five courses of squared ragstone, and then a third double course of bonding-tiles. Above this the wall has been rebuilt, and is probably mostly of post-Roman date. On the outer face, part of the sandstone plinth can be seen at the bottom, with Roman walling above it, but the wall has been rebuilt to a lower level, so that the uppermost course of bonding-tiles survives only in the inner part of the wall.

Immediately to the south of this, a portion of the purely Roman wall has been preserved in the basement of the Toc H Club, 40-41, Trinity Square (**W8**). This is not normally available for inspection, as it is in the Club's sitting-room, and for that reason it can never be visited during week-ends or after 6 p.m. Permission to view it at other times may possibly be granted by the Warden, if prior application is made. The external face of the wall can be seen here, with its sandstone plinth, courses of squared ragstone and triple bonding-course of red bricks.

Other portions of the Roman city wall are preserved on private property in the cellars of No. 1, Crutched Friars (**W14**, *Plate* 41) and the Three Tuns public house, 36, Jewry Street (**W17**). A small portion of the Roman wall is also preserved in the basement of the Sir John Cass College (**W16**). These remains are not accessible to the public except by special permission.

Nowhere in the City of London is very far from anywhere else, and a walk along the line of the wall from this area to the north-western corner of the walled city, where most of the other Roman remains are to be seen, will give the energetic visitor a good idea of the way in which the city wall has influenced the lay-out of the modern streets. The line of the wall is followed through a series of minor thoroughfares: Jewry Street, Duke's Place, Bevis Marks, Camomile Street, Wormwood Street and London Wall. At intervals it is necessary to cross a busy highway which marks the position of one of the old city gates: Aldgate, Bishopsgate and Moorgate. The city wall itself has disappeared, however, except that a portion of the core of the mediaeval wall is visible as the north wall of All Hallows Churchyard (**W29**). The vestry of this church is built on one of the bastions of the city wall (**B11**).

For those who do not wish to walk, a bus can be taken from Aldgate to St. Paul's, or the District train from Aldgate or Tower Hill to Moorgate. Users of the large underground car park, under the new road which forms the western end of

London Wall, will have the opportunity of seeing a fine piece of the Roman city wall which is preserved there (**W37**). Unfortunately, pedestrians are not admitted under the regulations of the car park. The wall survives from the triple levelling-course of tiles at the bottom to the height of the car park, and contains a triple and double course of bonding-tiles, which can be seen passing through the ragstone rubble concrete of the interior of the wall.

A good view can be obtained of the fine piece of city wall in St. Alphage Churchyard, which is of exceptional interest, from the upper pedestrian way north of the new road of London Wall (**W40**). The view of its section at the eastern end shows clearly that the base of the wall is double. The outer wall is the original fort wall of the early second century, and the inner (southern) wall is the thickening which was added when the Roman city wall was built, to bring it to the standard thickness of the new wall. (See p. 97.) The original facing of the fort wall has been removed and the core has been refaced at an unknown but early date. Above this are successive mediaeval rebuildings, which can best be seen from the small garden on the north side of the wall. A portion built with courses of squared flint can be paralleled in the precinct of Westminster Abbey, and is almost certainly of the reign of Henry III. The brickwork battlements at the top represent the final phase of rebuilding, when the city wall was repaired in 1477, in the mayoralty of Sir Ralph Jocelyn. The diaper pattern of black and red bricks, best seen on the south face of the wall, is characteristic of this period. (See *Plate* 38.)

The lay-out of the wall in this area, with its change of direction through 90 degrees at the Cripplegate corner bastion, representing the north-west corner of the earlier fort, can be clearly seen from the upper pedestrian level. The bastions are however worth a closer examination, if time permits, although no part of the visible structures is earlier than the Middle Ages. The narrow apertures filled with later brickwork in Bastion 14 may be mediaeval arrow-slits.

Visits to this area should if possible be arranged so that the west gate of the Roman fort (**G7**) is reached between 12.30 and 2 p.m. on a week-day[3], when it is open to the public. It is possible to arrange visits for small parties at other times, including Saturdays, if application is made well in advance to the Keeper of Guildhall Museum. The remains of the Roman gate

are reached by an entrance on the north side of the road of
London Wall, at the western end of the underground car park.
The northern half of the gate, with a portion of the double wall
adjoining it to the north, is preserved in a subterranean compartment beneath the road. The outer wall is the original fort
wall, as at St. Alphage, and the inner the thickening which was
added to it when the fort defences were incorporated in the new
city wall, probably about a century later. The fort wall has its
original facing of squared blocks of ragstone in regular courses,
and the body of both walls is of ragstone rubble concrete. The
lower part of the walls of the northern guard-room is preserved,
with a narrow doorway at the south-east corner. These walls are
of ragstone with a plinth of massive blocks of sandstone – like
the ragstone, probably brought from Kent. The central spine of
the double gateway is represented by two blocks of masonry.
The gravel roadway was too incomplete to be preserved, and it
has been replaced by a modern gravel surface on the same level.
The gate was eventually blocked by a ragstone wall of uncertain
date, and the bottom of this has been preserved on the south
side of the gateway.

To the south of the gate, the outer (fort) wall and the inner
(thickening) wall can be seen on the west side of Noble Street
(**W44–47**), which is to be laid out as a sunken garden. The
walls of a small intermediate turret (**W45**) and the corner
turret of the fort (**31**) can also be seen. At the time of writing,
the gravel surface of the perimeter road of the fort is visible in
several places to the west of Noble Street. The junction of the
corner of the fort with the city wall (**W48**) and with a small
portion of the wall of the corner bastion (**B15**) may also be
observed. It may be noted that the south-westerly alignment of
the modern building to the west perpetuates the line of the
city wall, although the wall itself has gone. The Roman city
wall is pierced by a brick-lined culvert for drainage near the
point where it meets the fort wall, and at a lower level below this
can be seen the V-shaped ditch of the fort at its south-west
corner, cut into the natural brick-earth (*Fig.* 31).

Provided that the necessary arrangements have been made in
advance, a visit to the Roman fort and associated remains can
conveniently be combined with a visit to the bastion and
portion of city wall preserved beneath the yard of the General
Post Office in King Edward Street (**B19, W55**). Permission to

view these can only be obtained by writing to the Postmaster, the G.P.O., St. Martin's-le-Grand.

There are also several Roman structures which have been preserved in the central part of the City. The remains of the temple of Mithras (248) have been rebuilt from the original material on a terrace outside Temple Court, 11, Queen Victoria Street, about sixty yards to the north-west of its original position. In some respects the reconstruction is rather misleading, as the earth floor has been replaced by crazy paving, and the shape of the wooden water-tank in the corner of the building has been reproduced with pieces of ragstone. The orientation has been changed from west-east to north-south, and the placing of the remains on a high podium may possibly give a wrong impression of the nature of this low-lying building.

A portion of a patterned mosaic pavement has been preserved in the basement of Selborne House, 11, Ironmonger Lane (151). This is a private office, and the pavement can only be seen by prior arrangement, through the courtesy of the owners, Messrs. Peat, Marwick, Mitchell and Company.

A restored mosaic pavement has been preserved in the Bank of England (171), but unlike the Ironmonger Lane pavement, which is in its original position, this has been lifted and relaid. It can be seen far below at the foot of the main staircase from the entrance hall of the Bank, which is accessible to the public during normal hours of business.[4]

In Lower Thames Street, the wall with the brick seat and part of the hypocaust of the western apsidal room of the bath-building (353) have been preserved. (See *Plate* 61.) The compartment in which these are contained is not at present open to the public, but it can be visited on week-days by small parties if application is made well in advance of the proposed visit to the Keeper of Guildhall Museum. It is impossible at present to arrange week-end visits, as the only access is from an office building which is closed on Saturdays and Sundays.

Outside Londinium and beyond the limits of our map, though in the City of London, is the fragmentary pavement of plain red tesserae which is preserved at the eastern end of the crypt of St. Bride's Church in Fleet Street. It belonged to a Roman building which extended under the apse of the first church. This is the only undoubted Roman building known on the north bank of the Thames between the city wall and Westminster.[5]

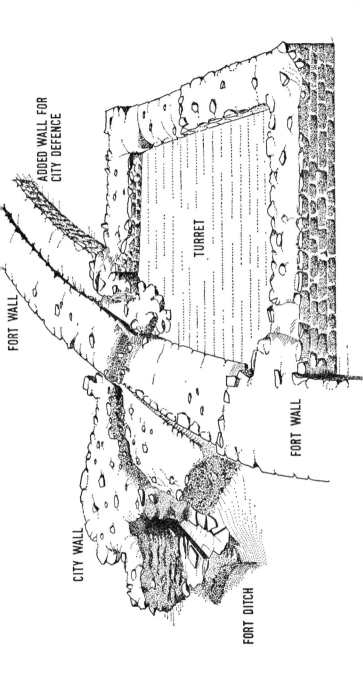

ADDED WALL FOR CITY DEFENCE

FORT WALL

TURRET

FORT WALL

CITY WALL

FORT DITCH

FIG. 31   The south-west corner of the Roman fort at its junction with the city wall, as preserved and partially restored, Noble Street (31 and **W48**). *Drawn by Miss W. Mumford.*

161

Museums

No study of Roman London can be complete without visits to the museums which contain the principal collections relating to it. The British Museum has the great collection formed by Roach Smith before 1856, and a number of very important finds acquired from other sources. Its possessions include the tomb-stone of Classicianus, the Procurator, which has been restored (*Plate* 6), the central medallion (*Plate* 66) and ornamental border of the mosaic from Leadenhall Street, the early legionary helmet (*Plate* 97), and many objects illustrating the daily life of Roman London.

The London Museum, at present housed in Kensington Palace, also contains a rich collection relating to daily life, with some exceptionally fine specimens, such as the legionary dagger from Copthall Court (*Plate* 99). The Museum is particularly fortunate in possessing material illustrating the religions of Londinium. It includes the Mithraic and other marble sculptures found in Walbrook in 1889 (*Plates* 84–5), the wine-jug from Southwark with a graffito referring to a temple of Isis at Londinium, and a silver plaque with a representation of the three Mother Goddesses (*Plate* 89). In the same category may be mentioned the curse written on a lead tablet (*Plate* 102). The Roman boat found on the site of County Hall is in store at Lancaster House.

Guildhall Museum is at present using the ambulatory of the Royal Exchange as its exhibition gallery. This is the museum of the Corporation of London, and its collections are limited to the history and antiquities of the City – unlike the London Museum, which includes the whole of Greater London in its sphere of interest. Since the City includes Londinium, however, Guildhall Museum is particularly rich in objects illustrating the daily life of Roman London. A special feature is the collection of craftsmen's tools of Roman date, which are remarkably like the corresponding tools used in modern times. Individual specimens of note are the wooden ladder and leather 'bikini' trunks from a well of the first century (*Plates* 113, 116), the sculptured figure of a legionary soldier (*Plate* 95) and the group of the three Mother Goddesses (*Plate* 88). The most important exhibits are probably the finds from the temple of Mithras in Walbrook, which include the fine marble sculptures of pagan deities and the mysterious silver box and infuser (*Plates 75–83*). The Bucklersbury mosaic pavement (*Plate 65*) is at present still fixed to the wall of the old museum, now the book-store of Guildhall Library.

Guildhall Museum and the London Museum are about to be merged into a new Museum of London, which will eventually be housed in a new building, to be built between Aldersgate Street and the city wall, north of the new road of London Wall. The combined resources of the two existing museums will be particularly impressive in the Roman section, which will contain one of the most important Romano-British collections in the country. It is hoped that the space and facilities available in the new building will at last make it possible to illustrate the subject of Roman London in a worthy manner.

The Cuming Museum in Walworth Road, Southwark, also contains considerable Roman collections from the southern suburb of Londinium, which occupied the southern bridge-head and extended in a line of ribbon development along Stane Street.

The visitor with an interest in Roman London should remember that the above museums are likely to be the reposi-tories of up-to-date information on this subject, and the answering of serious enquiries is one of their proper functions. Museum staff welcome these but (contrary to general belief) are often pressed for time, and therefore usually prefer specific questions to vague requests for information of an all-embracing character.

Owing to its location in the City of London, Guildhall Museum or its successor, the new Museum of London, is the likeliest source of up-to-date information concerning facilities for visiting the surviving monuments of Roman London, and members of its staff will always be glad to give advice to intend-ing visitors.

REFERENCES

1. Certain Roman structures which have been preserved but are quite inaccessible to the public at all times have been omitted from this account. They include a piece of the basilica beneath Messrs. Blurton's shop in Gracechurch Street (220): portions of the walls of the basilica beneath the National Provincial Bank (213) and the Bank of Australia and New Zealand (211) in Cornhill: and a portion of the city wall which forms the north face of the basement area of the General Post Office, on the south side of the churchyard of St. Botolph, Aldersgate (Postman's Park) (W51).

2. The fine tomb-stone with the Greek inscription, exhibited here on loan from the Port of London Authority, was found near Tilbury in Essex, where material from the excavations for the Underground Railway had been dumped, but there is a very strong probability that it is an antiquity imported into this country within the last three hundred years.

3. The west gate of the Roman fort is open between 12.30 and 2 p.m. Mondays to Fridays only. (See p. 158.)

4. The Bank's other mosaic pavement has been relaid in its Rotunda Museum, not open to the public.

5. The so-called Roman bath in Strand Lane is not generally accepted as being of Roman date, and a place so remote from the Roman city would be a most unlikely site for a bath-house. It is more likely to be a water-tank of the sixteenth or seventeenth century.

1   London in the second century, *reconstruction by A. Sorrell.*

2   London in the third century, *reconstruction by A. Sorrell.*

3   London in the third century, *reconstruction by R. W. Nicholson.*

6   Tombstone of Classicianus, the Procurator, reconstructed.

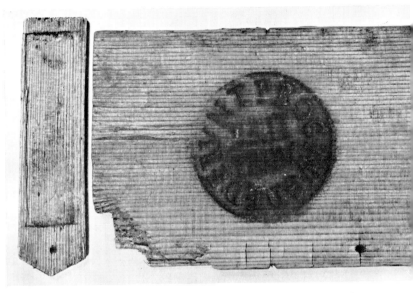

7 Writing-tablet with procuratorial stamp, and label, Walbrook.
(*Length of tablet, 6 in.: label, 4½ in.*)

8 Roof-tile with stamp P P BR LON, Leadenhall Street.
(*Length of stamp, 3½ in.*)

9 Memorial to the wife of a slave of the province, Ludgate Hill.
   (*Height 3 ft. 11 in.*)
10 Stamped silver ingot, early fifth century, Tower of London.
   (*Length 4 in.*)

11 Corroded mass of coins of the late third century, Newgate Street.
12 Barbarous coins of late third-century hoard, Newgate Street, after cleaning. (*Actual size.*)

13 Gold medallion commemorating the arrival of Constantius
Chlorus at London in A.D. 296.

14   Coins of the London Mint, A.D. 288–325 (1–15) and 383–388
(16). 1, 2, *Carausius*: 3, 4, *Allectus*: 5, *Diocletian*: 6, *Constantine I
as Caesar*: 7, 8, *Constantine I as Augustus*:

9, *Licinius I*: 10, *Crispus as Caesar*: 11, *Constantine I*: 12, *Constantine II as Caesar*: 13, *Constantine I*: 14, *Constantine II as Caesar*: 15, *Helena*: 16, *Magnus Maximus* (*gold solidus*). (*Actual size.*)

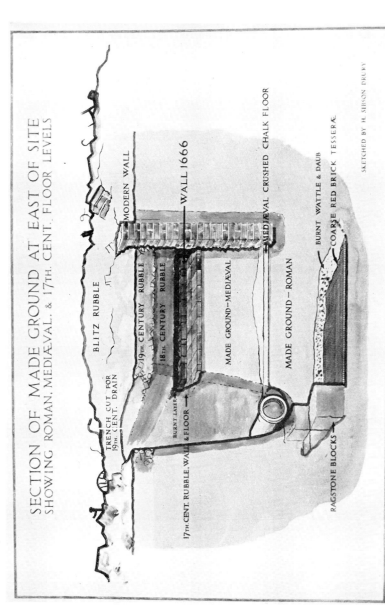

15 Section, St. Swithin's House, Walbrook, showing Roman tessellated
    floor, medieval chalk floor and ...

Newgate Street.

walls (*B*) and eighteenth-century walls (*A*), Minster House, Martin Lane.

18 Ancient stream-bed, Newgate Street.
19 Roman planking attached to piles, probably the revetment of a
    stream-bank, St. Mary-le-Bow church.

20　Roman wooden platform, Bucklersbury House, Walbrook.
21　Roman timber structure on piles, Bucklersbury House, Walbrook.

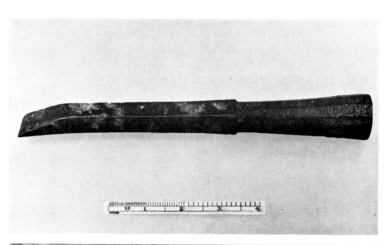

22 Roman chisel found in wooden pile supporting a timber structure, Prince's Street.

23 Wooden piles continuing line of Roman roadway, Bucklersbury House, Walbrook.

24 Roman wooden piles, Bucklersbury House, Walbrook.
25 Roman gravel road in section, Bucklersbury House, Walbrook.

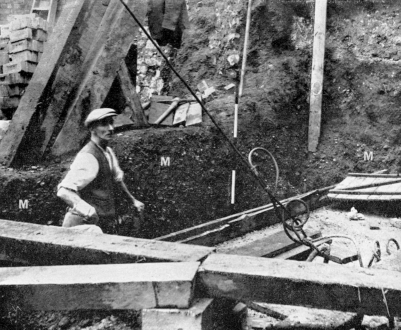

26 Roman gravel road in section, south of Newgate Street.
27 Roman road metalling (M), 15–18 Lime Street.

28 'London Stone' after removal from wall of St. Swithin's church.
29 Roman chalk platform on piles, forming a terrace, Lambeth Hill.

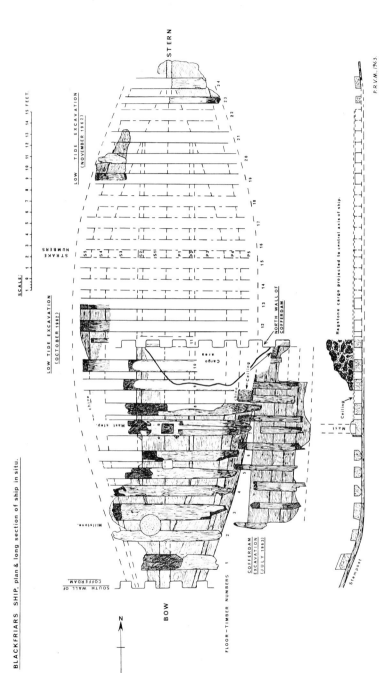

BLACKFRIARS SHIP, plan & long section of ship in situ.

SCALE

1 0 1 2 3 4 5 6 7 8 9 10 11 12 13 14 15 FEET

STERN

LOW TIDE EXCAVATION
(NOVEMBER 1962)

24
23
22
21
20
19
18
17
16
15
14
13
12

NORTH WALL OF
COFFERDAM

LOW TIDE EXCAVATION
(OCTOBER 1962)

STRAKE NUMBERS

S5 S4 S3 S2 S1 P1 P2 P3 P4 P5

Cargo area

Ceiling

chine

Mast step

Millstone

COFFERDAM
EXCAVATION
(JULY 1963)

SOUTH WALL OF
COFFERDAM

FLOOR-TIMBER NUMBERS 1 2 3 4 5 6 7 8 9 10 11

BOW

N

Ragstone cargo projected to central axis of ship.

Ceiling

Mast

Stempost

P.R.V.M. 1963

30 Plan and section of Roman barge, Blackfriars.

31 Bottom timbers of Roman barge, Blackfriars, 1963.
32 Leather with decoration representing a dolphin, from Roman
    barge, Blackfriars. (*Width, 7 in.*)

33   Coin of Domitian found in mast-step of Roman barge, Blackfriars. (*Actual size.*)

34   Mast-step of Roman barge, Blackfriars, with coin placed there for luck.

35   South-west corner of Roman fort with corner turret (*B*), Noble Street.

36   West wall of Roman fort with internal turret (*B*), from east. (*A*) is the fort wall, (*C*) the thickening added when the city wall was built.

38 City wall, St. Alphage churchyard, with double Roman wall at base (fort wall on right, later thickening on left).

37 West gate of Roman fort: northern half seen from south.

40 Roman and mediaeval city wall, Cooper's Row: internal face from west.

39 Roman and mediaeval city wall, Trinity Place, from south.

41 Roman city wall, in cellar of 1 Crutched Friars: internal face from wes[t]
42 Roman city wall, Cooper's Row: internal face from north-west.

43 Roman Newgate, *reconstruction by A. Sorrell*.

44 Roman and mediaeval city wall, Cooper's Row: section from north.

45 Internal turret of Roman city wall, Cooper's Row, from north.

46 Corner bastion, St. Giles Cripplegate, from east. (Visible structure mediaeval and later.)

47 Wardrobe Tower (built on bastion) and Roman city wall, Tower of London, from west.

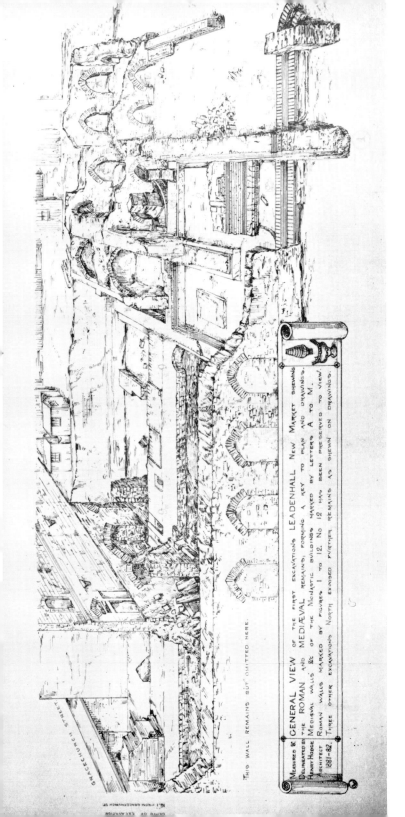

GRACECHURCH STREET

THIS WALL REMAINS BUT OMITTED HERE.

MEASURED & GENERAL VIEW OF THE FIRST EXCAVATIONS LEADENHALL NEW MARKET SHEWING
DELINEATED BY THE ROMAN AND MEDIÆVAL REMAINS; FORMING A KEY TO PLAN AND DRAWINGS.
HENRY HODGE MEDIÆVAL WALLS &c OF THE MONASTIC BUILDINGS MARKED BY LETTERS A TO M.
ARCHITECT ROMAN WALLS MARKED BY FIGURES 1 TO 12. No 12 HAS BEEN PRESERVED TO VIEW.
1881-82. THREE OTHER EXCAVATIONS NORTH EXPOSED FURTHER REMAINS AS SHEWN ON DRAWINGS.

48   Remains of Roman basilica, Leadenhall Market, 1881–2, *drawn by Henry Hodge.*

50 Brick pier of basilica resting on northern part of double east–west wall, *drawn by Henry Hodge, 1881.*

49 Eastern portion of Roman basilica, from east, *drawn by Henry Hodge, 1881.*

52 Brick pier with adjoining wall, 42 Lombard Street, probably part of the forum.

51 Northern sleeper wall of basilica with remains of brick pier on stone footings, 52 Cornhill.

54   Painted wall-plaster from site of basilica, Leadenhall Market. (*Length* 5½ *in.*)

53   Roman wall under street frontage of 42 Lombard Street.

55 Section through foundation of the long wall of Knightrider Street. (*See p.* 146.)

56 Roman brick culvert in the long wall of Knightrider Street. (*See p.* 14f

57 Massive Roman ragstone wall in Bush Lane, during demolition.
58 Flue passage in Roman bath-house, Huggin Hill, 1964.
(*See p.* 142.)

59 Roman bath, Threadneedle Street.
60 Blocked flue channel (*A*) and platform for tank (*B*) of Roman bath-house, Cheapside.

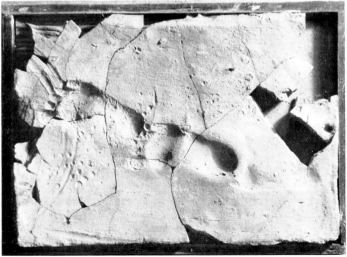

61 Roman hypocaust and brick seat, Lower Thames Street.
62 Roman tile with impressions of child's foot, from bath-house, Cheapside.

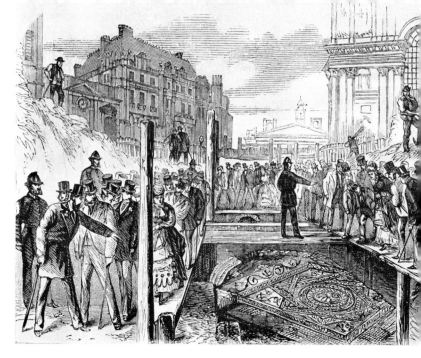

63 Crowds visiting mosaic pavement in Bucklersbury, 1869.
64 Roman mosaic pavement found in Old Broad Street, 1854.

65   Roman mosaic pavement from Bucklersbury. (*Drawing.*)

66   Roman mosaic representing Bacchus on tiger, Leadenhall Street.

67   Roman mosaic pavement, Ironmonger Lane.

68 Roman mosaic pavement, Bank of England.
69 Roman mosaic pavement, Bank of England.

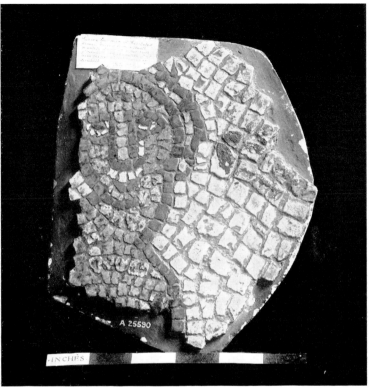

70 Portion of mosaic pavement representing female head, Cornhill.
71 Border of mosaic pavement, Crosby Hall.

72   Temple of Mithras, Wallbrook, from west.   73   Temple of Mithras, Wallbrook, from east.

74   Marble sculptures and stone vessel in temple of Mithras, Walbrook (as found).

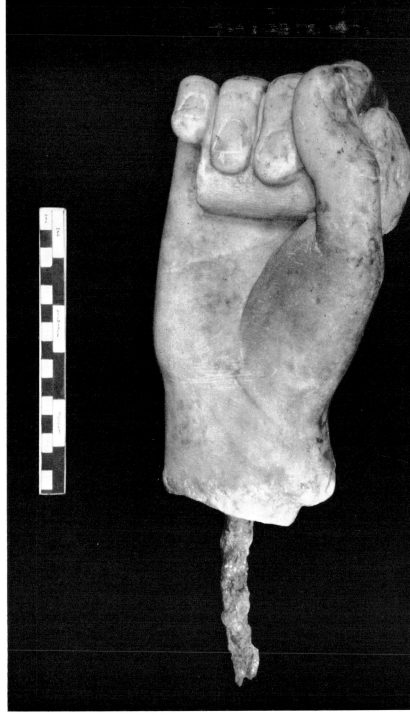

75 Marble hand of Mithras, holding sacrificial knife, from temple
of Mithras, Walbrook.

76   Marble head of Serapis, from temple of Mithras, Walbrook. (*Height, $12\frac{3}{4}$ in.*)

77 Marble figure of Mercury, from temple of Mithras, Walbrook. (*Height, 10 in.*)

78 Marble head of Mithras, from temple of Mithras, Walbrook.
(*Height*, $14\frac{1}{2}$ *in.*)

79 Dioscurus in oolite, found near temple of Mithras, Walbrook.
(*Height, 22 in.*)

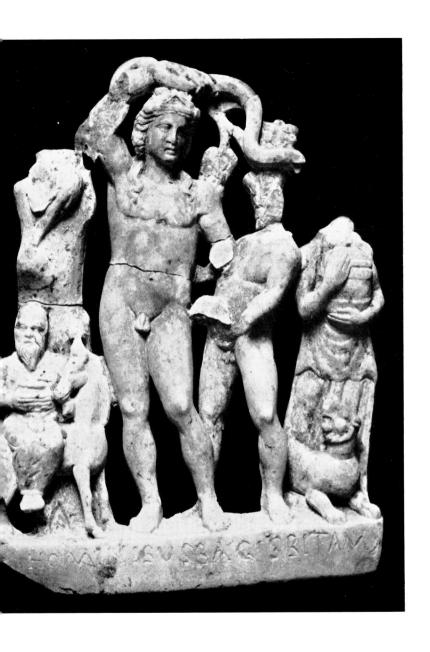

80 Bacchus with Silenus, satyr, maenad and panther, in marble, from temple of Mithras, Walbrook. (*Height, 13½ in.*)

81 Silver strainer or infuser and container, from temple of Mithras, Walbrook. (*Height of container 2½ in.*)

82 Lid of silver container of infuser, from temple of Mithras, Walbrook.

83 Decoration round wall of silver container from temple of Mithras, Wallbrook. (*Periphotograph.*)
(*Height,* 2½ *in.*)

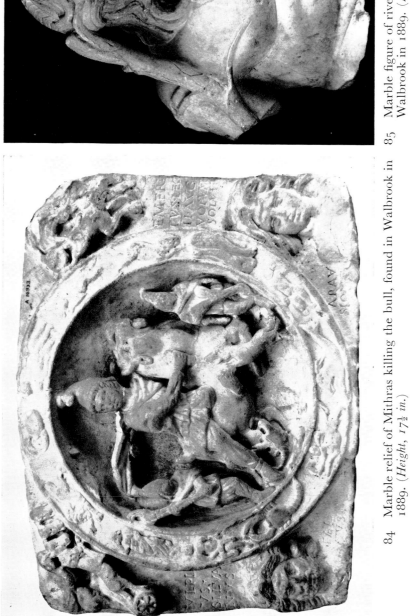

84 Marble relief of Mithras killing the bull, found in Walbrook in 1889. (Height, 17½ in.)

85 Marble figure of river god, found in Walbrook in 1889. (Height, 14 in.)

86   Altar of Diana from Goldsmiths' Hall.
     (*Height, 23 in.*)

87   Figure of Atys (?) from Bevis Marks.
     (*Height, 27 in.*)

88 Mother-Goddesses found near St. Olave Hart Street. (*Breadth, 33 in.*)
89 Silver plaque representing Mother-Goddesses, found in Moorgate.
    (*Scale in inches.*)

90   Bronze head of Hadrian, from the Thames near London
Bridge. (*Height about 16½ in.*)

91   Bronze fore-arm from well, Seething Lane. (*Length 19 in.*)
92   Bronze figure of archer, found in Queen Street. (*Height 11 in.*)

93 Capital with sculptured faces, found re-used as building material in Camomile Street bastion.

94 Sculpture of lion attacking a deer, found re-used as building material in Camomile Street bastion. (*Height, 28 in.*)

95 Figure of soldier, found re-used as building material in Camomile Street bastion. (*Height, 52 in.*)

96 Tombstone of soldier of Second Augustan Legion, from Ludgate
Hill. (*Height, 84 in.*)

1N ⌊__⌊½__⌋1

97   Bronze helmet of legionary soldier, found in London, probably in the Thames.

98   Spear-head with centurial inscription, found in well, Bucklersbury House, Walbrook. *(Length, 9¾ in.)*

99 Legionary soldier's dagger and frame of sheath, from Copthall Cour

100   Relief from tombstone representing civilian and boy, found in
       London.

101 Tile with scratched inscription in colloquial Latin, from Warwick Lane.

102 Lead sheet with Latin curse on two individuals, from Prince's Street. (*Length, 4¾ in.*)

103   Wooden tablet with writing in ink, found in pit or well, Queen Victoria Street. *(Length, 10½ in.)*
104   Portion of wooden writing tablet with *LONDINIO* on one side, from the Walbrook. *(Length, 5¾ in.)*

105 Wooden writing tablet, formerly covered with wax, and iron *stili* used for writing on such tablets, Bank of England.

106   Millstone of the kind turned by an ass, Prince's Street.
107   Relief from Ostia showing method of using millstones of type found in Prince's Street (*Pl.* 106).

108 Roman well with frame consisting of a wooden barrel, Queen Street.

109   Fragments of Roman oak water-pipe, from Bank of England.

110 Roman timber-lined well or pit with bronze jug in the filling, Queen Street.

111　Roman well consisting of square frame and barrels, Lime
Street. *Drawn by I. Noel Hume.* (*Scale in feet.*)

112 Typical Roman well with square oak frame, Queen Street.

113   Ladder found in first-century well, Queen Street.

114 Wooden spoon found in first-century well, Queen Street.
115 Wooden dipper found in first-century well, Queen Street.

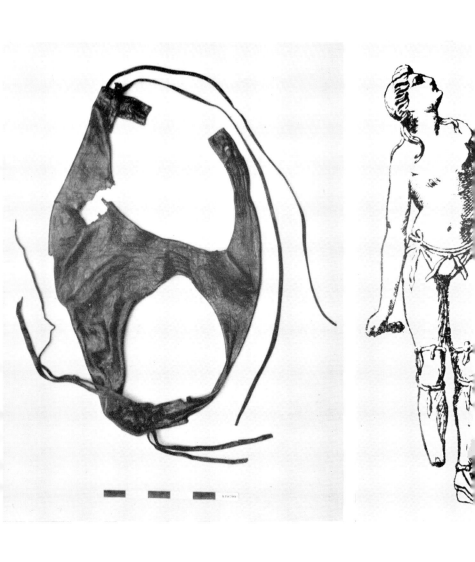

116 Leather 'bikini'-type trunks found in first-century well, Queen Street. (Nos. 113–116 from the same well.)

117 Girl, probably an acrobat, wearing trunks similar to No. 116, drawn from Roman bronze figure, Rennes Museum.

118 Bowl of South Gaulish Samian ware, A.D. 50–75, from refuse pit, King William Street. (*Diameter, 8½ in.*)

119 Bowl of Central Gaulish Samian ware, A.D. 100–120, found in Wormwood Street. (*Diameter, 7⅝ in.*)

120   Roman pottery, including complete amphora and wine jar,
from pre-Boudiccan pit, Walbrook. (*Foot-rule indicates scale.*)

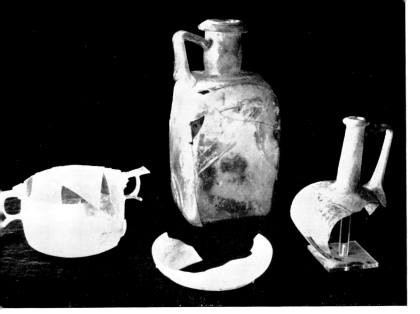

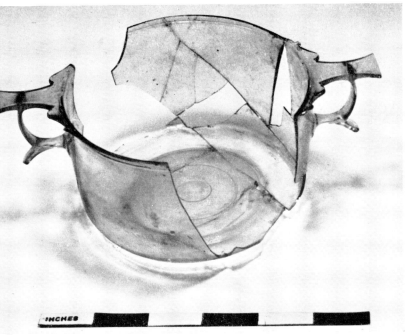

121 Roman glass from refuse pit of about A.D. 60–80, Walbrook.
122 Fine glass bowl imported from the East, from refuse pit of
about A.D. 60–80, Walbrook.

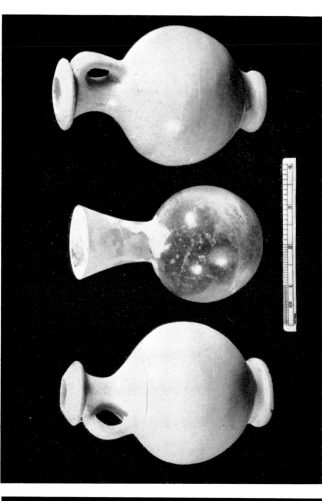

124 Pottery and glass vessels from fourth-century grave, the Minories.

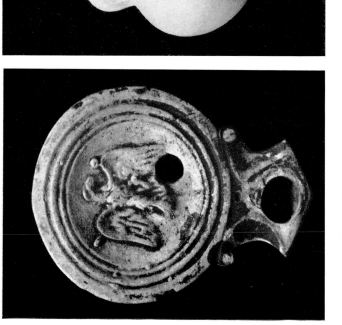

123 Pottery lamp from refuse pit of mid-first century, Lime Street. (*Length*, $3\frac{2}{3}$ *in.*)

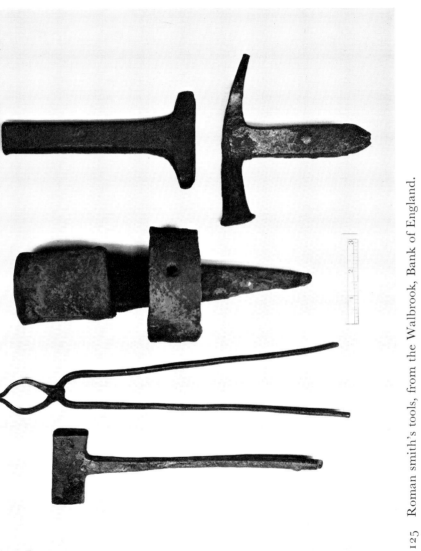

125 Roman smith's tools, from the Walbrook, Bank of England.

126 Roman docker's tools, from the Walbrook, Bucklersbury House.
127 Roman boat-hook from the Walbrook, Bucklersbury House.
   (*Length*, 9½ *in.*)

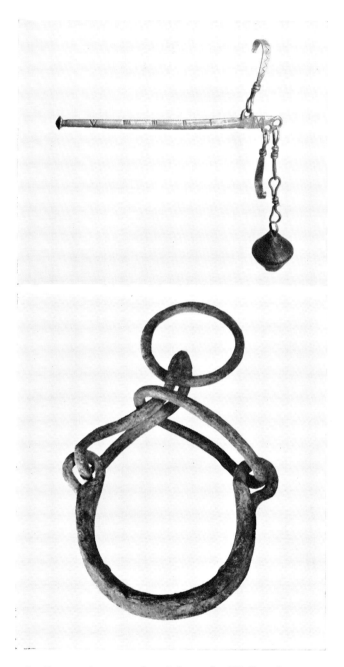

128 Roman brass steelyard from the Walbrook, Queen Victoria
Street. (*Length, 6 in.*)

129 Roman iron shackle from the Walbrook, Bucklersbury House.
(*Width, 4¼ in.*)

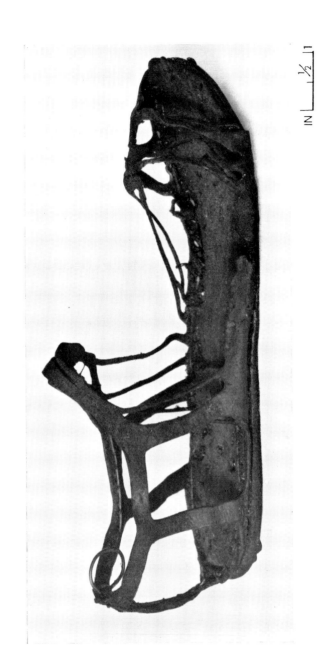

IN |___| ½ |___| 1

130   Roman leather sandal, found in London.

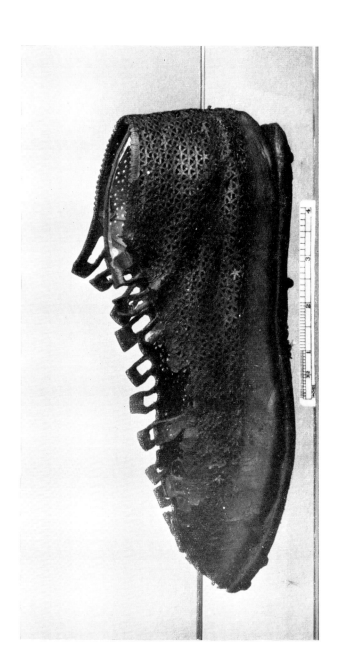

131 Roman leather shoe from the Walbrook, Bucklersbury House.

132   Roman coins, Claudius-Antoninus Pius, from Bucklersbury
House, showing the range of the Walbrook series, which
ends in A.D. 155. (*Actual size.*)

133   Roman bronze brooches, mid-first to mid-second century, from the Walbrook, Bucklersbury House. (*Actual size.*)

134   Roman pewter cup, box and spoons, from the Walbrook, Bucklersbury House. (*Actual size.*)

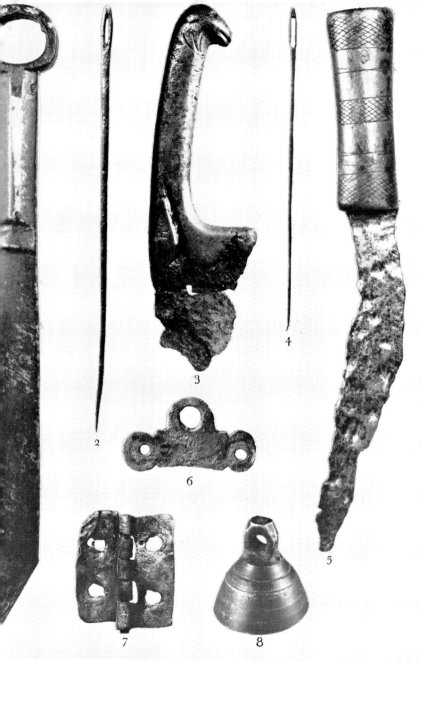

135   Roman knives, needles, brass fitting, hinge and bell, from the
Walbrook, Bucklersbury House. (*Actual size.*)

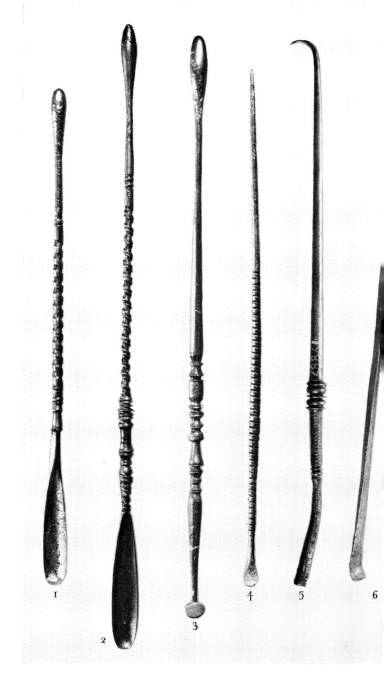

136 Roman surgical or toilet instruments, from the Walbrook, Bucklersbury House. (*Actual size.*)

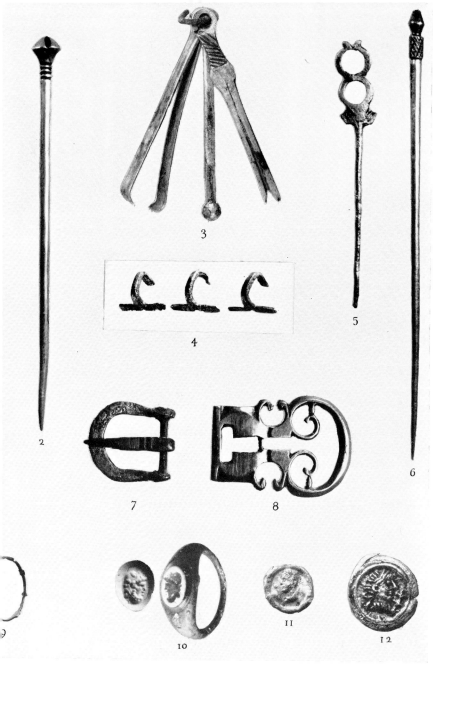

137 Roman hair-pins, toilet set, dress-hooks, buckles, rings and studs, from the Walbrook, Bucklersbury House. (*Actual size.*)

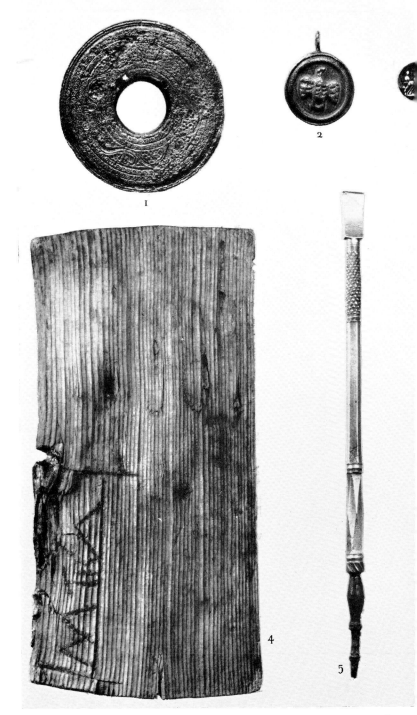

138   Roman ink-well cover, seal-box lid, seal, writing tablet and
stili, from the Walbrook, Bucklersbury House. (*Actual size.*)

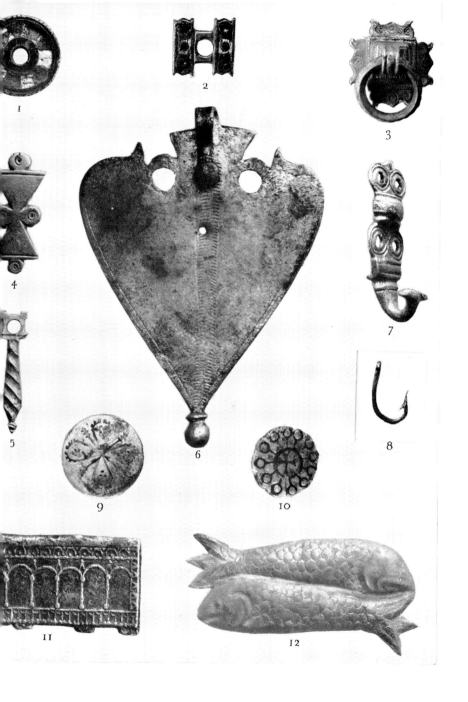

139 Roman brass casket fittings, pendant, toggle, fish-hook, studs, decorated pewter fitting and bronze ornament representing fishes, from the Walbrook, Bucklersbury House. (*Actual size.*)

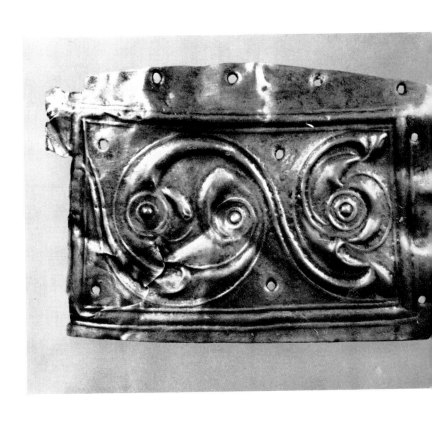

140 Brass plate with repoussé decoration in late Celtic style, found
near the mouth of the Walbrook. (*Length, 4 in.*)

Notes to the Plates

NOTE. Acknowledgement is gladly made to the Copyright owners as indicated at the end of each note, to whom thanks are due for the courtesy of reproduction.

1 **Reconstruction of Roman London in the second century by Alan Sorrell,** *from original drawing in London Museum*
Some details of the street lay-out are incorrect, but the picture gives a good general impression of Londinium at this period. The fort can be seen to the north-west of the city (background, centre).

London Museum

2 **Reconstruction of Roman London in the third century by Alan Sorrell,** *from original drawing in London Museum*
This shows the city after the building of the great defensive wall. It now seems unlikely, however, that there was a continuous riverside wall of the same character, as shown here.

London Museum

3 **Reconstruction of the central and western part of Roman London in the third century, by Robert W. Nicholson**
This shows the Roman bridge (the exact position of which remains unknown), the basilica and forum to the north of it, and the city wall with the gateway at Bishopsgate behind. To the left, on the far side of the Walbrook, is the fort, now enclosed by the city wall. Further to the left are the gateways at Aldersgate and Newgate. The oblong building with pillars in the centre of the picture is placed where a fragmentary inscription of a temple to the state cult was found, but there is no evidence that the temple itself stood here.

National Geographic Magazine, National Geographic Society, Washington D.C., U.S.A.

4 **Portion of inscription from tombstone of Classicianus, found in 1852 with architectural fragments re-used as building material in bastion, Trinity Place** (Map B2)

Engraving by A. H. Burkitt

5 **Lower portion of inscription from tombstone of Classici-anus, Procurator of Britain, as found re-used as building material in remains of Bastion, Trinity Place, 1935** (Map **B2**) (See *Pl.* 6, *Fig.* 4, p. 41 and p. 42)
Guildhall Museum

6 **Tombstone of Classicianus, Procurator of Britain, A.D. 61–c. 65, as reconstructed. Found re-used as building material in Bastion in Trinity Place in 1852 and 1935** (Map **B2**) (See also pp. 40–2)
Length about 7 ft. 6 in.
Inscription: DIS [M]ANIBVS [C. IVL. C.F. F]AB. ALPINI CLASSICIANI
———————————————————————————
PROC. PROVINC. BRIT[ANNIAE]
IVLIA INDI FILIA PACATA I[NDIANA]
VXOR [F.]
('Sacred to the memory of C. Julius Fabius Alpinus Classicianus . . . . Procurator of the Province of Britain, set up by his wife, Julia Pacata Indiana, daughter of Indus')
The British Museum

7 **Wooden frame of wax writing tablet with branded inscription:** PROC AVG DEDERVNT / BRIT PROV **('issued by the Imperial Procurators of the Province of Britain');** (See p. 42), **also small wooden label with recessed surface for wax; both from the Walbrook**
The British Museum

8 **Fragment of Roman roof-tile with stamp** P P BR LON, **found on site of Lloyd's Building, Leadenhall Street** (See pp. 43–4)   (*Length of stamp, 3½ in.*)
London Museum

9 **Memorial to Claudia Martina, wife of Anencletus, slave of the Provincial Council, found in Ludgate Hill, 1806** *Height 3 ft. 11 in.* Inscribed 'D.M. CL. MARTINAE AN XIX ANENCLETVS PROVINC. CONIVGI PIENTISSIMAE H.S.E.' ('In memory of Claudia Martina, aged 19, set up by Anencletus, slave of the Province, to his most devoted wife; she lies here').
Guildhall Museum

10 **Silver ingot with stamp** EX OFFE HONORINI **('From the Workshop of Honorinus') found with gold coins of**

Arcadius and Honorius (Mints of Rome and Milan) at the Tower of London in 1777

Length, 4 in. The ingot was evidently part of a small hoard of the early fifth century, and has no connection at all with the London mint, which was not functioning at that date. We do not know the location of the mint of Londinium, and there is no reason to believe that it was anywhere near the Tower.

The British Museum

11 **Corroded mass of nearly 600 barbarous British copies of the much debased coins of the late third century, deposited after A.D. 276 in a small pit in gravel metalling, possibly a road, south of Newgate Street, 1961** (Map **17**)

Professor W. F. Grimes and Guildhall Museum

12 **Selection from the coins found in the Newgate Street hoard (*Pl.* 11), after cleaning**

The coins are mostly copies of *antoniniani* of the usurping Emperors in Gaul, A.D. 259–73, but the hoard is dated by a later coin, the copy of an *antoninianus* of Tacitus, struck in A.D. 276. The first three obverses in the second row and the first two reverses in the third were struck from the same dies, and were therefore probably made locally. (*Actual size.*)

Professor W. F. Grimes and Guildhall Museum

13 **Gold Medallion found near Arras, commemorating the arrival of Constantius Chlorus at London in A.D. 296, after the defeat of Allectus**

$1\frac{2}{3}$ *in. in diameter.* Constantius is shown about to enter the city, welcomed by a personification of Londinium marked *LON*, while one of his warships lies nearby on the Thames. Constantius is described as REDDITOR LUCIS AETERNAE ('the Restorer of the Eternal Light'). The medal has the mint-mark of Trier (*PTR*).

Photograph of electrotype copy in Guildhall Museum

14 **Coins of the London Mint (all bronze except No. 16) with mint-marks in exergue of reverse:** *ML* – MONETA LONDINENSIS (1–3): *QL* – QUINARIUS (?) LONDINII (4): *LON* – LONDINII (5): *PLN* (6–11) and *PLON* (12–15) – possibly PRIMA LONDINII (the single workshop or *officina* of the London Mint taking the title of 'first') rather than PERCUSSA or PECUNIA LONDINII ('struck at London' or 'London money') as has been suggested: *AVG OB* – AUGUSTAE OBRYZUM ('Augusta – pure gold') (16). *Actual size.*

(1–2) *Carausius*, antoniniani, reverses with Pax, A.D. 288–9, 293

(3–4) *Allectus*, antoninianus and quinarius, reverses with Pax and galley, A.D. 293–6

(5) *Diocletian*, follis, reverse with Genius of the Roman People, A.D. 296–7

(6) *Constantine I* as Caesar, follis, reverse with Genius of the Roman People, A.D. 307

(7) *Constantine I*, reverse with Emperor on horseback, before him a captive, A.D. 312–13

(8) *Constantine I*, reverse with Sun-god, A.D. 313

(9) *Licinius I*, reverse with Genius of the Roman People, A.D. 316–17

(10) *Crispus*, son of Constantine I, as Caesar, reverse with Sun-god, A.D. 317–18

(11) *Constantine I*, reverse with two Victories placing shield on altar, A.D. 317–20

(12) *Constantine II*, son of Constantine I, as Caesar, reverse with standard between two captives, A.D. 319–20

(13) *Constantine I*, reverse with altar surmounted by a globe and three stars, A.D. 320–2

(14) *Constantine II*, son of Constantine I, as Caesar, reverse with VOT X in wreath, A.D. 322–3

(15) *Helena*, mother of Constantine I, reverse with Securitas holding branch, A.D. 324–5

(16) *Magnus Maximus*, gold solidus, reverse with two emperors facing, holding globe, and Victory facing behind them, A.D. 383–8

The British Museum

15 **Section, site of St. Swithin's House, Walbrook, showing Roman floor of red tesserae overlaid by a fire deposit, probably early second century, with mediaeval chalk floor above, and tiled floor of house destroyed in Great Fire of 1666 above that** (Map 266)
Drawn by H. S. Drury, Guildhall Museum

16 **Roman foundations which were still in use in the twentieth century, site of Minster House, Martin Lane, 1954–5. The brick walls of the surviving eighteenth century cellars (A) rest on mediaeval chalk walls (B), which were themselves built on Roman foundations (C)** (Map 302)
View from south.

Guildhall Museum

17 **Floor (F) and wall (W) of a Roman building revealed**

briefly by the mechanical grab in the side of a builders' excavation south of Newgate Street, 1961 (Map 6)

This is a typical example of the conditions in which observations must often be made on a building site. Photographs were taken, and an examination made of the structure, during the intervals when the grab had swung away to discharge its load before returning to its work of excavation and destruction.

Guildhall Museum

18 **Ancient stream-bed, marked by a band of black mud, extending across a large site south of Newgate Street, 1961** (Map 12)

The view is to the north towards Newgate Street.

Guildhall Museum

19 **Roman wooden planking attached to piles, believed to be part of the revetment of a stream-bank, found beneath the crypt of St. Mary-Le-Bow Church, 1915** (Map 63)

Guildhall Museum

20 **Portion of a Roman wooden platform, Bucklersbury House site, 1954** (Map 250)

It lay at a depth of about 17 ft. below street level.

Guildhall Museum

21 **Massive timber structure supported on piles, seen in section in the south-east corner of the Bucklersbury House site, Walbrook, 1955** (Map 252)

View from west.

Guildhall Museum

22 **Roman iron chisel, found driven into a wooden pile supporting an early timber structure, said to have been 28 ft. below modern street level, National Provincial Bank, Prince's Street, 1929–30** (Map 178)

The National Provincial Bank

23 **Wooden piles continuing line of north edge of Roman roadway, the gravel metalling of which can be seen in section in the background** (Cf. *Pl.* 25), **S.E. corner of Bucklersbury House site, Walbrook** (Map 251)

View from N.W.

Guildhall Museum

24 **Massive wooden piles of early Roman date, found on site of Bucklersbury House, Walbrook, 1955** (Map 251)

Guildhall Museum

25 **Roman gravel road, seen in section in the south-east corner of the Bucklersbury House site, Walbrook, 1955,** View to east (Map **251**) (See also *Fig.* 18, p. 123)

Guildhall Museum

26 **Roman gravel road, with drainage gully adjoining eastern edge, seen in section on site south of Newgate Street, 1961.** View to north (Map **10**) (See also pp. 127 ff.)
The western portion of the road has been destroyed by later intrusions.

Guildhall Museum

27 **Gravel metalling** (*M*) **of Roman roadway, site of Nos. 15–18, Lime Street, 1932** (Map **232**) (See also p. 117)

Guildhall Museum

28 **'London Stone', now preserved in a niche in the south wall of the Bank of China, Cannon Street, photographed in 1961 after it had been removed from a similar position in the wall of St. Swithin's Church on the same site**
It is of Clipsham Limestone, artificially shaped, and is evidently only the top of the great stone which once stood near the middle of the present Cannon Street (Map **268**). There is no evidence that it was a Roman milestone, as has been suggested, or even of Roman date, but it stood beside a Roman street, and apparently was in existence in Anglo-Saxon times. (See pp. 123 f.)

Guildhall Museum

29 **Chalk platform on wooden piles, a Roman terrace above the river front, Lambeth Hill, Upper Thames Street, 1961** (Map **116**)
View to north.

Guildhall Museum

30 **Plan and longitudinal section of the Roman barge found at Blackfriars, 1962–3** (Map **26**)
A portion of the port side, which had collapsed outwards, is shown in the plan as it was found. The starboard side had collapsed inwards over the bottom of the ship, and is not shown. (*Drawn by P. R. V. Marsden.*) (See pp. 49–50.)

Guildhall Museum

31 **Bottom timbers of Roman barge as excavated in a coffer-dam near Blackfriars Bridge, 1963.** From the S.E. (Map **26**)
The iron clench nails securing the planks of the bottom can be

seen in the cross-ribs. On the right is the square mast-step cut in one of the ribs, and on the left is an unfinished mill-stone. The starboard side had collapsed over the bottom, and a portion of this remains in the centre.

Guildhall Museum

32 **Piece of stitched leather of uncertain use, with perforated ornament representing a dolphin, found lying in the bottom of the Roman barge at Blackfriars**

Guildhall Museum

33 **Copper coin** (*as*) **of Domitian, struck in A.D. 88–9, found in mast-step of barge at Blackfriars**

The reverse side, which lay uppermost, has a representation of Fortuna, goddess of luck, holding a cornucopiae and a ship's rudder, and it seems likely that the coin was selected as a luck-offering for that reason. (See p. 49.)

Guildhall Museum

34 **Mast-step of Roman barge at Blackfriars, containing coin of Domitian as found**

It had evidently been placed there for luck, as was the custom in recent times.

Guildhall Museum

35 **South-west corner of Roman fort, Noble Street, from N.E.** (Map **31, W47, B15**) (See also *Fig.* 31, p. 161)

It shows the curve of the fort wall (A): the corner turret (B): a portion of the inner thickening added when the city wall was built (C): the city wall at its junction with the corner of the fort (D): the end of the wall of the corner bastion (E) cut by the modern brick wall. (See p. 97.)

Guildhall Museum

36 **Portion of west wall of Roman fort, Noble Street, from east** (Map **W45**)

It shows the fort wall (A): an intermediate turret of the fort (B): and portions of the inner wall added as a thickening when the city wall was built (C).

Guildhall Museum

37 **West gate of Roman fort as excavated in 1956, showing the northern half of the gateway from the south** (Map **G7**) (See pp. 99, 159).

In the foreground is the gravel metalling of the roadway (cut on the right by a later pit) with the north guardroom behind.

Professor W. F. Grimes and Guildhall Museum

38 **Roman and mediaeval city wall adjoining St. Alphage
Churchyard, showing double Roman wall at the base.
The outer (on the right) is the earlier fort wall, and
the inner the thickening added when the city wall was
built** (Map W40)
View of outer side from east. The Roman facing has gone, and the
lower part of the wall has been roughly refaced, perhaps in
Anglo-Saxon times. Above are mediaeval rebuilds, one identified
as thirteenth century, with the brickwork battlements built in
1477 at the top.

Guildhall Museum

39 **Roman and mediaeval city wall, Trinity Place, showing
the inner side of the wall from the south** (Map W6)
The Roman wall with its courses of bonding tiles survives to a
height just above the modern street level of Trinity Place (seen
on the left). Above this the wall is mediaeval. The original facing
of the Roman wall survives on the left, the portion adjacent to
Trinity Place.

Guildhall Museum

40 **Roman and mediaeval city wall, Cooper's Row, after
demolition of Barber's Warehouse in 1961-2, showing
the internal face of the wall from the west** (Map W9)
The lower portion of the wall (to about the top of the ranging
pole) is Roman, and above this are successive rebuilds, with a
round-headed mediaeval embrasure near the top right-hand
corner.

Guildhall Museum

41 **Portion of the Roman city wall preserved in the cellar
of No. 1, Crutched Friars (Roman Wall House), showing
the internal face of the wall seen from the west** (Map
W14)
The facing of squared blocks of ragstone survives here practically
intact, and two courses of bonding tiles (one triple and one
double) can be seen, as well as part of the triple levelling-course
of brick at the bottom.

Guildhall Museum

42 **Portion of Roman city wall, Cooper's Row, as exposed
during rebuilding in 1962** (Map W9)
View from N.W. of the lower part of the wall, interior face, showing triple course of tiles with offset, corresponding in level with
the plinth on the exterior. Above are four courses of squared

ragstone blocks, and then a triple course of bonding-tiles with an offset. The edge of the uppermost course has been mostly removed, but the tiles are visible in the wall behind. Above this the ragstone facing blocks have been removed, showing the ragstone rubble concrete of the interior of the wall.

Guildhall Museum

43 Reconstruction of Roman Newgate, by Alan Sorrell (Map G9)
View as seen from S.W. From original water-colour in Guildhall Library. It is uncertain whether the western bastions of the city wall shown here had been built in Roman times. (See pp. 68 ff.)

The Roman and Mediaeval London Excavation Council

44 Roman and mediaeval city wall, Cooper's Row, seen in section from the north, 1962 (Map W9)
The lower and thicker portion is Roman, and courses of bonding-tiles can be seen running through it. A modern brick wall has been built against its western face on the right.

Guildhall Museum

45 Internal turret of Roman city wall, Cooper's Row, 1962 (Map W10)
View from north. The modern brick wall on the left had been built against the internal face of the Roman city wall, cutting through the walls of the turret except at foundation level. The purpose of the turret was probably to house a stairway giving access to the ramparts. A portion of the original cement floor remains.

Guildhall Museum

46 Corner Bastion, near St. Giles Cripplegate (Map B12)
View from east. The whole of the visible structure is mediaeval and later, but it has usually been assumed that the buried lower portion and foundations are late Roman. It belongs, however, to the western group of hollow bastions, of which the Roman origin is now doubtful. (See pp. 69 f.)

Guildhall Museum

47 Wardrobe Tower (Tower of London) from the west (Map B1)
A portion of the base of the Roman city wall, up to the first triple course of bonding tiles, is seen in the foreground, with the remains of the tower behind it on the outside of the wall. The upper part was rebuilt, probably in the twelfth century, but the base is a

surviving portion of the earlier bastion, probably of late Roman date.

Guildhall Museum

48 **Roman and mediaeval remains on the site of Leadenhall Market,** *drawn by Henry Hodge, 1881–2* (Map 220, 222) (See also *Fig.* 24, *A, E, F.*)
View from south. The double southern wall, cross-walls and the eastern apse of the Roman basilica can be seen, and also the wall and pavement east of the apse and the drain to the south of it.

Guildhall Library

49 **The eastern wall of the basilica from the east, with fragments of the superstructure of the southern east-west wall and the wall of the eastern apse (behind, on right).** *Water-colour drawing by Henry Hodge, 1881* (Map 220)

Guildhall Library

50 **The brick pier of the basilica resting on the northern part of the double east-west wall, but overlapping the edge of the southern part.** *Water-colour drawing by Henry Hodge, 1881* (Map 220)
View from S.E. This is the pier still preserved in the basement of No. 90, Gracechurch Street.

Guildhall Library

51 **Northern sleeper wall of the basilica, with remains of a brick pier on stone footings, found on the site of No. 52, Cornhill, 1929** (Map 214) (See *Figs.* 21, 22, pp. 134 f.)
View from N.W.

Guildhall Museum

52 **Brick pier on rubble foundation, with a short length of brick wall adjoining its north face – the central one of three piers found on site of No. 42, Lombard Street in 1925** (Map 241) (See also *Fig.* 24, P.)
View from east. This is probably part of the forum building.

Guildhall Museum

53 **Roman wall of rubble with courses of brick, found under Lombard Street frontage of No. 42, Lombard Street, 1925** (Map 241) (See also *Fig.* 24, P.)
View from north.

Guildhall Museum

54 **Wall-plaster with painting of a floral spray, from the site of the basilica, Leadenhall Market** (Map 218–220)
? Late first or second century A.D. The leaves are of dark and light grey-green and the buds yellow, on a red background.

London Museum

55 **Section through the foundation of the mysterious long wall of Knightrider Street** (Map 93. See also 94–98, p. 146, and *Pl.* 56)
View to west. The foundations had been laid in a boarded trench, and cut through the filling of a pit which had itself been dug into a deposit of clay and gravel filling an irregular hollow, probably a gravel quarry.

Guildhall Museum

56 **Roman brick culvert through ragstone wall, Knightrider Street, north of St. Nicholas Church, 1955.** View to south (Map 97) (See also p. 146)

Guildhall Museum

57 **Massive Roman ragstone wall in Bush Lane, immediately east of Cannon Street Station, being demolished by workmen, 1960–1.** View to south (Map 273. See also p. 145 and *Fig.* 28 B, p. 147)

Guildhall Museum

58 **Arched flue passage and channel in the hot room of a Roman bath-house, found in 1964 in Huggin Hill, Upper Thames Street** (See *Fig.* 26, p. 141)
This and other flues admitted hot air which circulated beneath the floor of the room. The curved wall is the western portion of the northern apse of the hot chamber, seen from the south-east. The bath-building was found too late for inclusion in the Map and Gazetteer, but lay immediately to the west of 121, which evidently formed part of the same building. (See p. 142.)

Guildhall Museum

59 **Roman bath with steps in the corner, found on the site of No. 62, Threadneedle Street, 1895.** View to east (Map 182)

Guildhall Museum

60 **Portion of Roman bath-building, Cheapside, 1955, showing blocked flue channel** (*A*) **and platform for hot water tank** (*B*) (Map 55. See also *Fig.* 25, *F.* p. 139)
View from north. This flue channel was filled with tiles set on their edges, and a new one was made at a higher level (*C*). This in its turn was blocked with rubble and a facing of tiles.

Guildhall Museum

61 **Roman floor with hypocaust and brick seat forming**

part of a partition wall, still preserved in Lower Thames Street (Map 353) View to east.
The room was heated by hot air which passed from a furnace through the hollow space beneath the floor, and it may well have formed part of a bath-house. (See p. 142)

Guildhall Museum

62 **Roman tile or brick with impressions of a child's foot made while the clay was soft, found in the flue channel of the Roman bath-building in Cheapside** (Map 55)

Guildhall Museum

63 **Londoners examining the Roman mosaic pavement found in Bucklersbury in 1869** (See *Pl.* 65; Map 194)
The pavement was visited by 33,000 people in three days.

The Illustrated London News of 29 May 1869

64 **Roman mosaic pavement found under the old Excise Office, Old Broad Street, 1854** (Map 323)

From C. Roach Smith: Illustrations of Roman London

65 **Mosaic pavement found in Bucklersbury in 1869. ? Early third century A.D.** (Map 194)
Length, 17 ft. 2 in.
Original in Guildhall Museum: illustration from 'Description' by J. E. Price, 1870

66 **Central medallion of mosaic pavement, representing Bacchus riding on a tiger, found in Leadenhall Street in 1803** (Map 329)

The British Museum

67 **Mosaic pavement found on the site of No. 11, Ironmonger Lane, in 1949. ? Late third century A.D.** (Map 151)
A portion of the pavement has been preserved *in situ*.

Guildhall Museum

68 **Mosaic pavement found on the site of the Bank of England in 1934. ? Late second or early third century A.D.** (Map 171)
Decorated portion 4½ ft. square.

The Bank of England

69 **Mosaic pavement found on the site of the Bank of England in 1933. ? Late second or early third century A.D.** (Map 171)

The Bank of England

70 **Fragment of mosaic pavement, probably of late date, representing a female head, found at a depth of 14 ft. in Cornhill, 1844** (Map 187)

London Museum

71 **Border of mosaic pavement found on the site of Crosby Hall** (Map 325) *23¾ in. by 13½ in.*
The design is in black and white, with red tesserae at the leaf-tips.
In private possession. Guildhall Museum photograph

72 **Temple of Mithras, Walbrook, view from west, 1954** (Map 248)
The eastern end, where the sculptures were found, had not been excavated when this photograph was taken.

Professor W. F. Grimes and Guildhall Museum

73 **Temple of Mithras, Walbrook, view from east, 1954** (Map 248)
Within the apse at the western end is a raised sanctuary. The south wall is visible on the left, and two sleeper walls run the length of the building. Each of these supported a row of seven columns, which divided the interior into a central nave and two side aisles. The block of concrete in the centre is modern.

Professor W. F. Grimes and Guildhall Museum

74 **Group of sculptures with an inverted stone basin, as found in the temple of Mithras, Walbrook, 1954** (Map 248)
They had been carefully buried beneath a floor which, from coin evidence, had probably been laid during the reign of Constantine, when Christianity triumphed over its pagan rivals. The pagan sculptures had presumably been concealed to save them from destruction at the hands of the Christians. (See pp. 62 f.)

Professor W. F. Grimes and Guildhall Museum

75 **Colossal right hand of Mithras holding knife hilt, in Italian marble, found in the temple of Mithras, Walbrook, 1954** (Map 248)
Length, 10¼ in. (excluding iron shank). Second century A.D. In view of its great size (more than twice life-size) it is unlikely that the hand came from a group representing the bull-sacrifice, since such a group could only have been accommodated in a very much larger building. It is more likely that the hand alone served as a symbol of the sacrificial act.

Professor W. F. Grimes and Guildhall Museum

76 **Head of Serapis, Graeco-Egyptian God of the Under-World, in Italian marble, found in the temple of Mithras, Walbrook, 1954** (Map 248)

Height, 12¾ in. Late second century A.D. On the head is a *modius* or corn-measure, symbol of fertility and the riches of the earth.

Professor W. F. Grimes and Guildhall Museum

77 **Figure of Mercury, in Italian marble, found in the temple of Mithras, Walbrook, 1954** (Map 248)

Height, 10 in. Second quarter of second century A.D. Mercury is accompanied by a ram, since he was a god of the flocks and herds, and in his left hand he holds a purse, since he was a god of merchants and travellers. Below his left foot is a tortoise – an allusion to his invention of the lyre, which he made from a tortoise's shell.

Professor W. F. Grimes and Guildhall Museum

78 **Head of Mithras in Italian marble, found in the temple of Mithras, Walbrook, 1954** (Map 248)

Height 14½ in. Late second century A.D. Probably from a group representing Mithras sacrificing the bull. (Cf. *Pl.* 84.)

Professor W. F. Grimes and Guildhall Museum

79 **Sculptured relief with Dioscurus, in British oolite, found about 60 ft. south of the temple of Mithras, Walbrook**

Height, 1 ft. 10 in. Second or third century A.D. There seems little doubt that this fragment originally came from the temple, and it is an example showing the fate of those sculptures which were not concealed.

Guildhall Museum

80 **Group representing Bacchus, accompanied by Silenus on an ass, a satyr, a maenad and a panther, in Italian marble, with inscription 'HOMINIBVS BAGIS BITAM', found in the temple of Mithras, Walbrook, 1954** (Map 248)

Height, 13½ in. ?Mid-third century A.D. Bacchus holds a serpent in his right hand, and behind this is a vine. Originally a figure of Pan was seated on the tree, but only the lower part with its goat-foot remains. Silenus holds a wine-cup and the maenad the *cista mystica.* The inscription has been interpreted as 'HOMINIBUS VAGIS VITAM' ('Life to wandering men'). This sculpture was found *above* the floor which sealed the other sculptures, and evidently stood in the temple in the fourth century, perhaps during the revival of paganism under Julian. (See **p.** 63.)

Professor W. F. Grimes and Guildhall Museum

81 **Silver strainer or infuser, with its decorated silver container, found unstratified in the temple of Mithras, Walbrook, 1954, in circumstances strongly suggesting that it had been concealed in the north wall of the temple**

Height of container, 2½ in. Late third or fourth century A.D. The purpose of this object is unknown, but it seems more likely to have been used as an infuser, perhaps to prepare some herbal drug, than as a strainer for the honey used in certain Mithraic rites, as has been suggested.

Professor W. F. Grimes and Guildhall Museum

82 and 83 **Details of decoration on lid and round wall of silver casket which contained the strainer or infuser found in the temple of Mithras, 1954**

Diameter, 3⅛ in. Height, 2½ in. Late third or fourth century A.D. The subjects represented are mostly scenes of conflict between animals, and between men and animals. There are also enigmatic scenes of griffins seizing boxes, which they are apparently trying to open, and of men emerging from boxes.

Professor W. F. Grimes and Guildhall Museum
Periphotograph of wall by F. Fox, F.R.P.S.

84 **Relief in marble showing Mithras slaying the bull, found in Walbrook in 1889, no doubt when foundations were dug in the temple of Mithras** (See pp. 7, 63.)

Height, 17½ in. Late second or third century A.D. The relief bears the inscription: VLPIUS SILVANVS EMERITVS LEG[IONIS] II AVG[VSTAE] VOTVM SOLVIT FACTVS ARAVSIONE. The first part means 'Ulpius Silvanus, veteran of the Second August Legion, paid his vow', and the last two words 'made at Arausio' (Orange in Provence). It is likely that 'factus' refers to Silvanus, as being either initiated into some Mithraic grade, or discharged from the army (*factus emeritus*) at Orange, rather than to the making of the sculpture itself.

London Museum

85 **Figure of river-god in Italian marble, found in Walbrook in 1889, no doubt when foundations were dug in the temple of Mithras**

Height, 14 in. Mid-second century. This sculpture, with the bull-slaying relief (*Pl.* 84) and the headless figure of a Genius (also in marble) were said to have been found 'in the middle of the Walbrook at a depth of about 20 ft'. The finds of 1954 in the temple were at approximately the same depth, and were adjacent to concrete foundations which had been laid in 1889.

London Museum

86 **Altar of Diana, found on the site of Goldsmiths' Hall, Foster Lane, 1830. Second century A.D.** (Map 38)
Height, 23 in.
The Worshipful Company of Goldsmiths and the Warburg Institute

87 **Figure of Atys (?), wearing Phrygian cap and holding bow, oolitic limestone, third century A.D., found in Bevis Marks before 1859**
Height, 27 in.
The British Museum

88 **Group of the three Mother-Goddesses found lying on a tessellated pavement near St. Olave's Church, Hart Street, during sewer excavations, 1839–41. ? Second or third century A.D.** (Map 350)
Breadth, 33 in. The three Mother Goddesses were Celtic deities, and it is likely that this sculpture originally stood in a shrine or temple.
Guildhall Museum

89 **Silver plaque, with representation in repoussé of the three Mother-Goddesses, found on the site of Nos. 55–61, Moorgate, 1929** (Map 134)
$4\frac{1}{2}$ in. by 4 in. The plaque probably ended in a feather-like ornament, and is likely to have been attached to a crown used in religious ritual.
London Museum

90 **Colossal bronze head of Hadrian, dredged from the Thames near London Bridge in 1834**
Heignt, including neck, about $16\frac{1}{2}$ in. A bronze hand found in Lower Thames Street, also in the British Museum, may possibly be part of the same statue. Two other bronze hands in Guildhall Museum, however, bear witness to the fact that there were several such statues in Roman London. (See *Pl.* 91.)
The British Museum

91 **Fore-arm of Roman bronze statue, found in a well to the east of Seething Lane**
Length, 19 in.
Guildhall Museum

92 **Bronze figure of archer with silver eyes, found in Queen Street in 1842, at a depth of 12-13 ft., second century A.D.**
Height about 11 in.
The British Museum

93 **Small capital with sculptured faces, forming part of a larger architectural fragment, ? second–third century A.D.** Found re-used as building material in core of bastion of the city wall, Camomile Street, 1876 (Map **B10**)
Guildhall Museum

94 **Sculptured group representing a lion attacking a deer, probably second century A.D.,** found re-used as building material in core of bastion of the city wall, Camomile Street, 1876 (Map **B10**)
Height, 28 in.
Guildhall Museum

95 **Stone figure of Roman legionary soldier, ? late first–early second century A.D.,** originally from a tomb, but found with other Roman sculptured and architectural fragments re-used as building material in the core of a bastion of the city wall, Camomile Street, 1876 (Map **B10**)
Height, 52 in.
Guildhall Museum

96 **Tombstone of legionary soldier of the Second Augustan Legion, found in 1669 when Wren rebuilt St. Martin's Church, Ludgate Hill, ? second century A.D.** (Map **G10**)
Height, 84 in. Inscribed D.M. VIVIO MARCIANO LEG. II AVG. IANUARIA MARTINA CONIVNX PIENTISSIMA POSVIT MEMORIAM ('In memory of Vivius Marcianus of the Second Augustan Legion: Januaria Martina, his most devoted wife, set up this monument').
The Ashmolean Museum

97 **Bronze helmet of legionary soldier found in London, probably in the Thames, first century A.D.**
On each side is a plume-holder and attachment for cheek-piece. On the neck-guard are inscribed the names of successive owners.
The British Museum

98 **Spear-head with inscription of punched dots:** Ɔ. VER. VICT. (*CENTURY OF VER[VS] VICT[OR]*). **Found in well with pottery of late first century, site of Bucklersbury House, 1954** (Map 246)
Guildhall Museum

99 **Legionary soldier's dagger and frame of sheath, all of iron, found in Copthall Court in 1911.** From its condition evidently from the Walbrook or its eastern tributary, probably first or early second century A.D.

London Museum

100 **Figure of civilian wearing the toga, and boy wearing a short cloak, represented on stone memorial slab.** ? Second or third century A.D; Details of provenance unknown, but found in London.

Guildhall Museum

101 **Tile found in Warwick Lane, with inscription scratched with stick before the clay was fired: '*AUSTALIS DIBVS XIII VAGATVR SIB COTIDIM*'** ('Austalis has been wandering off on his own every day for the last fortnight') *Length of tile, 16¼ in.*

Guildhall Museum

102 **'The London Curse' – A sheet of lead with inscription incised on both sides solemnly cursing two individuals; it would originally have been nailed to a shrine. Found in Prince's Street** *4½ in. by 3 in.* The inscription reads: '*T[ITVS] EGNATIVS TYRANVS DEFIC[T]VS EST ET P[VBLIVS] CICEREIVS FELIX DEFICTVS E[S]T*' 'Titus Egnatius Tyranus is hereby solemnly cursed; likewise Publius Cicereius Felix'.

London Museum

103 **Wooden tablet with writing in ink, probably about A.D. 80–100, found in timber-lined pit or well, site of Temple House, Queen Victoria Street** *Length about 10½ in., width 2 in.* It is evidently a letter, apparently written by someone in Durobrivae (Rochester), and refers to a slave who appears to have run away with something that had been entrusted to him. There is a reference to London. (The last word in the third line is *Londinio*.) The tablet has been folded in half. (*J.R.S. L. pp. 108 ff.*)
(*Infra-red photograph by M. B. Cookson.*) *Guildhall Museum*

104 **Portion of wooden writing tablet from the Walbrook, probably in Lothbury, with *LONDINIO* written on one side, first–second century A.D.** *Length, 5¾ in.* On the other side of the tablet an inscription cut through the wax into the wood beneath has been read by Sir Ian Richmond. It is a letter from Rufus, son of Callisunus, to his servant Epillicus and others of his household, and appar-

ently concerns the realisation of an estate. There is a request for an inventory, and the final instruction is 'See that you turn that slave girl into cash'. (*Ant. Journ.*, Vol. XXXIII, pp. 206 ff.)

The British Museum

105 **Wooden tablet formerly covered with wax and used for writing with iron stili, also shown. From the Walbrook, site of the Bank of England** (Map 168)
Traces of writing can be seen where the point of the *stilus* cut through the wax surface into the wood beneath.

Guildhall Museum

106 **Large millstone, of the kind turned by an ass and used for corn-grinding on a fairly large scale, as in a baker's establishment. Found in Prince's Street, 1928–9** (Map 175)
Height, 22 in.

Guildhall Museum

107 **Relief from tomb at Ostia showing the method of using large millstones of the type found in Prince's Street** (See *Pl.* 106)

The Soprintendenza alle Antichità

108 **Roman well, apparently of the third century, with frame consisting of a wooden barrel, Bank of London and South America, Queen Street, 1953–4** (Map 91)

Guildhall Museum

109 **Fragments of oak water-pipe, found on the site of the Bank of England, 1927** (Cf. similar find nearby in 1933, Map 170)
Water-tight junctions between the lengths of timber were made by means of iron collars.

London Museum

110 **Excavation of a timber-lined well or pit showing a Roman bronze jug found in the third century filling, Bank of London and South America, Queen Street, 1953–4** (Map 91)

Guildhall Museum

111 **Roman well, late first century, Lloyd's Site, Lime Street, 1951–2**
The upper portion is a square frame of planks and the lower two barrels – an unusual arrangement.

Drawing by I. Noel Hume, Guildhall Museum

112 **A typical Roman well with square frame constructed of oak planks, Bank of London and South America, Queen Street, 1953–4** (Map 91)

Guildhall Museum

113 **Wooden ladder (length 15 ft.) found in a similar square timber-lined well of the first century A.D., Bank of London and South America, Queen Street, 1953–4** (Map 91)

The ladder is shown here as exhibited in the Royal Exchange.

Guildhall Museum

114 **Wooden spoon or scoop found in the first century filling of the same well, Bank of London and South America, Queen Street, 1953–4**

Guildhall Museum

115 **Wooden dipper found near the bottom of the first century filling of the same well, Bank of London and South America, Queen Street, 1953–4**

Guildhall Museum

116 **Leather 'bikini'-type trunks found in the first century filling of the same well as Nos. 113–115, Bank of London and South America, Queen Street, 1953–4** (Map 91)

The trunks were fastened with laces at the hips, and on one side the original knot remains tied. It is more likely that they were worn in exercise than as a bathing costume – perhaps by a girl performer, such as an acrobat. (Cf. *Pl.* 117)

Guildhall Museum

117 **Roman bronze figure of a girl wearing trunks similar to No. 116. She also wears knee protectors, and is probably an acrobat**

(Drawing of figure in the Rennes Museum, from the *Revue Archéologique*, Vol. XIX, p. 216.)

Revue Archéologique

118 **Samian bowl (Dragendorff Form 29), made by Primus of La Graufesenque or Montans, South Gaul, A.D. 50–75, found in a refuse pit in King William Street**

Diameter, $8\frac{1}{2}$ in., height, $3\frac{1}{2}$ in. It bears the stamp PRIMI MA ('by the hand of Primus'). This imported red ware with its characteristic glossy surface was made in a mould. It changed in form and decoration according to fashion, and can be closely dated.

Guildhall Museum

119 **Samian bowl (Dragendorff Form 37), made at Lezoux, Central Gaul, A.D. 100-20, found in Helmet Court, Wormwood Street, Bishopsgate**
Diameter, 7⅝ in., height, 3⅝ in. Its moulded decoration represents animals and gladiators. It was made by an anonymous potter whose work can be recognised, and who has been given the name *X* 3 by archaeologists.

London Museum

120 **Complete amphora and wine-jar, with similar broken vessel, from pre-Boudiccan refuse pit, site of St. Swithin's House, Walbrook, 1950**
The complete vessels were apparently thrown into the pit immediately before Londinium was burnt by Queen Boudicca's tribesmen in A.D. 60. (See pp. 37f and *Fig.* 3, p. 38.)

Guildhall Museum

121 **Roman glass from refuse pit of about A.D. 60-80, site of St. Swithin's House, Walbrook, 1950**

Guildhall Museum

122 **Fine glass bowl with delicately cut handles, an import from the East, found in refuse pit of about A.D. 60-80, site of St. Swithin's House, Walbrook, 1950**
Analysis of a fragment has shown that it is rich in antimony, a characteristic of glass from the eastern limits of the Roman Empire.

Guildhall Museum

123 **Pottery lamp with eagle moulded in relief, from refuse pit of mid-first century, Lloyd's site, Lime Street, 1951-2**

Guildhall Museum

124 **Pottery jugs and glass flask, fourth century, found in an inhumation grave, 28-35, The Minories**
Complete Roman vessels are seldom found except in graves, where they were carefully buried containing refreshment, etc., for the deceased. Pottery and glass in rubbish pits, on the other hand, are almost invariably broken, but can sometimes be restored.

Guildhall Museum

125 **Roman smith's tools, including anvil, from stream of Walbrook, site of Bank of England, 1933-4** (Map 168)
These probably belong to the earlier phase of occupation of this site, before about A.D. 160.

Guildhall Museum

126 **Iron case-opener, docker's hook (for handling sacks and bales) and crane-hook, first to mid-second century, from the Walbrook, site of Bucklersbury House, 1955** Although the Walbrook was much too narrow ever to have served as a dock, except perhaps at its mouth, goods of many kinds seem to have been handled in great quantities on its banks during the first hundred years or so of London's existence.

Guildhall Museum

127 **Roman iron boat-hook, first to second century A.D. From the stream-bed of the Walbrook, Bucklersbury House, 1955** *Length* $9\frac{1}{2}$ *in.*
Guildhall Museum

128 **Roman brass steelyard, used by traders for weighing goods, found in or near the stream-bed of the Walbrook during excavations for the 'Travolator' at the Bank Station, 1959** (Map 190)
Length, 6 in. The object to be weighed was hung from the lead weight on the right, and a movable weight suspended from the bar indicated the weight of the object by its position on the scale when equilibrium was attained. By reversing the steelyard and using the other hook as fulcrum a scale of heavier weights could be used.

Guildhall Museum

129 **Iron shackle for a prisoner, from the Walbrook, site of Bucklersbury House, 1955, probably first century or first half of second century** *Width* $4\frac{1}{4}$ *in.*
Guildhall Museum

130 **Roman leather sandal found in London**
Ancient leather in London is normally preserved only in water-logged soil, such as the stream-bed of the Walbrook or the filling of wells.

Guildhall Museum

131 **Roman leather shoe with pierced decoration and with loops for lacing, probably first–second century A.D., found in the stream-bed of the Walbrook, site of Bucklersbury House, 1955**
Guildhall Museum

132 **Roman coins from the stream of the Walbrook, Bucklersbury House, 1955.** (Map 247.) **They were selected from more than 160 found on this site, and show the**

range of date of the whole series, which ends abruptly in A.D. 155 (See p. 93 and *Ant. Journ.*, XLII, pp. 38–52) *Actual size*
(1) Barbarous dupondius of Claudius (A.D. 41–54). (2) Dupondius of Domitian (A.D. 86). (3) Silver denarius of Trajan (A.D. 112–14). (4) Sestertius of Titus struck in reign of Vespasian (A.D. 77–8). (5) As of Sabina, wife of Hadrian (? *c.* A.D. 128–38). (6) Dupondius of Hadrian (A.D. 119–21). (7) As of Antoninus Pius (A.D. 154–55). The reverse of this coin represents Britannia and commemorates the suppression of a revolt of the Brigantes.

Guildhall Museum

133 **Bronze brooches, some enamelled, from the stream-bed of the Walbrook, Bucklersbury House, 1955.** (Map 247.) **They range in date from mid-first century A.D.** (*No.* 11) **to mid-second century** (*Nos.* 8–10) *Actual size*
Such brooches were used by both sexes for fastening cloaks, etc. (4) is a chatelaine brooch which originally had a rod between the projections at the straight end for the suspension of toilet utensils.

Guildhall Museum

134 **Roman pewter cup, box and spoons, from the Walbrook, Bucklersbury House, 1955** (Map 247) *Actual size*
The handle of the spoon (3) is of iron.

Guildhall Museum

135 **Roman knives, needles, brass fitting, hinge and bell, from the Walbrook, Bucklersbury House, 1955** (Map 247) *Actual size*
The knife-handles are of solid iron (1), brass (3) and bone (5). The needles, fitting and hinge are all of brass, and the bell is bronze.

Guildhall Museum

136 **Roman surgical or toilet instruments from the stream-bed of the Walbrook, Bucklersbury House, 1955** (Map 247) *Actual size*
All are of brass (*orichalc*), (1) and (2) being decorated with a silver inlay. (1) and (2) may be surgeon's curettes: (3) and (4) may be surgical probes; but all four may have been used to extract ointments or cosmetics from flasks and to apply them to the skin. (6) is a similar instrument combined with a pair of tweezers, and could have been used either for surgical or toilet purposes. (5) has a hollow socket and a hooked point, and is certainly a surgical instrument. (Cf. J. S. Milne, *Surgical Instruments in Greek and Roman Times*, p. 87 and *Pl.* XXIV.)

Guildhall Museum

137 **Roman hair-pins of brass and bronze (1, 2, 5, 6): brass toilet set (3), dress-hooks (4), buckle (7), military buckle (8), and ring (9): iron signet ring with onyx intaglio (10): brass studs (11, 12); from the Walbrook, Bucklersbury House, 1955** (Map 247) *Actual size*

(3) consists of tweezers, instrument for pushing back cuticle of nail (or 'ear-pick') and nail-cleaner. (5) is in the form of a caduceus. (9) has a representation of a bearded head and the letters A-M-I-C-A ('sweet-heart') round the hoop. The cameo of (10) represents a triple bearded head, with Zeus on one side, Pan on the other, and a satyr (?) above. The studs (11 and 12) have repousse representations of laureate heads and palm-branches (?).

Guildhall Museum

138 **Roman bronze ink-well cover (1), brass seal-box lid (2), agate seal (3), portion of wooden writing tablet (4) and *stili* of brass and iron, from the Walbrook, Bucklersbury House** (Map 247) *Actual size*

(1) is engraved with a design of a vine with grapes. (2) has the emblem of the imperial eagle riveted to its centre. Seal-boxes were used to protect the seal on a document, and it is likely that this example was for official use. (3) is of dark-green and red agate, presumably from a signet ring, and represents a chariot drawn by four horses. (4) has an incised inscription MTRA on the back, presumably an abbreviation for the name of the addressee or owner. (5) and (6) were used for writing on the wax-covered surface of a similar writing-tablet.

Guildhall Museum

139 **Roman brass casket-fittings (1–5), pendant (6), toggle (7), fish-hook (8), studs (9–10): decorated pewter plate, probably from box or casket (11): bronze ornament in form of two fish (12); from the Walbrook, Bucklersbury House, 1955** (Map 247) *Actual size*

(1) and (2) are enamelled. (6) is probably a horse ornament. (7), (9) and (10) may be from military equipment (*Arch. Journ.*, CXV, p. 85). (9) and (10) are decorated with niello. (12), which is made from a thin sheet of bronze and is hollow beneath, probably represents the sign of the Zodiac.

Guildhall Museum

140 **Brass plate with repoussé decoration in late Celtic style, but of the early Roman period, found in black silt near the mouth of the Walbrook, under Upper Thames Street** *Length 4 in.*

Guildhall Museum

Gazetteer

The numbers in the gazetteer refer to the large map in the pocket. They are divided into four sections:

1 — 363	General	G1 — G10	City Gates
W1 — W61	City Wall	B1 — B21	Bastions

The following abbreviations are used in the notes:

G.M. = Observations by staff of Guildhall Museum
O.D. = Ordnance Datum (Newlyn)

General

1 *Newgate Street, General Post Office, formerly site of Christ's Hospital, 1908–9*

The beds of two streams were observed on this site, cut through the brick-earth into the gravel to depths of 30 and $31\frac{1}{2}$ ft. below the present surface. The fillings were of black mud with remains of reeds and rushes, and the lower part at least contained material of the Roman period only. The eastern stream appeared to have been artificially canalised to some extent. A wall of ragstone 8 ft. thick, quite different from the mediaeval walls on the site and believed to be Roman, was found resting in the bed of this stream on its eastern side, and apparently following its course. The area between the streams appeared to have been used as a brickfield in Roman times. In places the surface had been burnt red to a depth of about 1 ft., and there were many pits which may have been dug to obtain the material. One of these contained a quantity of prepared clay. A horizontal hole filled with wood-ash seen in section may have been part of a flue.

Arch., LXIII, pp. 275, 282–6, *Pl. XLVII.*

2 *Warwick Square, Nos.* 3–9, 1881

Roman remains, including a wall, a brick pavement and a well were found at a depth of about 19 ft. The portion of wall seen was 5 ft. long, 3 ft. wide and 6 ft. high.

Arch., XLVIII, pp. 221*ff.*   *R.C.H.M., p.* 145.

3 *Newgate Street, S. side, W. of Warwick Lane,* 1961

A culvert of Roman bricks was observed during the builders' excavation on the W. side of the ancient watercourse, towards which it ran, like the similar drains associated with the Roman building east of the stream (4).

G.M.

4 *Newgate Street, S. side, W. of Warwick Lane,* 1961

A section of rammed gravel road-metalling was exposed here during the builders' excavation about 126 ft. east of the kerb-line of Warwick Lane. It seemed to be at or near the southern edge of the main Roman E.–W. road – at this point about $8\frac{1}{2}$ ft. south of the building frontage. There were indications of a possible ditch nearly 4 ft. wide here, but only a small portion was seen, and the hollow seen in section might equally well have been a pit. To the south of the probable road-edge, gravel layers extended for at least 17 ft. These were not closely packed but interspersed with clay and other deposits, and probably represented spills of material at times when the road was made up.

G.M.

5 *Newgate Street, Nos.* 10–13, 1962

A layer of Roman gravel metalling $10\frac{1}{2}$ in. thick was seen in section beneath the old building frontage. It lay immediately below the cellar floor and immediately above the natural brick-earth, the surface of which lies at 43 ft. above O.D. This metalling is presumably part of the southern edge of the main Roman road to Newgate. (*See Fig.* 20, *p.* 129.)

G.M.

6 *Newgate Street, S. side,* 1961

The builders' excavation revealed portions of a Roman building, with a ragstone wall running N.–S. towards an E.–W. wall. To the west of it was a floor of brick tiles laid in pink cement, through which an open drain ran to the west. Above this were two more floors on which bricks were laid, one consisting of yellow cement and the other of *opus signinum*. To the south another N.–S. wall formed an angle with the E.–W. wall. Adjoining it to the west was a pavement of small tiles set in *opus signinum* in a herring-bone pattern, 7 in. lower than the tiled floor to the north, with which it formed a step. 20 ft. to the south of the E.–W. wall was another brick drain leading west, and 3 ft. south of this a portion of an E.–W. wall of brick. A few yards to the N.E. of the building were two stoke-holes separated by a wall of bricks and burnt clay. They contained pottery sherds of the late first century. (*See Fig.* 20, *p.* 129.) *G.M.*

7 *Paternoster Square, N.W. corner,* 1884
A portion of a plain pavement and hypocaust pillars were found, as well as a number of flue-tiles.
J.B.A.A. XL, pp. 123, 210.   *R.C.H.M., p.* 135.

8 *Paternoster Square, N. side (then W. corner of Paternoster Square and Rose Street),* 1883
A portion of Roman pavement was found at a depth of 17 ft. below ground level.
R.C.H.M., p. 135.

9 *Paternoster Square, approximately* 190 *ft. E. of Warwick Lane,* 1961
A mass of gravel metalling observed here during the builders' excavation first indicated the presence of a Roman N.–S. road, of which a good section with the eastern edge of the road was later seen and plotted by more accurate methods as the excavation proceeded further north (10).
G.M.

10 *Newgate Street, behind Nos.* 14–29, *near the E. edge of the buildings of Paternoster Square,* 1961
A road with gravel metalling and a distinct camber was observed in section in the builders' excavation, running in a northerly direction. A drainage gully, also seen in section, adjoined the roadway on the eastern side. The western part of the road had been destroyed by later intrusions, and it was impossible to ascertain its width at this point. (*See Pl.* 26.)
G.M.

11 *Newgate Street, W. of Ivy Lane, opposite Greyfriars Passage,* 1961
As the builders' excavation cleared the northern part of the site, a careful watch was kept for further traces of the Roman N.–S. road (10). The only indication seen was a small section of gravel metalling about 24 ft. to the south of the old building frontage of Newgate Street. This lay too far to the south to be part of the main E.–W. road, and it seems very probable that it was a surviving portion of the N.–S. road. Unfortunately, the three sections of

metalling that were seen (**9, 10, 11**) do not define with certainty
the precise alignment of the road.

G.M.

12 *Newgate Street, S. side, N. of Paternoster Row*, 1961
The course of an ancient stream was seen passing from north to
south right through this large site. Its bed was clearly defined by a
band of black mud of peat-like consistency in marked contrast to
the reddish gravel on either side. (*See Pl.* 18.) Its eastern limit
coincided very closely with the boundary between the Wards of
Farringdon Within and Castle Baynard in the central and
southern parts of the site. In the northern part towards Newgate it
curved from the N.E., and another branch apparently joined it
from the N.W., probably approximately following the boundary
at the north end of Castle Baynard Ward. These two branches are
evidently continuations of the two streams observed on the site
of the General Post Office north of Newgate St. in 1908–9. (See
Arch. LXIII, pp. 275, 282–5. *Pl. XLVII.*)

G.M.

13 *Ave Maria Lane, E. side*, 1962
The continuation of the stream seen to the north of Paternoster
Row (**12**) was observed on this site, and the western edge of the
filling of black mud, seen in section on the face of the builders'
excavation, was found to lie 63 ft. east of the old building line at a
point 105 ft. north of the junction of the Ave Maria Lane and
Ludgate Hill building frontages. (*See Fig.* 20, *p.* 129.)

G.M.

14 *Newgate Street, S. side, opposite Roman Bath Street*, 1961
In spite of a careful watch, no certain traces of the main Roman
E.–W. road could be identified on this site. Artificial layers of
gravel were seen during the builders' excavation 15–20 ft. south of
the building line, but these were thin and interspersed with
layers of occupation debris. Moreover, the earliest gravel deposit
overlay wooden piles, which were clearly an earlier feature,
whereas it might be expected that the road would have preceded
any other development in this part of Roman London. If these
deposits were connected with the road at all, they can only have
represented a spread of material from its southern edge, spilled
during road-making or repair. Sections in trenches immediately
south of the building line, however, did reveal a much thicker mass
of gravel, more like the metalling of a road. At a point about

170 ft. from Panyer Alley this extended about 10 ft. to the south of the building line. No trace of the usual drainage gully was seen, however, and the exact position of the road is uncertain. It is likely that most of it lay under the modern Newgate Street. (*See Fig.* 20, *p.* 129.)

G.M.

15 *Newgate Street, W. of St. Paul's Station, formerly No.* 48, 1961

On this spot, formerly occupied by No. 48 Newgate Street, a thick deposit of gravel, resembling the metalling of a Roman road, was observed in section in the builders' excavation, 18–20 ft. south of the building line. This may have been part of the E.–W. road or of the possible N.–S. road seen in the southern part of the site (17). Its position must be very near the junction of these two roads, if the N.–S. road were heading in the direction of Aldersgate. (*See Fig.* 20, *p.* 129.)

G.M.

16 *Newgate Street, W. of Panyer Alley,* 1961

A mass of gravel resembling road metalling was seen here during the builders' excavation, and measurements were taken to fix approximately the eastern limits of this in two places, as shown on the map. The impression given was that of a N.–S. road in the general direction of Aldersgate (i.e. N.N.E.), but no trace of a continuation of such a road on a reciprocal line to the south was found on the southern edge of the site. Instead a tessellated pavement (20) was seen very near the position where the road should have been. Metalling was again found further east (17), but if this formed part of the same road, and its direction was in fact towards Aldersgate, it must have been about 40 ft. wide. It may of course be that there were two roadways at different dates, one lying beside the other and replacing it. Another possibility is that this mass of gravel formed the floor of a courtyard which was parallel with the nearby roadway to the east (*See Fig.* 20, *p.* 129.)

G.M.

17 *Paternoster Row, W. of Panyer Alley,* 1961

Several sections of rammed gravel resembling road metalling were seen in the builders' excavation immediately north of Paternoster Row, and Professor W. F. Grimes was able to clean back and investigate the final section revealed by the builders. A gully or pit was seen cutting into the gravel near its eastern edge, and in this was found a hoard of barbarous radiate coins of the late

third century. (*See Pl.* 11, 12.) There was a much slighter gully to
the east on the edge of the gravel. The western side of the supposed
road had been removed by later building excavations, and in the
western portion of the remaining gravel had been cut another
gully or trench of uncertain date.
J.R.S., LII (1962), *p.* 179.

18 *Paternoster Row,* 1834–41
In this area was found a stone wall running in the direction of
the centre of St. Paul's, with surviving top at a depth of 18 ft.
Coins of Vespasian and Domitian were also found. A few years
later (in 1839–41) a fine mosaic pavement, extending for 40 ft.,
was found at a depth of 12 ft., and subsequently destroyed. It
had a design of birds and beasts in compartments within a border
of guilloche and rosettes. At a greater depth was found a skeleton
in a framework of tiles.
Arch., XXIX, p. 155.   *R.C.H.M., p.* 135.   ROACH SMITH: *Illustrations, pp.* 57–8.

19 *Paternoster Row, corner of Canon Row,* 1843
During the building of the Religious Tract Society's premises, a
small portion of a tessellated pavement of white and grey tesserae
was found at the N.E. corner of the site. It apparently extended
beneath the road. Coins of Claudius, Faustina and Commodus
were also found.
Gent. Mag., 1843, *II, p.* 81.   *R.C.H.M., p.* 135.

20 *Paternoster Row, E. of Canon Alley,* 1961
Builders' excavations near the S.E. corner of the big site between
Newgate Street and St. Paul's Churchyard revealed a Roman
pavement of coarse red tesserae under the north frontage of
Paternoster Row. There was no sign of any associated walls.
A curious feature was that the pavement lay in the line of the
apparent N.–S. road (**16**). (*See Fig.* 20, *p.* 129.)
G.M.

21 *St. Paul's Churchyard, N.E. corner,* 1841
A hypocaust with pillars of tiles supporting a tessellated pavement
(since destroyed) was found at a depth of 18 ft. The mosaic was
a variegated pattern of rosettes on a white ground. Coins of
Constans, Constantius, Magnentius, Decentius and Valens were
found 'beneath the ruins'. Another account says that a pavement

of tiles, varying from 7 in. to 8 in. square with four or five 23 in. square, about 3 in. thick, was found at a depth of 19–20 ft.
Arch., *XXIX*, *pp.* 272–3.   *Gent. Mag.*, 1841, *II*, *p.* 264.
R.C.H.M., *p.* 141.

22 *St. Paul's Cathedral, N.W. corner*, 1672
During the excavation for foundations at the N.W. corner of the cathedral, four Roman pottery kilns were found, at a depth of 26 ft. according to a contemporary account, but this is probably exaggerated. They were made of loam, 'naturally crusted hardish by the heat burning the loam red, like brick'. One is described as being 5 ft. high and 5 ft. wide, and to have been 'full of the coarser type of pot . . . viz. lamps, bottles, urns and dishes'. Drawings of some of the pots have survived, and one jar at least seems to be of first century date. A sketch of the kiln shows a dome-shaped structure with four flues arranged cross-wise.
MS. of John Conyers (*Brit. Mus. Sloane MSS.* 958, *fol.* 105).
R.C.H.M., *p.* 140.

23 *Ludgate Square* (*formerly Holiday Yard, Creed Lane*), *after* 1666
In digging foundations for a new building after the Great Fire, a 'Roman Aqueduct' is said to have been found. This was 'carried round a Bath which was built in a round Forme with Nitches at an equal Distance for Seats'.
STOW: *Survey of London, Strype's edition*, 1755, *II, Appendix Ch. V, p.* 693.
J. LELAND: *Collectanea* (*ed. Hearne*), *I, LXVI.*   *R.C.H.M.*, *p.* 132.

24 *Carter Lane, No.* 56, *before* 1909
In excavating for foundations a massive wall was found running diagonally across the site from N.W. to S.E. It was 8 ft. thick, and constructed of ragstone with courses of bonding-tiles. According to Norman and Reader it coincided with the parish boundary for a short distance, and therefore must have been on the line of the diagonal property boundary. It might be expected that it would follow this boundary in a south-easterly direction to Creed Lane, for such a massive wall must have determined the line of later boundaries. Norman and Reader note that it marks the south-western limit of Roman building, and suggest that it is in fact the continuation south of Ludgate of the Roman city wall, which it so closely resembles.
V.C.H., London, I, p. 69.   *Arch., LXIII, pp.* 305 *f.*
R.C.H.M., p. 113.

25 *Printing House Lane, site of 'The Times' ' new office*, 1960

Two walls of ragstone and yellow mortar, containing fragments of Roman brick, were found on the northern edge of Printing House Lane. There was no evidence of date, but the E.–W. wall lay beneath two later stone walls, presumably mediaeval, one of chalk and the other of ragstone, and the very hard character of the earlier walls suggested that they might be Roman. There remains, however, a strong element of doubt.

The E.–W. wall was a curious structure, battered on its southern face, which was covered with a layer of yellow cement $\frac{3}{4}$ in. thick. The north face was vertical and had no layer of cement covering the ragstone. Lying against it near its base were two horizontal timbers, one above the other, both oblong in section and standing on their narrow sides. At the western end, the base of the foundation rose at an angle of 45°, and its sloping under-surface was faced with squared ragstone blocks. The wall was 5 ft. 4 in. thick at one point, but at least 7 ft. thick at the eastern end of the portion. It is possible that the extra thickness was the beginning of another N.–S. wall. To the S.W. of the battered wall were wooden piles in black gravelly mud.

G.M.

26 *Blackfriars Bridge*, 1962–3

During the construction of the Blackfriars underpass, the remains of an ancient wooden ship were found in the river mud between Blackfriars Bridge and the railway bridge. One portion was examined at low tide in 1962, and another portion (near the southern end of the vessel) was subsequently enclosed in a coffer dam and could be excavated. This portion was removed to Guildhall Museum in August, 1963. The ship was a barge-like craft without a keel, probably about 55 ft. long, carvel-built with planks of varying thickness secured to the massive ribs with huge iron clench-nails. In the mast-step was a copper coin (*as*) of Domitian, dated to A.D. 88–9, which had presumably been put there for luck, as was the common practice in recent times. A millstone lay in the bows, and a quantity of ragstone was found lying in the bottom of the ship, perhaps ballast but more probably the remains of a cargo of building material brought from the Medway. Other objects found in the ship included fragments of sandals and a piece of leather with a design cut to represent a dolphin. (*See Pl.* 30–4.)

G.M.

27 *N. of Falcon Square*, 1956

Excavations by Professor W. F. Grimes revealed the fragmentary walls of a Roman stone building, which apparently fronted the perimeter road north of the gate of the fort, and was presumably one of the military buildings. Earlier occupation (pre-fort) was represented by pits, gullies and possible hut sites.

J.R.S., XLVII (1957), *p.* 220.

28 *E. of Bastion* 14 (*formerly Windsor Court*), 1957

Excavations by Professor W. F. Grimes revealed further remains of the perimeter road, just within the west wall of the fort, with walls of a Roman building fronting it. Traces of this building had also been found further south, nearer the west gate.

J.R.S., XLVIII (1958), *p.* 144.

29 *Wood Street – Silver Street*, 1956

Excavations by Professor W. F. Grimes in the area of the presumed H.Q. building of the Roman fort, in the N.W. angle of Wood Street and Silver Street, revealed only pits and gullies earlier than the fort. Higher Roman levels, including any foundations of buildings in the fort, had all been destroyed.

J.R.S., XLVII (1957), *p.* 220.

30 *Noble Street, No.* 1 (*Shelley House*), 1960–1

A small portion of a ragstone wall, over 9 in. thick, was found running approximately N.–S. Only the east face and the strata on the east side were undisturbed. Here a yellow clay containing many pieces of Roman painted wall-plaster surrounded and overlay the wall. The plaster had red and black lines painted on a white background.

About 23 ft. east of the wall was an area of gravel metalling, only 1 in. thick at the south edge, but thickening to 6 in. to the north. Two pottery sherds of the second century were found above the gravel surface at the south end of the metalled area, and in the metalling itself was a lump of *opus signinum*. Cutting into the gravel was a pit containing pottery of the twelfth century. There seems little doubt that the metalling was of Roman date, and it may therefore have formed part of the surface of the Roman fort. If so, it is perhaps more likely to have been part of a courtyard than a roadway. The south edge was found, so it cannot have been part of a N.–S. road, and the presence of the ragstone wall to the west, if of the same date, would preclude the possibility of an E.–W. road at this point, unless it terminated at the building represented by the wall fragment.

G.M.

*31 *Noble Street*, 1949

The foundations of an internal corner turret 12–15 ft. long were found within the rounded angle of the S.W. corner of the Roman fort during Professor Grimes's excavation on behalf of the Roman and Mediaeval London Excavation Council. Just to the north of this, a reinforcing wall had been built against the inner face of the west wall of the fort, in order to bring it up to the standard thickness of the Roman city wall when it was incorporated in the latter. (*See Fig.* 31, *p.* 161, *and Pl.* 35.)

J.R.S., XL (1950), *p.* 109. *Pl. IX.*   R. L. S. BRUCE-MITFORD: *Recent Archaeological Excavations in Great Britain*, 1956, *pp.* 127–30.

**See note at end of Gazetteer.*

32 *Wood Street, site of Nos.* 92–100, 1950–1

During the excavations of the R.M.L.E.C. on this site the position of the S. gate of the fort was found. There was apparently a break in the line of the wall just west of Wood Street, and immediately to the north was part of the gravelled roadway which formed the main N.–S. road of the fort. This converged on the line of the modern Wood Street and coincided with the northern part of it. The fort ditch was continuous, but holes for the timber supports of a wooden bridge were found where it ran across the line of the roadway. The structure of the S. gate and of the bridge, however, had been almost obliterated by later disturbances.

J.R.S., XL (1950), *p.* 109; XLI (1951), *p.* 134.   R. L. S. BRUCE-MITFORD: *Recent Archaeological Excavations in Britain*, 1956, *pp.* 127–8.

33 *Wood Street, site of St. Alban's Church*, 1962

Excavations by Professor W. F. Grimes on the site of the ruined church revealed the ragstone walls of two Roman buildings, probably barracks, parallel with the main N.–S. road (*via praetoria*) of the Roman fort. The western building consisted of a single row of rooms with a corridor 9 ft. wide on the west side and a narrower verandah on the east. Facing it, on the opposite side of a N.–S. gravel street, was the second building, which was apparently similar in plan, with a verandah on the west side. Post-holes, pits and gullies of an earlier occupation were also found, containing pottery at least as late as the late first century. These had been filled with clay when the fort was built.

J.R.S., LIII, *p.* 139.

34 *Aldermanbury, site of Barrington House*, 1951

The curve of the ditch at the S.E. corner of the fort was found in the R.M.L.E.C. excavation on the site of Barrington House, immediately west of Aldermanbury. Only the commencement of the curve to the north was seen, the actual corner lying under the street. The wall of the fort had been almost completely destroyed at this point, only a few stones of the foundation remaining. Pottery in the filling of the ditch ranged in date from the late first century at the bottom to the end of the second or early third century at the top.

R. L. S. Bruce-Mitford: *Recent Archaeological Excavations in Britain,* 1956, *p.* 128. *J.R.S., XLII, p.* 97.

35 *St. Martin's-le-Grand, E. side (site of Post Office of* 1825*),* 1845 *and* 1913
A Roman tile inscribed P. P. BRI.LON was found here about 1845, and in 1913 traces of a wattle-and-daub house destroyed by fire were found in the S.W. corner of the site. There were also numerous bricks, roofing-tiles and pieces of painted plaster. Numerous rubbish-pits, a well and traces of a foot-path were found nearby. The latter passed between the pits from the E. side of the site in the direction of Aldersgate. It has been suggested that the pits were originally dug for clay.
Arch., LXVI, p. 246.   *R.C.H.M., p.* 139.

36 *Foster Lane, St. Vedast House,* 1962
Traces of gravel metalling, presumably part of the main E.–W. Roman road, were observed during the builders' excavation on this site. It overlay the natural brick-earth, the surface of which lay at about 43 ft. above O.D., and survived to a thickness of 18 in. The upper levels had evidently been removed in post-Roman times.
G.M.

37 *Cheapside, Nos.* 137–44 *(Cheapside House),* 1957
A patch of packed gravel was seen on the southern edge of the site in the edges of the builders' trenches. It was dirty and packed in layers, and had the appearance of road metalling. Mr. N. C. Cook noted that it was approximately opposite the E. end of St. Vedast Church, Foster Lane. Mr. P. Marsden independently recorded a similar patch of rammed gravel in the foundation trench about 10 ft. to the east. There is little doubt that this metalling formed part of the main Roman road which had been detected at several points on the S. side of Cheapside. There were no further traces in the trenches to the west, but this area appeared to have been disturbed by mediaeval and later building.
G.M.

38 *Goldsmiths' Hall, Foster Lane,* 1830

An altar with a figure of Diana in relief was found on this site, and is still preserved in Goldsmiths' Hall (*Pl.* 86). Associated with it is said to have been a mass of stonework 'more like natural rock than masonry, and so hard that it had to be blasted with gunpowder'.

Gent. Mag., 1831, *I, pp.* 390, 452.   *R.C.H.M., p.* 120.

39 *Gresham Street, Nos.* 2–12, *site of Wax Chandlers' Hall,* 1956–7

The gravel metalling of a Roman road is said to have been seen on this site during the builders' excavation, but there is no record of its exact position or alignment. It is said to have run across the site in a north-westerly direction towards Aldersgate.

40 *Gresham Street, corner of Wood Street (N. side of former church of St. Michael),* 1843–4

A mosaic pavement of white and grey tesserae was found on the W. side of Wood Street on the N. side of St. Michael's, Huggin Lane, and apparently extending beneath the church. Short portions of Roman walls were also observed in sewer excavations just north of this pavement.

Plan by ROACH SMITH *in Guildhall Library.*   *R.C.H.M., p.* 121, *Fig. p.* 122.

41 *Wood Street, W. side, former site of Huggin Lane,* 1851

During excavations for a new sewer in Huggin Lane, a tessellated pavement was found at a depth of 10 ft. from the modern surface. It was laid on a bed of concrete 9 in. thick, and extended from the frontage of Wood Street 45 ft. up Huggin Lane, according to a City Sewer Plan. A large fragment was exhibited a few days later to the Society of Antiquaries by E. B. Price, who described it as being of 'white half-inch tesserae with occasional stripes of grey', and remarked that portions of a coarse red brick pavement were also found. He observed that he had seen large quantities of a similar white mosaic in Lad Lane in 1843 (**42**), and at the corner of Maiden Lane and Wood Street in 1844 (**40**). A portion adjoining the N. side of St. Michael's had evidently extended beneath the church, and it was now found on its S. side.

Proc. Soc. Antiq. (Series I), II, p. 184.   *City Sewer Plan,* 273.
R.C.H.M., p. 123.

42 *Gresham Street, corner of Wood Street,* 1843 *and* 1923

A complex of wall fragments and also tessellated and tiled floors were found in sewer excavations in 1843.

A wall running N.N.E. with cross-wall to the S.E. was recorded by Roach Smith at the junction of Gresham St. and Wood St. A brick wall recorded by Mr. F. Lambert in 1923 ran N.W.–S.E. under the building line at the N.E. corner of the junction – i.e. almost parallel with the cross-wall recorded by Roach Smith. A tile pavement, apparently the floor of a hypocaust, adjoined this on the north, and pavements adjoined both sides of Roach Smith's walls. Roach Smith also recorded fragments of three walls approximately parallel, running N.N.E. by N. – i.e. more nearly in alignment with the fort.

ROACH SMITH: *plan in Guildhall Library.* *J.R.S.*, *XII* (1922), *pp.* 257–8. *R.C.H.M.*, *pp.* 121–2.

43 *Wood Street, S. of Goldsmith Street (Goldsmith House)*, 1961
Fragmentary remains of several ancient structures were observed. The best defined lay just to the east of the centre of the site, and consisted of portions of two parallel ragstone and chalk founda-tion walls 2½ ft. thick and about 22 ft. apart. The southern terminated on the west with a return to the north, probably forming a rectangular compartment with the northern wall. There was no dating evidence, but the alignment is approximately the same as that of the Roman fort to the north and the presumed line of the Roman road to the south. This building overlay an earlier structure with a floor of *opus signinum* sunk into the natural brick-earth, and fragmentary ragstone walls (not marked on the map). A number of sherds of the late first century were found on this floor. About 40 ft. to the S.W. of the corner of the later structure, a short piece of another ragstone wall was seen, with alignment approximately N.W.–S.E. To the north of this, near the centre of the site, were the burnt remains of a daub and timber building, the base of which had been constructed of bricks of unfired clay laid on sleeper beams. It overlay a rubbish pit of the period Nero–Vespasian, and in the debris above was pottery of the late first–early second century. Beneath the building was a dumped layer of brick-earth, through which the rubbish pit had been cut, and under the brick-earth was an earlier rubbish pit which contained pottery of the period of Nero.
G.M.

44 *Blossoms Inn*, 1930 *and* 1955
In 1930 much Roman pottery was found on the site, ranging in date from the Claudian period to the fourth century, but no structures were detected.

Excavations by Professor W. F. Grimes in 1955 revealed traces

of Roman timber buildings on foundations of rafting, made necessary by the waterlogged character of the site. At a depth of about 14 ft. below street level were found four wall-slots meeting at right angles on a large post-hole. These had evidently been partition walls dividing a building into rooms. A series of successive floors, surfaced with oyster shells or fragments of amphorae, suggested that the building had remained in use for a long time.
Guildhall Library Report, 1930–1, *p.* 15.   *J.R.S.*, *XLVI* (1956), *p.* 140.

45 *Gresham Street, Nos.* 20–38 (*formerly King Street, Nos.* 26–7), 1960
Traces of Roman ragstone walls 3 ft. thick, with courses of bonding-tiles, were recorded during the builders' excavation. The position of the fragments observed – mostly in section – indicated the lines of two parallel walls about 10 ft. apart, apparently forming the corner of a room or courtyard round which ran a corridor. The alignment was unusual, being approximately N.E.–S.W., suggesting that these remains were part of the same house as a wall observed on the same alignment on the opposite side of King Street (site of Nos. 13–14) in 1956, and another fragment further south, on the site of No. 33, recorded in 1938 (**48** and **46**). Neither an associated floor nor an occupation layer could be found, and therefore the date of the building within the Roman period is unknown.
G.M.

46 *King Street, No.* 33 (8–9 *Lawrence Lane*), 1938
A fragment of a wall, probably Roman, of ragstone rubble with light sandy mortar, was observed in a builders' excavation. It is said to have run approximately N.W.–S.E. The bottom was in natural sand at a depth of 14 ft. 3 in. below the level of the modern pavement of Lawrence Lane. A section to the south of the wall showed the top of the natural soil 1 ft. above this, and above were dark sandy and gravelly layers presumed to be Roman occupation levels or debris.

    In the extreme S.W. corner of the site, under the Lawrence Lane frontage, an underpinning hole, 4 ft. by 5 ft., was dug through dumped gravel, resembling road material, 6 ft. thick with traces of horizontal layering. Its top was at a depth of 10 ft. 6 in. below the pavement level of Lawrence Lane.
MS. notes by Mr. F. COTTRILL.

47 *King Street, Nos.* 34–5, 1955

In the N. central part of the site was a layered accumulation of gravel 4 ft. thick, which seemed to form part of a road or courtyard which had been re-metalled nine times. A timber-lined well containing pottery of the third–fourth centuries in its lower filling cut through the metalling near the N. edge of the site. There seems to have been a trace of similar gravel metalling in the S.W. corner also.

During trenching for the retaining wall on the W. edge of the site, the workmen cut through a 14 in. layer of burnt daub resting on wood-ash at a depth of 4 ft. below the level of the basement. It contained pottery of the first half of the second century.

G.M.

48 *King Street, Nos.* 13–14, 1956

The S.E. corner of a ragstone building was exposed, one wall running N.E. and the other N.W. At a lower level on the same site was uncovered an earlier path of rammed gravel, apparently running approximately N.–S.

Observations by Mr. P. MARSDEN.

49 *King Street, Atlas Assurance site, N. of Provident Place,* 1963

Excavations were carried out by the staff of Guildhall Museum to investigate the possible existence of an E.–W. and a N.–S. Roman road on the site, suspected as a result of the observation of gravel metalling on sites to the west and north (**47** and **48**). A layered deposit of gravel nearly 3 ft. thick was found in the southern part of the site overlying the natural soil. It was very similar to the deposits seen between King Street and Lawrence Lane (**46** and **47**) and may form part of an E.–W. road. A much thinner layer of metalling in the northern part of the site had the appearance of a minor N.–S. road, with a shallow drainage ditch along its western edge, and a width of about 20 ft. It was not constructed until the early second century and did not continue in use for very long. (See **48**.) In neither case could the exact alignment of the supposed road be ascertained.

No Roman buildings were found, but a scatter of burnt daub and fragments of red and white wall-plaster showed that there were wattle and daub houses in the neighbourhood in the late first and early second centuries.

50 *King Street, No.* 7, 1926–7

Seven or eight occupation levels, none apparently later than the reign of Trajan, were found between 14 and 18 ft. below the surface. On the original gravel surface were fragments of pre-Flavian Samian, including a stamp of *Murranus*, coarse pottery and the stumps of bushes. There was evidence of two fires, one above the earliest occupation level and one over the fourth. A small stream apparently flowed E.S.E. in the southern part of the site.

Mr. G. HOME *in 'Morning Post'*, 27 *January* 1927.   *R.C.H.M.*, *p.* 123.

51 *Cheapside, Nos.* 100–16, *Sun Life Assurance Company building, western end against Milk Street*, 1955–6

A small fragment of patterned mosaic pavement of poor quality, with a *guilloche* ornament, was exposed and destroyed by the mechanical grab at the western end of this site. A photograph was taken, but the precise position could not be recorded.

G.M.

52 *Cheapside, Nos.* 110–16, *Sun Life Assurance Company building*, 1956

A portion of gravel metalling was seen near the northern edge of the site, adjacent to Russia Row. It was made up of numerous layers, with thin bands of dirt between them, to a height of 7 ft. 8 in. above the natural clay on which it rested. At this point it was covered and cut away by modern concrete foundations. A layer of rubbish consisting mostly of oyster shells was seen on the uppermost layer, and from this came pottery of the late first-early second century.

G.M.

53 *Cheapside, Nos.* 100–16, *Sun Life Assurance building*, 1955–6

A hollow filled with black silt, evidently the bed of a stream or a pond, was seen in the builders' cutting on the N. edge of the site. If the former, its general direction was apparently south-easterly. The water tank of the bath-house (**55**) was eventually submerged by black silt in which was found a quantity of Roman pottery, none of it later than the second century. All of this area seems to abound in springs, and a deposit of wet black gravel in the S.E. corner of this site suggested that there may have been an early stream which flowed into the channel seen on the opposite side of the road under St. Mary-le-Bow. If so, it was covered by dumped material and built over in the early Roman period, for a deposit of clay containing pottery of the early second century overlay the gravel, and on this was burnt daub. The stream, whether dammed or driven underground, now presumably supplied the bath-house tank until the latter was swamped and submerged by the rising water-levels of the later second century. *G.M. (Excavations Register* 356 *and* 326.)

54 *Cheapside, Nos.* 100–16, *Sun Life Assurance Company building (formerly Honey Lane Market)*, 1955

Excavations by Professor W. F. Grimes revealed a succession of Roman floors and occupation levels, with post-holes and hearths, probably the remains of timber houses. At a higher level were short stretches of later stone walls, apparently belonging to buildings of simple plan which might possibly be shops.

J.R.S., XLVI (1956), *p.* 139.

55 *Cheapside, Nos.* 100–16, *Sun Life Assurance Company building,* 1955

The foundations of a Roman bath-building were uncovered during the builders' excavation, and recorded by the staff of Guildhall Museum as they came to light. Its alignment was approximately N.N.E., with furnace flue and sudatorium at the N. end, caldarium and tepidarium in the middle, and frigidarium at the S. end, with plunge bath adjoining it on the east. A large wooden water tank was found about 15 ft. to the N.E. There was some evidence of a late first or early second century date, with a rebuilding and enlarging during the second century, and abandonment during the third century. (*See Fig.* 25, *p.* 139, *and Pl.* 60.)

I. NOEL HUME: *A Roman Bath Building in Cheapside*, 1956.

56 *Milk Street (formerly Honey Lane Market)*, 1861

A portion of a tessellated pavement of red and yellow tesserae, about 7 ft. by 4 ft., was found while excavating trenches for new walls at a depth of 17 ft. About 30 ft. to the north were found the remains of a thick wall, apparently Roman. Fragments of wall-paintings were also found.

London and Middlesex Arch. Soc. Trans., II (Proceedings of Meetings), p. 68. *R.C.H.M., p.* 122.

57 *Cheapside, Nos.* 100–16, *Sun Life Assurance Company building, eastern end and alley adjoining*, 1956

A pavement of herring-bone tiling was seen in the builders' cutting protruding from beneath the northern wall of the old Henekey's Tavern (demolished 1955–6). Adjoining this to the west were the remains of a N.–S. wall, the bottom of which consisted of tiles on a ragstone footing. 1 ft. to the west of this was

another N.–S. wall of tiles, which apparently made a corner with
an E.–W. wall seen in the W. face of the builders' cutting. The
room which these walls enclosed had a floor of *opus signinum*. These
two structures seem to have belonged to different buildings, and
it was impossible to ascertain whether they were contemporary.
A rim-sherd of the early second century came from a level overlying
the herring-bone pavement, and a fragment of a small amphora,
probably of the late first century, was found in a black, burnt
deposit below it.
Guildhall Museum Excavations Register 311 *and* 311A.

58 *King Street, No.* 39, 1935
In the S.E. corner of the site were found two patches of coarse
cement flooring at a depth of 16 ft. below pavement level.
Occupation and clay layers continued to a depth of 19 ft.
J.R.S., XXVI (1936), *p.* 256.   *MS. note by* Mr. F. COTTRILL.

59 *Cheapside, S.E. corner of Lawrence Lane,* 1960
Excavations in the bombed cellar were carried out by Professor
W. F. Grimes, who found an accumulation of 4–6 ft. of clay and
other material deposited in the Roman period. Fairly high in
this was the corner of a stone building, most of which lay beneath
the street. A portion of a channelled hypocaust was found, and
there was evidence of quarters of much more flimsy construction
behind the stone building.
J.R.S., LI (1961), *p.* 185.

60 *Cheapside, N.E. corner of Bread Street,* 1595
During excavations for a vault a pavement was found at a depth
of 15 ft., 'and at the further end at the channel, was found a tree
sawed into five steps, which was to step over some brook running
out of the west towards Walbrook, and upon the edge of the said
Brook, as it seemeth, there were found lying along the bodies of
two great trees, the ends whereof were then sawed off, and firm
timber as at the first when they fell, part of the said trees remain
yet in the ground undigged. It was all forced ground, until they
went past the trees afore said, which was about seventeen foot
deep or better, thus much hath the ground of this City in that
place been raised from the main.'
JOHN STOW: *A Survey of London,* 1603, *Kingsford ed., Vol. I, p.* 345.

61 *Cheapside, W. of St. Mary-le-Bow,* 1955
Excavations by Mr. George Rybot and other volunteers under
the direction of Professor W. F. Grimes, on a site which had been
cleared by bombing, uncovered part of the gravelled Roman
E.–W. road. Its southern edge lay about 15 ft. to the south of the
street frontage at a point approximately 100 ft. west of the tower
of St. Mary-le-Bow. A considerable part of the road here lay
beneath the roadway of Cheapside and at this point the southern
edge was parallel with the modern street. This is probably merely
a local irregularity, since the general course of the Roman road
was converging on Cheapside, but the possibility of a branch
road beginning to diverge to the left at this point must be borne in
mind. The main road, however, is likely to have continued in
approximately the same line as it followed east of St. Mary-le-
Bow, crossing to the north side of Cheapside on its way to
Newgate.
J.R.S., XLVI (1956), *p.* 139.   (*Measurements kindly given by Professor
Grimes in advance of publication.*)

62 *Cheapside, St. Mary-le-Bow Church,* 1671–80
Sir Christopher Wren, during excavations for the new church
after the Great Fire, found at a depth of 18 ft. below the street
level 'a Roman Causeway of rough Stone, close and well rammed,
with Roman Brick and Rubbish at the Bottom, for a Foundation,
and all firmly cemented'. It was 4 ft. in thickness, and seems to
have been undoubtedly part of the Roman E.–W. road. The
foundations of the Wren tower were laid on this rammed gravel.
WREN: *Parentalia,* 1750, *p.* 265.   *R.C.H.M., p.* 139.

63 *St. Mary-le-Bow Church,* 1915
An excavation beneath the Norman crypt near the eastern end
of the church revealed two oak piles with planks across their face
extending in a south-south-westerly direction. (*See Pl.* 19.) Parallel to
them was another plank on its edge 4 ft. to the east. The underlying
gravel dipped from a depth of 21 ft. below the street level of Bow
Lane between the planks, to 25–26 ft. in the area to the east of them.
This dip appeared to be the bed of a stream, with the planks and
piles forming the revetment of its W. bank. Above the gravel and
covering the piles was a thick layer of peat-like silt, indicating
that the original stream-banks were eventually swamped. In this
deposit, approximately level with the tops of the piles at a depth
of 18 ft. below street level, were found three fragments of a first
century Samian bowl (*Drag.* 29), which from the description

appears to have been of Flavian date. In view of the line of the ward boundary in this area – which may indicate the course of a later (Anglo-Saxon) stream – and of the discovery of a deposit like stream silt at the N. end of the Aldermary House site (**89**), it is as likely that the stream followed a meandering course eastward to the Walbrook, as that it continued southward to the Thames.

J.B.A.A. (N.S.), XXI (1915), *pp.* 281–93.

64 *Cheapside, Nos. 67–8 (Queen Street, Nos. 1–5),* 1937–8

The gravel metalling of a Roman road was observed in three places on this site, with its top at a depth of about 13 ft. below the pavement level of Queen Street, and its bottom at a depth of about 17 ft. 3 in. resting on a layer of yellow clay 3–6 in. thick, beneath which was greyish-brown natural clay. The gravel was hard and coarse, with horizontal layering. From a low level in it came the base of a Samian cup (*Drag.* 27) with an encircling groove (a pre-Flavian feature). The road was at least 26 ft. 6 in. wide. To the south of it was a square timber-lined well.

MS. notes and plan by Mr. F. COTTRILL.

65 *Cheapside, Nos.* 72–3, 1930

The discovery of oak-piles and camp-sheathing, apparently associated with early Roman pottery, suggested that a tributary stream of the Walbrook may have passed through the site in Roman times. A very early occupation of this area was indicated by the Samian ware found, which included the stamps of potters of the Claudian period.

Guildhall Library Annual Report, 30 *April* 1931, *p.* 14.

66 *Cheapside – Friday Street (now part of New Change House),* 1844 *and* 1886

A fragment of a coarse tessellated pavement was observed 16–18 ft. deep on the site adjoining St. Matthew, Friday Street on the south. When the church was pulled down in 1886 part of the same or another pavement was found at a depth of about 14 ft. (or 18 ft.), 13 ft. from the S. wall of the church and the same distance from the E. wall. It was of rough red tile tesserae. (Later it was preserved on the N. side of the church of St. Vedast, Foster Lane.)

London and Middx. Arch. Soc. Trans., III, p. 339.   *J.B.A.A., XLII, p.* 435.   *R.C.H.M., pp.* 119–20.

67 *New Change, New Change House (Nos. 1–14 Bread Street)*, 1954

A cutting made by Professor Grimes on the E. side of Friday Street (which formerly ran through the site) revealed a fragment of a Roman stone building, but showed that occupation here during the Roman period had consisted mainly of timber-framed huts with clay and gravel floors.

J.R.S., XLIV (1954), *p.* 99.

68 *Watling Street, Gateway House*, 1954

In the N.W. corner of the site, over the whole width of the 5 ft. foundation trench, extending along the latter for about 45 ft., were intermittent traces of a mortar floor overlying tile rubble, at a depth of 2 ft. 7 in. below basement level. The floor was covered with burnt wood, etc., and over this lay 3 in. of rammed gravel, from which came one fourth century sherd.

G.M.

69 *Watling Street, Gateway House*, 1954

The corner of a substantial Roman building, out of alignment with the other Roman structures on the site, was found beneath the eastern end of St. John the Evangelist, Friday Street. North of this, on the extreme edge of the site, was seen a portion of a wall on approximately the same alignment, standing to a height of 4 ft., with a double course of bonding-tiles. Further west and apparently on the alignment of **70** was the corner of another ragstone building or room, with a mortared slot at the corner, presumably to hold a door post.

G.M.

70 *Watling Street, Gateway House*, 1954

Fragments of a ragstone wall, 2 ft. 4 in. thick, were found along the N. side of the eastern part of the site, running E.–W. nearly parallel with modern Watling Street, appearing at basement level at its highest point, and terminating at depths varying from 8 ft. 3 in. to 5 ft. 2 in. below basement level. Another wall 3 ft. thick ran parallel with this, about 13 ft. to the south, but did not extend so far to the west, making a right-angled turn to the south about 60 ft. west of Bread Street. This was of ragstone with yellow mortar. An offset wall ran to the south about 16 ft. west of Bread Street. Parallel with the E.–W. wall was a short length of another, also with yellow mortar, about 6 ft. further south. (*See Fig.* 19, *p.* 127.)

G.M.

71 *Watling Street, Gateway House,* 1954
In the S.E. of the site two parallel E.–W. walls of ragstone were found, about 32 ft. apart, with offsets indicating a partition wall between them. In the room thus enclosed was found a fragment of poor quality mosaic in green and white, probably of late date. In the same area were found traces of the corner of another ragstone structure, apparently earlier, but post-dating a refuse pit of *circa* A.D. 60–80. This wall was subsequently covered by a mortar floor at a depth of 3 ft. below basement level, and was cut by a drainage gully running E.–W. North of the later room was found a floor of coarse red tesserae on a mortar base at a depth of 4 ft. 5 in. below basement level. Further north still, at about the same level, was a floor of *opus signinum* resting on ragstone rubble and overlaid with rammed gravel. (*See Fig.* 19, *p.* 127.)
G.M.

72 *Watling Street, Gateway House,* 1954
About 68 ft. west of Bread Street were traces of a ragstone wall running N.–S. with offsets to the west. On the E. side was a plinth, terminating at 5 ft. 10 in. below basement level. The wall post-dated a refuse pit of about A.D. 60–80. To the west, in the central part of the site, were traces of two floors of *opus signinum,* the lower at 5 ft. below basement level overlaid by a burnt level, and the upper about 1 ft. above the first. Further south was a scrap of a coarse red tessellated pavement at a depth of 2 ft. below basement level. (*See Fig.* 19, *p.* 127.)
G.M.

73 *Watling Street, about* 1833
During excavations for a sewer, a roadway is said to have been found somewhere in Watling Street, at a depth of about 20 ft. It had a substratum of chalk and a pavement of flint. It should be noted that its position in Watling Street is quite unknown, and that it was at a much greater depth than the supposed Roman roadway encountered at the junction of Queen Victoria Street and Watling Street (**92**).
Gent. Mag., 1833, *II, p.* 422.   *R.C.H.M., p.* 145.
V.C.H. (*London*), *I, p.* 34.

74 *Watling Street, Watling House,* 1954
Near the N.W. corner of the site was found a room about 14 ft. by 6 ft., with ragstone walls and a floor of coarse red tesserae at a

depth of 4 ft. 9 in. below basement level. Flavian sherds were found beneath the floor. The N. wall of the room seemed to continue the line of an E.–W. wall recorded on the Gateway House site. Near the N. edge of the site traces of another E.–W. wall were seen, and these seemed to continue the line of the northernmost wall on the Gateway House site. Adjoining the N. wall of the small room was another wall continuing to the east (probably of a later extension). Adjacent to this on the south was a floor of coarse tesserae at a depth of 3 ft. 9 in. below basement level. This was overlaid at the edge by a moulding of *opus signinum*. (*See Fig.* 19, *p.* 127.)

G.M.

75 *Watling Street, Watling House,* 1954

To the south of the small room (**74**) were found traces of the ragstone walls of a larger room about 20 ft. by 16 ft., and over these lay the hypocaust of a later building at a depth of about 3 ft. 5 in. below basement level. The hypocaust floor was covered with burnt wood ash, suggesting a destruction by fire of the later building. Towards the eastern side of the site was found an E.–W. wall in a line with the N. wall of the larger room. (Dating evidence: a Claudian Samian sherd was found in the foundation trench of this wall, and five Flavian sherds came from an overlying layer of tiles.) A short piece of another wall was seen, parallel with this E.–W. wall, and about 7 ft. to the north. (*See Fig.* 19, *p.* 127.)

G.M.

76 *Watling Street, Watling House,* 1954

On the eastern edge of the site, at a depth of 9 ft. below basement level, portions of three E.–W. walls of ragstone were seen, the northernmost with yellow mortar, the other two with pale mortar. Traces of a mortar floor were seen just north of the southernmost wall, at a depth of 6 ft. On the southern side of this wall was an indication of a plinth at a depth of 6 ft. 2 in., and this overlay a pit containing pottery of the late first and early second centuries. (*See Fig.* 19, *p.* 127.)

G.M.

77 *Watling Street, Watling House,* 1954

Near the western edge of the site were found three ragstone walls of a room, appearing at depths from 2 ft. to 7 ft. below basement level. A concrete offset, sealing the wall, was seen along the inside of the N.–S. wall at a depth of 7 ft. A portion of tessellated floor was seen inside the room at a depth of 3½ ft. below basement level, overlying a layer 1 ft. thick of burnt wall-plaster, daub, etc., in yellow-brown clay. The southern E.–W. wall only appeared at a depth of 7 ft., and was overlaid by a layer of burnt wood, oyster-shells, etc. (*See Fig.* 19, *p.* 127.)

G.M.

78 *Watling Street, Watling House,* 1954

In the S.E. corner of the site were found the ragstone walls of another room, with N.–S. wall in alignment with that of the room to the north, but with the room enclosure lying to the west instead of the east of this line. Within the room was a trace of an *opus signinum* floor at a depth of 1 ft. 3 in. below basement level. There were indications of an offset wall to the east, and north of this was a floor of *opus signinum* on mortar at a depth of 1 ft. 6 in. below basement level. This was overlaid with clay and wall-plaster. Traces of a mortar floor were seen on the south, also at a depth of 1 ft. 6 in. The N.–S. wall continued to the south, and there was another wall off-set to the west, parallel with the S. wall of the room. In the compartment enclosed by these two walls was a layer of burnt clay, containing fragments of a pot of about A.D. 50–70 at a depth of 2 ft. 7 in. to 3 ft. Immediately to the south was a floor of *opus signinum* at a depth of 1 ft. 8 in. overlaying pottery of about A.D. 90–120. (*See Fig.* 19, *p.* 127.)

G.M.

79 *Watling Street, Watling House,* 1954

On the S. edge of the site, adjoining Cannon Street, was a wall 2 ft. thick running E.–W. At the W. end was a corner, with a wall 1 ft. 6 in. thick off-set to the south, at a depth of 3 ft. 9 in. below basement level. At the E. end the wall joined a N.–S. wall 1 ft. 10 in. thick, which showed at a depth of 4 ft. 11 in. below basement level. (*See Fig.* 19, *p.* 127.)

G.M.

80 *Watling Street, Watling House,* 1954

A small portion of a wall was seen in section on the S. edge of the site, evidently running approximately N.–S. The base was of ragstone rubble resting on a foundation of gravel with mortar. On the top of the ragstone was a single course of tiles, and above this the wall was of *clay*, faced on the west with wall-plaster. On the E. side the clay was reddened with fire, and against it lay a thick deposit of burnt wood, daub and tile. On the W. side, near the foot of the wall, was a layer of tile debris overlying clay, both

deposits resting against the wall, and presumably post-dating it. From the layer of tile debris came fragments of Claudian pottery. It is therefore possible that this building was destroyed in the Boudiccan revolt. (*See Fig.* 19, *p*, 127).
G.M.

81 *Sermon Lane*, 1844
A wall about 70 ft. long, parallel with the road, and apparently turning under the houses on the E. side at each end was found in a sewer excavation at a depth of 14 ft.
R.C.H.M., p. 141.

82 *Knightrider Street, W. of Sermon Lane (formerly Little Knightrider Street*), 1845(?)
During sewer excavations at the junction of Sermon Lane and Little Knightrider Street, the corner made by two stone walls was encountered. One of these ran eastward approximately in the line of the street; the other to the south at a right angle with it. Some distance to the west another N.–S. wall was encountered running across the street. This is described in a note on the City Sewer Plan where the walls are marked as 'old stone and tiles wall'.
City Sewers Plan 81.

83 *Carter Lane, S. side, E. of Sermon Lane*, 1960
Six trenches cut in this area by Professor W. F. Grimes showed that the natural surface had been cut away by Roman quarry-pits, sometimes to a depth of 22 ft. below modern street level. There was little sign of any structures earlier than mediaeval.
J.R.S., LI (1961), *p.* 185.

84 *Cannon Street, Bracken House ('Financial Times' building*), 1955
Excavations by Professor W. F. Grimes showed that gravel had been dug on this site in Roman times. A quarry-pit 40 ft. wide and 5 ft. deep ran across the area examined.
J.R.S., XLVI (1956), *p.* 140.

85 *Cannon Street – formerly Little Friday Street*, 1845
Walls found in sewer excavations are recorded on a City Sewers Plan in this position. No further details seem to be known.
City Sewers Plan 373.   *R.C.H.M., p.* 111; *p.* 124, *Fig.* 43 (155).

86 *Cannon Street, Fire Station,* 1906

A small Roman bath, 14½ ft. by 8¾ ft. with long axis N.–S., was found with its bottom at a depth of 16 ft. 9 in. below street level on the N. edge of the site, bisected by the building line of the Cannon Street frontage. The tile walls stood to a height of 3 ft., and the bottom was of *opus signinum* over white mortar which rested on a base of sandstone rubble. Brick steps built with the walls gave access to the bath at its S.W. corner.

Arch., LX, pp. 214 *ff.*   *R.C.H.M., p.* 111 *and Fig.* 33, *p.* 112.

87 *Cannon Street, N. side, W. of Bow Lane,* 1877

A mosaic pavement was found at a depth of 12 ft. below the modern street level, when foundations were dug for new buildings two or three doors west of the junction of Cannon Street with Bow Lane. It was of white and black tesserae with a border of red.

J.B.A.A., XXXVIII, p. 260.   *R.C.H.M., p.* 111.

88 *Watling Street, Nos.* 67–9, 1961

A small excavation at the rear of this building revealed the remains of a tessellated pavement, much disturbed and broken, made of coarse red brick tesserae with a few white ones also. It lay 65–75 ft. behind the frontage of Watling Street at 40½ ft. above Ordnance Datum.

G.M.

89 *Queen Street, Nos.* 10–15, *Aldermary House,* 1960

Seven Roman wells were recorded on this site. As on the site of the Bank of London and South America on the opposite side of Queen Street, they were of two types – square wells with sides supported by a box-like wooden framework of planks, and round barrel wells. In addition there were several mediaeval and later wells, and others that could not be dated. Immediately to the north is the appropriately named *Well Court.* On the northern edge of the site adjacent to this was a hollow filled with black peat-like mud, resembling a pond or stream-bed. It seems possible that it was a southern continuation of the stream observed in various places on the N. side of Cheapside, and it may have determined the boundary between Cheap and Cordwainer Wards as it flowed eastward to the Walbrook. Its course, however, is by no means certain.

Guildhall Museum Excavations Register 604, 612, 624, 626, 642, 644, 645.

90 *Queen Street, opposite Well Court, 1836–41*
Walls were found crossing the street, and in the middle, opposite
Well Court, was a red tessellated pavement, 14 ft. square, at a
depth of 13 ft. In the same excavation were found two thin bands
of pure gold, apparently armlets.
Arch., XXIX, p. 155.

91 *Queen Street, No.* 82 (*Queen Victoria Street, Nos.* 40–66), *Bank of*
London and South America, 1953–4
Fourteen Roman timber-lined wells were found on this site during
the builders' excavation – as well as eleven mediaeval and later
wells. The Roman wells were both square and round, the former
having the upper portion supported by a box-like frame of oak
planks, and the latter by a barrel-like structure. (*See Plates* 108, 110
and 112.) In a square well near the northern edge of the site, filled
before the end of the first century, were found a wooden ladder,
a pair of leather trunks, a wooden spoon and a wooden dipper.
(*See Plates* 113–16.)
J.R.S., XLV (1955), *pp.* 138–9.

92 *Queen Victoria Street, at junction with Watling Street,* 1869
During excavations for Queen Victoria Street an ancient roadway was found between St. Mary Aldermary and St. Antholin
Budge Row, at a depth of 10 ft. 3 in. below the surface. It is said
to have been 14 ft. in width and nearly in line with the modern
Watling Street. The metalling, which was hard and well made,
was of rough stones and gravel, cambered on the surface. In the
upper part were found quantities of Roman pottery.
J. E. PRICE: *Description of a Roman Tessellated Pavement in Bucklersbury,*
1870, *p.* 77.   *R.C.H.M., p.* 145.   *V.C.H.* (*London*), *I, p.* 34.

93 *Peter's Hill, upper end near Knightrider Street,* 1863 *and* 1961
During excavations for drainage in 1863, a Roman wall was
found 'almost at the upper extremity of St. Peter's Hill'. The
footing stood in gravel and sand, and above this were 3 ft. of
rubble wall, 3 ft. 8 in. thick at the base. Then came courses of
Roman bricks to a height of 3 ft. 10 in., then rubble again for a
further 2 ft. 2 in., diminishing in thickness to 2 ft. 9 in. at the top,
which lay 5 ft. 10 in. below the surface of the ground. The wall
did not lie parallel with Knightrider Street which veered northwards near this point, and it was carefully measured to record its
alignment. A few days later, a continuation of the wall was found

on the N. side of Knightrider Street, tending 'to the exact line of the front wall of the parish church a little to the eastward' (i.e. St. Mary Magdalen, which formerly stood on the N. side of Knightrider Street). (See **94**.)

The eastern end of this stretch of wall was seen in the builders' excavation of 1961. (*See Pl.* 55.) The footings here overlay an artificial deposit of clay and gravel which filled a large hollow, possibly a gravel quarry. Above this the foundations cut through a large refuse pit containing pottery of the late first century. They were of ragstone and white cement, and had evidently been laid in a boarded trench, as impressions of vertical timbers were seen in both faces of the wall. (Cf. **99**.) These posts, of which only the holes remained, seem to have been squared off at the ends, and did not penetrate below the base of the ragstone foundation. The wall survived to a height of about 5 ft. 6 in. above the footings, but the upper 1 ft. 6 in. was of a different build, and had refuse layers containing pottery of the late third–fourth centuries piled against its N. face.
Arch., *XL*, *pp.* 48–9.   *R.C.H.M.*, *p.* 141.   *G.M.*, *August* 1961.

94 *Knightrider Street, at bottom of Knightrider Court,* 1844 *and* 1863
A brick-lined culvert of horseshoe form, made of tiles 12 in. long set radially, was found in a wall of Kentish rag, during excavation for a sewer in 1844, in front of No. 15, Little Knightrider Street. The culvert was filled in with earth.

The same wall, or its continuation immediately to the east, was seen during further sewer excavations in 1863, on the N. side of Knightrider Street, tending to the exact line of the front of St. Mary Magdalen's Church, which then stood on the S.W. corner of Old Change. It was also noted that it seemed to be a continuation of the wall recorded at the top of Peter's Hill. (See **93**.)
J.B.A.A., *I*, *p.* 253.   *Arch.*, *XL*, *pp.* 48–9.   *R.C.H.M.*, *pp.* 125, 141.

95 *Knightrider Street, W. of Old Change,* 1961
A further length of 24½ ft. of the southern face of this long ragstone wall was exposed. Above the foundation a single course of neatly squared ragstone blocks remained. They were set in a yellow cement, and the wall was of very solid and tough construction. Above the squared blocks and set back 1½ in. was a course of Roman bricks, approximately level with the surface of Queen Victoria Street to the south of the site. The rest of the wall had previously been destroyed.
G.M.

96 *Knightrider Street, at junction with Old Change,* 1961
Another portion of this wall was uncovered when a sewer was diverted at the junction of Old Change and Knightrider Street in 1961. It extended westwards from the eastern edge of Old Change for 29 ft. The N. face of the foundation had survived and was carefully examined for impressions of timber posts. None were present, presumably because the foundation was laid here in firm gravel. As elsewhere on this wall there was no trace of any cross-wall to the north. The section at the western end of the wall (**93**) was visible at the same time as this stretch, and it could be confirmed that both were in alignment.
G.M.

97 *Knightrider Street, N. side, opposite St. Nicholas Church (site of Old Change House),* 1955
During the builders' excavation a Roman culvert of radially set tiles was observed opposite St. Nicholas Church, in a ragstone wall. It was an arched structure with internal height of 3 ft. $\frac{1}{2}$ in. and width at base of 2 ft. (*See Pl.* 56.) The wall ran right across the site from Distaff Lane to Old Change, a distance of more than 125 ft. It survived to a height of 6 ft., and had been used in places as the foundation for walls of the eighteenth and nineteenth centuries. A single course of Roman tiles remained at one point, immediately overlaid by modern brickwork. Only the northern face of the wall was seen, and it was impossible to expose an adjacent section. It was noticed, however, that the ground beneath the wall changed from brick-earth at the eastern end of the site to clean ballast at the western end. At a point 15 ft. west of the culvert, the brick-earth dipped away, leaving a gully filled with alternate layers of sand and ballast, each about 1 in. thick. These overlay a layer of sand about 8 in. thick that rested on ballast. It extended for about 9 ft., and appeared to have been deposited by running water.
G.M.

98 *Knightrider Street, N. side, opposite E. end of St. Nicholas Church (site of 'Financial Times' building),* 1956
A continuation of the Roman wall recorded on the site of Old Change House in 1955 was observed here in the following year. A length of about 6 ft. of the N. face was visible at one time, and this was carefully examined for impressions of timber posts like those found in the wall further east (**99**) and later (in 1961) seen in the wall much further west (**93**). No traces of these could be found, and there were no facing stones. In close association with

the wall, and level with the uppermost remaining course, was found a small bronze 'knee' brooch (Collingwood Group V) of the middle of the second century (Guildhall Museum Excavations Register 365). The wall survived here to a height of about 9 ft., and a length extending for 14 ft. 3 in. west of Distaff Lane was seen. Further east it had been destroyed.

G.M.

99 *Friday Street, bottom end,* 1906

A slightly curved or angled wall, running diagonally across the junction of Friday Street and Knightrider Street, was found with its foundation resting on ballast at a depth of 21 ft. below street level. It had been built between boarding with upright posts 4 ft. apart, which had left an impression on both sides of the wall. It was 4 ft. thick and 9 ft. high, the top lying 12 ft. below street level. At an earlier date, a continuation of this wall had been found while constructing a sewer in Friday Street.

Arch., LX, pp. 219 *ff.   R.C.H.M., p.* 120 *and Fig.* 40.

100 *Peter's Hill, upper end,* 1845 *and* 1961

A wall was marked on a City Sewers Plan further south than **93**, and the two are identified in the Royal Commission's Report. The detailed account given of the latter portion of wall and its position, however, rules out this possibility, and a second Roman wall was in fact seen in the builders' excavation of 1961, 30 ft. 7 in. south of wall **93**. It ran E.–W. right across Peter's Hill approximately parallel with the wall to the north. The foundations were 4 ft. 4 in. wide and composed of ragstone and hard white cement. They had been set into the undisturbed gravel. A single course of squared ragstone blocks and a course of red bonding tiles remained above the foundation, where the wall was 4 ft. thick.

R.C.H.M., p. 141, *and Fig.* 43, *p.* 124 *(Plan A* 168).   *G.M.,* 1961. *City Sewers Plan* 373.

101 *Old Change Hill (formerly Lambeth Hill),* 1845

The position of a wall is indicated in this street on a City Sewers Plan.

City Sewers Plan of 1845.   *R.C.H.M., p.* 125.

102 *Queen Victoria Street, W. of St. Nicholas Church,* 1961

A portion of an E.–W. ragstone wall was seen in section 80 ft. west of the W. wall of St. Nicholas Church. It seems likely that it was a continuation of the wall (**101**) seen under Old Change Hill in 1845. It was 4 ft. thick, but the N. face had been cut away by a modern foundation, so that originally it must have been somewhat thicker. The surviving N. edge was 32 ft. 4 in. south of the S. edge of the Knightrider Street wall (**96**). The two walls were very similar in structure, and this find, in conjunction with the two other pieces of wall (**100** and **101**) found further west, suggests that there may possibly have been a second wall, approximately parallel with the long Knightrider Street wall (**93–99**), lying 30–32 ft. to the south of it.

G.M.

103 *Bread Street, junction with Knightrider Street (now under Queen Victoria Street),* 1844–5
A mass of masonry was found during sewer excavations at this point, and its position is indicated on a City Sewers Plan. An engraving published in the *Illustrated London News,* 20 July 1844, shows a Roman wall apparently parallel to the sewer.
R.C.H.M., p. 108.   *City Sewers Plan* 373.

104 *Great Trinity Lane, junction with Queen Victoria Street (now under Queen Victoria Street),* 1845
Portions of immense walls, with some layers of bonding-tiles, were found during sewer excavations. There were remains of fresco paintings on some of these.
J.B.A.A., I, p. 254.   *R.C.H.M., p.* 145.

105 *Little St. Thomas Apostle, now part of Cannon Street,* 1848
During sewer excavations, the remains of great walls of chalk, stone and flat bricks, stucco painted in red and green, drain tiles and other Roman remains were found. There was a considerable quantity of charred wood and ashes at a depth of 16 ft.
J.B.A.A., X, p. 195.   *R.C.H.M., p.* 141.

106 *Cannon Street, at junction of Queen Street,* 1850
Fragments of a tessellated pavement in black and white were found. The exact position is not recorded.
Proc. Soc. Ant. (Ser. I), II, p. 93.   *R.C.H.M., p.* 111.

107 *Cannon Street, W. of Tower Royal,* 1852
Below the mediaeval fragments of Tower Royal were found Roman walls, 3 ft. thick, built of ragstone, chalk and tiles on a

foundation of wooden piles. A little to the west was a pavement of plain red tesserae. 60 ft. north of the street frontage were three piers 6 ft. apart, built of tiles 14½ in. by 11 in.

J.B.A.A., X, pp. 190*ff.   Illus. Lond. News,* 1852, *I, p.* 308. *R.C.H.M., p.* 111.

108 *Great St. Thomas Apostle,* 1846
A few yards from Queen St. a Roman mosaic pavement was seen, 7 ft. below street level. It had a pattern in red, white, yellow and black tesserae, and probably formed part of a large pavement. It was subsequently destroyed.

J.B.A.A., II, p. 350.   *R.C.H.M., p.* 141.

109 *Peter's Hill, lower portion, near Upper Thames Street,* 1845(?)
A wall in the lower part of Peter's Hill was indicated on a City Sewers Plan of 1845. No further details are known, but it seems likely that this was a continuation of the cement retaining wall of the upper terrace seen in 1961 on the site to the east (**110**).

R.C.H.M., p. 141 (*Plan A* 169).   *City Sewers Plan* 373.

110 *Lambeth Hill, W. side (E. of Peter's Hill),* 1961
Two chalk platforms supported by piles formed an upper and lower terrace. The former, seen only in the N.W. corner of the site, was about 20½ ft. above O.D., and had an E.–W. retaining wall of cement, 3 ft. thick, on its S. edge. This survived to a height of 3 ft. – 2 ft. short of the difference in level between the two terraces, which was presumably its original height. It contained a large squared block of stone, evidently re-used material. A sandstone block, 3 by 3 by 1 ft., with a bevel on the N. side as if for a plinth, lay on the upper platform 30 ft. north of the retaining wall. The lower terrace, at about 9½ ft. above O.D., extended to the N. frontage of Thames St. Two re-used stone blocks were exposed in the body of its chalk platform. The whole site was curiously clear of pottery and other datable refuse, but in the W. part of the site there was structural evidence that the lower terrace was of the Roman period. (See **116**.) (For the lower chalk platform, see *Pl.* 29.)

G.M.

111 *Lambeth Hill, W. side (S. end of the new road and W. of this),* 1960–1
During excavations for the new road, four parallel rows of oak piles about 1 ft. apart were uncovered, crossing the trench from

east to west. The piles were 4–6 in. in diameter and pointed at both ends, with their tops about 14½ ft. below the level of Upper Thames Street. They presumably formed the foundation of a wall about 5 ft. thick. Building debris, consisting of *opus signinum*, Roman bricks, a fragment of white tessellated pavement which had been re-used as building material, and wall-plaster painted red, white and black – probably the remains of the fallen wall – lay to the south of the piles, mixed with brown river silt, as if the wall had collapsed as a result of the encroachment of the river.

In the subsequent builders' excavation, a row of piles was found about 47 ft. to the west, continuing the line of the northernmost row. Parallel with this, and about 12 ft. to the south, was a multiple row of piles.

G.M.

112 *Lambeth Hill,* 1961

Builders' excavations exposed two portions of Roman wall, 3 ft. thick, constructed of ragstone with a double or triple course of bonding-tiles. Both ran approximately E.–W., but were not quite in alignment, as the western end of the eastern portion curved slightly to the north of the western portion. The eastern end of the latter was squared off, as if for the edge of a doorway.

It is an interesting fact that the boundary between the former parishes of St. Mary Mounthaw and St. Mary Somerset seems to have coincided with the Roman walls, even following their kink. There was also archaeological evidence that part of the wall at least had been visible in the early Middle Ages, for refuse layers containing imported Pingsdorf pottery of the eleventh–twelfth centuries lay piled against it.

G.M.

113 *Upper Thames Street, bottom of Lambeth Hill,* 1961

In the middle of the roadway at the bottom of the old Lambeth Hill (30 ft. east of the new road) a ragstone wall was seen during the builder's excavation, running approximately N.–S. It had three double courses of red bonding-tiles and stood about 7 ft. high. The northern part was only 1½ ft. thick, but to the south, near the southern edge of the site, it had widened to more than 4 ft. 4 in. The original thickness of this southern portion could not be ascertained, as the W. face had been destroyed by the old sewer. In the body of the wall was a squared ragstone block, evidently re-used.

Nearly 10 ft. to the east of the narrow portion of the wall, and apparently parallel with it, was the foundation of a massive wall,

12 ft. thick, and built of very hard white cement, ragstone and broken Roman tiles.

G.M.

114 *Upper Thames Street, at foot of Lambeth Hill*, 1841
Workmen excavating for the sewer in Upper Thames Street met no impediment between Blackfriars and Lambeth Hill, but at the foot of the latter were obstructed by a great wall 'which formed an angle at Lambeth Hill and Thames St.'. It was 8–10 ft. thick, with its upper part 9 ft. below street level, and was constructed of ragstone, flint and lime, bonded at intervals with courses of tiles. It contained much re-used material. The footings were a course of hewn sandstones 3–4 ft. by 2 ft. by 2½ ft. cemented with *opus signinum*, at a depth of about 17 ft. below street level. These were laid on a stratum of chalk and stones supported by oak piles about 6 ft. above O.D. (cf. **110**, **116**), so that there seem to have been two artificial terraces here sloping slightly towards the river – at about 7–9½ ft. and 18–20½ ft. above O.D. The wall is said to have continued with occasional breaks as far as Queenhithe, and Roach Smith believed it was the city riverside wall. This seems unlikely as it did not continue to the west, but 'formed an angle', and similar massive walls were found to the north (**115**, **113**). It may possibly have formed a quayside, however. From Roach Smith's account, the wall was on the line of the Thames Street sewer, so it cannot have been identical with the wall found in 1924 (**115**) as is suggested in the Royal Commission's Report. The position of the wall described by Roach Smith is in fact clearly shown on a City Sewers Plan, with its broken eastern end near the middle of Upper Thames Street opposite the entrance to Brook's Yard. A dotted line marks the position of a N.–S. wall running up Lambeth Hill at a right angle to the great E.–W. wall – evidently the W. side of the wall seen in 1961 (**113**). Notes on the plan record that both walls were 8 ft. below the surface.
C. ROACH SMITH: *Illustrations of Roman London, pp.* 18–19.
R.C.H.M., pp. 92–3.   *Arch., XXIX, p.* 150.   *City Sewers Plan* 315.

115 *Upper Thames Street, E. of Lambeth Hill*, 1924
During the construction of a sewer under Brook's Yard from Upper Thames Street, two Roman walls were seen running E.–W. The southern wall, which was half under the pavement and half under the building line, was about 8 ft. thick, and was believed to have been the supposed river wall seen by Roach Smith in 1841 (**114**). Excavations in 1961, however, showed that

this wall did not continue to the foot of Lambeth Hill, where Roach Smith saw his wall (probably nearer the middle of Upper Thames Street), and that it was almost certainly part of the structure with thick walls which was seen in 1961 (113). The southern wall seen in 1924 was of ragstone rubble concrete, with its foundations laid between two rows of contiguous piles. The tops of these were about 14 ft. below the road level of Upper Thames Street, and a few inches above them was a course of tiles. A second course occurred 2 ft. higher.

The second wall was about 15 ft. north of the first, and was 5 ft. thick. This also had its foundations laid between two rows of piles, but these were not contiguous. A thick bonding course occurred just above the heads of the piles, and above this the wall was battered on both sides and finished with a flat top 2 ft. wide, about 14 ft. below the modern surface. On the S. face of the wall was a mass of puddled clay.

R.C.H.M., p. 93.

116 *Upper Thames Street, Lambeth Hill, E. side,* 1961

A retaining wall of ragstone overlay the gravel, forming three steps rising from west to east at the N. edge of the lower chalk platform. (See **110**.) The bottom step was 3½ ft. high, and the total height of the steps 6½ ft.

The stepped wall extended at least 12 ft. from south to north, and at its southern end was a line of large squared stone blocks running from east to west. These were evidently re-used in this position, for one had a channel for a cramp, and another, which had evidently once formed part of a plinth, had a bevelled edge – both of these features being upside down. The wall was, however, clearly of Roman date, and provided evidence for the Roman date of the chalk platform, for the upper course of a characteristic double line of bonding-tiles extended over the row of stone blocks which overlay the chalk platform. The latter was overlaid by the wall for about 4 ft. from its northern edge.

There was a ragstone wall with a foundation of piles aligned with the western edge of the stepped wall, extending from 8 to 18 ft. to the south of it. To the west of this, at a lower level *beneath the chalk platform*, were traces of earlier walls on a different alignment (not shown on map). (*For the lower chalk platform, see Pl.* 29.)

G.M.

117 *Old Fish Street Hill (E. of Lambeth Hill),* 1845

During sewer excavations near the entrance into Upper Thames Street, a wall was found running parallel with the street towards

Upper Thames Street. It was 3–4 ft. thick and lay at a depth of 16 ft. Another wall crossed it at right angles, and through this ran an arched culvert 3 ft. wide and 3½ ft. high, with tiles set horizontally in the upper part of the arch. The position of the cross-wall is shown on a City Sewers Plan. The walls were built on large hewn stones, many of which had been previously used, laid on wooden piles. About 16 ft. from the culvert, by the side of the wall parallel to the sewer, were 'several tiers of tiles each 2 ft. by 1½ ft. placed upon massive hewn stones'.

J.B.A.A., I, pp. 45–6.   *R.C.H.M., p.* 119.   *City Sewers Plan* 373.

118 *Fye Foot Lane*, 1845(?)
During sewer excavations two stone walls were found running E.–W. across the street. The southern wall was 4 ft. thick, and the northern 5 ft. Further north, a Roman pavement was found at a depth of 4 ft.
Information from a City Sewers Plan, indicated on a map in Guildhall Museum.

119 *Bread Street Hill*, 1845
During sewer excavations in the lower part of Bread Street Hill, near Upper Thames Street, two walls were found crossing the street.
R.C.H.M., p. 123.   *City Sewers Plan* 373.

120 *Huggin Hill, Upper Thames Street*, 1845
On a City Sewers Plan, two walls were recorded crossing the street.
R.C.H.M., p. 123.   *City Sewers Plan* 373.

121 *Little Trinity Lane, Nos.* 10–12, 1929–30
A ragstone wall with courses of tiles, 5 ft. thick, with its base set in London Clay at a depth of 15½ ft. below the modern surface, was observed running E.–W. from Huggin Hill across the site for over 36 ft. 10 ft. to the south of this was a 2 ft. wall parallel with it, and there were traces of other walls at right angles. The two E.–W. walls rose almost to the surface where they passed under Huggin Hill, and the larger was pierced with an arched culvert of voussoir tiles. About 40 ft. to the north was another Roman ragstone wall parallel with these, underlying the S. wall of Painter-Stainers' Hall, and over 20 ft. long. Its western end abutted against a wall built entirely of large tiles set in mortar

containing crushed tile. These foundations were at a considerably
higher level than the two walls found further south and must have
belonged to another building. The difference in level suggested
that the slope towards Upper Thames Street was considerably
steeper in Roman times.

There seems no doubt that the more southerly building formed
part of the bath-house found to the west of Huggin Hill in 1964,
too late for inclusion in the map. (*See Plan, Fig. 26, p.* 141.)
J.R.S., XIX (1929), *p.* 200.   *Guildhall Library Annual Report* 1930–
31, *p.* 15.   *Unpublished plan by* Mr. G. C. DUNNING.

122 *Skinners' Lane* (*formerly Maiden Lane*), *E. of Garlick Hill,* 1848
During sewer excavations a Roman pavement was found here,
but no further particulars are known.
R.C.H.M., p. 132.

123 *Upper Thames Street, opposite Vintners' Hall,* 1839
During sewer excavations in the middle of the street, the remains
of a wall were found running parallel with the line of the river, at
a depth of 10 ft. from the surface. It was built of alternate layers
of flint, chalk and flat tiles, and was believed to be Roman. It
seems to have formed part of the long wall observed by Roach
Smith (**114** and **124**), although the description of its structure is
a little different. If, however, the supposed river wall was not
defensive, but merely a series of quays, as now seems likely, some
variation of the structural details might be expected.
R.C.H.M., p. 93.

124 *Upper Thames Street, at junction with Queen Street, about* 1839
C. Roach Smith observed what he believed to be the river wall
at this point, and noted that it was precisely similar in character
to the wall which he subsequently saw at the foot of Lambeth
Hill (**114**).
C. ROACH SMITH: *Illustrations of Roman London, p.* 19.
Arch., XXIX, p. 151.   *R.C.H.M., p.* 93.

125 *St. Martin Vintry,* 1956–7
A Roman pier was found resting on a sleeper wall running E.–W.,
which consisted of three courses of ragstone capped by a double
course of tiles. Over the top of the wall was a layer of pink *opus
signinum.* The pier was constructed of Roman tiles, some whole
and others broken, set in yellowish mortar. The sides were

covered with a layer of *opus signinum* 1 in. thick, overlaid with plaster. A concave moulding at the top was painted red, and the sides between this and a tile offset at the base were painted white with splashes of red. A few sherds of pottery of the late first or early second century came from the loose filling around the pier.

Several walls of stone and tiles were seen in builders' trenches in the northern part of the site. One of these, an E.–W. wall close to the western edge, had a plaster facing on its S. side.

G.M.

126 *Basinghall Street, S. of Church Alley*, 1861

In excavations for the foundations of the Sewers Office to the north of Guildhall, a tessellated pavement of irregular cubes of grey slate and white marble was found.

J.B.A.A., XVII, p. 325. *R.C.H.M., p.* 122.

127 *Guildhall, rear of*, 1951

Between the third and fourth buttresses from the west a stratum of silt was observed during the builders' excavation. There were a quantity of rushes in the deposit, and these lay in a N.–S. direction, suggesting that the silt was in the bed of a stream which flowed in a southerly direction. This must have been drained or diverted before the first Guildhall was built, but the silt contained a few small fragments of twelfth century pottery, indicating that the stream-bed was still open at that date. (*See also* **128**.) Immediately to the west of the stream, Roman pottery of the third century and a coin of Postumus were found in the filling of a mediaeval pit, which had been cut through Roman levels where another coin of the late third century was found.

G.M.

128 *Guildhall, site of Council Chamber*, 1882–3

When the foundations were dug for the Council Chamber, an ancient stream-bed was found. Its direction was from N.W. to S.E., and it seems likely that it continued in this direction and met the tributary which flowed into Lothbury between Coleman Street and Moorgate (**155**). There was still so much water in the ground that a table of concrete had to be prepared as a support for the Council Chamber, but the open stream obviously cannot have survived the building of the fifteenth century Guildhall. It is possible, however, that it was not a Roman stream-bed, but was produced by a diversion of the stream which flowed

about 80 ft. to the W. (**127**) when the first Guildhall was built
in the very early Middle Ages.

Arch., LXIII, p. 314 *and Fig.* 25, *p.* 315.

129 *Guildhall,* 1951

A trial-hole revealed a Roman foundation on the E. side of
buttress No. 3 on the S. side of Guildhall. The mediaeval buttress
terminated at a depth of about 10 ft. 6 in. beneath the basement
floor of the Comptroller's office, and under it were the remains of a
substantial Roman wall, consisting of a course of squared ragstone blocks resting on two courses of bonding-tiles, one of which
appeared to be a re-used roofing-tile. Below these was a base of
ragstone rubble bound with mortar.

On the S. side of the hole at the same depth was seen a level of
broken Roman tiles on a similar base, springing from the N.–S.
wall, and apparently forming part of an E.–W. wall at right
angles to it.

G.M.

130 *Gresham Street, Nos.* 71–5, *at junction with Aldermanbury,* 1908

Over the greater part of the site, the natural surface of brick-
earth lay at a depth of 13 ft. below the present ground level,
beneath an accumulation of made earth. At the N.E. corner,
however, it fell a few feet deeper, and the lower part of the
depression was filled with black mud, in which were piles in a
sloping position as if they supported the bank of a stream. It
seems likely that the water which supplied it was eventually
drained or canalised by the fort ditch to the N.W. In view of the
fact that a culvert was necessary in the city wall near its junction
with the S.W. corner of the fort (**W48**), it is possible that this
stream continued to flow in some form at quite a late date.

To the south, under the building line of Gresham Street, were
Roman pits about 3 ft. in diameter dug into the brick-earth. They
contained only a few fragments of Roman pottery and a quantity
of oyster-shells. It was suggested that these were not ordinary
refuse pits, but that the brick-earth had been dug for use. There
were indications of fires nearby, and it is possible that bricks
were fired here.

Arch., LXIII, p, 314, *and Fig.* 25, *p.* 315.

131 *Aldermanbury, Fountaine Court,* 1911

When foundations for a new building were dug at the E. end of

Fountaine Court, immediately N.W. of St. Lawrence Jewry
Church, a deposit of black mud was found resting on the gravel.
It was 2½ ft. thick and lay at a depth of 14½ ft. below the present
surface. The excavation continued to a depth of 21 ft., or 4 ft.
into the natural gravel, and water rose in this to within 9 in. of
the top of the gravel. It has been suggested that the black deposit
represented the northern side of the stream-bed which was found
on the site to the south (**130**).
Arch., LXIII, pp. 314–15, *Fig.* 25.

132 *St. Lawrence Jewry Church,* 1671
When Sir Christopher Wren built the chancel for the new church,
he was obliged to drive piles 12 ft. deep for its foundations after
digging for 7 ft. It is likely that the marshy hollow which he
encountered was the ancient stream-bed which was later found
to the N.W. (**130** and **131**). The trend of the stream here seems
to be to the S.E., and it is likely that it determined the alignment
of the Roman buildings found in King Street (**45, 46** and **48**) and
in Ironmonger Lane (**151**).
Arch., LXIII, pp. 314–15, *Fig.* 25.

133 *Coleman Street, S. of Nun Court,* 1843
A brick pavement apparently vitrified by heat was found in this
area at a depth of 20 ft.
J. E. PRICE: *A Roman Tessellated Pavement found in Bucklersbury,* p. 54.
R.C.H.M., p. 114.

134 *Moorgate, Nos.* 55–61, 1929
Mr. G. C. Dunning observed here what appeared to be the
embankments of brooks running eastwards into the Walbrook.
The bottom was of river gravel with a layer of black mud above it.
Above the mud was a Roman deposit 5 ft. thick, in the lower
part of which was a rectangular system of camp-sheathing held
together by piles driven into the gravel. From this site came a
small votive silver plaque with repoussé figures of the Mother-
Goddesses, now in the London Museum. (*See Pl.* 89.) The pottery
found here was almost all of the second century, and earlier
forms were quite rare.
J.R.S., XIX (1929), *p.* 199.   *Guildhall Library Annual Report,* 1929–
30.

135 *Moorgate Street, near the Swan's Nest Public House in Great Swan Alley, about* 1835–6

During excavations, presumably for the new Moorgate Street, a pit 2¾ ft. to 3 ft. square was found on the Coleman Street side of the excavation. It was boarded on each side with planks placed upright but discontinued towards the bottom where the pit became circular. It is said to have contained 'a store of earthen vessels', including a Samian bowl (Drag. 35), apparently closely packed. At the bottom were an iron bucket handle and hook, with a coin of Allectus. The pit was more than 30 ft. deep, and there seems little doubt that it was originally dug as a well.

ROACH SMITH: *Illus. Rom. Lond., p.* 142.   *R.C.H.M., p.* 135.

136 *Moorgate, No.* 30, 1951

A bed of black, peat-like silt was seen in a small building excavation on this site, overlying the natural sandy ballast. From its lower levels came a few sherds of Roman coarse pottery with animal bones and shells of whelks and oysters. The upper levels contained fragments of mediaeval tiles. A Roman bronze coin of the fourth century was said by the workmen to have been found in the silt, but its patina was unlike that of coins from similar deposits.

From this discovery, and similar observations of silt on the sites of 55–7 Moorgate (**134**) and 5 Copthall Avenue (**138**), it seems likely that a major tributary of the Walbrook flowed through this area in Roman times, but its course remains uncertain.

G.M.

137 *Moorgate, Nos.* 20–8 (*between Great Swan Alley and Copthall Close*), 1936

Towards the eastern end of the site large quantities of Roman pottery 'wasters' were found, indicating the proximity of a kiln. The spoilt pots, which must have been made nearby, included shouldered jars of grey ware, open pans with reeded horizontal rims and platters with upright walls. In addition to this coarse pottery, there are also said to have been wasters of fine micaceous ware, and of black glossy ware imitating Samian bowls (Drag. 29 and 37) in form, and decorated with incised designs of concentric circles and parts of circles. The damaged pots all seemed to belong to the late first or early second century. The ground sloped rapidly eastwards towards the bed of the Walbrook.

Guildhall Library Report, 1936, *pp.* 14–15.

138 *Copthall Avenue, No.* 5, 1962

Builders' excavations in all parts of this site between Great Swan Alley and Copthall Close revealed black silt-like mud of a considerable thickness, containing pottery of the third and fourth centuries. This seemed to indicate the close proximity of a large tributary of the Walbrook, although the actual stream-bed was not seen. It is most unlikely that such a thick deposit could be the result of flooding from the main stream about 120 ft. to the E., and it is more probable that it came from the same watercourse as the flood-silt seen on the site of No. 30 Moorgate (**136**).

G.M.

139 *Copthall Avenue, formerly Little Bell Alley*, 1851–2

A note on a City Sewers Plan records that vertical oak piles with horizontal planking, believed to be the embankment of the Walbrook, were found in Little Bell Alley between London Wall and New Court. A position on or near the Ward boundary between Coleman Street and Broad Street Wards, which runs up Copthall Avenue north of Great Swan Alley, is a likely enough place in which to find the main stream of the Walbrook, which must in any case be very near. It must be remembered, however, that General Pitt-Rivers made a very similar discovery of piles with horizontal planks attached 60 ft. to the east (See **142**.)

R.C.H.M., p. 115.

140 *Copthall Avenue, Nos.* 10–12, 1906

It was observed on this site that the strata sloped towards Drapers' Gardens, and at a little more than half-way across the site gave place to washed gravel and sand, which became deeper as it approached Drapers' Gardens, where it was in places 6–7 ft. deep. Presumably this was the stream-bed of the Walbrook. Over the whole were 5–6 ft. of black mud, extending to the top of the undisturbed levels at 11 ft. 9 in. below the street level. Many piles were found.

Arch., LX, Pt. 1, *p.* 232.

141 *Copthall Avenue, Nos.* 4–6, 1904

It was observed on this site that the ground fell in the direction of Drapers' Gardens, presumably towards the bed of the Walbrook. It is stated, however, that only the side of the stream was found, and that the main part evidently extended under the Gardens. The eastern edge of this site is also the Ward Boundary, which was evidently determined by the position of the stream.

Arch., LX, Pt. 1, *pp.* 231–2.

142 *Copthall Avenue, No. 20, extending behind Nos.* 14–54, 1866
During excavations here for a wool warehouse, General Pitt-Rivers (then Colonel Lane-Fox) observed a layer which he described as peat, 7–9 ft. thick, 10–13 ft. below the surface. It contained great quantities of animal bones, including those of *Bos longifrons*, red deer, boars and goats. A number of wooden piles were found in the peat and penetrating the gravel beneath, some in rows, others in irregular groups. Horizontal wooden planks were nailed on the W. side of a row of piles running N.–S., and another plank was seen on the S. side of an E.–W. row. These are remarkably like the timber revetments of the banks of the Walbrook seen further down-stream, and it is just possible that the N.–S. row of piles represents the E. bank of the stream. It is more likely, however, that the stream flowed further west under Copthall Avenue. (See **139**.) It is possible that the piles on this site formed part of the foundations of wooden buildings, but the horizontal planks are in that case difficult to explain. Bronze pins, *stili*, iron knives, leather shoes, and coins of Vespasian, Nerva, Trajan, Hadrian and Antoninus Pius were found in the peat, with Roman pottery and tiles, one of which had the stamp P.PR.BR.
Anthropological Review, V, pp. LXXIff.   *R.C.H.M., p.* 130 and *Fig.* 48, *p.* 131.

143 *Throgmorton Avenue, No.* 2, 1880
During excavations on the site of the Submarine Telegraph Company, at the junction of London Wall and Throgmorton Avenue, a Roman road is said to have been found crossing the site diagonally, at a depth of 15 ft. It was of hard gravel, about 9 in. thick, and was 12 ft. broad. Roman remains were found at the same depth. Unfortunately there is no indication in the report whether the road was crossing the site to the N.W., approximately at right angles to the tributary of the Walbrook to the south, presumably after crossing a bridge – or to the N.E., approximately parallel with the stream. In either case, it must have been a minor roadway leading only to the perimeter road of the city, since there is no evidence of a gateway in this part of the city wall.
Arch. Journ., XXXVII, p. 331.   *R.C.H.M., p.* 130.

144 *Great Winchester Street, No.* 22, 1940
Six shafts dug in a line W.–E., 25 ft. south of the roadway, preparatory to the building of a basement air-raid shelter, gave some indication of the position of an eastern tributary of the Walbrook

and the eastern limit of its valley. The two most westerly shafts had water in the bottom at a depth of 19–20 ft., and a wooden pile was found. In one of them there was a sharp dip in the strata. These shafts may well have been in or near the stream-bed. Other shafts to the east were drier but contained alluvial mud mixed with Roman pottery of the first to the third century, to a depth of 24 ft., where there was a layer of compressed vegetation on a sub-soil of London Clay. A shaft 74 ft. to the east of the first two, however, encountered red Quaternary gravel at a depth of only 12 ft. below the street level, and evidently had been sunk to the east of the edge of the valley.

London and Middlesex Arch. Soc. Trans., N.S. X, 1951, pp. 150–4.

145 *Great Winchester Street, Winchester House,* 1962–3

The eastern tributary of the Walbrook was observed in the western part of the site. The stream-bed itself was not revetted and was ill-defined, but its position could be located fairly satisfactorily by noting the position of the lowest point in the mud-filled valley. The black silt of the flood-deposits extended eastwards to about the middle of the site.

G.M.

146 *Finsbury Circus, Nos.* 1–6 *(Britannic House), northern part of the site (formerly Nos. 4–6 Finsbury Circus and Nos. 34–40 Finsbury Pavement), c.* 1920

Excavations on this site showed that the gravel was overlaid by grey clay containing many pebbles, apparently the silt of a stream. There was no well-defined bed, however – apart from a shallow depression 7 ft. wide, containing fewer reeds than elsewhere, which crossed the S.W. corner of Nos. 34–40 Finsbury Pavement – and it is likely that the stream meandered in various places at different times. In all parts of the site there were traces of reeds, forming a bed 1 ft. thick above the clay. Among these, on the S. and E. sides of the area, were found a few Roman objects, none of which were earlier than the latter part of the second century. They included pottery fragments of the late second and third centuries: a white jug, probably of the fourth century: and coins of Licinius and Constantine. Immediately above the reed-bed was a black marshy deposit containing antiquities of the fifteenth century.

Arch., LXXI, pp. 97–8, 106–8, *Plan p.* 76.

147 *Eldon Street, Nos.* 26–31, *and Finsbury Circus, Nos.* 16–18, *c.* 1915

During building excavations on this site, the bed of a stream was found, almost parallel with Eldon Street. Along its southern side were the remains of a wooden gutter. The bed was cut through undulating gravel which deepened towards the eastern end of the site. In the southern bank was a cremation burial in a coarse urn, probably of the late second or early third century. Nearby, on the surface of the gravel, were fragments of a Castor ware pot of the third century. From the same level came a coin of Antoninus Pius, two bronze armlets (one of recognisably late type) and fragments of a Samian dish (Form 80) of the Antonine period. Above the gravel was a black marshy deposit, 4 or more feet thick, which contained antiquities ranging in date from the end of the fourteenth to the first half of the sixteenth century.

Arch., LXXI, pp. 94–7, 107, *Plan p.* 76.

148 *Blomfield Street, No.* 23, *with No.* 4 *London Wall Buildings,* 1901–2
Wooden pile structures were observed here, apparently constructed in the flood-silt of the stream, which contained Roman pottery sherds at its lowest levels. The structures were platforms made by fixing planks against short piles, forming compartments which were filled with earth and rubbish. The northernmost group consisted of two platforms with a timber-lined channel or pit between them. This contained water-laid sand or silt, and it is not unlikely that it was an artificial channel for the stream, possibly diverting it from its natural course for some industrial purpose such as milling. The channel had a wooden floor, so was not merely a revetted stream-bed of the kind found elsewhere in the Walbrook. As only a small portion was seen, however, it is possible that it was merely a large tank. No man-made object was found in it, so it was presumably kept clear of silt until the abandonment of the site. The upper filling of the platforms contained pottery of the first and early second centuries, together with pieces of vitreous matter and burnt flints with traces of fused material. It was uncertain whether these finds, suggesting industrial activity of some kind, formed part of an occupation level or had been brought from elsewhere for the filling of the platforms.

Arch. Journ., LX, pp. 137*ff.* (*esp.* 187–205) *and* 222*ff.* R.C.H.M., *pp.* 145–7.

149 *New Broad Street, Nos.* 46–7 (*County House*), *formerly Nos.* 13–14 *Blomfield Street,* 1925
A line of stout oak posts, irregularly placed but roughly parallel with Blomfield Street, was seen in the northern part of the site. It was thought that this might be the remains of the embankment of the Walbrook, and the bed of the stream was believed to be

between the posts and Blomfield Street. It is more likely, however, that the actual position of the stream was west of this site, and that the supposed stream-bed was the eastern edge of the flood-silt, which has commonly been mistaken for the stream itself. The corresponding western edge on the opposite side of Blomfield Street (148) was seen to be about 70 ft. west of the street, so the flood-plain here seems to have been 160–170 ft. wide. In the silt west of the posts were found fragments of Roman pottery, including a ring-necked jug of the first century, and Samian ware of the first and second centuries, together with an iron knife and the linch-pin of a cart.

M.S. notes by Mr. Q. WADDINGTON *in Guildhall Museum.*
R.C.H.M., p. 147.

150 *Austin Friars, site of Dutch Church,* 1951–2
Excavations by Professor W. F. Grimes on the site of the bombed church showed that there had been Roman occupation of the site, although no stone walls of the Roman period were found. Quantities of Roman wall-plaster mingled with clay suggested that there were less substantial houses with clay walls here. This may account for the lack of records of Roman buildings in this part of the city, which was perhaps a relatively poor quarter with few ragstone walls, tessellated pavements and other recognisable structural remains.

151 *Ironmonger Lane, No.* 11, 1949
During the builders' excavation, a tessellated pavement with a geometrical pattern and traces of three ragstone walls were found. (*See Pl.* 67.) Pottery of the mid-second century was found in rammed gravel beneath the pavement. Further west on the site, however, were traces of another tessellated pavement on the same level, and this overlay a pink mortar floor dated by an underlying pit of the first half of the third century. The building is therefore probably of the later third century.

A portion of the patterned tessellated pavement has been preserved *in situ* in the basement of the premises of Messrs. Peat, Marwick and Mitchell.

Near the S.W. corner of the site, black silt containing late Roman pottery was found in an underpinning hole, apparently indicating the presence of a stream.

D. DAWE and A. OSWALD: 11 *Ironmonger Lane,* 1952, *pp.* 112–14.

152 *Old Jewry, St. Olave,* 1888
A Roman pavement of red tesserae, measuring 20 ft. by 3 ft.

was found on the site of St. Olave, Old Jewry, at a depth of 16 ft. There was also a wall parallel with the present line of frontage 12 ft. below the surface. It was 3 ft. thick and 12 ft. in height, but the foundations were not reached. Much of the soil was black mud, presumably a flood deposit, containing Roman pottery.
V.C.H., London, I, p. 124.   *R.C.H.M., p.* 140.

153 *Old Jewry, Nos.* 27–32, 1953
Trial holes revealed a wall foundation of ragstone, ballast, mortar and broken tiles, running roughly N.–S., approximately at right angles with St. Olave's Court, in the S.W. corner of the site, 6 ft. east of the old N.–S. building line and 7 ft. 9 in. east of the new. The foundation trench had been cut into a refuse deposit of the early second century at the S. edge of the site, and (further north) into a refuse pit of Flavian date. It therefore belonged to a building not earlier than the second century. The foundation wall was 3 ft. 2 in. in height, with a thickness of more than 2 ft. (Only part of its thickness was revealed by the trial hole.)
G.M.

154 *Old Jewry, between Frederick's Place and St. Olave's Court,* 1952
In a small excavation about 15 ft. by 12 ft., approximately 12 ft. west of the building line of Old Jewry, the gravel metalling of a Roman road or courtyard was encountered at a depth of 6 ft. 2 in. below the modern basement level. The camber suggested that it was part of an E.–W. road, but not enough was seen to determine with any certainty either the direction of the road or whether it was in fact a road rather than a gravelled courtyard.
G.M.

155 *Moorgate, Nos.* 1–5, *site of the Northern Assurance Company* (*between Coleman Street, Moorgate and Lothbury*), 1907
A western arm of the Walbrook was found just east of the lower end of Coleman Street. It was a depression filled with black mud and rushes, from which came a Samian pot with stamp of the period of Domitian. On either side of the depression was a chalk wall, possibly mediaeval, and at the S. end adjoining Lothbury was a wooden enclosure 3 ft. square in the centre of the stream-bed. It seems likely that it was a well, and it is possible that the stream-bed was covered at some period in Roman times. The chalk walls were 28 ft. apart, but the actual stream-bed must in normal times have been much narrower, probably only a few feet wide.
Arch., LXIII, p. 312.   *R.C.H.M., p.* 114, *Fig.* 34.

156 *Moorgate, No. 2 (Founders' Court),* 1927

West of Founders' Court was found the base of a wall of chalk and flint rubble, about 4¼ ft. thick, running approximately N.–S., with a pink cement floor on either side of the wall, 13½ ft. below the modern pavement level. A second pink pavement capped the wall 7 in. above the first. There were indications of the brick pillars of a hypocaust on the W. side of the wall.

About the middle of the site the wall appeared to turn to the west, and the line of this return wall was continued to the east by a double row of piles. The foundations of the building had been laid in the black sludge, and other groups of piles were found to the north and west.

R.C.H.M., p. 132.

157 *Moorgate, No. 2 (Founders' Court), E. side,* 1927 *and* 1930

A tessellated pavement was found at a depth of 19 ft. 8 in. at the N.E. corner of Founders' Court. It consisted of a border 3½ ft. wide of red tesserae, with a fragment of the edge of a pattern in smaller (½ in.) black tesserae at the S.E. corner of the excavation. At the W. edge the red border came to a well-defined end, indicating the former presence of a wall running approximately N.–S., but inclined slightly more towards the N.E. than the modern building line of Founders' Court. A deposit described as alluvial, sealed by the floor, contained pottery of the first and early second century with burnt animal bones and oyster shells. The pre-Antonine date of the pottery from this layer beneath the floor was confirmed by further finds in 1930. To the west the ground dropped towards what had apparently been the bed of a feeder of the Walbrook, where the black alluvium went down to a greater depth. Fragments of mosaic from this site are preserved in the London Museum (A. 30. 157).

R.C.H.M., pp. 130–1.   *J.R.S., XXI* (1931), *p.* 239.

158 *King's Arms Yard, site of Bank of England Canteen,* 1959

Black mud containing Roman pottery of the first and early second centuries, leather and metal objects was found in the builders' trenches in various parts of the site, resting on the ballast and brick-earth. The ballast was higher on both W. and E. sides of the site, and dipped towards the centre, where the black silt was much thicker – evidently the stream-bed of the Walbrook. Wooden piles were observed on the W. side of the stream, and two planks on their edges were seen in section 9 ft. 9 in. apart, apparently extended in a southerly direction beside the stream. There were also the remains of tree-trunks and branches, which may well have been growing when they were submerged by the silt.

G.M.

159 *Tokenhouse Yard*, 1867 *and* 1889

Piles connected by camp-sheathing, probably part of the embankment of the Walbrook, were reported by General Pitt-Rivers (then Colonel Lane-Fox) in 1867.

In 1889, the bed of the Walbrook was found in this area at a depth of 20 ft., and a few coins of the early Empire and pieces of pottery were found.

Anthropological Review, V (1867), *LXXVI.*   *Arch. Review, IV, p.* 292.
R.C.H.M., p. 144.

160 *Lothbury, No.* 6 (*site of the Royal Bank of Canada*), 1931–2

In the Bank are preserved two small fragments of tessellated pavement which were found on the site. One is of coarse red tesserae, and the other is a patterned mosaic with small red, black, white and yellow tesserae. The ornament seems to be a portion of a guilloche. They presumably belong to the same building as the pavement found on the adjacent site to the north (**157**), and may well be part of the same pavement. The Bank also possesses a few iron tools and a bronze 'ear-pick' or *ligula*, which, from their condition, came from the flood-silt that on the adjacent site lay beneath the tessellated pavement. The small quantity of pottery of the late first and early second centuries in the Bank's collection probably came from the same deposit. (Cf. **157**.)

161 *Lothbury, in roadway between No.* 5 *and public lavatories*, 1963

A tunnel in the roadway revealed a Roman wall of ragstone with a double course of bonding tiles. It was about 2 ft. thick, with an offset of 2 in. immediately above the bonding-course on the southern side. The base of the tunnel was at a depth of 12 ft. 9 in., and the wall continued below this level, and to a height of 2 ft. above it.

G.M.

162 *Lothbury, opposite Founders' Court*, 1834–6

Remains of a tessellated pavement were found at a depth of about 11 ft. below the modern road during sewer excavations opposite Founders' Court.

Arch., XXVII, p. 147.   *R.C.H.M., p.* 130.   T. MORGAN: *Rom.-Brit. Mosaic Pavements, p.* 181.

163 *Lothbury, opposite St. Margaret's Church*

A Roman pavement is said to have been found at a depth of 16–17 ft. below the modern road of Lothbury, opposite St. Margaret's Church.

Proc. Soc. Antiq. (2nd S.), *XVI, p.* 36.   *R.C.H.M., p.* 130.

164 *Lothbury, near St. Margaret's Church,* 1834–6

At a lower level than the pavement found opposite Founders' Court 11 ft. below the modern road (see **162**) in the sewer excavations, were found wooden piles, and coins of Domitian and Antoninus Pius, apparently from a stream-bed. This is said to have been 'beyond the church of St. Margaret', but the position of the Roman Walbrook indicated by the more recent excavation on the site of the Bank of England was opposite the eastern end of the church.

Arch., XXVII, p. 147.   *R.C.H.M., p.* 130.

165 *Lothbury, S.W. corner of Tokenhouse Yard,* 1843

At a depth of from 12 to 18 ft. were found a number of curiously fluted piles, with fragments of Samian ware and coins of Nero and Vespasian.

Gent. Mag., 1843, II, *p.* 533.   *R.C.H.M., p.* 130.

166 *Throgmorton Street, near the corner of Bartholomew Lane,* 1856

A deep ditch was found containing the remains of cask hoops. Probably a series of barrel wells had been constructed here, but it is uncertain whether they were Roman or mediaeval.

Arch. Journ., XIII, p. 274.   *R.C.H.M., p.* 144.

167 *Bank of England,* 1805

A patterned mosaic pavement, now in the British Museum, was found near the N.W. angle of the building, at a depth of 11 or 12 ft. below the level of the street. Its position was about '20 ft. west of the W. gate of the Bank opening into Lothbury, and the same distance south of the carriage-way'. It is 11 ft. square, with a pattern of four acanthus leaves in a circle, in red, black and grey on white. The edges are said to have shown traces of fire. The pavement has been tentatively dated by Dr. David Smith on stylistic grounds to the early third century.

Arch., XXXIX, pp. 495–6.   *R.C.H.M., pp.* 106–7.   *Gent. Mag.,* 1807, I, *p.* 416.

168 *Bank of England,* 1933–4

The stream-bed of the Walbrook was observed running across the site in approximately the position indicated. From it came a quantity of iron tools, leather, bronze-work, etc. (*See Pl.* 125.)
The Old Lady of Threadneedle Street, XII, December 1936, *plan opposite* p. 283.

169 *Bank of England,* 1927

A Roman concrete floor about 3 in. thick with a surface of pounded tile was found 12½ ft. below the pavement level of Lothbury, in the courtyard a little west of the old main entrance. Another floor was found a few feet to the S.E. at a slightly lower level. About 10 ft. further east, at a depth of 20½ ft., resting almost immediately on the undisturbed clay, was another concrete pavement 4½ in. thick. On its N. side was a double timber-framed structure, consisting of boarding on 6 in. by 4 in. sills. Between the two frames, which stood vertically like walling, the space was filled with building rubbish lying on black earth. Fallen timbers, perhaps from a roof, were lying on the original floor in a layer of clay. Two higher occupation levels were seen above this, and between the levels of the upper and lower pavements were found fragments of leather and pottery of the first century, with little or nothing of a later date.
R.C.H.M., p. 107.

170 *Bank of England,* 1933–4

An oak water-pipe, 6 in. by 6 in., was found in the N.E. part of the site, south of the E. entrance on Lothbury. It lay in a line approximately N.E.–S.W. (Cf. *Pl.* 109.)
The Old Lady of Threadneedle Street, XII, December 1936, *plan opposite* p. 283.

171 *Bank of England,* 1933–4

A square tessellated pavement with a circular central panel, borders in meander and guilloche pattern, and leaf ornaments in the spandrels, was found during building excavations in 1933, at a depth of 20 ft. or more below modern street level. (*See Pl.* 69.) Pottery found beneath it was of the early second century, and the pavement is therefore of this date or later. About 60 ft. to the south, and at a level 8 ft. higher, was another paved area with plain tesserae only. In the following year a second patterned mosaic pavement was found to the S.E. of the first, also at a depth of 20 ft. or so. (*See Pl.* 68.) The decorated portion is 4½ ft.

square, with floral ornaments in squares and a guilloche border, surrounded by plain red tesserae. Like the first pavement, it overlay pottery of the early second century, but both mosaics have been tentatively dated by Dr. David Smith on stylistic grounds to the late second or early third century. They have been restored, and the first (and larger) pavement is now preserved in the basement of the Bank, while the second is set in the floor of the Bank's Cupola Museum (not open to the public).

J.R.S., XXIV (1934), *p.* 211; *XXV* (1935), *p.* 216.

172 *Bank of England*, 1933–4

To the south and east of the tessellated pavements were a number of Roman wells, approximately in the positions shown. Several staves from a barrel-well bore stamped letters, one reading L.E.FL.

J.R.S., XXIV (1934), *pp.* 211, 221.

173 *Prince's Street, Grocers' Hall*, 1834

A pavement of concrete with a thin coating of red earth was found at a depth of 17 ft. 6 in., and is noted in a MS. record of sewers in the City Engineer's office at Guildhall.

R.C.H.M., p. 121.

174 *Prince's Street*, 1834–6

Wooden piles found beneath this street appeared to belong to the ancient embankment of the Walbrook. Pottery and bronze utensils were found there, as well as a sharpening steel with a bronze handle in the form of a horse's head.

Arch., XXVII, p. 143.   ROACH SMITH: *Illustrations of Roman London, p.* 141.   *V.C.H., London, Vol. I, p.* 119.   *R.C.H.M., p.* 136.

175 *Prince's Street, No. 5, site of Midland Bank*, 1928–9

The excavation on this site was in narrow shafts, so that observation was limited. A very thick deposit of black mud containing Roman pottery was found, apparently lying directly on blue clay at a depth of 30–35 ft. In the bottom 10 ft. of the black mud were roughly squared piles which did not penetrate the clay. One had been driven into the base of a Samian cup with the stamp of *Callus*, a potter of the Flavian period, and so can hardly have been earlier than the reign of Vespasian. On the other hand, no pottery later than the first century was found in the level immediately above the piles. No system of arrangement of the piles could be discovered, but there seems little doubt that they were connected with the embankment of the Walbrook. Higher levels of black mud above the tops of the piles contained Antonine pottery. A gravel deposit was seen at the W. end of the site, sloping down to the east. This may have been part of the W. bank of the stream.

On the eastern edge of the site, at a depth of 32 ft., below the system of piles, was found a large mill-stone of the type which would have been used in a baker's shop (*See Pl.* 106.)

Antiq. Journ., IX (1929), *pp.* 219*ff.*

176 *Poultry, Nos.* 33–5, *site of the Midland Bank* (*formerly Chapel Place*), 1925

A series of groups of wooden piles were found, some of which had planks attached. They seemed to be the remains of long rectangular structures enclosed with boarding, the tops of which were about 18 ft. below the level of the pavement. A thick deposit of black mud seemed to indicate the presence of a stream, the direction of which is not clear, and it has been suggested that the rectangular structures may have been the piers of a bridge. In the black mud were found pieces of Samian, including one with the stamp MAIOR.I, part of a wooden bowl, leather, etc. Traces of a possible ditch, running N.W.–S.E., were seen in the western part of the site.

R.C.H.M., p. 136.

177 *Poultry, Nos.* 33–5, *site of Midland Bank extension*, 1936

A number of oak piles were found in the S.W. corner of the site. They stood in black mud which probably indicated the position of a tributary of the Walbrook. Nearby was a square timber-lined well, from the bottom of which came a sestertius of Commodus.

J.R.S., XXVII (1937), *p.* 241, *and MS. notes by* Mr. F. COTTRILL.

178 *Mansion House Street, corner of Prince's Street, site of the National Provincial Bank*, 1867 *and* 1929–30

In 1867 a portion of a mosaic pavement was found at a depth of 18 ft. below the surface. The design consisted of a square within a circle, the central ornament being a vase, around which were portions of the foliage of a tree and an object resembling an archway with human figures. The circle was enclosed with two bands of black tesserae, which separated it from an elaborate scroll with foliage and flowers. The entire design was bordered with a guilloche pattern in black, red, brown and white. The pavement was laid on concrete with a hypocaust.

In 1929–30, excavations to a deeper level took place when the present building was constructed. A structure of 9 in. piles was found, with baulks of timber 1 ft. square resting on the top. The direction of the timbers was very nearly N.E.–S.W., and the surface which they formed was 28 ft. below the present level of the street. Driven into one of the piles was an iron chisel stamped with the name of its maker, unfortunately illegible. (*See Pl.* 22.) This is still in the possession of the Bank, with other antiquities from the same excavation.

London and Middlesex Arch. Soc. Trans., III, pp. 217–8.   Morgan: *Rom.-Brit. Mosaic Pavements, pp.* 193–4.   *R.C.H.M., p.* 135. *Guildhall Library Annual Report,* 1929–30.

179 *Royal Exchange, fore-court,* 1841
A shaft sunk between the Royal Exchange and Bank Buildings (which formerly stood west of the Royal Exchange) revealed a wall 7 ft. thick and 14 ft. high, with its base at a depth of 20 ft. below the modern street level. It appeared to run in the direction of the Bank. A fine Samian vase with figures in appliqué, now in the British Museum, was found in the same shaft.
Arch., XXIX, p. 273.   *R.C.H.M., p.* 115.

180 *Royal Exchange,* 1841
Foundations of Roman buildings were found 'running in a diagonal direction from N.E. to S.W.' near the centre of the Royal Exchange. 30 ft. further west was found a mass of masonry of tiles and mortar, two sides of which still retained traces of wall-plaster with a painted pattern. This overlay a gravel-pit, in the filling of which were coins of Vespasian, Domitian, and a plated denarius of Septimius Severus. (A more doubtful find of a coin of Gratian was recovered after being taken away.)
Tite: *Cat. Antiq. Roy. Exch., p.* xxxix.   *Arch., XXIX, pp.* 267*ff*; *XXXIX, pp.* 497–8.   *R.C.H.M., pp.* 137–9.

181 *Bartholomew Lane,* 1841
A piece of tessellated pavement found here, probably when the church of St. Bartholomew was destroyed, was preserved by the City authorities. According to another account, however, it was found in a cellar, apparently not *in situ*. The pattern consisted of a scroll of ivy-leaves in black upon a white ground.
Arch., XXIX, p. 155.   Tite: *Cat. Antiq. Roy. Exch., p.* xxxi. *R.C.H.M., p.* 107.

182 *Threadneedle Street, No.* 62 (*now the eastern end of No.* 63), 1895
A rectangular bath (5 ft. 3 in. by 5 ft. 3 in. by 2 ft.) built of rough stone mixed with broken tiles was found at a depth of just over 17 ft. The floor was of *opus signinum* and the walls were plastered, the whole resting on a substructure of concrete. Access was by two steps forming a quarter of a circle in the N. corner of the bath. (*See Pl.* 59.)
Arch. Journ., LII, pp. 198–9.   *Arch., LX, pp.* 218–19.   *R.C.H.M.,*
p. 144.

183 *Threadneedle Street, No.* 53 (*former site of the French Protestant Church*), 1841
Coarse red tessellated pavements were found under the church opposite its entrance, and on either side running under the street, at a depth of 12 ft. There was also a patterned mosaic 6 ft. by 5 ft. – apparently the floor of a passage 6 ft. wide. About 6½ ft. to the north was a square mosaic with a central rosette. Both pavements are now in the British Museum. The walls had disappeared but pieces of painted wall-plaster were found. A quantity of charcoal and some charred barley lying on the pavements suggested that the building had been destroyed by fire.
Arch., XXIX, p. 400.   ROACH SMITH: *Illustrations of Roman London,*
pp. 55–6, *Pls. IX and X.*   *R.C.H.M., pp.* 143–4, *Pl.* 50.

184 *Threadneedle Street, Nos.* 28–9, 1910
A floor of *opus signinum* on a foundation of rough pieces of ragstone and white mortar was found just to the north of Merchant Taylors' Hall. A small Roman stone drain ran beneath the floor.
Arch., LXIII, p. 323.   *R.C.H.M., p.* 144.

185 *Threadneedle Street, opposite Nos.* 43–7, 1849
During sewer excavations in Threadneedle Street a massive wall of ragstone and chalk was encountered. It was about 12 ft. thick, running approximately parallel to the modern street, with its top about 10 ft. below the surface.
R.C.H.M., p. 144.   *City Sewers Plan* 217.

186 *Finch Lane,* 1847
Walls of houses and the remains of tessellated pavements were observed running across Finch Lane. About half-way along the Lane traces of an extensive patterned mosaic pavement were seen on the W. side of the street at a depth of 13 ft. A portion which was preserved had a double guilloche in black, red, yellow and white, enclosing a square.
J.B.A.A., II, pp. 205–6.   *R.C.H.M., p.* 119.

187 *Finch Lane, W. side,* 1844–5

Part of a tessellated pavement was found between Finch Lane and the Royal Exchange. It represented a female head in red, white, black and green tesserae. Fragments of other pavements were also observed. It seems reasonably certain that the mosaic described is the fragment preserved in the London Museum, said to have been found at a depth of 14 ft. on the northern side of Cornhill in 1844. It is a crude representation of a female head and shoulder in red, white, black, grey and yellow tesserae (not green, as stated in the earlier report). The style suggests a late date. (*See Pl.* 70.)

J.B.A.A., I, p. 64.   *R.C.H.M., p.* 119.   *London Museum Catalogue,* '*London in Roman Times*', *p.* 39 (*A*25590).

188 *Cornhill, No.* 15, 1926

During the clearance of this site a wall was found running north by west under Cornhill. It was about 4 ft. thick, and stood to a height of 3 or 4 ft. on gravel at a depth of 14 ft. below the modern street level. It was built of ragstone and some tiles, with a double bonding-course of tiles.

R.C.H.M., p. 116.

189 *Lombard Street, No.* 79, 1935

A ragstone wall running N.–S. was seen in section at a depth of 4 ft. to 6 ft. 3 in. below basement level. It consisted of ragstone rubble with hard sandy buff cement, and had a double bonding course of bricks 5 ft. to 5 ft. 4 in. below basement level. The wall is said to have gone down to a depth of 15 ft. below the level of the basement, and according to one of the workmen it turned east near the N. edge of the site.

J.R.S., XXVI (1936), p. 256, *and MS. notes by* Mr. F. COTTRILL.

190 *Queen Victoria Street, E. end,* 1959–60

During tunnelling excavations for the Travolator at the Bank Station, black Walbrook mud containing metal antiquities and pottery of the early Roman period was encountered, as well as substantial wooden piles and horizontal timbers. The piles were closely set in rows running not quite at right angles with the kerb line of Queen Victoria Street. These presumably were to support the foundations of Roman buildings immediately to the west of the Walbrook, and were situated just to the north of the mosaic pavement found when Queen Victoria Street was constructed in 1869. The alignment of the rows of piles has no relationship with the mediaeval street plan, and may be parallel with the western branch of the Roman Walbrook, for the stream probably forked near this point.

Information from Engineer's plan, British Railways.

191 *Bucklersbury, Nos. 1–2, now part of 76–80 Cheapside,* 1963

The grey silt seen in the southern and central part of the site of Nos. 76–80 Cheapside did not extend over the north-eastern area immediately south of Bucklersbury. Here the natural soil was brick-earth at about 31 ft. above O.D. A few inches higher was a burnt deposit, and at a still higher level another burnt layer with its bottom about 4 ft. above the natural soil. About 16 ft. to the west was a square timber-lined well, the filling of which contained pottery of about A.D. 200. Unfortunately its stratigraphical relationship with the two burnt layers could not be determined, and the latter could not be dated. A Roman quern, however, was found in a burnt deposit a few feet to the S.E. of the well. (*See plan, Fig.* 17, *p.* 121.)

G.M.

192 *Cheapside, Nos. 76–80,* 1963

The gravel metalling of a Roman roadway was observed during the builders' excavation in several places in the central part of the site. It overlay grey silt at about 31 ft. above O.D. in the eastern part, dropping to 27 ft. 3 in. above O.D. opposite No. 78. The natural ground level descended sharply into the valley of a small stream which apparently flowed in a south-easterly direction across the S.W. corner of the site. Unfortunately the whole area was much disturbed, and it was impossible to see how the road crossed the stream. There appeared to be a road surface just north of No. 9 Pancras Lane at about 34 ft. above O.D., with more metalling lying above it. The total surviving thickness was 4 ft. in the eastern part of the site, and 4 ft. 9 in. further west. No edge of the road was seen, but from the distribution of the remaining patches of gravel, the roadway cannot have been less than 29 ft. wide, and could hardly have been more than 35 ft. Piles indicated the presence of timber structures immediately to the north and south of it, and a curious feature was the presence of a few posts 4 in. or 5 in. in diameter, in the silt and extending up into the gravel, near the centre of the roadway itself. These must have formed part of a fairly slight structure which was earlier than the road, or contemporary with an early phase when the road was very much narrower. (*See plan, Fig.* 17, *p.* 121.)

G.M.

193 *Queen Victoria Street, near junction with Bucklersbury*, 1869

During the construction of Queen Victoria Street, the workmen cut through two Roman walls of tiles at a distance of 90 ft. in a westerly direction from the mosaic pavement (**194**). They were at a depth of $17\frac{1}{2}$ ft. from the surface of the modern roadway at Bucklersbury, and ran nearly in a line with it, directly towards the stream of Walbrook. They were each 2 ft. 9 in. in thickness and were 2 ft. 3 in. apart. In the space between them had been laid a drain of flue tiles laid to fall towards the stream, and over this was a tiled pavement with a skirting of mortar against the walls. The structure rested on a foundation of chalk blocks supported by wooden piles driven into the clay or silt beneath. A drawing indicates that the walls were just over 3 ft. high, and above them were later walls of chalk and stone, probably mediaeval. It seems likely that the whole structure was in fact a drain, and as it was in the immediate vicinity of the Roman E.–W. road, it is probable that its purpose was the drainage of this important road in an area that must have been subject to flooding. It is possible that it replaced here the usual shallow drainage gully or gutter beside the road. (*See Fig*, 29, *p.* 149.)

J. E. Price: *A Description of the Roman Tessellated Pavement in Bucklersbury*, 1870, *pp.* 66–7.   R.C.H.M., *p.* 109.

194 *Queen Victoria Street, N. of Bucklersbury*, 1869

A fine patterned mosaic pavement, now in Guildhall Museum, was found during the construction of Queen Victoria Street, at a depth of 19 ft., parallel to the stream-bed of the Walbrook (*Pl.* 63, 65). Below was a hypocaust, and in the N.E. corner a drain. At the S.E. corner was a portico, evidently a doorway, to the east of which was the concrete floor of a passage. Part of a wooden paling adjoining this may indicate a verandah facing the Walbrook. The walls enclosing the pavement were of tile with blocks of chalk and ragstone on a chalk foundation, which was laid on square piles. The pavement has been tentatively attributed by Dr. David Smith on stylistic grounds to the early third century.

J. E. Price: *Description of a Roman Tessellated Pavement in Bucklersbury*, 1870.   R.C.H.M., *p.* 109.

195 *Queen Victoria Street, National Safe Deposit Co.'s premises*, 1872–3

The stream-bed of the Walbrook ran in a southerly direction just west of the centre of the site, approximately parallel to the eastern side of the triangular site.

J. E. Price: *Roman Antiquities Recently Discovered on the Site of the National Safe Deposit Co.'s Premises*, *p.* 53.   R.C.H.M., *p.* 137.

196 *Bucklersbury, site of National Safe Deposit Company,* 1872–3

Traces of a gravel roadway were found in a line with Bucklers-bury on the southern side of the site, extending to the eastern side of the stream-bed, with similar traces continuing on the western side, apparently indicating a crossing of the stream at this point. Adjoining the roadway at the S. corner of the site was a timber flooring at a depth of 25 ft., supported by massive oak timbers, and running parallel with the stream.

J. E. PRICE: *Roman Antiquities found on National Safe Deposit Co.'s Premises, pp.* 53–4.   *R.C.H.M., p.* 137.

197 *George Street, Nos.* 13–14, 1961

In the northern part of No. 14 George Street, deposits of gravel were found overlying the natural brick-earth and gravel. These were clearly artificial, for a thin spread of material from one of the gravel deposits extended to the south and overlay a pit containing pottery sherds of the first century, at a point about 20 ft. south of the northern edge of the site. Since the Roman E.–W. road, which skirted the S. side of the forum and crossed the Walbrook near Bucklersbury, should pass across the northern edge of this site, it seems likely that these deposits were either the remains of the metalling of the road itself, or a spread of material from its southern edge spilled during road-making or repair. They do not therefore define the position of the road, except that it can be said with some certainty that the very thin layer of gravel overlying the pit must have been merely a spread, and that the southern edge of the roadway lay to the north of this point.

London and Middlesex Arch. Soc. Trans., Vol. XXI, *Pt.* 1 (1963), *p.* 70.

198 *Lombard Street, W. end,* 1785

During excavations for a sewer trench a pavement of rough stones was found at a depth of 9 ft., and below this at 12 ft. a pavement of red, black and white tesserae. Further east was a wall about 10 ft. high and 18 ft. long, with its top at a depth of 10 ft. In it were two flues, one semi-circular and one rectangular.

Arch., VIII, p. 117.   *V.C.H., London, I, p.* 81, *Fig.* 30.   *R.C.H.M., p.* 128.

199 *Lombard Street, opposite St. Mary Woolnoth,* 1785

A pavement of coarse red tesserae was found during excavations at a depth of 10–15 ft. Several other pavements were also found in this part of the street and a little further east, together with channelled tiles and painted stucco.

Arch., VIII, p. 117.   *V.C.H., I, p.* 81, *Fig.* 30.   *R.C.H.M., p.* 128.

200 *Lombard Street, near the W. entrance of Change Alley*, 1785
A wall was found on the N. side of the sewer excavations at a
depth of 14 ft. There was 'rough work' for 2 ft. at the top, and
below this were regular layers of flat bricks at smaller intervals.
Near this wall, but at a depth of only 9 ft., was a pavement of
flat tiles.
Arch., VIII, p. 117.   *V.C.H., I, p.* 81, *Fig.* 30.   *R.C.H.M., p.* 128.

201 *Lombard Street, No.* 15, *site of Coutts' Bank*, 1958–9
A wall of ragstone, chalk and flint was found running parallel
with Abchurch Lane, and part of a wall, apparently of the same
building, was found at right angles with this in the N. part of the
site. The bottom of the foundations were at a depth of 18 ft. and
the top 14½ ft. below the street level of Abchurch Lane. Overlying
these walls was fire debris containing pottery of the late first to
early second century. At the N.W. corner of the site was found a
deep room, with walls of ragstone with a small quantity of chalk,
their base being at a depth of about 20 ft. below street level.
This was on the same alignment, and may have formed part of
the same building.
Observations by Mr. P. MARSDEN.

202 *Lombard Street, No.* 15, *site of Coutts' Bank, southern end*, 1958–9
On the southern edge of the site was found a wall, 2 ft. thick, of
ragstone and flint, faced with knapped flints. This was not in
alignment with the walls found in the N. part of the site, being
inclined more to the west – i.e. roughly the same alignment as
the basilica. Adjoining this wall on the N. side a small area of
rammed gravel metalling was observed about 92 ft. to the south
of the Lombard Street frontage and 27 ft. west of Abchurch Lane.
Observations by Mr. P. MARSDEN.

203 *Lombard Street, near the N. end of Abchurch Lane*, 1785
Two stone walls crossing Lombard Street from N.–S. were found
during sewer excavations, one opposite Abchurch Lane, and the
other a little to the east of it. Further east was a tile pavement,
and 'a piece of solid archwork composed of stones of irregular
form' at a depth of 20 ft., on the S. side of the sewer.
Arch., VIII, p. 117.   *V.C.H., I, p.* 81, *Fig.* 30.   *R.C.H.M., p.* 128.

204 *Lombard Street, W. of Nicholas Lane*, 1937
During excavations for a new sewer, a piece of Roman walling
running at right angles with the street was found a few feet west
of Nicholas Lane, according to one account. It stood 7½ ft. high,

and had five courses of bonding tiles. Another account, apparently of the same find, describes a wall of the same height and 3 ft. thick, built of ragstone rubble with yellow tile bonding-courses, running N.–S. at a depth of 14–15 ft. below the modern street level, and gives its position as about 11 ft. west of the corner of Birchin Lane – which would be directly opposite Nicholas Lane.
Guildhall Library Report, 1937, *p*. 17.   *J.R.S., Vol. XXIX* (1939), *p*. 217.

205 *Lombard Street, E. of Nicholas Lane,* 1785
During sewer excavations opposite the end of Birchin Lane, stone walls were found on the S. side of the sewer, running approximately in the same direction as Lombard Street. Other E.–W. walls were found east of Birchin Lane on the N. side of the sewer, and opposite the Church of St. Edmund the King a wall crossed the street at right angles with these.
Arch., VIII, pp. 117–18.   *V.C.H., I, p.* 81, *Fig.* 30.   *R.C.H.M., p.* 128.

206 *Lombard Street, opposite the end of Clement's Lane,* 1937
During sewer excavations a portion of Roman walling 3 ft. thick, running in the direction of the line of the street, was encountered. Only the lower portion of the masonry remained. This presumably made an angle with the wall observed in 1785 crossing the street at right angles opposite the Church of St. Edmund the King (**205**), if both were contemporary.
Guildhall Library Report, 1937, *p.* 17.

207 *Birchin Lane, S. end,* 1785
Walls of rubble with bonding-courses were found, apparently roughly in alignment with Birchin Lane, during excavations for a sewer in 1785. There was also a pavement of coarse red tesserae, about 5 ft. long, sloping northwards.
Arch., VIII, p. 119.   *V.C.H., I, p.* 81, *Fig.* 30.   *R.C.H.M., p.* 107.

208 *Birchin Lane, centre,* 1785
Fragments of a figured tessellated pavement were found to the north of the plain pavement (**207**). The tesserae were about $\frac{1}{4}$ in. square and were of various colours.
Arch., VIII, p. 119.   *V.C.H., I. p.* 81, *Fig.* 30.   *R.C.H.M., p.* 107.

209 *Birchin Lane, N. end,* 1785

A wall was found crossing the sewer trench E.–W., with a pavement of chalk stones lying to the south of it at a depth of 14 ft.

Near the N.W. corner of the lane was another wall, running N.–S., on the W. side of the sewer. At the N.W. corner was seen the border of a pavement in black, white and red tesserae. There were also fragments of wall decoration in painted stucco in this area.

A portion of another decorated tessellated pavement with a representation of a sea-horse (now in Guildhall Museum) was found in Birchin Lane in 1857.

Arch., VIII, p. 119, *and plan, p.* 117.   *R.C.H.M., p.* 107.

210 *Cornhill, No.* 36, *at N.E. corner of Birchin Lane, about* 1922

A wall was found about $4\frac{1}{2}$ ft. back from the frontage, with its top about 9 ft. below the level of the pavement. There was, however, some doubt as to its Roman date.

A second wall is said to have been found running diagonally across the extreme N.W. angle of the site.

London and Middlesex Arch.Soc. Trans.,N.S., V, pp. 50–1.   *R.C.H.M., p.* 116.

211 *Cornhill, Nos.* 69–73, 1897 *and* 1959

The ragstone walls of a rectangular compartment, 22 ft. by 20 ft., with a buttress on the N. side of the N. wall, and apparently with an offset on the S. side of both E.–W. walls, are recorded on an architect's plan of the building of the Bank of Australia and New Zealand (1897). A continuation of these walls to the west was found during the sinking of trial holes on the site of No. 73 Cornhill in 1959, and the discovery of a portion of another N.–S. wall after a further interval of 22 ft., showed that there was a second compartment to the west, practically identical with the first, with a thickening of the N. wall that suggested the presence of another buttress. The western N.–S. wall, however, was at least 7 ft. thick, whereas those of the eastern compartment were only 4 ft. 6 in. It may therefore be an outside wall, ending the series. The wall fragments seen in 1959 were of ragstone faced with squared blocks, and several courses of tiles were seen in the S. wall. A portion of the N. face of the latter has been preserved. (*See Fig.* 24, *C, opposite p.* 138.)

(*Plans in Guildhall Museum.*)

212 *Cornhill, Nos.* 45–7, 1923–4

A ragstone wall about 5 ft. thick, with four courses of brick ran

across the site in a westerly direction. The western face of a
N.–S. wall of ragstone with brick courses at a different level was
seen on the eastern edge of the site, and the northern face of
another E.–W. wall, parallel with the first, was observed on the
southern edge under St. Michael's Church. There were indications of a projection from this to the north, suggesting the
existence of another cross-wall running N.–S., and a hole sunk
on this line near the centre of the site passed through a wall at a
lower level, and perhaps of earlier date. Two other wall fragments
were observed at the western end of the site, and Mr. G. C.
Dunning has shown that these and the cross-walls fit into the
probable plan of the western end of the basilica. A loose brick
stamped P.P.BR.LON. was found on this site. (*See plan, Fig.* 24,
G, opposite p. 138.)
London and Middlesex Arch. Soc. Trans., N.S., V, p. 189*ff.* *J.R.S.,*
XXI (1931), *pp.* 236*ff.* *R.C.H.M., p.* 116.

213 *Cornhill, No.* 50, 1891
A series of walls of rubble with fragments of Roman brick were
found extending to a depth of 21½ ft. below pavement level, and
standing 9 ft. high. The Royal Commission Report states that
the plan published in *Archaeologia* is incorrect, and that the
original plan shows that the walls were parallel and in alignment
with the basilica. It has been suggested that the curved cross-wall
was originally straight, the effect of curvature being due to the
breaking away of the outer edge. The walls seem to have been
foundations, but a pier of the superstructure, built of tiles on a
block of ashlar sandstone, was seen standing on the southern wall
under St. Michael's Church. On the N. edge of the site, running
west under Cornhill was another wall with the beginning of a
cross-wall to the north. (*See plan, Fig,* 21, *p,* 134.)
Arch., LX, pp. 223*ff.* *Proc. Soc. Antiq.* (*2nd S.*), *XIV, pp.* 6*f.*
R.C.H.M., p. 115.

214 *Cornhill, No.* 52, 1929
Two ragstone walls 5 ft. and 6 ft. in thickness were found on the
site, 20 ft. apart, running E.–W., and evidently continuations of
those found in 1891 on the site of 50 Cornhill (**213**). On the
N. side of the northern wall were two cross-walls, 4 ft. thick and
21 ft. apart, passing under Cornhill. The southern E.–W. wall
was a sleeper wall with a course of bonding-tiles, and carried a
pier of solid brick on stone footings, identical in construction

with the pier at the corner of Gracechurch Street and Leadenhall Avenue. (*See Pl.* 51.) Between the walls was an *opus signinum* floor 6 in. thick, 11 ft. below the level of Cornhill. This overlay brick-earth from the foundation trenches of the walls and rubbish, including pottery, all of the Flavian period, with potters' stamps of *Cosius and Rufinus, Marius, Monticus and Crestus.* (*Figs.* 21–2, pp. 134f.)

J.R.S., XXI (1931), *pp.* 236–8.

215 *Cornhill, Nos.* 56–7, 1922

On the demolition of these premises, a length of 6 ft. or 7 ft. of Roman walling, with courses of bonding-tiles and faced with squared ragstone, was revealed passing at a slight angle under the northern wall of St. Peter's Church. The top of the wall was about 9 ft. 6 in. below the level of the pavement, and it extended to a depth of 17 ft. The thickness could not be ascertained as the southern face lay under the church. A small piece of plaster with red paint remained adhering to its northern face. The wall appeared to be a continuation of one found under Gracechurch Street (**217**). (*See Fig.* 24, *opposite p.* 138.)

Ant. Journ., II, p. 260.   *R.C.H.M., pp.* 115 *f.*   *J.R.S.,* XI (1921), *pp.* 219–20.

216 *Gracechurch Street, E. of St. Peter's Church,* 1848–9

While sinking a shaft for a side entrance to the sewer, a N.–S. wall of Kentish ragstone, 5 ft. thick, with its top at a depth of 10 ft. from the surface, was encountered on the western side of Gracechurch Street. A similar E.–W. wall, apparently making a right angle with it, was found while tunnelling for the sewer in Gracechurch Street, and the positions of both walls are marked on a City Sewer Plan with the following note: 'In the inside of those two walls there was an old pavement which extended from wall to wall; it was $1\frac{1}{2}$ in. thick and it laid upon a bed of concrete 6 in. thick a specimen of which I brought to the office.' This was evidently the same E.–W. wall as the one found in 1922 beneath the eastern half of the roadway, when another N.–S. wall of a slighter character was found (**217**). (*See Fig.* 24, *opposite p.* 138.)

City Sewer Plan 210.

217 *Gracechurch Street, E. of St. Peter's Church,* 1922

During excavations for telephone wires two Roman walls were found under the roadway opposite the northern portion of St. Peter's Church. The more important one was 4 ft. 6 in. thick, and ran E.–W., approximately in line with the wall found on the site

of Nos. 56–7 Cornhill (**215**). The base was not reached at a
depth of 16 ft. At a depth of 10–11 ft. were five rows of tiles
between courses of squared ragstone, and a few feet higher up
were two rows. The upper part of the south side was plastered
and painted in black, yellow and red, apparently with a design
of panels. The other wall ran to the south at right angles with the
first, and had evidently been added later, as the plaster continued
behind the junction. It was 2 ft. 9 in. thick, and built of ragstone
with a double course of bonding-tiles at a depth of 12 ft. 6 in.,
where traces of a white cement floor were found. On the W. side
a later floor of coarse red tesserae had been laid 4 ft. above the
original floor. (*See Fig.* 24, *opposite p.* 138.)
Ant. Journ., II, pp. 140–1.   *R.C.H.M., p.* 121.

218 *Leadenhall Street, N. of Leadenhall Avenue,* 1881
Fragmentary walls are recorded on H. Hodge's plan on the
northern edge of Leadenhall Avenue and on the sites to the north
of it. This area seems to have been incompletely excavated,
and only short pieces of wall are shown. These are set at
various angles and strongly suggest the presence of curved walls.
(*See Fig.* 24, *opposite p.* 138.)
R.C.H.M., pp. 40f., *Plan, Pl.* 5, *opp. p.* 40.

219 *Leadenhall Market, S. of Leadenhall Avenue,* 1881
On the site of the London Metal Exchange a portion of ragstone
wall running E.–W. is recorded on H. Hodge's plan. On it rested
limestone blocks 2 ft. 3 in. wide and 11 in. thick. To the south
was a concrete floor at a depth of about 15 ft. 3 in. below pavement level. A cross-wall of ragstone ran N.–S., and just to the
west of this were found loose inscribed bricks like others found built
in the E.–W. wall to the south (**220**). (*See Fig.* 24, *B, opposite p.* 138.)
  Loftus Brock observed two distinct floor levels, the lower being
of red tesserae and covered with the ashes of a great fire, while
the upper was of concrete.
R.C.H.M., pp. 40f., *Plan, Pl.* 5, *opp. p.* 40.

220 *Leadenhall Market,* 1881–2
Foundations of the southern wall of a great building were found
running the length of the western portion of the Market, from
Gracechurch Street to Whittington Avenue. At the eastern end
(at the S. end of Whittington Avenue) was an apse, and to the
south of this were rectangular compartments. The main S. wall

was apparently double for part of its length, probably representing two periods, of which the southern half may represent the outer wall of the original structure. Resting on the northern half, but also overlying the edge of the southern half, a rectangular brick pier was found beneath the pavement and frontage of Gracechurch Street, and is still preserved in the basement of Messrs. Blurton's shop. The northern half of the wall seems therefore to have been a sleeper wall carrying an arcade in a larger and later building. A small apsidal wall adjoining it on the north was probably a foundation only, intended to give additional strength at this point. (*See Fig.* 24, *opposite p.* 138.) Pavements of two periods also are described – one of ordinary brick tesserae, covered with the ashes of a great fire, and above this the concrete of a second floor. A fragment of white tessellated pavement is also mentioned, apparently overlying the foundation apse on the N. side of the S. wall.

Drawings and plan by H. HODGE, *Guildhall Library.*   *R.C.H.M.,* *pp.* 40–1, 127, *Plan, Pl.* 5, *opp. p.* 40.

221 *Gracechurch Street, between St. Peter's Alley and Corbet Court,* 1883–4 *and* 1964

The continuation of the supposed sleeper wall of the basilica was found in 1883–4, with an apse adjoining its northern face – presumably a foundation arch. Traces of cross-walls to the north were found under the Gracechurch Street footpath and about 20 ft. further west. Adjoining the E.–W. wall to the south was a sloping buttress which appeared to be the end of the southern E.–W. wall seen on the E. side of the street. Further south, beneath the Gracechurch Street footpath was found the W. end of another wall with a finished face. The foundation of the E.–W. (sleeper) wall beneath the southern side of St. Peter's Alley was seen in 1964 extending to a depth of 32 ft. below the modern pavement level. It was 6 ft. thick and consisted of intensely hard ragstone rubble concrete, containing some broken brick. (*See Fig.* 24, *A, opposite p.* 138.)

Another wall was observed in 1883–4 about 33 ft. south of this wall and not quite parallel with it, running under Corbet Court to the west. This was thought to be the southern wall of the extended basilica, but it now seems much more likely, allowing for a slight error in alignment, that it was a continuation of the northern wall of **229**. When the site of Corbet Court was excavated in 1964, only one small portion of ragstone foundation remained, and this was consistent both with the re-alignment shown here and the position previously recorded. The N.–S. wall of **229A**, however, encroached on the line of this wall as

shown by Hodge, so it seems reasonably certain that the re-alignment is correct, and that the wall had no connection with the basilica. (*See Fig.* 24, *R, opposite p.* 138, *and Fig.* 27, *C, p.* 145.)
Plan by H. HODGE *in Guildhall Library* (*R.C.H.M., Pl.* 5, *opp. p.* 40).
G.M.

222 *Leadenhall Market, eastern portion,* 1881–2
About 31 ft. to the east of the eastern apse and adjacent wall of the great basilica (**220**) was a much narrower brick wall, about 2 ft. thick, with painted plaster on both sides. Adjoining it on the western side was a portion of pavement with tiles in a herring-bone pattern, at a depth of 13 ft. 2 in. below the modern level of Gracechurch Street. This corresponds in level with the earlier floors found within the basilica. The top of the wall was levelled about 1 ft. 1 in. higher, evidently before the road (**232**) was constructed. A section drawn by Hodge immediately to the north of this area shows a portion of gravel, probably metalling of this road, at a higher level.

To the south, passing through the thick E. wall of the basilica, was a drainage channel or flue, running E.–W., and consisting of tile walls on a base of concrete where it emerged on both sides of the thick wall. The eastern end, within the building, dipped down. (*See also Fig.* 24, *opposite p.* 138.)
Drawings by H. HODGE *in Guildhall Library.*   *R.C.H.M., Pl.* 5, *opp. p.* 40.

223 *Whittington Avenue (uncertain date)*
Two portions of pavement were found on the site of the Green Yard, between Whittington Avenue and East India House (now part of Lloyd's building). The one to the west was of herring-bone type, and the one to the east of tesserae. Presumably the herring-bone pavement was a continuation of the one recorded by H. Hodge 50–60 ft. further south (**222**). Like the latter, it must have been earlier than the road (**232**), which probably passed over it at a higher level.
Plan in Guildhall Library.   *R.C.H.M., p.* 128.

224 *Lime Street, Nos.* 4–6, *Lloyd's Building,* 1925
During excavations on the western side of the site, Roman foundations and the lower courses of partition walls were found, as well as a Roman tiled floor.
R.C.H.M., p. 128.

225 *Birchin Lane, Nos.* 19–21, 1935

Road metalling consisting of hard compact gravel with some brick fragments was seen in two places on the site. It contained some blocks of worked stone near the bottom, which was at an irregular depth varying from 15–21 ft. below pavement level. It seemed to form part of a N.–S. road, which must have been more than 30 ft. wide. From occupation levels and refuse deposits below it came eight potter's stamps of the following dates: Tiberius – Nero (1), Tiberius – Vespasian (2), Claudius – Nero (1), Claudius – Vespasian (2), Claudius – Domitian (1), Nero – Vespasian (1). The construction of the road cannot therefore be earlier than the reign of Nero, and is more probably of Flavian date. East of the road was a robber trench 4 ft. wide, containing powdered cement and lumps of ragstone, apparently following the line of a N.–S. wall just east of the road. (*See Fig.* 24., *X, M, opposite p.* 138.) (See also **299** for a possible southern continuation of this road.)

MS. notes by Mr. F. COTTRILL.

226 *George Yard, Nos.* 9–12, *before* 1912

A portion of an ancient stream-bed was observed when the Bank was built on this site. It apparently flowed N.–S., but inclined slightly towards the west. This seems to be the continuation of a stream-bed seen on the site of No. 50 Cornhill (**213**). It is likely to have been drained and filled in at an early date, since the extended basilica was constructed above it. This stream was also found further to the S.W. on the site of Nos. 34–7 Nicholas Lane (**287**).

Arch., LXIII, p. 318–19, *Fig.* 26.

227 *St. Michael's House, Nos.* 1–2, *S. of St. Michael's Alley,* 1932

Two ragstone walls 5 ft. thick and another 3 ft. thick to the east of these were found crossing the site N.–S. In the opinion of Mr. G. C. Dunning, who recorded them, they seemed to belong to a series of rooms and a colonnade overlooking the forum from the west. The foundations cut through an occupation layer and rubbish pit of middle or late first century date. (*See also Fig.* 24, *J, K, L, opposite p.* 138.)

J.R.S., XXIII (1933), *p.* 204.

228 *Gracechurch Street, Nos.* 7–9, 1912

A Roman wall, 4½ ft. thick, with base 27 ft. below the surface, of ragstone bonded at 3 ft. intervals with double layers of tiles, ran N.N.E., and then turned at right angles and passed under the

street. Beneath the lower of the two bonding-courses were 5 ft. of rough ragstone built on 2 ft. 6 in. of flints lightly set in occasional splashes of mortar. This foundation seemed to have been laid in a trench cut in the original surface. A small piece of much thinner wall ran north from the E.–W. wall, parallel with Gracechurch Street and close to the roadway. The position of these finds is shown as it is recorded, but it seems likely that the E.–W. wall was really in line with the southern E.–W. wall of **229,** and the N.–S. wall may well have been a continuation of the building line of **237.** (*See also Fig.* 24, *opposite p.* 138.)
Arch., LXIII, p. 320 (*Plan, p.* 329).   *R.C.H.M., p.* 121.

229 *Gracechurch Street, No.* 85, 1934
A portion of a large rectangular structure with an inner compartment was found. The outer walls were of ragstone rubble with some flint and contained courses of bonding-tiles. They were on foundations of flint rubble, usually mortared to the bottom. The outer walls on the north and east (partly discovered in 1908) were 3 ft. 3 in. thick and had external square buttresses of brick at intervals of about 10 ft. The outer wall on the south had no buttresses but was considerably thicker (4 ft. 6 in.). It was possibly a continuation of the E.–W. wall found on the west of Gracechurch Street (**228**). The inner walls were also of ragstone rubble with bonding-courses, and had foundations of flint rubble. Traces of a cement floor were seen in the N. part of the building in both outer and inner compartments. There were walls of a small extension in the S.E. corner, apparently continuing to the south, and between the inner and outer walls was observed a short stretch of another N.–S. wall at a slightly higher level. The S. external wall cut through a pit said to have contained Flavian and earlier pottery. (*See also Fig.* 24, *Q*, *opposite p.* 138, *and Fig.* 27, *p.* 145.)
J.R.S., XXV (1935), *pp.* 215–17.

229A *Gracechurch Street, No.* 6, *and Corbet Court,* 1964
A builders' excavation revealed an E.–W. wall of ragstone with two triple courses of bonding-tiles on a foundation of flints and cement. This was in line with the northern E.–W. wall of the internal compartment of **229**, and seemed to be a continuation of it. A layer of debris piled against the N. face of the wall contained pottery of about A.D. 60–80. Above this was a layer of white cement overlaid with a deposit of clean brick-earth, which in turn was covered by Roman building rubble, possibly from the destruction of the building. A similar N.–S. wall with one triple course of bonding tiles joined the E.–W. wall at its western end.

To the west of this, outside the building or compartment formed by the two walls, was a white cement floor laid on broken tiles, slightly above the internal layer of white cement and at about 41 ft. above O.D. Overlying it were layers of gravel concrete, above which was Roman building debris. A small portion of an earlier foundation of ragstone and clay, probably of an E.–W. wall (not shown on the map), was seen in section in the natural brick-earth under the layers of make-up beneath the white cement floor.

G.M.

230 *Gracechurch Street, Nos.* 83–7, 1934

At various places two cement floors were observed. The earlier one was of whitish sandy cement, of thickness 3–8 in., and lay at a depth varying from 18 ft. 3 in. below ground level where it bordered the wall **231**, to 16 ft. at a distance of 52 ft. west of the wall. Two intermediate observations suggest that this floor gradually sloped from the centre of the site down towards the wall. Overlying the white floor was make-up of gravel and brick-earth, of varying thickness; and on this was laid a later floor of pink cement, $1\frac{1}{2}$–4 in. thick, at depths varying from 14–16 ft. below ground level. With this floor the slope seems to have been in the opposite direction, viz. from the wall towards the centre of the site, and probably also from north to south. At one point some occupation debris overlay the white floor beneath the make-up of the pink floor. A sketch by Mr. F. Cottrill of a jug-neck, said by a workman to have come from this debris, indicates a form of the third century. If this evidence can be trusted, it gives a *terminus post quem* for the later floor.

MS. notes and section by Mr. F. COTTRILL.

231 *Gracechurch Street, No.* 85 (*E. end of site, adjoining Lime Street Passage*), 1934

A robber trench marked the position of a N.–S. wall near the E. edge of the site, and from its position and alignment this could be the internal wall of the E. side of the forum. Portions of two large rectangular buttresses, 23 ft. apart, remained on the W. side of the wall, of which only one small section survived, immediately south of the northern buttress. Its footings, at a depth of 21 ft. below ground level, consisted of ragstone without mortar, with a 2 in. layer of mortar 1 ft. 5 in. above the bottom. The wall itself consisted of ragstone rubble 3 ft. 9 in. thick. The buttress adjoining was 5 ft. 9 in. thick, and consisted of ragstone rubble with a single tile course. 1 ft. above this, at a depth of 18 ft., a

white cement floor adjoined the W. face of the buttress. On the east of the wall, opposite the southern buttress, was an offset wall running to the east. A portion of rubble which might belong to a third buttress was seen in the N.E. corner of the site. (*See also Fig. 24, H, opposite p.* 138, *and Fig.* 27, *p.* 145.)
J.R.S., XXV (1935), *p.* 215, *and Fig.* 21, *p.* 217.

232 *Lime Street, Nos.* 15–18 (*site of Pewterers' Hall*), 1932
The gravel metalling of a Roman N.–S. road was observed in the N.W. corner of the site. It was at least 25 ft. wide and made up to 8 ft. in thickness. It overlay an early occupation layer resting on the brick-earth, containing pottery of A.D. 50–80, including potters' stamps of *Perrus, Pontus* and *Maccarus*. West of the road, in the extreme N.W. corner of the site, were the footings of a wall running parallel with the road. This probably represented the E. boundary of the forum. (*See also Fig.* 24, *YI, opposite p.* 138.)
J.R.S., XXIII (1933), *p.* 205.

233 *Lime Street, Nos.* 15–18 (*site of Pewterers' Hall*), 1932
Part of a rectangular compartment, believed to be part of a bath-building, measuring 11 ft. by 8 ft. internally, was found about 50 ft. east of the Roman road (**232**). It had a thick concrete floor and solid tile walls 3 ft. thick, standing to a height of 2 ft. above the floor. It was sealed by a burnt layer attributed to the Hadrianic fire. The alignment seems to have been that of the buildings within the forum area rather than that of the forum and basilica.
J.R.S., XXIII (1933), *p.* 205.   *Unpublished plan by* Mr. F. COTTRILL.

234 *Gracechurch Street, Nos.* 17–19, 1934–5
A wall was found running E.–W. about 10 ft. south of the N. wall of the site. It was faced with undressed ragstone blocks set in yellowish-brown cement, laid in five courses to a height of 2 ft. 3 in. The uppermost course had a level top (at a depth of 7 ft. below basement level), and it is possible that this was merely a sleeper wall, but more probable that it had been deliberately demolished and levelled. Above was clean brown clay 1 ft. thick. 11½ ft. to the west was a block of similar masonry, apparently all that had been left by stone robbers. (*See also Fig.* 24, *opposite p.* 138.)
MS. notes by Mr. F. COTTRILL.

235 *Gracechurch Street, Nos.* 17–19, 1934–5

In the western part of the site the nearly complete plan of a Roman building, possibly a temple, was recovered. Its orientation was 10° E. of N., and at the northern end was an angular apse. The northern compartment, excluding the apse, was 28 ft. by 29 ft., and there was access through a doorway from the compartment to the south, which was 23 ft. by 29 ft. This was entered by a doorway in the eastern wall. The foundations were of flint rubble with yellowish-brown mortar, sometimes resting on a layer of unmortared ragstone blocks, and were 3 ft. thick. Above, the walls were built of flanged roofing tiles, broken and laid in regular courses, with the face of the wall formed by the upturned flanges. The bottom of the foundation was 10–14 ft. below basement level. There was little dating evidence, but a jug-neck of early type (Claudius – Nero) came from a rubbish level sloping up against the wall. The building seems to have been deliberately dismantled and the level of its site raised, presumably when the forum was constructed. (*See also Fig.* 24, *T, opposite p.* 138.)

J.R.S., XXVI (1936), *p.* 254 *and Fig.* 28.

236 *Gracechurch Street, Nos.* 17–19, 1934–5

In the eastern part of the site were traces of a fairly complex building. The walls rested on a foundation of flint rubble set in yellowish-brown pebbly concrete, with its bottom about 23½ ft. below street level. Some ragstone was seen in the easternmost N.–S. wall. The foundation was about 3 ft. thick. Above were courses of brickwork, containing broken roofing tiles with their flanges turned upwards on the face of the wall. The N.–S. wall on the west had a triple bonding-course above the flint rubble, with a plinth on the E. side level with its top. Above were more courses of brick. A bead-rim sherd (first century) was found in a dark layer against the wall overlying the plinth. There was some evidence of an ancient demolition of the building. (*See also Fig.* 24, *S, opposite p.* 138.)

MS. notes by Mr. F. COTTRILL.

237 *Gracechurch Street, Nos.* 15–16 (*S. of Bell Yard*), 1912

A wall 2 ft. thick was found with its base 16½ ft. below the surface. The base was of ragstone with two courses of tiles at the top. Below the wall was a mass of flint and mortar more than 4 ft. thick. From its depth this appeared to have been built at a later date than the wall north of Bell Inn Yard (**228**), after the surface had been artificially raised. (*See also Fig.* 24, *N. end of building S, opposite p.* 138.)

Arch., LXIII, p. 320, *Plan p.* 329.   *R.C.H.M., p.* 121.

238 *Gracechurch Street, Nos.* 17–19, 1934–5

Near the S.E. corner of the site, a layer of gravel and sand containing brick fragments, 2 ft. 10 in. thick, was seen in section. At a depth of 7 ft. 10 in. below the level of the basement it was overlaid by a layer of white cement 1 in. thick. Above this was mixed soil with building rubbish, and over this a layer of pinkish coarse cement at a depth of 4 ft. 4 in. The gravel was seen extending from about 16 to 23+ ft. west of Gracechurch Street, but may have extended further in either direction. In it was a dark layer of carbonised matter.

MS. notes by Mr. F. COTTRILL.

239 *Lombard Street, All Hallows Church, now part of Barclays Bank,* 1939

A Roman E.–W. wall of brick with pink mortar and a course of ragstone, 4 ft. thick, was found overlying Antonine pottery (*Drag.* 38), and was presumably of the mid-second century or later. This made an angle with a similar N.–S. wall on the edge of Gracechurch Street. Immediately to the south were three brick piers with yellow mortar, of which the two easternmost had additions in pink mortar. Overlying the yellow mortar piers but flush with the pink mortar additions was a white cement floor, which overlay Hadrianic and earlier pottery. About 10 ft. to the south was a single column base and core, which stood on the cement floor, and probably rested on a similar pink mortar pier. S.W. of this was a T-shaped pier of brick with yellow mortar, its E. and S. arms in alignment with the walls and piers described above, but its W. arm aligned with an earlier building to the west (see **240**). To the south were traces of a wall running N.–S. in a line between this pier and the central pier found in 1925 (**241**). There were traces of another E.–W. wall (the foundation trench of a robbed wall only), probably earlier, to the north, and also two more yellow mortar piers in a line at right angles to that of the other three. (*See also Fig.* 24, *N, P 1, opposite p.* 138.)

Plan and MS. notes by Mr. A. H. OSWALD.

240 *Lombard Street, All Hallows Church, now part of Barclays Bank,* 1939

The E.–W. wall (**239**) which is probably part of the forum building, intersected an earlier N.–S. wall in the same alignment as the buildings to the north, on the site of 17–19 Gracechurch Street (**234, 235, 236**). This wall had been heavily robbed, apparently in the second century, as the pottery in the robbing was exclusively of that century or earlier. Parallel with it, to the S.E., was another wall, from which ran two E.–W. walls to the

east. (*See Fig.* 24, *U, opposite p.* 138.) This appeared to be a southern continuation of the building observed on 17–19 Gracechurch Street (**236**). It was clear that it was earlier than the brick piers to the east, but probably survived until the building of these, since a portion of one is on the same alignment. A yet earlier E.–W. wall (not shown on the map) was intersected by the eastern N.–S. wall. (*See Fig.* 24 *Z.1, opposite p.* 138.)
Plan and MS. notes by Mr. A. H. OSWALD.

241 *Lombard Street, No.* 42, *at N. angle of Lombard Street and Gracechurch Street,* 1925
A wall was found running at a slight angle with the N. frontage of Lombard Street. It was of rubble alternating with courses of brick on the N. face and set in yellow mortar. (*See Pl.* 53) About 8¼ ft. north of the wall were two complete piers and part of a third, made entirely of brick set in red mortar, standing on rubble foundations. In the corridor between the piers and the wall were traces of a mortar bed, probably for a pavement, a few inches above the level of the footings of the piers. The second pier had a short length of broken wall adjoining it about the middle of its N. face. (*See Fig.* 24, *P, opposite p.* 138, *and Pl.* 52.)
London and Middlesex Arch. Soc. Trans., N.S., V, pp. 317–23.
R.C.H.M., p. 129.

242 *Lombard Street, W. of entrance of All Hallows Church,* 1933
An extension of the wall found in 1925 (**241**) was observed. Its face was about 7 ft. south of the building line from which it diverged only very slightly. The wall was 4 ft. thick with the top of its footings about 11½ ft. below the pavement. It was constructed mainly of red tiles 1½ in. thick with 1½ in. joints of pink or buff cement, but in one part the tiles were replaced by ragstone rubble, roughly coursed, from a depth of 7 ft. 7 in. to about 9 ft. 3½ in., the tilework continuing again below this. Immediately east of this, however, all of the wall that was visible was of tiles. There was an offset of 8 in. on the N. side of the wall at a depth of 9 ft. 8 in. below pavement level. (*See also Fig.* 24, *opposite p.* 138, *which shows the old building frontage to which reference is made. The map shows the present frontage.*)
J.R.S., XXIV (1934), *p.* 211.   *MS. notes by* Mr. F. COTTRILL.

243 *Lombard Street, Nos.* 54–8, *site of Barclays Bank,* 1960–1
The earliest features on the site were a U-shaped trench running

approximately N.N.E., containing pottery of the Claudian period in its filling, and two parallel E.–W. walls of ragstone, brown mortar and courses of bonding-tiles. The southern wall and an off-set wall to the south were overlaid by the later building described below. To avoid confusion, only the N. wall of the earlier structure has been marked on the map. It is possible that the southern wall may be a continuation of the earliest wall on the site of All Hallows (*See Fig. 23, p. 137, where the earliset walls are marked C, and Fig. 24, opposite p. 138, where they are marked Z.*)

The first building was succeeded by a second, of ragstone and white mortar (*Fig. 23 B*), perhaps part of the large, complex structure apparently antedating the forum on the sites to the east (**236, 240**). There were indications of a suite of rooms with a corridor to the south and probably to the west. The westernmost wall (*Fig. 23, A*), unfortunately not stratigraphically related to the rest of the building, overlay the Claudian ditch, and a layer of occupation debris of the period Claudius–Nero, with a burnt level, possibly Boudiccan, had accumulated against it. Within the building, overlying a floor of gravelly earth, was occupation debris of A.D. 60–80. It was buried beneath a layer of almost clean brick-earth, 3 ft. thick, containing sherds of about the end of the first century. This probably represents make-up to level the site after the demolition of the building. To the south, underlying the roadway, was seen a similar ragstone wall, running E.–W., which may have been part of the same building, though it apparently continued the line of the supposed forum wall (**241, 242**). A small portion of another wall of ragstone, evidently of later date than the structures described above, was observed on a higher level further west, running approximately N.–S. (**245**).

G.M.   *J.R.S., LII, pp.* 178–9, *Fig.* 25, *p.* 180.   *London and Middlesex Arch. Soc. Trans., XXI, Pt.* 1 (1963), *pp.* 72ff.

244 *Lombard Street, Nos.* 54–8, *site of Barclays Bank, northern portion, W. of Ball Alley,* 1960–1

An area of hard gravel metalling with two surfaces was found immediately to the west of Ball Alley. It was more than 8 in. thick, and its upper surface lay at about 43½ ft. above O.D. The gravel had been mixed with cement. It had no camber and could not be traced in either a southerly or a westerly direction, so it is unlikely to have been a road. As it did not lie far above the natural brick-earth, it was probably of early date, and may well have formed part of a courtyard round the building to the north found in 1934 (**235**). A small portion of an E.–W. wall, presumably part of the southern wall of this building, was found about 18 ft. N.W. of the metalling. It consisted of four courses of Roman brick set in brown cement. Its top lay about 44 ft. above O.D., and was overlaid with Roman building rubble 2 ft. 2 in. thick. On this was a layer of yellow cement 3 in. thick. A portion of a ragstone foundation-wall running approximately N.–S. was seen to the west under Ball Alley, but the period of this was uncertain. (*See Fig.* 23, *p.* 137, *and Fig.* 24, *opposite p.* 138.)

G.M.

245 *Lombard Street, Nos.* 54–8 (*site of Barclays Bank*), 1960–1
To the west of the building **243** was seen a small fragment of the foundation of a later Roman wall, running N.–S., and cutting into the clay make-up which overlay the remains of the earlier building. This was presumably part of the forum building. It was 4 ft. 4 in. thick, and mixed with the fragments of ragstone of which it was composed was a quantity of pitch, which had evidently been spilt over the stones while the wall was being built. (*See Fig.* 23, *p.* 137, *and Fig.* 24, *opposite p.* 138.)

G.M.

246 *Queen Victoria Street, N.W. corner of Bucklersbury House site*, 1954
A Roman well consisting of two wooden barrels, one above the other, was observed during the builders' excavation. The upper barrel, which was destroyed by the builders, was 5 ft. 4 in. in height; the lower, which was excavated by the staff of Guildhall Museum, was only 1 ft. 10 in. high, with an internal diameter of 2 ft. This may have been cut down from a larger barrel. It contained pottery of the late first century, a brass knife-handle and an iron spear blade with an inscription in punched dots, 'Ɔ.VER.VICT', indicating that it belonged to the Century commanded by an officer named VER[US]VICT[OR]. (*See Pl.* 98.)

Guildhall Museum Excavation Register 220.

247 *Walbrook, Bucklersbury House*, 1955
The line of the Roman stream-bed, in its earlier stages flowing between banks revetted with piles and planks, was observed passing through the site. The stream-bed shown on the map is the revetted bed of the first and second centuries, which seems to have narrowed immediately north of the Mithras temple site from a width of 12–13 ft. to only about 8 ft. The revetment of the east bank was deflected slightly to the west where this occurred. Further south the width was nearly 14 ft. The revetted banks seem to have collapsed soon after the middle of the second

century, and thereafter the stream became a mere runnel flowing at ever higher levels as the relative water level rose and the stream silted. The position of the stream changed slightly at different periods, and the earliest bed seems to have been a little to the west of the Roman revetted stream.

The point at which the western tributary joined the main stream is unknown, but it seems likely that it was at the place where the stream-bed widened.

For finds from the stream-bed and its banks on this site see *Plates* 126, 127, 129, 131–9.

G.M. See also R. L. S. BRUCE-MITFORD: *Recent Archaeological Excavations in Britain*, 1956, *pp.* 137*ff.*, *for account by Professor W. F. Grimes.*

248 *Walbrook, Bucklersbury House, Temple of Mithras*, 1954
During excavations by Professor W. F. Grimes on behalf of the Roman and Mediaeval London Excavation Council, a basilican temple was found. It had a rounded apse at the W. end, a central nave, and two side aisles separated from the nave by sleeper walls, bearing settings for the bases of seven columns on each side. At the western end within the apse was a raised sanctuary, and at the eastern end was a narthex slightly wider than the main part of the temple, with which it communicated by a double door-way opening on to three steps down into the nave. These had wooden risers. The narthex could not be excavated owing to its proximity to the street of Walbrook. In the S.W. corner of the southern aisle was a wooden tank, which was covered in a later phase of the occupation of the building. A succession of seven floors of earth and gravel had been laid because of flooding from the Walbrook. The last but one of these, dated by coin evidence to the reign of Constantine, overlay carefully buried marble sculptures of Mithras and other deities. The building of the temple has been attributed to the latter part of the second century. (*See pp.* 62–4, 143–4, *Plates* 72–83).

J.R.S. XLIV (1954), *p.* 99; *XLV* (1955), *pp.* 137–9. R. L. S. BRUCE-MITFORD: *Recent Archaeological Excavations in Britain*, 1956, *pp.* 139–42 (*account by Professor W. F. Grimes*).

249 *Walbrook, Bucklersbury House, Roman building N. of temple*, 1954
A Roman wall 3 ft. in thickness running N.–S. was found during the builders' excavation north of the temple. The fragment seen was 8 ft. long and built of ragstone and sandstone rubble, with a course of bonding-tiles above an offset on the W. side. A few inches lower on the E. side was a small piece of pavement of

coarse red tesserae, laid directly in earth at a level of 21.45 ft. above O.D. – several feet higher than the uppermost floor of the temple. A cutting further east showed that there were a number of rammed floors of sand and gravel below this level. Pottery sherds of the third to fourth century were found against the W. face of the wall in the filling of a gully which appeared to be the builder's trench.

Guildhall Museum Excavation Register 214.

250 *Walbrook, Bucklersbury House, wooden structures S. of the Temple of Mithras,* 1954

A small square timber-framed well or tank was found about 15 ft. south of the temple. It was $2\frac{1}{2}$ ft. square internally, and had a cement bottom on which two tiles had been set. The filling contained pottery of the late third to early fourth century. A few feet to the west of this, a portion of a timber platform about 6 ft. wide and of unknown length, was observed at a depth of about 17 ft. below street level. (*See Pl.* 20.) Pottery overlying the platform was probably Antonine. Beneath its boards were found a number of pupae, identified as those of 'Latrine Flies' (*Teichomyza fusca* and *Fannia sp.*). It is possible therefore that this structure was either a latrine or a workshop in which urine was used for some industrial process, such as fulling.

Another square, timber-framed well of about the same size as the first was seen a short distance to the south-west. In it were found an iron arrow-head and a wooden bucket, apparently associated with pottery of the third to fourth century.

A wooden barrel, believed to be Roman, was seen further west, near the stream. The filling of this contained only leather fragments, with nothing datable.

Guildhall Museum Excavation Register 222, 235, 218 *and* 213.

251 *Walbrook, Bucklersbury House, Roman road at S. end of Walbrook,* 1955

A gravelled road was seen in section, with its southern edge just over 32 ft. north of the retaining wall at the S.E. corner of the site. It was about 20 ft. in width, and consisted of a series of metalled surfaces one above the other, about 6 ft. in thickness, with the upper levels above this disturbed. The base rested on timbers supported by massive beams laid horizontally, and these in turn seem to have been carried by vertical piles driven into the grey clay beneath. Other piles were seen at the same depth adjoining the N. edge of the road and continuing its line westward towards the Walbrook stream. There was a timber retaining

wall on each side of the mass of metalling, and a timber-lined gully adjoined this at a high level to the south. The bottom of the gravel road was about 26–7 ft. below the level of the modern pavement. (*See Fig. 18, p. 123, and Plates 23 and 25.*)
Guildhall Museum Excavation Register 291.

252 *Walbrook, Bucklersbury House site, piles and timber structure in S.E. corner of site,* 1955
At the S.E. corner of the site, directly within the retaining wall perimeter, a massive timber platform supported on piles was found, extending about 10 ft. to the north of the south retaining wall. (*See Pl.* 21.) A small quantity of first century pottery was found close to one of the vertical piles. The timbering apparently extended as far as a gully adjoining the S. edge of the gravel roadway (**251**), but a modern intrusion made it impossible to plot more than the first 10 ft. North of the intrusion, however, was what appeared to be a continuation of the timber platform adjoining the gully.
Guildhall Museum Excavation Register 291, *and Day Book, April* 1955–*March* 1956, *p.* 51.

253 *Budge Row, eastern end, at southern extremity of Bucklersbury House site,* 1955
Massive piles driven close together were seen near the presumed line of the western edge of the revetted Roman stream, but at a higher level. Around them was a sandy deposit containing pottery of the third century, and over them lay a mixed filling, which in one area consisted of 7 in. of chalk rubble. A base of a Castor ware vessel was found in black silt 2 ft. 3 in. below the chalk capping.
Guildhall Museum Excavation Register 296, 301, 302.

254 *Budge Row,* 1853
During sewer excavations the remains of a Roman wall were found at a depth of 15 ft. It was constructed of rubble, layers of tile and concrete.
J.B.A.A., IX, p. 84.   *R.C.H.M., p.* 110.

255 *Cannon Street, Temple House,* 1958
A line of squared wooden piles was observed running just north of Budge Row, roughly in line with Watling Street, but as these probably formed part of a complex of posts their alignment may not signify very much. Patches of clean ballast were seen where

the grab had been working along the line of Budge Row, overlying a thin layer of black pebbly mud, from which an amphora handle was recovered. This layer was immediately above the clay sub-soil. The patches of ballast may possibly indicate the continuation of the metalled road seen on the east of the Walbrook.

Guildhall Museum Excavation Register 436 *and Notebook* 5, *p.* 22.

256 *Cannon Street, Temple House,* 1958
In the trench for the retaining wall along the Cannon Street frontage, about 12–15 ft. north of the pavement, wooden piles were seen, in not very even lines, running roughly E.–W. The pile tops were about 7 ft. below the old basement floor.
G.M.

257 *Cloak Lane,* 1846
Wooden piles and some concrete pavement are said to have been found here, and a fragment of a tombstone with an inscription is also said to have come from sewer excavations in this street.
J.B.A.A., II, p. 341.   *R.C.H.M., pp.* 113, 172.

258 *Cloak Lane,* 1888
During excavations for the District Railway under the site of St. John the Baptist, Walbrook, a Roman tile floor of herring-bone type was found at a depth of 21 ft. A portion has been preserved in Guildhall Museum. Nearby was a 'a large quantity of stout oak piling and the sill of a bridge which crossed the brook from east to west.' It is rather doubtful if there was in fact a Roman bridge at this point, but another Walbrook crossing for a road south of Budge Row is by no means unlikely.
R.C.H.M., pp. 113 *f.*

259 *College Street, Dowgate Hill, Dyers' Hall,* 1839
Remains of a pavement, apparently of tile tesserae about 1 in. square, were found in excavating for the rebuilding of Dyers' Hall, at a depth of 13 ft. 8 in. according to one account, and 15–16 ft. according to Roach Smith. Pottery and coins were also found. 'The lower part of the ground in which the above were found, for 4½ ft. in thickness, appeared to be the sediment of water, probably the ancient Walbrook, and in it, scattered over the surface, was a large quantity (20 cwt.) of animal bones.'
ROACH SMITH: *Illustrations of Roman London, p.* 59.   *R.C.H.M., p.* 114.   *Gent. Mag.* (1839), *II, p.* 636.

260 *Upper Thames Street, S. of Innholders' Hall,* 1958

The bed of the Walbrook was seen in section in a sewer trench north of Upper Thames Street, about 130 ft. west of Dowgate Hill. It is interesting to note that the Ward boundary at this point coincides with the stream-bed. The stream was 20–21 ft. wide, with the W. bank marked by vertical wooden piles about 2 ft. apart, and the E. bank by two large horizontal timbers placed one above the other. The stream-bed lay at a depth of 22–25 ft. below the modern street level, but the bottom was not reached. There were, however, sufficient pottery sherds of the first to third century to indicate that this was the Roman stream. Its direction at this point seemed to be very slightly east of south.

J.R.S., XLIX (1959), *p.* 125.

261 *Upper Thames Street, bottom of Dowgate Hill,* 1959

A mass of chalk walling with a little flint was cut through by a sewer shaft. It was impossible to determine its direction, and it may have been a chalk platform of the type later encountered near Lambeth Hill. (*See* **110**, **116**.) It seems likely that it was a river embankment, but its date is quite uncertain. It is perhaps more likely to be mediaeval than Roman. The top was about 9 ft. below the modern road surface, and it extended below the bottom of the sewer shaft.

Guildhall Museum Excavation Notebook, 1 May 1959.

262 *Upper Thames Street, S. side, site of Public Cleansing Depot,* 1959

Roman river gravels were seen on this site in two distinct layers. The lower consisted of fairly large pebbles and contained pottery of the first and second centuries. This occurred in lens-shaped heaps, evidently deposited on the river bottom by dumping from boats. It included a considerable quantity of Samian ware, in which more than 200 potters' stamps were found. The upper river gravel consisted of smaller pebbles and was much more muddy, suggesting that the river was more sluggish when it was formed. It contained pottery of the third and fourth centuries in much smaller quantities. Unlike the earlier gravels, which evidently reached Upper Thames Street, the later deposit petered out before the northern edge of the site was reached. In the northern part of the site it was overlaid directly by a deposit of river silt which contained Pingsdorf and other imported pottery of the early Middle Ages. The position of the later Roman river bank is therefore obscure, but in the earlier period it evidently lay under Thames Street at this point, which is opposite the mouth of the Walbrook. Piles and large timbers

were seen in an excavation under the northern edge of the old
road, and near the middle of the new widened roadway. A few
piles were seen well out into the river bed on the site of the Public
Cleansing Depot. These were driven into the gravel of the first
and second centuries, but were overlaid by the later Roman gravel.
Observations by Mr. P. MARSDEN.

263 *Walbrook, St. Swithin's House,* 1949–50
The mortar-covered skirting moulding and wall-plaster (yellow,
black and magenta) of two walls forming the angle of a room
were found in approximate alignment with the modern street of
Walbrook. The *opus signinum* floor rested on a wooden 'builders'
raft'. The remains of a timber partition wall were also found.
Associated pottery suggested a date late in the first century.
Guildhall Museum booklet – Discoveries on Walbrook, 1949–50.

264 *Walbrook, St. Swithin's House,* 1949–50
Walls of ragstone blocks interspersed with courses of bonding-
tiles were observed during the builders' excavation, standing in
one corner to a height of 3 ft. They evidently belonged to a
Roman building in approximate alignment with the modern
street of Walbrook. A large square pivot stone, probably to carry
a door leading to a corridor, was found near the corner of an
inner room. The floor was of *opus signinum*, resting on a loose
filling of ragstone rubble, from which came a single pottery sherd
which must antedate the building. This was a fragment of Samian
ware (Curle Type 21) of Antonine date. From the building a
square wooden gutter ran down towards the Walbrook. A little
to the north was a square timber-lined well, 10 ft. in depth, and
lined with square-cut timbers mortised together. The bottom was
lined with chalk rubble, in which was found a sestertius of
Postumus (A.D. 259–268), which must have been deposited during
the construction of the well.
Guildhall Museum booklets – Discoveries in Walbrook, 1949–50;
Finds in Roman London, 1949–52.

265 *Walbrook, St. Swithin's House,* 1949–50
Approximately midway between Walbrook and St. Swithin's
Lane were found the remains of a wattle and daub hut with a
clay floor, on which lay pottery of the early second century. It
had apparently been destroyed by fire, probably the great
Hadrianic fire.
Guildhall Museum booklet – Discoveries in Walbrook, 1949–50.

266 *St. Swithin's Lane, St. Swithin's House site,* 1949–50
The ragstone foundations of a fairly large house with remains of
a floor of coarse red tesserae laid on *opus signinum* were revealed
in small portions by the grab at the E. end of the St. Swithin's
House site, in approximately the same alignment as the lower
part of St. Swithin's Lane. The house seemed to have been
destroyed by fire, and quantities of burnt wattle and ash lay on the
floor. It may have been burnt in the great Hadrianic fire, as
pottery of the late first and early second century seemed to be
associated with the building.
Guildhall Museum booklet – Discoveries in Walbrook, 1949–50.

267 *Cannon Street, site of St. Swithin's Church,* 1960–1
Excavations by Professor W. F. Grimes showed that the natural
surface was overlaid by 4–6 ft. of Roman deposits. A burnt layer
containing daub, tile-fragments, plaster and pottery suggesting a
date in the second century rather than the first, was observed.
The Roman road was located near the S. edge of the site, with
gravel metalling about 4 ft. thick, and a gully along its N. edge,
which was 5 ft. inside the church wall in the eastern part of the
site. Post-holes along the N. side of the gully suggested an early
timber building. This had been succeeded by a Roman building
with foundations of knapped flints, cut into the burnt level and
therefore of later date. It had a corridor 11 ft. wide internally, on
its S. side adjacent to the street. To the north were small compartments, much damaged by the church vaults.
   A flint wall, which appeared to be a continuation of the
southern external wall of the Roman building, was subsequently
seen in the builders' excavation about 6 ft. from the W. wall of
the church, suggesting that it extended right across the site. The
gravel of the roadway was also seen again in section to the south
of the Roman wall.
The Times, 31 December 1960.   *J.R.S., LI* (1961), *p.* 185.   *G.M.*

268 *Cannon Street, former position of London Stone*
A small portion of London Stone was until 1960 incorporated in
the S. wall of St. Swithin's Church, but until 1742 it stood on the
S. side of Cannon Street in approximately the position shown –
now in the middle of the widened road. It is not unlikely that the
base, and perhaps even the main part of the stone, is still buried
here. The portion removed from the church wall is shaped
artificially to a rounded top, and is evidently merely the upper
part of the great stone which Stow describes as being deep-
rooted in the ground. It is of Clipsham Limestone, and is quite

featureless apart from two grooves worn in the top. From the time of Camden, it has been suggested that it was a Roman milestone, possibly the central milestone of the Province, from which all distances were measured. Modern archaeologists have been sceptical of this, and there is no evidence of a Roman date, though the stone was certainly in existence in the early Middle Ages, and according to Stow it was mentioned in a Gospel book given by King Athelstan to Christ's Church, Canterbury. In excavations for rebuilding after the Great Fire, mosaic pavements and other Roman remains were found in the adjoining ground to the south, and the stone certainly stood beside a Roman road.

STOW: *Survey of London (Kingsford ed.)*, I, *p*. 224.   *R.C.H.M.*, *p*. 111. WREN: *Parentalia*, *pp*. 265 *f*.

269 *Cannon Street, near Bush Lane, before* 1755

According to Strype, 'in Canning Street nigh Bush Lane was found pretty deep in the Earth, a large pavement of Roman mosaic work'. A piece of this was given to the Repository in Gresham College. This pavement presumably belonged to the same building as those recorded by Wren after the Great Fire, and remains which have subsequently been found in Bush Lane.

STOW: *Survey of London*, *Strype's edition*, 1755, *II Appendix,Ch. V*, *p*. 692. *R.C.H.M.*, *p*. 111.

270 *Bush Lane, N. portion,* 1840–1

The northern portion of Bush Lane was intersected by five walls, indicated on a sewer plan as approximately parallel to Cannon Street. From south to north they are shown as 10 ft. 7 in., 3 ft., 3 ft., 3½ ft., and 4 ft. thick respectively. The northernmost wall ran under the pavement of Cannon Street.

R.C.H.M., *p*. 110, *Fig*. 32.

271 *Bush Lane, central portion, near Gophir Lane,* 1840–1

At the junction of Bush Lane and Gophir Lane (formerly Cross Lane) was found a massive wall 20–22 ft. in width crossing Bush Lane diagonally (approximately to the N.N.W.). It was built of flints and ragstone, with occasional masses of tiles, the flints preponderating on the N. side, and the ragstone on the S. – suggesting two dates. The top of the wall was 6 ft. below the level of the modern pavement, and the sewer excavation continued to a depth of 15 ft., apparently without reaching the bottom. Adjoining the N. side of the wall was a pavement of white tesserae and a floor of lime and pounded brick supporting the tiles of a hypocaust.

An E.–W. wall 10 ft. thick is also indicated on a Sewer Plan further south in Bush Lane, with a note that it was 6 ft. below the surface. Its position does not quite accord with any of the walls found in 1961. (See **273**.)

City Sewer Plan 27.   *Arch.*, *XXIX*, *pp.* 156, 405.   *R.C.H.M.*, *p.* 110.

272 *Bush Lane, W. side, S. of Bush Lane House (formerly Scotts Yard)*, 1840–1

A portion of wall 8 ft. thick, at a depth of 8 ft. descending to 13 ft., was found opposite the great wall (**271**) with alignment approximately N.N.E. It was built of tiles and mortar, and adjoining it, at a depth of 13 ft., were pavements of lime and gravel. From the description, it seems likely that it was one of the N.–S. walls seen in the excavations to the south in 1960–1 (**273**), but its position is indicated on the Sewer Plan somewhere between them.

City Sewer Plan 27.   *Arch.*, *XXIX*, *p.* 157.   *R.C.H.M.*, *p.* 110.

273 *Bush Lane, W. side*, 1960–1

Massive walls of ragstone and brick, $8\frac{1}{2}$ and $6\frac{1}{2}$ ft. thick, were found running approximately N.–S. and E.–W. in the northern part of the site. (*See Pl.* 57.) The exact alignment is almost N.N.E., as was the wall found in Scotts Yard in 1840–1 (**272**). With another N.–S. wall running under Cannon Street Station, they formed a compartment 42 ft. across, with a floor of white cement at 24 ft. above O.D. Another E.–W. wall over 6 ft. thick ran from the eastern wall across Bush Lane. (*See Fig.* 28, *B*, *p.* 147.) The hypocaust and floors of a later Roman building on a different alignment (not shown on the map) overlay this structure.

In the southern part of the site were two E.–W. walls of ragstone with courses of bonding-tiles, about 3 ft. thick and 33 ft. apart. The area between them was occupied by a massive platform of flint and ragstone rubble concrete 6–7 ft. thick, with its upper surface at about 17 ft. above O.D. The pottery from the layers overlying this and piled against the northern wall was of the late first century. On the N. side of this wall was an apse, the

curved wall of which ran across Bush Lane. A brick structure
seen in section in the eastern half of the apse did not continue to
its western side, and may have been part of a central pier or the
base of a pedestal. (*See Fig.* 28, *A*, *p.* 147.)
London and Middlesex Arch. Soc. Trans., XXI, Pt. I (1963), *p.* 72.
J.R.S., LII, p. 179, *Fig.* 26, *p.* 181.

274 *Cannon Street Station*, 1960–1
In a hole excavated beneath the arches of the station, a short
piece of a massive Roman wall was seen. It was 6 ft. thick and
built of ragstone with white cement. It was similar in structure
to the walls between the railway station and Bush Lane (**273**)
but was on a different alignment, being approximately at right
angles to the wall under the western part of the station, found in
what was then Turnwheel Lane in 1850 (**275**). (*See also Fig.* 28,
p. 147.)
G.M.

275 *Cannon Street Station (then Turnwheel Lane)*, 1850
During excavation for a sewer, a wall was found running across
the lane, with its top at a depth of 6 ft. from the surface. It was
5 ft. thick, and built of Kentish ragstone and chalk. At a depth of
10 ft. from the surface, an oak timber 14 in. by 12 in. lay in a
horizontal position close against the face of the wall.
Note on City Sewer Plan 375.   *R.C.H.M., p.* 112.

276 *Cannon Street Station*, 1868
A network of timber piles was found, and above this were massive
foundations. An immense external wall ran nearly in line with
Bush Lane – possibly a continuation of the eastern wall seen
running under the station from the Bush Lane site (**273**), or a
wall parallel with this further west. It was 200 ft. long, 10 ft.
high and 12 ft. thick, and built of ragstone, chalk and mortar.
At an angle were foundations of flint and rubble, 8 ft. wide,
supporting walls 3 ft. thick, built of tiles 18 in. by 12 in. These
were connected with cross-walls 2 ft. 6 in. thick, built of flat tiles
14 in. by 11 in., also set on rubble footings, which were 4 ft. thick.
Nearer Cannon Street were remains of a series of apartments,
floored with red concrete, and with plain and patterned tessellated pavements. A short distance in front of the central apart-
ment in this series was a square piece of paving of bricks set on
edge, herring-bone fashion. Some of the rooms were decorated
with wall-painting. Many tiles stamped PP.BR.LON. were

found, strongly suggesting that this was a public building. Several wooden drains were found running beneath the foundations towards the river.

London and Middlesex Arch. Soc. Trans., III, pp. 212–17.   *R.C.H.M., pp.* 112–13.

277 *Bush Lane, lower end,* 1964

Several Roman walls of ragstone with double and triple courses of bonding tiles were encountered during tunnelling for a sewer. They mostly stood more than $6\frac{1}{2}$ ft. high, and the only foundation reached consisted of rows of timber piles. From north to south, the remains comprised (1) three sides of a room in which was a brick construction like a drain: (2) two walls with a facing of *opus signinum*, apparently curving and possibly part of an apse: (3) several more walls, one of which had a construction of bricks and cement, resembling the *pila* of a hypocaust, built against it. No dating material was found. The walls were quite different in structure from the massive wall found a few yards to the north in 1961.

G.M.

278 *Suffolk Lane*

During excavations for a sewer in the nineteenth century, ragstone walls 3 ft. thick were found and recorded on a City Sewer Plan. The first of these crossed Suffolk Lane from east to west 47 ft. north of Upper Thames Street. 15 ft. further north was another E.–W. wall, and a third apparently crossed the street diagonally in a northerly direction.

City Sewer Plan 302.

279 *Upper Thames Street, S.E. corner of Suffolk Lane,* 1863

A wall which was regarded as part of the river-wall was found near the S.E. angle of Suffolk Lane.

Arch., XL, p. 48.   *R.C.H.M., p.* 93.

280 *Upper Thames Street, near foot of Suffolk Lane,* 1927

In driving a tunnel for electric-power cables along the N. side of Upper Thames Street, two heavy composite baulks of timber were cut through on either side of the foot of Suffolk Lane, 20 ft. apart and at a depth of 15–20 ft. below the pavement level. The construction was said to slope towards the river. The timbers were not at the same level, so it is unlikely that they formed slips.

About 18 ft. further east, a flint wall 2½ ft. thick, set in white mortar, was encountered crossing the trench. About 17 ft. east of the wall another timber construction, lighter than the first, was found. It consisted of timbers running both across the trench and longitudinally. Projecting into the trench at this point was the drum of a stone column 2 ft. in diameter.

R.C.H.M., p. 143.

281 *Abchurch Lane,* 1855

During sewer excavations a 36 ft. length of wall of ragstone, chalk and flints, was found in the south part of the Lane, north of King William Street. The exact position and orientation are unknown, but the new sewer, which evidently followed its line for 36 ft., ran northwards for nearly 70 ft. up the middle of Abchurch Lane from a point just north of the alley which goes through to Nicholas Lane.

City Sewer Plan 153.   *R.C.H.M., p.* 106.

282 *Nicholas Lane, S. of King William Street, about* 1920

During repairs to a sewer a pavement of coarse red tesserae was found, overlying a burnt layer.

Arch., LXXI, p. 58.   *R.C.H.M., p.* 135.

283 *Cannon Street, Nos.* 143–7, 1961

On the eastern half of No. 145 Cannon Street, a gravel deposit 1 ft. thick was observed extending to about 6 ft. north of the old building frontage. It overlay the natural brick-earth and seemed to be an artificial deposit. It had the appearance of Roman road-metalling, and probably represented either the N. edge of the Roman road or a spill of road material immediately adjacent to it.

Elsewhere on the site was a fire-level containing burnt daub and pottery of the Flavian period. In view of the presence of Hadrianic fire deposits on sites immediately to the north and east, however, there seems little doubt that this also should be attributed to the same great fire. (See *Ant. Journ., XXV, p.* 55.) Cutting into it were ragstone foundations of a later date. An earlier thin burnt level, possibly representing the Boudiccan fire, lay a few inches above the natural soil.

London and Middlesex Arch. Soc. Trans., XXI, Pt. I (1963), *p.* 70.

284 *Nicholas Lane,* 1850

During excavations for a sewer the quoin-end of a wall 7 ft.

thick, built of Kentish ragstone, chalk and flints, was found with its top at a depth of 9 ft. below the surface, 30 ft. from the line of frontage in Cannon Street. 2 ft. or 3 ft. deeper, and apparently forming the foundation stone at the corner, was an inscribed slab, evidently re-used, since the lettered face lay downwards. It was 3 ft. long, 2½ ft. wide and 1 ft. thick, with well-cut letters 6 in. high, as follows: NVM C———— PROV———— BRITA————. This inscription, apparently to the divinity of the Emperor (*Numini Caesaris*), and set up by the Province of Britain (*Provincia Britanniae*), presumably came from a temple of the state cult. It was unfortunately lost from Guildhall before 1859. (*See Fig.* 5, *p.* 43.)

ROACH SMITH: *Illustrations of Roman London, p.* 29.   *R.C.H.M.,* *pp.* 135, 170.

285 *King William Street, corner of Clement's Lane,* 1920
A fragment of plain tessellated pavement of red and yellow tesserae, preserved in the London Museum, was found at a depth of 8 ft. in the roadway at the corner of Clement's Lane and King William Street, opposite the church. A portion more than 8 ft. by 6 ft. was seen, and it appeared to run through beneath the present road. At a deeper level on the same site were found fragments of a mosaic with a guilloche border in black, yellow, white and red tesserae (also preserved in the London Museum). This floor is said to have been 9 ft. below the first pavement, and beneath it was a rubbish pit containing a Samian bowl (*Drag.* 29) with a stamp of the potter *Felix* (Claudius-Vespasian) and a cordoned vase of the first century. Adjoining the lower pavement, at a depth of about 17 ft., was a fragment of a column shaft of oolitic stone, 9 in. in diameter, decorated with a scale pattern.
London Museum Catalogue, 'London in Roman Times', p. 39 (*A*22601 *a-e*), *p.* 38 (*A*22699), *and Pl.* ixB.

286 *Nicholas Lane, northern part,* 1847
The remains of a dwelling-house, 'decidedly Roman', are said to have been found. Openings in the walls contained decayed wood, 'probably of joists, door-posts, etc.' In the immediate vicinity of the house was found an urn of dark clay, at a depth of about 16 ft. below the surface. It contained burnt clay, charcoal, small pieces of iron and lead, and portions of the unburnt bones of a small animal. There were no human bones, and it seems likely that this was a domestic votive deposit, rather than part of a burial, as was suggested.
J.B.A.A., II, p. 341.   *R.C.H.M., p.* 135.

287 *Nicholas Lane, Nos. 34–7, before* 1912

An ancient stream-bed was observed on this site. It apparently ran in a south-westerly direction, and was evidently a continuation of the stream-bed seen on the sites of Nos. 9–12 George Yard (**226**) and No. 50 Cornhill (**213**). It is likely to have been filled in at an early date in the Roman period. (See **226**.)

Arch., LXIII, p. 319. *Fig.* 26.

288 *Clement's Lane,* 1841–78

During excavations for sewers in 1841, walls 3 ft. thick were found crossing the street at depths of 12–15 ft. They were built of flints, rubble and tiles. There were also fragments of pavements.

Later excavations (1865–78) brought to light a great quantity of Roman glass, glass slag, and an iron mould, suggesting that glass was manufactured here, and also a number of amphorae, five or six of which were found standing in a row.

In 1878 fragments of a tessellated pavement were found close to St. Clement's Church.

Arch., XXIX, p. 272. *J.B.A.A., XXXIV, pp.* 134, 254. *R.C.H.M., p.* 113. *London and Middlesex Arch. Soc. Trans., III, p.* 100.

289 *Lombard Street, Plough Court, site of Chase National Bank of New York,* 1955–6

Post-holes of Claudian date were found in many parts of the site. There were also traces of the foundations of a later first century ragstone building, with alignment approximately parallel with Plough Court, except in the S.E. corner of the site, just north of Lombard Court, where a wall of a similar character ran N.W.–S.E. The walls were about 2 ft. thick, and there was a gap, apparently for an entrance from the west, just west of Plough Court. This building was succeeded by a much smaller building on a different alignment (approximately the same as that of the basilica and forum) apparently before the end of the first century. There were also traces of brick walls and an *opus signinum* floor of a building apparently destroyed in the Hadrianic fire.

Notes by Mr. P. MARSDEN.

290 *Lombard Street, Nos.* 30–2, 1962

Gravel metalling more than 6 ft. thick was observed on this site during the builders' excavation, overlying the trampled surface of the natural brick-earth, at about 38 ft. above O.D. The metalling was in layers which were slightly cambered to the south. Among these were two distinct road surfaces, the upper at

43 ft. 5 in. above O.D. dropping to 42 ft. 6 in. near the southern
edge, and the lower at 41 ft. 3 in. dropping only to 41 ft. towards
the south. There seems little doubt that this was the southern part
of the main E.–W. Roman street. A short distance to the south,
the trampled surface of the natural brick-earth was overlaid by a
man-made layer of brick-earth and charcoal, and over this was a
layer 12 in. thick of burnt daub containing red and white painted
wall-plaster. Its position in the stratification corresponds with
that of the Boudiccan fire-level on neighbouring sites (*Fig.* 16, *p.*
119.) Since the early occupation layer and fire layer did not occur
beneath the roadway, which lay directly on the natural surface,
the E.–W. street seems to have been one of the earliest features of
Roman London, although in one place it overlay an earlier pit.
J.R.S., LIII (1963), *p.* 140.

291 *Gracechurch Street, opposite Nos.* 63–4, *c.* 1830–40
During sewer excavations in Gracechurch Street, walls 4 ft.
thick were found 22 ft. from the surface, continuing down to the
depth of the sewer. They ran under the street opposite the N.
and S. walls of St. Benet Gracechurch (then standing at the
corner of Fenchurch Street and Gracechurch Street). There is
unfortunately no record of their exact alignment, or of the
material of which they were made.
R.C.H.M., pp. 120*f.*

292 *Fenchurch Street, W. end,* 1921
In making a tunnel for telephone cables, a wall was discovered
towards the N. side of the street. It ran approximately E.–W.
about 60 ft. east of Gracechurch Street. The S. face had been
destroyed by a previous sewer excavation. Three courses of flint
surmounted by three courses of bricks were observed in the
remaining portion.
London and Middlesex Arch. Soc. Trans., N.S., IV., pp. 333–4.
R.C.H.M., p. 118.

293 *Gracechurch Street, Nos.* 59–60, *site of Midland Bank,* 1959
A burnt level containing pottery of the mid-first century, including a jug of coarse ware with stamp C.ALBUC, presumably of
the period of the Boudiccan revolt, was found in the S.W. part
of the site. In it were the burnt remains of timber and daub
houses. At a higher level, on the western edge of the site, was a
deposit of gravel, possibly the edge of a road, or spill from the
gravel make-up of an adjacent road under Gracechurch Street.

Towards the centre of the site, a fragment of Roman ragstone wall was seen, running N.–S., approximately parallel with Gracechurch Street. West of this was a cement spread associated with another probable foundation which showed traces of burning.

G.M.

294 *Gracechurch Street, opposite St. Benet's Place,* 1841

Roman pavements were found while digging foundations for two houses opposite St. Benet's Place. These were evidently on the W. side of Gracechurch Street, and were probably Nos. 31–2.

Arch., XXIX, p. 154.   *R.C.H.M., p.* 120.

295 *Gracechurch Street, No.* 42, *formerly Nos.* 61–6 *King William Street, (at the angle of the street, opposite the E. end of Cannon Street),* 1920

Three Roman walls were found running N.–S. The two eastern walls were of squared ragstone with one double bonding-course of brick remaining. Between them at the level of the top of the bonding-course was a white flooring 9¾ ft. below pavement level, overlying packed pebbles and tile fragments, beneath which was a 6 in layer of chalky mortar. On the E. side were traces of tiles laid as though to form a drain. The third wall, further west, was entirely of ragstone, and its base rose under the pavement as though to admit a broad arch. North of this stretch, after a gap of some feet, was a 20 ft. length of wall of a different type, which apparently extended right across the site. It was built of squared ragstone with double bonding-courses of bricks.

Arch., LXXI, pp. 60*f.*   *R.C.H.M., p.* 125.

296 *Gracechurch Street, S.W. corner,* 1831

During excavations for a sewer running from Great Eastcheap (now part of Cannon Street) into Gracechurch Street, a Roman road was found 3–5 ft. below the surface of Great Eastcheap (*See Fig.* 15, *p.* 115), its lack of depth being the result of the lowering of the surface in this area after the Great Fire of 1666. The road was 16 ft. wide (or 18 ft. according to another account) and from 6–7½ ft. thick, made of gravel concrete on a bed of loam, with supporting walls of ragstone and tiles, about 2½ ft. thick. It lay at this point under the southern foot-path and the roadway of Great Eastcheap. According to one account, 'In direction it apparently tended from Cannon Street in the direction of Little Eastcheap' (i.e. the present Eastcheap), but another observer claimed that it was 'inclining N.E. of Little Eastcheap towards Aldgate'. It has, therefore, been taken as evidence of a diagonal Roman road leading from the Roman London Bridge to Aldgate, but it is clear that the portion of road seen lay to the west of Old London Bridge, which probably lay to the west of the Roman bridge. The position of the road can be determined fairly accurately from the intersection of the lines of the sewer and Great Eastcheap, and from the measurements on the published section. It is wrongly placed at the top of Fish Street Hill in the map of the Royal Commission Report, and must have been about 80 ft. west of this position. As the position on the map is closely defined, it has not been ringed, but the alignment shown is one of strong probability only.

HERBERT: *Hist. of St. Michael, Crooked Lane, p.* 20.　　*R.C.H.M.,* *pp.* 116–17.　　*Arch., XXIV, p.* 192.　　*Gent. Mag.,* 1833 (*II*), *p.* 422.

297 *Gracechurch Street, S.W. corner,* 1831

When the sewer reached the N.E. corner of Great Eastcheap (now in the roadway at the bottom of Gracechurch Street), the foundation of a Roman building was found a little in advance of the nineteenth century building line. It was 2 ft. thick and built of ragstone, with a double course of tiles, mostly of white clay, about 5 ft. from the base. A flue tile with four apertures was taken from this wall, with two coins of Claudius. The wall is described as 'contiguous to the raised Roman way in Eastcheap' (see **296**). In the same area, two wells, which were believed to be Roman, and a massive architectural fragment, possibly from the architrave of a building, were also found, as well as two floors, one of coarse tesserae about 1 in. square, and the other of 'sandy and argillaceous earth mingled with pebble stones 3 in. thick, the whole covered with a thin coat of fine stucco of polished smoothness, painted red'.

Arch., XXIV, p. 192.　　*Gent. Mag.,* 1836 (*I*), (*N.S.V.*), *p.* 136. *R.C.H.M., p.* 117.

298 *King William Street, lower part,* 1831

During the construction of sewers under the line of approach to the new London Bridge (now King William Street), a piece of plain red tessellated pavement, about 14 ft. square, was revealed near the site of St. Michael's Church, under the roadway of Crooked Lane (which then followed a zig-zag course from the later Crooked Lane to Fish Street Hill).

Also, built into an old wall of the church, were massive fragments of Roman masonry 'of a sort of sandstone, the surface of which had been painted . . . a bright red'.

Arch., XXIV, p. 195.   HERBERT: *Hist. of St. Michael, Crooked Lane,*
p. 19.   *R.C.H.M., p.* 129.

299 *Crooked Lane,* 1961

In several places gravel deposits about 1 ft. thick, containing
indeterminate sherds of Roman pottery, were observed overlying
the natural gravel when the modern roadway had been removed.
These were possibly remains of the metalling of a Roman road,
for Crooked Lane lay on the line of a southern continuation of the
N.–S. road bounding the western side of the basilica and forum,
traces of which were seen east of Birchin Lane in 1935 (**225**).
Unfortunately, the basements on both sides of Crooked Lane
were very deep, so that the gravel layers survived only beneath
the narrow modern roadway, and gave no indication of the width
of the original deposit.

Trans. London and Middlesex Arch. Soc., XXI, Pt. I (1963), *p.* 72.

300 *Lawrence Pountney Lane,* 1846

During sewer excavations numerous Roman remains were found
between the churchyard and Cannon Street. Opposite No. 27 at
a depth of 3–4 ft. was a common red tessellated pavement, and
opposite Nos. 26 and 3 were bases of two columns, 15 and 19 in.
in diameter, at a depth of 8 ft., embedded in a thick layer of
debris of buildings. Near Cannon Street was a wall partly consisting of mill-stones of Andernach lava.

J.B.A.A., II, pp. 340, 345.   *R.C.H.M., pp.* 125, 127.

301 *Lawrence Pountney Lane, opposite churchyard,* 1846

A wall of ragstone and flints with tiles in masses and layers was
found 3 ft. below the surface opposite the churchyard. It continued to a depth of 10 ft. At the entrance to Church Passage was
a wall $4\frac{1}{2}$ ft. thick and bonded with tiles, at a depth of 3 ft.

J.B.A.A., II, pp. 340, 345.   *R.C.H.M., pp.* 125, 127.

302 *Arthur Street, Minster House,* 1954–5

In the N.E. corner of the site were traces of two successive
Roman buildings, the first of which had a floor of rough but
evenly set white tesserae laid on a bed of concrete 2 ft. thick.

The later building had been raised 1 ft. above this by a layer of
concrete through which ran moulded channels capped by red
building tiles. These were evidently flues through which passed
furnace-heated air to warm a floor above. A small number of

pottery sherds from one of the channels suggested that this part of the hypocaust had ceased to operate by the mid-third century.

Mediaeval walls had been built on the Roman foundations, and these in turn supported the arches of surviving eighteenth century cellars. The Roman foundations had therefore remained in service for seventeen hundred years. (*See Pl.* 16.)

G.M.

303 *Upper Thames Street, between Lawrence Pountney Lane and Arthur Street,* 1927

In driving a tunnel for electric power cables along the N. side of the street, a timber was cut through about 34 ft. west of the W. corner of Arthur Street.

R.C.H.M., p. 143.

304 *Miles Lane, W. side,* 1926

Traces of timber constructions were found all over the site of King William Street House, similar to those found on the E. side of Miles Lane (**306**), but of a less heavy character. A further line of timber-walling about 23 ft. to the south of the main line was seen.

R.C.H.M., p. 134.

305 *Miles Lane, E. side, about* 1920–1

On the northern part of the site of Nos. 2–4 Miles Lane (now Nos. 34–7 King William Street) was found the southern edge of a rectangular building 31 ft. wide, with external walls $3\frac{1}{4}$ ft. thick, entirely faced with brick, but patched in places with ragstone. The foundation was composed of 2 ft. of flints above 2 ft. of chalk. Within the building was a longitudinal wall enclosing a brick drain with a corbelled covering. Traces of timber work at the S. end of the brick building seemed to indicate that a wooden construction similar to that to the south had been destroyed when the building was erected.

Arch., LXXI, pp. 62–72.   *R.C.H.M., pp.* 132–4; *Fig.* 50, *p.* 133.

306 *Miles Lane, E. side, about* 1920–1

Remains of an extensive timber structure, resembling a wharf, were found on the southern part of the site. The main wall consisted of timber baulks laid one upon the other, running roughly E.–W., with a series of similar walls at right angles both to the north and south, those to the north being spaced at fairly regular intervals of 7–9 ft. To the south were another line of piling with camp-sheathing, and what appeared to be a chute. Datable pottery found within the main line of timbering was earlier than A.D. 100, whereas the pottery to the south of it extended to the middle of the second century (suggesting a late first century date for the structure).

Arch., LXXI, pp. 62–72.   *R.C.H.M., pp.* 132–4, *and Fig.* 50, *p.* 133.

307 *London Bridge Approach,* 1831

Under the S. abutment of the Thames Street land arch of the new bridge a line of massive chestnut and oak piles was found, forming a line of embankment, at a depth of about 10 ft. below the surface of the ground. A revetment of hurdlework was attached to the piles. This was of quite different character from the second embankment (**306**), where the piles are said to have been of elm.

Arch., XXV, p. 601.   *R.C.H.M., pp.* 129 *and* 130.

308 *King William Street, Regis House,* 1929

Timber structures, which were believed to be part of a wharf, similar to those found on both sides of Miles Lane (**304, 306**) were partially exposed in pits dug down to the gravel. There were massive oak baulks 18 in. square, some 20 ft. long, running E.–W. In some cases other timbers were jointed to these at right angles. To the south were camp-sheathing and piles. There was a mass of oyster-shells filling the spaces between the timbers, and this contained Samian pottery of a date later than A.D. 100.

Spread over the southern part of the site was a layer about 8 ft. thick of burnt debris containing pottery. It appeared to be a dump, covering the timbers, from a wide area occupied by wattle and daub huts, destroyed in the great fire of A.D. 120–130.

J.R.S., XIX (1929), *p.* 200.

309 *King William Street, Regis House,* 1929

Two walls 2 ft. thick and 20 ft. apart, built of solid brick with chalk foundations were found on the landward side of the timber embankment (**308**). They may have been part of a warehouse or shed adjoining the embankment (cf. **305**). Between the walls was found a moulded column base, but this was not *in situ*.

J.R.S., XXI (1931), *p.* 239.

310 *Lower Thames Street, bottom of Fish Street Hill,* 1834

During excavations for a sewer substantial masonry, presumed to be Roman, was found at the point where old London Bridge abutted. In the absence of more detailed information, a mediaeval date seems to be a possibility, but a portion of a massive Roman wall with courses of bonding-tiles was found a short distance to the east (**311**), and this masonry may have been part of the same structure.

R.C.H.M., p. 143.

311 *Lower Thames Street, No.* 125, 1911
Under the frontage line and adjoining pavement of No. 125, a thick wall, possibly a river-wall or embankment, was found resting on ballast at a depth of 24 ft. below the present surface. 'Large, roughly squared timbers, 12 ft. long and about 8 in. square rested on the top of the ballast, across the thickness of the wall, these being held in position by pointed piles driven in at intervals . . . On these timbers were laid large irregular sand-stones and ragstones bedded in clay and flints. Three layers of these stones showed on the face, above which was a bond of two (*the drawing shows three*) rows of yellow tiles. Some chalk with other stone formed the core, the whole being cemented with red mortar. The total height of the masonry remaining was 3 ft. and its width 10 ft. Some of the stones were apparently re-used . . .'
Arch., LXIII, pp. 309–10.   *R.C.H.M., pp.* 93–4.

312 *Monument Street, S. of the Monument,* 1833
In sinking a cess-pool south of the Monument, at the back of newly erected fruit warehouses in Pudding Lane, a floor of 'stone and brick broken very fine and mixed with lime' was found. Below this was loose made soil, and under this a culvert or aqueduct with sides of Roman bricks, and bottom apparently of roofing tiles, running southwards towards the Thames, and communi-cating on the north with a brick tank or bath coated on the inside with plaster covered with tesserae. On the E. side of the aqueduct was a transverse watercourse, consisting of semi-circular tiles 17 in. long (*?imbrices*), placed one on the other, forming a complete barrel.
Gent. Mag., 1834, *I, pp.* 95–6.   *R.C.H.M., p.* 134.

313 *Monument Street,* 1887
About 150 ft. east of the Monument, at a depth of 12 ft., a portion of a tessellated pavement laid on a bed of concrete 12 in. thick was found. It was of $\frac{1}{2}$ in. tesserae with an inscription in smaller black tesserae. A drawing of this by H. Hodge is reproduced in the Report of the Royal Commission, where it is transcribed as follows:—

WUNANI
NIIISTGNA+VS
IMNTESSELSTRAT
SEMDSTD

(It has been suggested that there is reference to the name
Egnatius and to the laying of the pavement, but the inscription as
reported is very obscure.)
Proc. Soc. Antiq. (Ser. 2), *XII, pp.* 128–9.   *Arch. Journ., XLV, p.* 184.
R.C.H.M., p. 134, *and Fig.* 88, *p.* 176.

314 *Pudding Lane, N. of Lower Thames Street,* 1836–41
A wall of ragstone and tiles, apparently about 2 ft. 8 in. thick,
was found in the middle of Pudding Lane, running to the bottom,
and possibly even into Lower Thames Street. Adjoining it was a
hypocaust, with two rows of tile pillars.
Arch., XXIX, p. 154, *Pl.* 18.   *R.C.H.M., p.* 136 *and Pl.* 44.

315 *Lower Thames Street, opposite Botolph Lane,* 1834
During excavations for a sewer, oak and chestnut piles were
found all along the line of the trench, but these were much closer
and larger at the end of Botolph's Wharf gateway and warehouse –
i.e. at the foot of Botolph Lane – than in other places.
KELSEY: *Description of Sewers, p.* 90.   *R.C.H.M., p.* 143.

316 *Old Broad Street, Winchester House,* 1792
A circular Roman pavement was found during sewer excavations
behind the old Navy Pay House (Winchester House). A quantity
of burnt corn and charcoal, with pottery and plated coins, lay
upon it.
Arch., XXXIX, p. 493.   *R.C.H.M., p.* 109.

317 *Camomile Street, at junction with Bishopsgate,* 1707
During the rebuilding of premises in Camomile Street adjoining
Bishopsgate, a mosaic pavement was found extending for 60 ft.
from Bishopsgate, and running under the foundations of houses
that had not yet been pulled down. It was 10 ft. broad, with the
N. edge 3½ ft. from the city wall. The colours of the tesserae were
red, black and yellow. The pavement apparently lay at a depth of
about 4 ft., and beneath it was a layer of rubbish 2 ft. thick.
Below this was a layer of clay, in which were buried at a further
depth of 2 ft. several urns containing bones. With them was found
a coin of Antoninus Pius. It seems clear from this account that the
pavement was of late Roman date, presumably laid after the
building of the city wall over burials which antedated the wall.

Woodward's letter to Wren, quoted in Gent. Mag., 1807, *I, p.* 415.
R.C.H.M., p. 111.

318 *St. Mary Axe, N. end,* 1849 *and* 1909

A tessellated pavement was found at the corner of St. Mary Axe and Bevis Marks while digging for sewers in 1849.

In 1909, a ragstone wall bonded with tiles was found in the middle of the road at the junction of St. Mary Axe, Camomile Street and Bevis Marks. It ran parallel with the city wall and 40 ft. from it.

Arch., LXIII, p. 321. *R.C.H.M., p.* 139.

319 *St. Helen's Place,* 1733

A Roman mosaic pavement which is said to have had an inscription, unfortunately not recorded, was found here by workmen. The tesserae were not more than 1 in. square. Human bones found at the same time were probably mediaeval.

Arch. Journ., XXXIII, p. 269. *R.C.H.M., p.* 139.

320 *Bishopsgate, Nos.* 31–3, 1908

A pavement of plain red tesserae was found on the site of a public house, immediately at the back of Nos. 31–3 Bishopsgate and in Gresham House Court. This must have adjoined one found in 1839 under what was then No. 101. It lay at a depth of 9 ft. or 10 ft. below the level of the modern roadway of Bishopsgate.

Arch., LXIII, p. 319. *R.C.H.M., p.* 108.

321 *Bishopsgate Street, Nos.* 19–27, 1875

A Roman mosaic pavement 4 yd. square was found here at a depth of 15 ft. below the modern pavement level and about 50 ft. west of the street.

J.B.A.A., XXXIII, p. 106. *R.C.H.M., p.* 108.

322 *Bishopsgate, No.* 15, 1895

A red tessellated pavement was found at a depth of 16–17 ft. below the level of the yard. The portion seen was about 6 ft. by 2 ft., and it extended northward under the wall of the house.

Proc. Soc. Ant. (2nd S.), *XVI, pp.* 36–7. *R.C.H.M., p.* 108.

323 *Old Broad Street, Nos. 23–7, Gresham House, formerly site of the old Excise Office,* 1854

When the old Excise Office was demolished, a Roman mosaic pavement was found beneath the vaults in the S.E. part of the building at a depth of more than 13 ft. (probably about 16 ft.) below the modern street level. There was a representation of a Bacchante on a panther in the central panel, with other compartments formed by stars of intersecting guilloches enclosing various ornaments, and with an outer border of lotus flowers. It was laid on a bed of hard cement with coarse concrete beneath resting on natural soil, and formed the floor of a room 28 ft. square. (*See Pl.* 64.)
To the north was another floor of red tesserae about 12 ft. square. *Arch., XXXVI, pp.* 203 *ff.* MORGAN: *Romano-British Mosaic Pavements, p.* 190. ROACH SMITH: *Illustrations of Roman London, p.* 54, *Pl. VII. R.C.H.M., pp.* 108–9, *Pl.* 39.

324 *Crosby Square, Bishopsgate, S.W. corner,* 1836

Under a house (No. 3) at the S.W. angle of the Square was found a mosaic pavement of yellow, red, white and black tesserae in a guilloche or scroll pattern, about 13 ft. below the surface. Beneath it was a layer of coarse mortar on a bed of hard ground 2 ft. thick. The site was intersected by ancient foundations running north and south, at depths of 12–14 ft., but as these are said to have been of chalk, they are much more likely to have been mediaeval than Roman.
Gent. Mag., 1836, *I, pp.* 369 *f. Arch., XXVII, pp.* 397–9. *R.C.H.M., p.* 116.

325 *Crosby Square, Bishopsgate, site of Crosby Hall,* 1908(?)

Two fragments of mosaic pavements, framed with inscriptions saying that they had been found in Crosby Hall at a depth of 11 ft., were in the possession of Messrs. Pimm's Ltd., at 88 Bishopsgate in 1963, and were said to have been formerly kept at the 'Ship and Turtle', Leadenhall Street. One of these – since presented to Guildhall Museum – is a portion of a guilloche border, 43¼ in. by about 21 in., in black, white and red tesserae, with an edge of coarse red tesserae. The other – to be offered for preservation in the reconstructed Crosby Hall in Chelsea – is a fragment of a vine-leaf scroll, 23¾ in. by 13½ in., in black and white, with red tesserae at the leaf-tips. (*See Pl.* 71.) The London Museum also possesses a piece of tessellated pavement that is said to be from the site of Crosby Hall, and was acquired by the Museum before 1913 (*A.* 11248).

326 *Leadenhall Street, Nos.* 130–8, 1882
Two portions of pavements were found at a depth of 11 ft. below street level on the site of Rochester Buildings, possibly belonging to the same building as those on the other side of the street.
Arch. Journ., XL, p. 107.   *R.C.H.M., p.* 128.

327 *Leadenhall Street, Nos.* 122–30, 1846
On the site of the old King's Arms Tavern a red tessellated pavement was observed extending over a large area. According to another account only a concrete pavement was found here, with quantities of painted wall plaster.
Arch., LXIII, p. 321.   *J.B.A.A., II, p.* 340.   *R.C.H.M., p.* 127.

328 *Leadenhall Street, site of Lloyd's Building, then East India House,* 1863
When East India House was pulled down, near the portico was found a room paved with red tesserae, with walls of ragstone rubble and chalk bonded with tiles, plastered and coloured in fresco. It is said to have been at a depth of 19 ft. 6 in. – 10 ft. deeper than the Bacchus mosaic found nearby. The orientation was about 40°, a different alignment from the basilica and other buildings to the south.
Arch., XXXIX, pp. 494 *f.*   *R.C.H.M., p.* 127.

329 *Leadenhall Street, pavement opposite Nos.* 17–19, 1803 *and* 1864
During sewer excavations in 1803 a mosaic pavement was found at a depth of 9½ ft. It formed the floor of a room more than 20 ft. square. The central portion, now in the British Museum, represents Bacchus riding on a tiger. (*See Pl.* 66.) On the opposite side of the street were foundations of tile and ragstone. In 1864 another portion of mosaic pavement was found nearby under the pavement at the entrance to the old East India House.
Arch., XXXIX, pp. 493–4.   *R.C.H.M., p.* 127.   T. MORGAN: *Romano-British Mosaic Pavements,* 1886, *pp.* 179–81.

330 *Leadenhall Street, under street near corner of Lime Street,* 1864
Three portions of Roman pavements found in the middle of the street during excavations for sewers have been recorded. They lay at a depth of about 11 ft. from the surface of the centre of the road. It seems likely that the westernmost portion at least was part of the same house as the mosaic floors discovered beneath the pavement nearby in 1803 and 1864 (**329**).
Plan in Guildhall Library.   *R.C.H.M., p.* 128.

331 *Lime Street, site of Lloyd's new building,* 1951–2
Traces of a substantial ragstone building, with a room heated by a
hypocaust at the northern end, were recorded. Near the S.W.
corner of the site, i.e. at the corner of Lime Street and Fenchurch
Avenue, were pavements of coarse red tesserae. The building
seems to have been destroyed by fire after A.D. 350. There was
some evidence of a last first to early second century origin, with a
major reconstruction and extension of the N. part of the building
in the late 3rd century. A small hoard of barbarous radiate coins
was buried, apparently at the time of the reconstruction. (*See Fig.
6, p.* 55.)
*Guildhall Museum booklet: Finds in Roman London, 1949–52, pp.
11–15.   Numismatic Chronicle, 6th Series, Vol. XV,
pp. 113–24.*

332 *Leadenhall Street, Nos.* 34–5 (*Albion House*), 1953
A trial-hole revealed a Roman pavement of coarse red and yellow
tesserae at a depth of about 16 ft. below the present street level.
A Roman coin, unidentifiable through corrosion, but of minim
size and therefore of the late third century or later, was found in a
black filling 6 in. above the pavement. At a level 3 ft. above it
were traces of a daub structure destroyed by fire. This was
presumably mediaeval, as a fragment of twelfth century pottery
lay upon it.
Guildhall Museum Excavation Note-book, August 1953

333 *Leadenhall Street, No.* 77, 1924
A small excavation revealed a wall of concrete, apparently
Roman, running parallel with Mitre Street. The visible portion
was at a depth of 16–18 ft. below street level.
R.C.H.M., p. 128.

334 *Fenchurch Street, rear of No.* 80A, 1911
Trenches cut at the back of No. 80A revealed a rough floor of
red tile and rubble walls.
Arch., LXIII, p. 320.   *R.C.H.M., p.* 118.

335 *Crutched Friars, Northumberland Alley,* 1787
A tessellated pavement, which passed into the possession of the
Society of Antiquaries, was found in Northumberland Alley at a
depth of 12 ft.
A pavement is also reported to have been found when digging

foundations for the East India Company's warehouse in North-umberland Alley, before 1805, at a depth of about 7 ft.
Arch., XXXIX, p. 501.   *Gent. Mag.,* 1807, *I, pp.* 416–17.
R.C.H.M., p. 116.

336 *Crutched Friars, No.* 1, 1905
A ditch about 8 ft. wide was found running N.–S. through the middle of this site, converging towards the north with the line of the city wall. It was cut into the ballast and was 6 ft. deep. The filling was of dark earth. No evidence of date was seen, and it cannot, therefore, be assumed that the ditch was Roman, but this seems probable, and an early date might be expected as it was cut deep into natural gravel and was on a different alignment from the city wall.
Arch., LX, p. 193, *Plan on p.* 194.   *R.C.H.M., p.* 123 *and Fig.* 42.

337 *Fenchurch Street, between Billiter Street and London Street,* 1853–4
A stone wall was discovered during sewer excavations, running diagonally across the street. A note on a City Sewers Plan says that it was built of flint, and there was a thickness of 3 ft. of made ground above it. It also records that the sewer was built on it. (The base of the sewer is at a depth of about 15 ft.)
R.C.H.M., p. 118.   *City Sewers Plan* 236.

338 *Fenchurch Street, Nos.* 46–8, 1923
Part of an important structure, possibly at some time a granary or warehouse, was found, with a chamber about 40 ft. by 25 ft. internally, divided across the middle into two equal compart-ments. The outer walls were entirely of brick, 2 ft. thick with four courses to the foot, set in undisturbed gravel and brick-earth. The floor was of tiles, about 9 in. square, apparently about 4 ft. lower than the original surface. It is possible that this was originally a hypocaust floor, although no *pilae* remained. Subse-quently sleeper walls of ragstone and bonding-tiles, about 4 ft. 6 in. high, 18 in. thick and 18 in. apart had been built across the chamber, evidently to support a damp-proof floor. The spaces between had, however, been packed with rubble, and a cement floor supporting a double layer of tiles had been laid over all. There were indications of adjoining rooms to the north and south. On the east, however, was undisturbed ballast.
J.R.S., XII, p. 257.   *R.C.H.M., pp.* 118–19.

339 *Fenchurch Street, near end of Mincing Lane,* 1833
Walls were found in sewer excavations at a depth of 12 ft. Others were found near the bottom of Cullum Street.
R.C.H.M., p. 117.

340 *Fenchurch Street, Nos.* 36–8, *1833 and* 1857
During sewer excavations in 1833, two tessellated pavements were found underneath the pavement opposite the entrance of No. 36. One had geometrical patterns in red, grey and white tesserae, while the other was of large red tesserae only. Fragments of plaster painted vermilion were also found. In 1857 another portion of tessellated pavement was found when digging the foundations for No. 37, at a depth of 11½ ft. It measured 3 ft. 4 in. by 2 ft. 6 in., and had a coloured design representing a peacock and vase within a guilloche and plain border. (It is now in the British Museum.) From the site of St. Gabriel's Church immediately to the west came two bronze fingers of a large statue (now in Guildhall Museum).
ROACH SMITH: *Illustrations of Roman London, p.* 58.   *J.B.A.A., 1st Series, XXIV, p.* 76.   *R.C.H.M., pp.* 117–18.

341 *Mincing Lane, W. side, northern end,* 1927
About 41 ft. S.E. of the junction with Fenchurch Street, a portion of Roman wall about 2 ft. thick was found under the pavement, running approximately N.–S. The foundation was of ragstone and chalk, and above was apparently a double course of tiles at a depth of 16½ ft. below street level.
R.C.H.M., p. 134.

342 *Mincing Lane, opposite the gateway into Clothworkers' Hall,* 1824
Remains of a hypocaust were found here in excavating for a sewer, at a depth of 18 ft. A vase full of charcoal was found in one of the flues.
R.C.H.M., p. 134.

343 *Mincing Lane, Nos.* 4–8, 1936
Near the N. end of the site (under No. 4), layers of gravel were seen, 4 ft. in thickness, extending from 11 to 15 ft. below pavement level. Beneath them was grey sand with occasional flecks of charcoal. The gravel was hard, brown, and laid in horizontal layers, with one dirty layer at a depth of 13 ft. 2 in. to 13 ft. 9 in.

below pavement level. There is little doubt that it was the metalling of a major E.–W. road.

J.R.S., XXVII (1937), *p.* 241.   *MS. notes by* Mr. F. COTTRILL.

344 *Fenchurch Street, Nos.* 31–4, 1935
Reddish gravel layers were seen in the E. part of the site, extending for 2 ft. below basement level – i.e. from 13 to 15ft. below street level. This seems to be a continuation of the road metalling seen on the site of Nos. 4–8 Mincing Lane (**343**). Neighbouring Roman walls seem to be approximately at right angles to the line of roadway produced by joining these patches of metalling; and if continued to the west, this skirts the S. front of the forum and would reach the Walbrook near the supposed crossing on the site of the National Safe Deposit Company (**196**). Other portions of gravel metalling have since been found on the same line (**344A, 290**).

J.R.S., XXVI (1936), *p.* 256.   *MS. notes by* Mr. F. COTTRILL.

344A *Fenchurch Street, No.* 22 *(corner of Fenchurch Street and Rood Lane)*, 1964
A piece of gravel metalling $7\frac{1}{2}$ ft. wide and 5 ft. thick was observed in a builders' excavation on the northern edge of the site, 3 ft. south of the old building-line. This was the only sign of gravel metalling on the site, and it lies exactly on the southern edge of the presumed course of the Roman roadway observed to the east (**343** and **344**) and west (**290**). Sandwiched among the layers of gravel was a single layer of yellow clay.
G.M.

345 *Fenchurch Street, Nos.* 31–4, 1935
Portions of a Roman wall were seen in section in holes to the south of the road-metalling (**344**). It ran approximately N.–S. at right angles to the supposed alignment of the road. The foundation was of rubble, consisting of flints, yellow cement and Roman brick. A cement floor adjoined it on the E. side, at a depth of about 5 ft. 2 in. below basement level – i.e. about 18 ft. 2 in. below present pavement level – a greater depth than the lowest level of the road nearby. South of the wall were traces of a rectangular timber structure in approximately the same alignment.
MS. notes by Mr. F. COTTRILL.

346 *Rood Lane, No.* 23, 1937
On the N. edge of the site a short length of E.–W. wall was seen,

built of coursed ragstone rubble with yellow cement. At the top
a single brick bonding-course remained. Both faces were rendered
in pink cement. The wall was about 8½ ft. long, with a return to
the north at the W. end and a return to the south at the E. end.
MS. notes by Mr. F. COTTRILL.

347 *Mincing Lane, W. side,* 1850
Two Roman floors were found 2 ft. apart. The upper, which was
at a depth of 12 ft. below the surface, was tessellated, and the
lower was of gravel, lime and powdered tiles. Between them were
found the base and capital of a column, and part of a stone
mortar.
J.B.A.A., VI, pp. 442–3.   *R.C.H.M., p.* 134.

348 *Mark Lane, Nos.* 26–8, 1935
On the N. edge of the site, a Roman bath or tank was found. It
was 5 ft. wide with a cement floor, and adjoining it to the north
was a mass of masonry 6 ft. thick.
J.R.S., XXVI (1936), *pp.* 255–6. *Unpublished plan by* Mr. F. COTTRILL.

349 *Mark Lane, Nos.* 26–8, 1871
'At the back of the archway adjoining the premises situated at
No. 27 Mark Lane', was found a pavement of common red
tesserae at a depth of 7–8 ft. One account says that it was 12 ft.
square, and another that it was 11 ft. by 6 ft. It was left *in situ*.
Illustrated London News, 13 May 1871.   *R.C.H.M., p.* 132.

350 *Seething Lane,* 1839–41
Tessellated pavements were found near St. Olave's Church and
throughout the street. Lying on one of them was part of a sculpture of the three Mother-Goddesses, now in Guildhall Museum.
(*See Pl.* 88.) Since the provenance of this is also given as Hart Street,
it seems likely that it was found at the northern end of Seething
Lane, very near the church. From the size of the sculpture, which
must originally have been at least 3 ft. in height and more than
3 ft. wide, it is likely to have stood in a temple or shrine.
ROACH SMITH: *Illustrations of Roman London, pp.* 33 *ff.*   *R.C.H.M.,*
p. 141.   *Arch., XXIX, p.* 154.

351 *Trinity Square, Inner Circle Railway,* 1882
During excavations for the District Railway foundations of
buildings were found, together with a red tessellated pavement

on a bed of concrete supported by a substructure of oak piling. With the piling were the roots of oak trees, suggesting that there had been a clearance of woodland before the building was erected. 'A wall, a platform or way on two sides, a gutter and some ducts' were also seen.

J.B.A.A., XXXVIII, p. 447.   *R.C.H.M., p.* 145.

352 *Eastcheap (formerly Little Eastcheap), site of St. Andrew Hubbard Church,* 1836
Traces of Roman work are said to have been seen in the foundations of the church (which was destroyed in the Great Fire), and fragments of Samian pottery were found. It was suggested that the church had been built partly on the remains of a Roman building. Foundations of houses are said to have been found all along the street at depths of 12–20 ft.

Gent. Mag., 1836, *I, p.* 137.   *R.C.H.M., p.* 117.

353 *Lower Thames Street, site of Coal Exchange, and of Nos.* 86–90, 1848 *and* 1859
The foundations of a Roman building were found at a depth of 12 ft. Near the centre was a double chamber, heated by a hypocaust with pillars of bricks 8 in. square, standing to a height of 2 ft. and carrying flanged roofing tiles supporting the cement floor. At each end was an apse. The chamber was divided into two compartments by a brick wall, in the western side of which was a recess, probably a seat. A doorway immediately north of the seat gave access from one compartment to the other. (The western compartment with its hypocaust and brick seat has been preserved. *See Pl.* 61.) Adjoining the heated chamber were rectangular rooms on the north, south, and east, and to the north and south of these were apparently corridors 10 ft. wide running E.–W. To the west was a drain of hollowed logs.

J.B.A.A., IV, pp. 38–49, 75; *XXIV, pp.* 295–7.   *R.C.H.M., pp.* 142–3, *and plan, Fig.* 55.

354 *Lower Thames Street, in roadway immediately S. of the Coal Exchange,* 1859
A wall about 7 ft. thick, built of ragstone, was encountered here, but no details of its construction have been recorded. It is possible that this was an embankment wall on the river-side.

J.B.A.A., XXIV, p. 296.   *R.C.H.M., p.* 94.

355 *St. Dunstan's Hill, Nos.* 15–16, 1937–8

Walling of ragstone rubble was seen at a depth of 10 ft. 6 in. below the pavement adjacent to the curved frontage, which it is said to have followed, with its face about 1 ft. from the edge of the site. The mortar contained fragments of brick and was presumably Roman.

On the E. edge of the site, two Roman walls making a corner were seen. They were of ragstone rubble with light brown mortar containing brick fragments, and the faces were of coursed undressed blocks. The surviving top of each was at a depth of 3 ft. below basement level. Adjoining the N. side of the E.–W. wall was a floor of plain red tesserae at a depth of 4 ft. below basement level, with a cement moulding at the junction of wall and floor.

Another similar but narrower E.–W. wall ran across the site 8 ft. 6 in. south of the first, extending from 5 ft. 9 in. to 8 ft. 6 in. below basement level.

MS. notes and plan by Mr. F. COTTRILL.

356 *St. Dunstan's Hill, before* 1840

In making a sewer, a Roman pavement was cut through near Cross Lane.

Nearby, 'under the old wall of the churchyard' of St. Dunstan's, was found a mass of concrete containing pounded brick (possibly *opus signinum*) 'and a cavity, which seems to have been moulded upon a wooden coffin, and contained some human remains . . . some roofing tiles, similar in shape to the ordinary Italian tiles were laid in a slightly arched form over the grave'. The Royal Commission Report suggests that this may well have been a Saxon burial, like the tombs of the early archbishops found at St. Augustine's, Canterbury.

HERBERT: *Hist. of St. Michael, Crooked Lane, p.* 19.   *R.C.H.M., p.* 139.   *J.B.A.A., XX, p.* 298, *Pl.* 19.

357 *Water Lane (Lower Thames Street),* 1927

A small shaft sunk in the lower part of the road cut through a wall of ragstone with light brown mortar, with its top 3½ ft. below the surface of the road. It ran N.–S., and may have turned west at its lower end.

R.C.H.M., p. 145.

358 *Great Tower Street, All Hallows Barking Church,* 1928–30, *and* 1936

A pavement of red tesserae each about 1 in. square was found beneath the tower of the church. It was dated by Mr. F. Cottrill on the evidence of underlying pottery as not earlier than the late second century, and presumably formed part of the late Roman building found under the centre of the church (**359**). It has been preserved *in situ* and can be seen from the crypt. The tesserae on the floor of the crypt to the east have been relaid, however, and are not in the position of an original Roman pavement. The genuine pavement beneath the tower is divided by a gully 1 ft. wide and 6 in. deep, in which a wooden partition wall was probably originally set. Part of a moulding in pink plaster with a light-red surface remains at the junction of the gully and the tessellated pavement, and traces of a vertical plaster face were observed rising from this. The partition is in alignment with the stone and mortar walls found to the east, being parallel with the N. wall of the rectangular compartment (**359**).

J.R.S., XXI (1931), *p.* 239; *XXVII* (1937), *p.* 241.

359 *Great Tower Street, All Hallows Barking Church,* 1930
Near the centre of the church, stone walls were found forming three sides of a room or corridor, 9 ft. wide and at least 20 ft. long. They were 2–3½ ft. thick, and rested on footings of large squared blocks of chalk in hard yellow mortar. There was a single bonding-course of flanged tiles 4 ft. above the foundations, and above this the walls were built of ragstone and flints. The foundations cut into, and therefore post-dated, an occupation layer of the Antonine period. Mr. G. C. Dunning was of the opinion that the stone building was probably of the third century, and that the earlier occupation layers on the site, ranging from Flavian to Antonine, with a little earlier pottery, were remains from plastered timber houses. The Roman stone walls were on the same alignment as the partition associated with the tessellated pavement under the tower (**358**). This is very near the alignment of the modern Great Tower Street, and is quite different from that of the Saxon and mediaeval church.

J.R.S., XXI (1931), *pp.* 239–40.   *MS. notes and plan by* Mr. G. C Dunning.

360 *Tower of London, S.W. of White Tower,* 1899
Roman remains, including masonry, tiles and part of a hypocaust flue, were found near the Cold Harbour Tower (no longer in existence) about 16 ft. to the south-west of the S.W. corner of the White Tower.

J.B.A.A., 2nd Series, V, *p.* 351; VI, *pp.* 26–32.   *R.C.H.M.,* p. 145.

361 *Tower of London, E. of White Tower,* 1956–7
During work on the plinth of the White Tower, part of a Roman

building was discovered and excavated by the Ministry of Works. The walls were of ragstone, and several rooms were found between the E. side of the White Tower and the Roman city wall. One of these had a floor of red tesserae, the others being mainly of cement. The relationship of the building to the city wall remains doubtful, since all the layers between the two had been destroyed by later foundations.

J.R.S., XLVII (1957), *p.* 220; *XLVIII* (1958), *p.* 144.

362 *Aldgate High Street*, 1938

Excavations made in connection with the extension of Aldgate East Underground Station exposed interesting sections of the ancient thoroughfare outside the city gate. The lowest layers of road-metalling, resting on virgin clay at a depth of 10 ft. below the present street level, are said to have been undoubtedly Roman. According to Mr. F. Cottrill, Mr. Quintin Waddington observed some of these layers of road-metalling near the Roman structure under No. 52 Aldgate High Street (**363**).

Guildhall Museum Annual Report, 1938.   *MS. notes by* Mr. F. COTTRILL.

363 *Aldgate High Street, No.* 52, 1938

During excavations for a District Railway tunnel, the S.W. angle of a Roman structure was found about 7 ft. south of the building-line on the S. side of Aldgate High Street. The wall is said to have been entirely of Roman brick, and was about 3 ft. high and 1 ft. 6 in. thick. It was fully described (with approximate measurements) to Mr. F. Cottrill, who did not, however, see it himself. Within the angle was Roman debris which contained a micaceous hemispherical bowl with a flange (cf. T. May: *The Pottery found at Silchester*, 1916, *Pl. XLVIII*, 61). It seems likely that this roadside structure was a Roman tomb.

MS. notes by Mr. F. COTTRILL.

Wall

W1 *The Tower of London, S. of Wardrobe Tower*, 1955

Excavations on behalf of the Ministry of Works, before the erection of a new Jewel House, exposed a portion of the Roman city wall, continuing the line previously known only as far south as the Wardrobe Tower. It stood to a height of several feet above the plinth. There was a crack running through the wall, appar-

ently the result of subsidence, and it had been broken off at the S. end. This portion of the wall had presumably fallen as a result of sinking, and any evidence for a junction with a river wall was lost, since the ground had been cleared to a depth lower than the wall-footing level, and made up with rubble when the Ordnance Offices were built. (A massive wall found running W.–E. and then turning south, between the Lanthorn and Wakefield Towers, appeared to be mediaeval from the character of the masonry, though the fill of earth which post-dated it contained only late Roman pottery.)
J.R.S., XLVI (1956), *pp.* 139–40.

W2 *Tower of London, Wardrobe Tower*
A length of Roman city wall, about 10½ ft. long and 3ft. high above the plinth, remains standing at the back of the Wardrobe Tower. The external face above the sandstone plinth consists of four courses of squared ragstone, three courses of brick bonding tiles and then two more courses of ragstone. On the internal face is an offset of three courses of brick corresponding in level with the plinth. (*See Pl. 47.*) The line of this fragment points to the south directly at the Lanthorn Tower.
J.B.A.A., XXXVII, p. 280; *XXXVIII, pp.* 129–30. *R.C.H.M., p.* 83.

W3 *Tower of London, internal turret N. of Bastion 1,* 1957
Excavations by the Ministry of Works revealed the flint and clay foundations of the Roman city wall, and showed that the change in alignment took place a few feet north of the Wardrobe Tower. At this point was found a rectangular foundation, apparently representing a small internal turret, measuring on the inside 9 ft. by 5 ft.
J.R.S., XLVIII (1958), *pp.* 142*f.*

W4 *Tower of London, Bowyer Tower,* 1911
An excavation in the floor of the Bowyer Tower revealed a small portion of the inner face of the Roman wall, including brick bonding-courses. This has been preserved beneath the modern floor.
R.C.H.M., p. 83.

W5 *Tower Hill,* 1936
During excavations beneath what was then the cellar floor of

No. 19, Tower Hill, were found the remains of a turret, not quite rectangular, built against the inner side of the city wall. It had an internal length (measured parallel with the wall) of 11 ft., and a width (measured at right angles to the wall) of 6 ft. The turret walls were 2 ft. 8 in. thick. Its purpose was probably to accommodate a stair-case giving access to the ramparts. The houses on this and the adjoining sites were destroyed by bombing, and the area has since been laid out as a garden, with the northern part of the turret visible.

F. COTTRILL: *London Wall through eighteen centuries*, 1937, *p. 28, and p. 25, Fig. 19.*

W6 *Trinity Place, S.*
An impressive stretch of the city wall can be seen here, but the upper part is mediaeval rebuilding. The clearance of the modern ruins south of Trinity Place down to basement level has revealed, however, a fine piece of the Roman wall with its courses of bonding tiles. (*See Pl. 39.*) At one point a considerable amount of the internal Roman face has survived, consisting of six courses of squared ragstone above a triple bonding-course of tiles; then comes a double bonding-course, above which are five more courses of squared ragstone. An engraving of 1852 shows the external face, with plinth, four courses of squared ragstone, a triple bonding-course of brick, six courses of ragstone, a double bonding-course, five courses of ragstone, a second double bonding-course and seven courses of ragstone.
ROACH SMITH: *Illus. Rom. Lond.*, Pl. I.　　R.C.H.M., *p. 83.*

W7 *Trinity Place, N.*, 1882
A stretch of 73 ft. of the Roman wall was destroyed during the construction of the Inner Circle Railway in 1882. A drawing by H. Hodge shows the external face with plinth, four courses of squared ragstone, a triple course of brick, six courses of ragstone, a double course of brick, four courses of ragstone and another double course of brick.
R.C.H.M., *p. 83.*

W8 *The Crescent, No. 6 (Nos. 40–1 Trinity Square)*, 1938
A stretch of the Roman wall, 40 ft. long and 11 ft. high, was uncovered and the inner slope of the Roman ditch was traced 12 ft. in front of it. A considerable portion of the external face of the wall can still be seen in the basement of the Toc H Club. It consists of plinth, four courses of squared ragstone, a triple

bonding-course of brick and then six more courses of ragstone. *J.R.S., XXIX* (1939), *p.* 216.

W9 *Coopers Row, Barber and Co.'s warehouse,* 1864 *and* 1961–2
In the rebuilding of the warehouses in 1864, a stretch of wall, 110 ft. long and standing to a height of 35 ft. above ancient ground level, was uncovered and preserved in the new building. This in turn was demolished in 1961, but the wall has been preserved and made more accessible. The upper part is mediaeval, and contains round-headed embrasures, possibly of the twelfth century. (*See Plates* 40, 44.) The triple course of bricks on the internal face, corresponding with the external plinth, was 6in. below the basement floor level of the 1864 warehouse, but was revealed during rebuilding in 1962 (*Pl.* 42). Mr. F. Cottrill noted in 1936 that somewhere in this stretch of wall there is a change of construction. Near the southern end there are three courses of ragstone between the levelling course and the first bonding-course, and 86 ft. further north there are four.
Arch., XL, pp. 297*ff.*; *LXIII, pp.* 259–61.   *R.C.H.M., p.* 83. *MS. notes by* Mr. F. Cottrill.

W10 *Coopers Row, Barber and Co.'s warehouse,* 1962
During building excavations on this site a portion of an internal turret came to light, and opportunity was given for a hasty excavation by the staff of Guildhall Museum to uncover the rest of it. (*See Pl.* 45.) The walls were 3ft. 7 in. thick at foundation level, where they were of clay and flints, and 2 ft. 10 in. above, where they were of ragstone with courses of bonding-tiles. The portion adjacent to the city wall had been destroyed, except at foundation level, but it was quite clear that it had been built at the same time as the wall, as it was on the same foundation, and the facing of the city wall gave place to an irregular roughened surface at the junction with the turret walls. A small portion of the cement floor of the turret remained. To the north, a section was cut through the internal bank of the city wall, which here consisted of a deposit of gravel with a layer of soil sandwiched in the middle. Fragments of Castor ware of Antonine date came from a layer of soil beneath the bank. (*See Fig.* 14, *p.* 109.)
J.R.S., LIII, pp. 139*f.,* Pl. *xv.*1.

W11 *Fenchurch Street Station, S. side,* 1841
During demolitions for the construction of the railway, a portion of the Roman wall 7½ ft. thick and 6–7 ft. high was uncovered.

A wood-cut shows two courses of squared stone, a double course of bricks, five courses of stone, a double course of bricks (carried through the wall), and above this three more courses of stone.
C. KNIGHT: *London, I, p.* 163.   *R.C.H.M., p.* 83.

W12 *Fenchurch Street Station, N. side,* 1881
When the railway was widened on the N. side, a further stretch of wall with a bastion, immediately adjoining **W11**, was destroyed. It was 40 ft. long and 8½ ft. thick above the plinth. A drawing by H. Hodge shows on the external face three courses of squared ragstone *below* the plinth, and above it four courses of ragstone, a triple bonding-course with set-back above the second brick, six courses of ragstone, a double bonding-course with set-back immediately above it, and finally three more courses of squared ragstone. The internal face is shown with the same courses and offsets, but with the usual triple course of bricks opposite the plinth. The foot of the faced walling was 18 ft. below the modern surface, and a roughly rectangular drain of Roman brick passed through the wall at about this level.
R.C.H.M., pp. 83, 85, *and Pl.* 24.   *J.B.A.A., 1st Series, XXXVI, p.* 463; *XXXVIII, p.* 132.

W13 *America Square, Nos.* 15–16, 1908
The demolition of these premises revealed a stretch of wall about 65 ft. long, and a further special excavation was carried out to examine it. The wall was 8¼ ft. thick, and stood to a height of 7 ft. above the plinth. The base was 16 ft. below street level. On the external face above the plinth were four courses of squared ragstone, a triple bonding-course, six courses of squared ragstone and a double bonding-course. The internal face had the usual offsets. The Roman ditch was observed at two points, about 12 ft. from the face of the wall. It was V-shaped in section, and about 10 ft. wide and 5 ft. deep. (*See Fig.* 12, *p.* 105.)
Arch., LXIII, pp. 261*ff.*   *R.C.H.M., pp.* 85, 94.

W14 *Crutched Friars, No.* 1 (*Roman Wall House*), 1905
On the sites of Nos. 18–20 Jewry Street and No. 1 Crutched Friars, a length of about 40 ft. of the inner face of the wall was revealed, standing to a maximum height of 8–9 ft., with the base 8½ ft. below the present ground level. Above the usual triple levelling-course of brick were four courses of squared ragstone, a triple bonding-course, six courses of squared ragstone and a

double bonding-course with the usual offsets. A considerable portion of this fragment has been preserved in the cellar of the modern building. (*See Pl.* 41.)

Arch., LX, pp. 191*ff.* *R.C.H.M., p.* 85.

W 15 *Jewry Street, Sir John Cass College,* 1900
On rebuilding the College, the foundations of the wall were found in the lower part of the site, beneath the old Cass School. The wall itself had previously been destroyed. At one point at least the foundation extended partly under the pavement of Jewry Street, and projected 7 ft. into the site. There is no record of Roman remains coming to light during the excavations just to the north of this, where houses were pulled down for an extension of the Sir John Cass Foundation.

Arch., LX, p. 193. *R.C.H.M., p.* 85.

W 16 *Jewry Street, Nos.* 32–5, *now part of Sir John Cass College,* 1933
The city wall was exposed for a length of 75 ft. It was 8 ft. thick, surviving to a height of 4 ft. above the plinth. The foundations were cut through the filling of a stream-bed which contained pottery of the late first century. A culvert of bricks had been constructed below the plinth, evidently to carry the water of the stream through the wall. The Roman city ditch was observed in section at several points, but its relationship with the earlier stream-bed is not clear. There was a layer of gravel on the 10 ft. berm between the wall and ditch. A fragment at the end of this stretch of wall has been preserved in the basement of the college.

J.R.S., XXIV (1934), *p.* 211. *MS. notes by* Mr. F. Cottrill.

W 17 *Jewry Street, No.* 36 (*the 'Three Tuns'*), *before* 1861
In the cellar of the public house is still preserved a large fragment of the Roman city wall, extending to a point about 17 ft. from the northern boundary of the Sir John Cass College. The sandstone plinth is just visible above the cellar floor, at a depth of about 8 ft. 10 in. below the level of the pavement. Above this are four courses of ragstone, with a damaged portion above containing patches of modern brickwork with at least one course of Roman bricks at the top. Above this again are six more courses of ragstone. The thickness of the wall is 7 ft. 10 in. above the plinth and 8 ft. 9 in. just above the cellar floor.

Gent. Mag., 1861, *I, p.* 646.

W18 *Jewry Street, N. end*, 1861

A stretch of wall lying just beneath the frontage of Jewry Street was found during re-building immediately south of Aldgate. The foundations are said to have rested on massive piles.

J.B.A.A., 1st Series, XXXVI, p. 163.　　*Gent. Mag.*, 1861, *I, p.* 646. *R.C.H.M., p.* 85.

W19 *Duke Street*, 1887

The widening of Duke Street on the N.E. side exposed a long stretch of the Roman city wall, lying partly beneath the footway of the old street, and partly beneath the frontage of the houses that were demolished. Its position was approximately in the middle of the present widened road.

J.B.A.A., XLIII, p. 203.　　*R.C.H.M., p.* 85.

W20 *Houndsditch, Nos.* 28–30, 1935

The core of the city wall was exposed in the S.E. corner of the site, and was seen in section at several points. It consisted of ragstone rubble, roughly coursed in alternate layers of ragstone blocks and hard cream-coloured cement mixed with small flints. The footings were of flints and puddled clay, level at the bottom which was about 15 ft. below pavement level. The masonry above oversailed the footings on the N. side by about 1 ft. There was a triple levelling-course of bricks with the top bricks about 7 ft. 9 in. below pavement level, and the bottom 4 ft. above the top of the footings.

J.R.S., XXVI, p. 254.　　*MS. notes by* Mr. F. COTTRILL.

W21 *Bevis Marks, Nos.* 17–18, 1880

In the rebuilding of the back of No. 31 Houndsditch, a length of about 70 ft. of the Roman city wall was removed. It stood to a height of 11¾ ft., and formed the boundary at the back of the houses in Bevis Marks. On the outer face were two courses of squared ragstone below the plinth and four above it. Above these was a triple bonding-course, followed by a course of ragstone, above which the face had been destroyed. On the inside face, above the triple levelling-course of bricks were four courses of ragstone, a triple bonding-course without a set-back, five courses of ragstone and another triple bonding-course.

J.B.A.A., XXXVII, pp. 86–7; *XXXVIII, pp.* 132–5.　　*R.C.H.M., p.* 85.

W22 *Bevis Marks, No.* 19, 1935

A length of more than 19 ft. of the city wall, running right across the site, was exposed and subsequently destroyed. The outer face was about 25½ ft. from the Bevis Marks frontage, and the thickness of the wall above the plinth was 7 ft. 11 in. The Roman masonry in parts came up to the underside of the ground floor of the modern building, 2 ft. 6 in. below pavement level. The top of the plinth was 4 ft. 4 in. lower than this. A double bonding-course ran through the wall, with its top 4 ft. below pavement level, and on the inner face of the wall there was an offset of 3 in. at this level, with an additional single course of bricks immediately above it, only one brick deep.

J.R.S., XXVI (1936), *p.* 254.   *MS. notes by* Mr. F. COTTRILL.

W23 *Bevis Marks, E. of Goring Street,* 1923

A stretch of the Roman wall about 120 ft. long immediately S.E. of Goring Street was revealed and destroyed. It was about 8½ ft. thick with a sandstone plinth 7½ ft. below modern ground level. There was a triple bonding-course. The wall stood on 5 ft. of brick-earth lying above the gravel.

J.R.S., XII, p. 258.   *R.C.H.M., p.* 85.

W24 *Bevis Marks, W. of Goring Street,* 1884

A contemporary drawing shows that the wall consisted on the external face of two courses of ragstone, the red sandstone plinth, four courses of squared ragstone, a triple bonding-course of tiles and five courses of squared ragstone. On the inside face three courses of tiles were level with the external plinth. The base of the plinth was about 7¼ ft. below modern pavement level, and the wall was 8 ft. 10 in. thick. It rested on a foundation of flint and puddled clay.

Ant. Journ., VII, pp. 518–20.   *R.C.H.M., p.* 85.

W25 *Camomile Street, E.,* 1905 *and* 1926

A stretch of city wall was revealed at the back of Nos. 58–60 Houndsditch and adjoining the churchyard belonging to the parish of St. Martin Outwich. The bottom of the plinth was at a depth of 8 ft. 4 in. below street level, and the height of the fragment was 14½ ft. above the base of the plinth. The external face consisted of four courses of squared ragstone above the plinth, followed by a triple bonding-course of tiles and two more courses of squared ragstone. Above this point only the core of the wall remained. This contained three double bonding-courses.

Arch., LX, pp. 187*ff.*   *R.C.H.M., p.* 86.

W26 *Camomile Street, middle,* 1876
A stretch of wall more than 60 ft. long was uncovered here. It was 8 ft. thick, with a foundation of flints and clay. The wall was destroyed above the plinth.
J. E. PRICE: *On a Bastion of London Wall,* 1880, *pp.* 23–5.
R.C.H.M., p. 86.

W27 *London Wall, E. of All Hallows Church,* 1905
A small portion of the wall was uncovered 45 ft. east of All Hallows Church. The plinth and two courses of squared ragstone were exposed.
Arch., LX, pp. 211*f.*   *R.C.H.M., p.* 86.

W28 *London Wall, All Hallows Church,* 1905
During the excavation of the bastion under the vestry, the lower part of the wall was uncovered. It consisted of the plinth with four courses of squared ragstone and a triple bonding-course.
The Roman ditch was found at a distance of 15 ft. from the N. face of the city wall, extending for more than 200 ft. It was 10 ft. wide, and 4½–5 ft. deep. (*See Fig.* 8, *p.* 71.) The wide mediaeval ditch had been cut from a higher ground level, and its southern edge just missed the buried Roman ditch, which had remained undisturbed. It is a curious fact that the modern property boundaries seem to follow the N. edge of the Roman city ditch.
Arch., LX, pp. 212*f.*; *LXIII, p.* 273.   *R.C.H.M., p.* 86.

W29 *London Wall, All Hallows Churchyard,* 1905
Here the city wall forms the N. boundary of the churchyard. When the external face was uncovered in 1905, Roman work was found remaining to a height of 12 ft. – i.e. to about the present ground level. Above the plinth were four courses of squared ragstone, a triple bonding-course, five courses of ragstone, a second triple bonding-course, six courses of ragstone, a double bonding-course, and three more courses of ragstone. Below the plinth a brick-lined culvert passed through the foundation. It lay in a hollow depression, the lower part of which was filled with sandy silt, like that of a stream-bed. This was cut by the Roman city ditch, so the stream was evidently of earlier date.
Arch., LX, pp. 207*ff.*, 213.   *R.C.H.M., pp.* 86–7.

W30 *London Wall, W. corner of Blomfield Street,* 1837 *and* 1841
During sewer excavations of 1837, a Roman arched culvert was found, passing through the substructure of the city wall and dis-

charging into a ditch 14 ft. south of London Wall. Inside the culvert, on the N. side, enclosed by three iron bars, were two human skeletons with Roman pottery and coins of Antoninus and Faustina. The bottom of the culvert was at a depth of $18\frac{1}{2}$ ft. below the present surface. Near the same spot, but 5 ft. lower, was found a second culvert in 1841. It seems likely that both afforded passage to one of the main tributaries of the Walbrook stream, the higher and later one being constructed after the earlier one had been blocked. If the burials were subsequent to the construction of the later culvert, they cannot, of course, be contemporary with the coins mentioned.

Cat. of Antiq. Roy. Exch., p. xxxi. Arch., XXIX, p. 152. R.C.H.M., pp. 87–9.

W31 *London Wall, opposite Carpenters' Hall, 1905*
A shaft sunk at this point on the outside face of the wall showed the plinth at a depth of $13\frac{1}{2}$ ft. below the modern street, resting on an unusually massive foundation of ragstone $5\frac{1}{2}$ ft. deep and projecting 2 ft. from the face of the wall. Near the bottom of the foundations, in sand overlying the undisturbed ballast, were two skulls, one partly embedded in the mortar of the Roman foundation – no doubt from earlier burials disturbed when the wall was constructed. Above the plinth were four courses of squared ragstone, a triple bonding-course of brick, five courses of squared ragstone, a second triple bonding-course and three courses of squared ragstone.

Arch., LX, pp. 170ff. R.C.H.M., p. 89.

W32 *London Wall, between Throgmorton Avenue and Moorgate Street*
A long stretch of city wall survived here until 1817, forming the back enclosure of Bethlehem Hospital. It is recorded that 75 yards of it were destroyed at that date when the road of London Wall was widened towards the north. A layer of Roman bricks was seen on the N. side of the wall level with the pavement. In 1905 telephone mains were laid in the core of the wall for a considerable distance east of Moorgate Street.

J. T. Smith: Ancient Topography of London, p. 28 (Engraving of view, 1812). Gent. Mag., 1817, I, p. 196. Arch., LX, p. 169. R.C.H.M., p. 89.

W33 *London Wall, W. of Copthall Avenue*
A branch of the Walbrook passed under the city wall just west of Copthall Avenue (formerly Little Bell Alley), and a red brick

arch for the transit of water was observed in 1835. It was 6 ft.
high and 4 ft. wide, and was supported on either side by massive
piles of elm 6 ft. long, between which the stream flowed. The
actual structure of the wall is not mentioned, however, and it is
by no means certain that the brick arch described was the culvert
which conducted the W. branch of the Walbrook into the city.
Builder, 1889, *II, p.* 236.   *R.C.H.M., p.* 89.

W34 *London Wall, E. of Moorgate,* 1930
A tunnel for telephone cables was cut through the Roman wall
which was exposed for a length of more than 105 ft. (The length
of 195 ft. given in the *J.R.S.* note seems to be a misprint, according
to Mr. Dunning's map references given in the same note.) It was
of Kentish ragstone in yellowish-white mortar, faced with squared
stones, and with three courses of red bonding-tiles passing right
through the core. There was a single course of tiles at 4 ft. below
street level, a double course at 6½ ft., and a triple course at 10 ft.
In the western part of the trench a triple facing-course of tiles
was seen on the internal face of the wall at a depth of 13 ft.
below street level. The plinth and foundations were not uncovered.
J.R.S., XXI (1931), *p.* 236.

W35 *London Wall, immediately W. of Moorgate,* 1882
A stretch of about 43 ft. of the wall was uncovered beneath the
street frontage. It was 9 ft. 2 in. thick, but this included 2 ft. of
mediaeval thickening on the inner face. It stood to a height of
4 ft. above the modern ground level and extended to a depth of
at least 8 ft. below it.
J.B.A.A., XXXVIII, pp. 424–6.   *R.C.H.M., p.* 89.

W36 *London Wall, E. of Coleman Street,* 1911 *and* 1920
A portion of wall with the outer face cut away was found on the
site of No. 123 London Wall, and nine years later the adjoining
portion was exposed on the demolition of No. 122, at the E. angle
of Coleman St. Here there was evidence of an early rebuilding
at some uncertain date. Above the plinth were five courses of
squared ragstone and a double bonding-course of brick. The
outer face had evidently fallen away above this point, and had
been made good by a battering plinth 6 ft. high, resting on a
foundation 2 ft. thick laid in front of the original face of the wall.
Above the batter the wall was again vertical, consisting of a double
course of bonding-tiles, above which were four facing-courses of

squared ragstone. The core of the repaired portion contained many fragments of brick and roofing tiles.

Arch., LXXI, pp. 73ff. *R.C.H.M., p.* 90.

W37 *London Wall, between Coleman Street and New Basinghall Street,* 1957

During the clearance for the new road (Route 11, the new 'London Wall'), a stretch of about 210 ft. of the Roman city wall was exposed, extending from about 60 ft. west of Coleman Street. Much of the external N. face had survived, standing 2–6 ft. above the footings with its chamfered sandstone plinth and levelling tile course. The thickness of the wall was 8 ft. 3–6 in. A particularly fine portion has been preserved in the underground car park beneath the new road.

The Roman city ditch was seen to be about 12 ft. wide and 4 ft. deep here. Gravelly layers south of the modern street (the former London Wall) suggested that there was a Roman street to the south of the city wall.

J.R.S., XLVIII (1958), *p.* 144.

W38 *London Wall, immediately E. of Aldermanbury Postern,* 1857

A portion of the wall revealed during excavations for the foundations of houses was of peculiar construction, consisting of a series of blind arches, apparently purely structural. A sketch reproduced by C. Roach Smith shows three of these arches built with radially set bricks of Roman type, seen from the N. side of the wall. Above them is a portion of a very uneven double bonding-course of bricks.

C. ROACH SMITH: *Illus. Rom. Lond., p.* 17. *R.C.H.M., p.* 90 *and Pl.* 23.

W39 *E. of St. Alphage Churchyard,* 1960

Excavations immediately north of St. Alphage Church and east of the churchyard revealed a section through the foundations of a ragstone wall 3½ ft. thick. This was in line with the wall of the Roman fort 37 ft. to the west (see **W40**) and was presumably its continuation. Everything above the bottom 2 ft. of the foundation had been removed, and there was no trace here of the foundation of the inner thickening wall which was added to the fort wall when the later city wall was built, as is found elsewhere in the fort area. Since its foundation was at a higher level it had been completely removed. A V-shaped cutting which may have been the bottom of the fort ditch was seen immediately to

the north, though its relationship to the ragstone foundation was puzzling as it appeared in the section. Its filling contained the shells of land mollusca so it was probably dry. Further north, about 17 ft. north of the wall, was the bottom of a V-shaped depression which appeared to be the Roman city ditch.
Guildhall Museum Excavations Notebook, 20 October 1960.

W40 *St. Alphage Churchyard*
A fine stretch of city wall has been preserved here, with the N. side exposed by the clearance of the bombed ruins which adjoined it. Traces of a rebuilding under Henry III have been identified in the N. face, and the wall is surmounted by the brick battlements built during the mayoralty of Sir Ralph Jocelyn in 1477. Only the core of the Roman wall remains, but this is of particular interest, as it can be seen clearly at the E. end that the lower part of the wall is double, the outer wall being the original wall of the Roman fort, and the inner the thickening wall that was added when the N. wall of the fort was incorporated in the city wall, to bring it to the standard thickness of the latter. No bonding-courses of brick occur in the fort wall and earlier archaeologists, such as Roach Smith, did not therefore recognise its Roman date. (*See Pl.* 38.)
R.C.H.M., p. 90.

W41 *E. of Nicholl Square, between bastions* 13 *and* 14, 1947
Professor W. F. Grimes observed here in 1947 that the foundations of the wall had been cut into the bank of an earlier wall, later identified as the W. wall of a Roman fort.
J.R.S., XXXVIII (1948), *p.* 92.

W42 *Windsor Court, Monkwell Street, behind Bastion* 14, 1948
Professor Grimes's excavation here revealed the wall standing to a height of about 4 ft. on the outside, with a bank of clay behind it, and traces of a gravel road surface beyond the bank. The usual sandstone plinth was here replaced by a deeper horizontal offset. The clay bank was an earlier feature, underlying the wall and cut by its foundations. Professor Grimes later found that it was the bank of the fort wall, to which an internal thickening wall had been added when the fort wall was incorporated in the thicker city wall.
J.R.S., XXXIX (1949), *p.* 107.

W43 *N. of Falcon Square*, 1956
The city wall adjoining the N. turret of the fort gateway was found to be double – as elsewhere in this stretch of wall – consisting of the original fort wall with a thickening wall added internally when the fort was incorporated in the new city wall. The thickening wall was inserted into a deposit which had accumulated between the N. wall of the turret and the fort wall, and was therefore evidently later than the deposit. Fortunately the latter could be dated with some precision, for it contained a worn coin of Commodus of A.D. 183–4. The deposit, and consequently the city wall, can hardly therefore be earlier than the end of the second century. A worn coin of Vespasian, probably of A.D. 71, came from a pit underlying the internal bank of the fort, which cannot therefore be much earlier than A.D. 80, but may well be considerably later. A date early in the second century seems most likely, in view of the other evidence (*Cf.* **33**).
J.R.S., *XLVII* (1957), *p.* 220.

W44 *S. of Falcon Square*, 1961–2
Excavation on behalf of the Roman and Mediaeval London Excavation Council revealed a number of pieces of both the fort wall and the inner thickening which was added when the city wall was built. A fine stretch of the fort wall was uncovered immediately to the north of the internal turret (**W45**). It is intended that these remains shall be preserved. (*See Pl.* 36.)

W45 *W. of Noble Street*, 1957
During excavations on behalf of the Roman and Mediaeval London Excavation Council the foundations of a rectangular internal turret of the Roman fort were found, and are now preserved. (*See Pl.* 36. *B.*) The turret is about 10 ft. by 12½ ft., and is situated between the gate and the S.W. angle of the fort. It is not bonded into the fort wall but is clearly contemporary with it. A careful search failed to reveal a corresponding turret to the north of the fort gate, and it was clear that none had existed.
J.R.S., *XLVIII* (1958), *p.* 144.

W46 *W. of Noble Street*, 1961–3
Between the S.W. corner of the fort and the internal turret (**W45**), excavations on behalf of the Roman and Mediaeval London Excavation Council revealed further traces of the internal thickening wall. The gravel metalling of the perimeter road was found with its edge 11–12 ft. to the east of this.

W47 *Noble Street, W. of junction with Oat Lane,* 1949

Excavations by the Roman and Mediaeval London Excavation Council showed a double foundation wall here, running N.–S. The inner wall came to an end just opposite the corner bastion, while the outer, which proved to be the wall of the earlier fort, curved through 90° to an easterly direction. (*See Pl.* 35, *walls C and A; and Fig.* 31, *p.* 161.) The inner wall was evidently a thickening wall added when the city wall was built to bring the fort wall to the standard thickness of about 8 ft. The fort wall and thickening wall were each approximately 4 ft. thick. (See also **31**.)

R. L. S. BRUCE MITFORD: *Recent Excavations in Britain, pp.* 126–7. *J.R.S., XL* (1950), *pp.* 107–9, *Pl. IX.*

*W48 *Noble Street, N.E. of St. Anne and St. Agnes Church,* 1958–9

Excavations under the direction of Professor W. F. Grimes revealed the Roman city wall at its junction with the S.W. corner of the earlier Roman fort. This portion has been preserved, but the actual junction was unfortunately pierced by a lift shaft of the modern bombed building. (*See Pl.* 35, *wall D, where the portion destroyed by the lift shaft has been restored.*) Inside the corner of the fort is the foundation of its corner turret (see **31**). Above the ditch of the fort is a later Roman brick-lined culvert, which pierces the city wall near its junction with the fort (*Fig.* 31, *p.* 161). (See also **W49**.) The filling of the gully associated with the culvert produced material ranging in date to the late third century.

J.R.S., XLIX (1959), *p.* 126; *L* (1960), *p.* 229.
**See note at end of Gazetteer.*

*W49 *E. of Aldersgate Street,* 1922

During excavations on the site of Alder House (formerly the site of the Castle and Falcon Hotel and its yard) in 1922, a piece of the city wall was found running E.–W. It survived in parts from the modern ground level down to the foundations, a depth of about 10 ft., and over its whole length the outer face had been repaired in later Roman times. The outer face was badly battered for about 20 ft. west of the bastion. No trace of a Roman ditch was found. At one point a brick-lined drain pierced the wall – presumably the same culvert that was found on the inside of the wall during the R.M.L.E.C. excavation of 1958, behind the bastion just west of the S.W. corner of the fort.

J.R.S., XI, p. 220.   *R.C.H.M., p.* 90.
**See note at end of Gazetteer.*

*W50 *W. of Aldersgate Street,* 1841

A section of wall was found in excavating for the French Pro-

testant Church, a site now occupied by the N.E. wing of the
G.P.O. building. It consisted of a foundation of flint and clay
1½ ft. thick and 11½ ft. below the surface of the ground. Above
this were 4½ ft. of rubble, a double bonding-course, 2½ ft. of
rubble, a second double bonding-course, and more rubble above.
This wall also ran under the roadway.
Arch., XXX, pp. 522–4. R.C.H.M., pp. 90–1.
See note at end of Gazetteer.

W51 St. Botolph, Aldersgate, churchyard, S. side (Postman's Park), 1887
A stretch of 131 ft. of the wall was exposed in clearing a site
for the G.P.O. buildings. This still survives, its inner face forming
the N. side of the basement area of the G.P.O. A total height of
14 ft. 4 in. of Roman work was seen. Above the footings was a
triple levelling-course, followed by five courses of squared ragstone, a double bonding-course of brick, five courses of ragstone,
a second double bonding-course, five courses of ragstone, a third
double bonding-course, two courses of ragstone, and at the same
interval a fourth double bonding-course visible in the core of the
wall.
Arch., LII, pp. 609ff. Builder, 1888, I (Vol. 54), p. 315.
R.C.H.M., p. 91.
See note at end of Gazetteer.

W52 G.P.O. site, King Edward St. (formerly Christ's Hospital site),
1907–9
A stretch of wall 10 ft. 2 in. high was found, with the plinth at a
depth of 13 ft. 8 in. below ground level. Above this point one
triple and two double bonding-courses remained. There were
indications of a bank built against the inner face, extending
16½ ft. from the wall, and remaining to a height of about 5 ft. (See
Fig. 13, p. 106.)
Arch., LXIII, p. 276. R.C.H.M., p. 91.
See note at end of Gazetteer.

W53 General Post Office Yard (Christ's Hospital site), 1907–9
A portion of wall adjoining the bastion was uncovered, and the
base of the plinth was found 9½ ft. below the ground level. Above
it were four courses of squared ragstone, a double bonding-course
of brick, five of ragstone, a second double bonding-course, and
two courses of ragstone. The thickness above the plinth was 8½ ft.
The Roman city ditch was found cut into the brick-earth at a
distance of about 10 ft. or 12 ft. north of the wall. It was about
12 ft. wide and 6½ ft. deep, and was cut to a sharp V-shape in
section. It was ignored when the bastion was built, and the base

of the latter passed straight through it to rest on the undisturbed
brick-earth beneath.

Arch., LXIII, p. 277.   *R.C.H.M., p.* 91.
*See note at end of Gazetteer.

*W54 *General Post Office, N. edge of building and yard (formerly site of
Christ's Hospital),* 1907–9

A long stretch of wall similar to **W53** was found here. At one
point, just below the base levelling-course of bricks, a floor of
large Roman tiles laid on a bed of clay extended for a distance
of 10 ft. to the south of the wall. As it was covered with brick-earth,
probably part of the internal bank of the wall, to a height of 3 ft.,
it presumably belonged to a building destroyed before the construction of the wall.

About $11\frac{1}{4}$ ft. to the north of the wall was the Roman city ditch.
This was much wider and deeper than the ditch cut by the bastion
further east (see **W53**). It was 25 ft. wide and 14 ft. deep, the
section showing that it had been produced by re-cutting the
original smaller ditch, the southern lip of which remained at a
distance of about $10\frac{1}{4}$ ft. north of the face of the wall.

Arch., LXIII, pp. 278–80.   *R.C.H.M., pp.* 91, 96.
*See note at end of Gazetteer.

W55 *General Post Office Yard, E. of Giltspur Street (Christ's Hospital
site),* 1907–9

A curved portion of wall (still preserved) adjoining the corner
bastion was found, the base of the plinth being 12 ft. below the
surface. It is said that the outer face 'bore evident marks of water
having stood against it for a long time'. Above the plinth were
five courses of squared ragstone, a double bonding-course of
brick, five courses of squared ragstone, and a second double
bonding-course. The thickness above the plinth was $7\frac{3}{4}$ ft. The
wall had apparently tilted outwards and cracked before the
bastion was added.

Arch., LXIII, pp. 286*ff.*   *R.C.H.M., p.* 91.

W56 *Newgate, No.* 122, *immediately N. of the Roman gate,* 1875

A portion of city wall adjoining the Roman gate was uncovered
and recorded, but at the time its true nature was unrecognised,
and there was considerable confusion arising from the discovery
of portions of the mediaeval gateway, one of which was believed
to be the city wall. The true Roman city wall was, however,
drawn in plan and section with the other remains. It was 8 ft.
thick, and had two double courses of bonding-tiles.

J.B.A.A., XXXI, pp. 76–80; *XXXII, pp.* 385–6.   *R.C.H.M.,
pp.* 91–2.

W57 *Central Criminal Court (Newgate Prison site),* 1903
Two stretches of the wall were uncovered, the northernmost
being 76 ft. in length. The base of the plinth was 11 ft. below the
pavement level of Newgate Street. Above were five courses of
squared ragstone and a double bonding-course of brick. A second
bonding-course remained in the inner face.
Arch., LIX, pp. 125 *ff.* *R.C.H.M., p.* 92.

W58 *Warwick Square, Nos.* 10–12, *before* 1880 *and* 1922
The internal sides of two portions of Roman city wall were
uncovered here in 1922. Of these, only the southern fragment
retained its facing, showing a double bonding-course with four
courses of squared ragstone above and below it. A fragment is
still preserved.
A portion of the wall was also found near here before 1880,
when a fragment preserved beneath the premises of Messrs.
Tylor and Sons in Warwick Lane was examined by J. E. Price.
He describes it as standing to a height of about 8 ft., with three
courses of bonding tiles at a distance of 1 ft. 2 in. from ground
level, and a double course apparently at a greater depth.
J. E. PRICE: *On a Bastion of London Wall,* 1880, *p.* 21 *n.* *R.C.H.M.,*
p. 92. *J.R.S., XII, p.* 258.

W59 *Old Bailey, rear of Nos.* 7–10, *W. of Amen Court,* 1900 *and* 1907–8
A fragment of the wall was found at the rear of No. 8 Old Bailey
in 1900, standing 8 ft. high, with the top 18 in. below pavement
level. It was 8¼ ft. thick above the foundation.
The remains of the wall behind Nos. 7–10 Old Bailey were
uncovered in 1907–8, on the demolition of the Old Bailey
Sessions House. The original base continued throughout, but at
the S.E. corner of the site the sandstone plinth was missing, and
the external face had been repaired in later times, the thickness
at the first bond being only about 7 ft.
Contrary to popular belief, the wall visible on the W. side of Amen
Court is not part of the city wall, which lies a few feet to the west.
London and Middlesex Arch. Soc. Trans., N.S., I, p. 354. *Arch.,*
LXIII, p. 295. *R.C.H.M., p.* 92.

W60 *Playhouse Yard, before* 1843
During excavations for a sewer, a portion of a wall 10 ft. thick
is said to have been found running N.–S. in a line with Ludgate.
It was of 'large unhewn stones embedded in a sort of grouting
composed of powdered bricks, lime and gravel'. The wall was

tunnelled through but not destroyed. Another account, however, describes three walls of the same massive character running N.–S. in Playhouse Yard, and it is possible that all three were part of the Blackfriars Convent. Nevertheless it is most likely that one of them was built on the foundations of the earlier city wall which the Black Friars were permitted to pull down. This seems to be confirmed by Roach Smith's observations further south (**W61**). The only Priory wall crossing Playhouse Yard which could be regarded as 'in a line with Ludgate' seems to be the one immediately east of Church Entry. This building line, consisting of the W. walls of the Priory Choir, Chapter House, School House and Infirmary, probably follows the earlier city wall. (See Clapham's plan of the Priory in *Arch.*, LXIII, *Pl.* XI.)
R.C.H.M., p. 92.   *Gent. Mag.*, 1843, *I, p.* 635.

W61 *'The Times' Office,* 1855
A very thick wall was found, and this was described by C. Roach Smith as being of three distinct constructions: 'that of the Roman city-wall; a reparation of considerable solidity, which might be Norman or Early English work; and, above all, the remains of a passage or window which probably belonged to the Blackfriars Monastery'. The fragment has since been destroyed. It is not unlikely that the W. wall of the Blackfriars Infirmary was built on the earlier city wall (see **W60**).
The Builder, 1855, *pp.* 221, 269.   *J.B.A.A.,* 1st Series, V, p. 155.
R.C.H.M., p. 92.

Gates

G1 *Tower Postern*
The Tower Postern is said by Stow to have been on the main line of communication from east to west of the city, but there is no evidence for its original date. It is, however, reasonably certain that there was a Roman gate in the eastern wall, south of Aldgate, and it may have been on or near this site. The mediaeval Tower Postern was undermined by the digging of the Tower Ditch, about 1190, and partly collapsed in 1440.
R.C.H.M., p. 97.

G2 *Aldgate*

The mediaeval gateway is shown on the sixteenth century plan of the Holy Trinity Priory as of rectangular form with two semi-circular towers projecting on the outer face. It is said that when it was rebuilt in 1610 'two heads done after antique models' were found. In 1907, during sewer excavations under the roadway on the S. side of Aldgate High Street, solid masonry was encountered. It was apparently of two periods, one mediaeval, and the other probably Roman. The latter portion consisted of ragstone with hard white mortar and fragments of Roman tile. At 10 ft. from the house-fronts, under the roadway, a face of dressed stones was found, running in a south-easterly direction. This may have formed part of the base of a flanking-tower. It was similar in character to the bases of the bastions, and was possibly part of a late Roman gate.

Arch., LXIII, p. 266.   *V.C.H., London, I, pp.* 52f.   *R.C.H.M., p.* 97.

G3 *Bishopsgate*

This gate is approximately on the line of Ermine Street, and the Roman wall changes direction at this point. It is likely, therefore, that it is of Roman origin. In 1905 a mass of ragstone rubble masonry was found at a depth of 5 ft. near the N. angle of Wormwood Street and Bishopsgate Street. It extended to a depth of 10 ft., 2 ft. into the ballast. The rubble contained some portions of Roman tile, and was apparently carefully faced on its S. side. It stood on a puddling of flint and clay. Cutting into the masonry was a culvert of later date, probably mediaeval. The masonry seems to have been Roman, and probably formed part of the S. face of a gatehouse projecting about 20 ft. on the inside of the city wall. A fragment of walling found in 1921 on the N. side of No. 108 Bishopsgate, apparently at right angles with the city wall, was of Roman work and may have been part of the gate.

London and Middlesex Arch. Soc. Trans., N.S., IV, p. 332.   *R.C.H.M., p.* 97.

G4 *Moorgate*

It is most unlikely that this was ever a Roman gate, for it gave access to no known Roman road, although a few Roman burials have been found in the area. It was a small postern in the Middle Ages, and was not made into a large gate until 1415. A mass of concrete consisting of broken bricks and tiles, ragstone, and septaria was found in 1925, about 10 ft. in front of the city wall, standing on a timber raft 3 in. thick, resting on 9 in. of rammed chalk, at a total depth of $14\frac{1}{2}$ ft. below the pavement. This was probably part of the mediaeval gate.

R.C.H.M., p. 97.

G5 *Aldermanbury Postern*
This postern is said to have been made in 1655, but it has been suggested that there may have been a gate of some kind here in Roman times, in view of the curious wall arches recorded nearby by Roach Smith in 1857. (See **W38**.) These, however, were not openings and were apparently purely structural, so it is difficult to see what connection they could have had with this conjectural gate.

V.C.H., London, I, p. 62.   *R.C.H.M., p.* 97.

G6 *Cripplegate*
This gate is mentioned in the Laws of Ethelred, *c.* 978–1016 (Thorpe: *Ancient Laws and Institutes,* I, p. 301), and it has long been surmised that it might be of Roman origin, although it apparently gave access to no known Roman road from the city. The discovery by Professor W. F. Grimes of the Roman fort has solved this problem and explained its true nature. It is in the centre of the N. wall of the fort, and was undoubtedly its N. gate, the line of modern Wood Street approximately coinciding with the *via praetoria* of the fort. Presumably it continued in existence as a city gate after the incorporation of the fort in the city wall.

R.C.H.M., p. 97.

G7 *Falcon Square, W. gate of Fort,* 1956–8
Excavations by Professor W. F. Grimes revealed part of the foundations of a double gate, of which the N. turret and central piers have been preserved. The N. turret is 15 ft. square, containing a guardroom $8\frac{1}{2}$ ft. square with a narrow doorway at the S.E. corner, and is built of ragstone with a plinth of massive blocks of sandstone. (*See Pl.* 37.) The two central piers are rectangular foundations of ragstone masonry. A portion of the N.W. corner of the S. guardroom was seen and recorded, but has not been preserved. Traces of the original metalling of the roadway were found (*Pl.* 37), but have now been replaced with similar modern gravel. The perimeter road of the fort was also seen and traced for some distance north of the gateway. The gate evidently continued in use after the construction of the city wall, but at a later stage, possibly in late Roman times, was blocked with a ragstone wall, a portion of which has also been preserved.

J.R.S., XLVII (1957), *pp.* 219*f.*; *XLIX* (1959), *p.* 126.

*G8 *Aldersgate, 1887 and 1939*

Aldersgate is mentioned in the laws of Ethelred, *c.* 1000, as Ealdredesgate. In 1887 a raised mound was found in the middle of what was assumed to be the Roman ditch, but may have been a marshy hollow observed in 1939. It was thought to have formed the support for a wooden bridge. Mr. A. H. Oswald in 1939 found a mass of ragstone masonry in the centre of the street, projecting to the north of the Roman city wall. No original facing remained. The bottom rested on black silt which had apparently accumulated after the building of the city wall. In places the structure seemed to have been keyed roughly into the wall, but it overlay the wall footings and was clearly of later date. On the E. side, just above the plinth level of the city wall, was a course of bonding tiles. To the east were two massive piers of characteristically Roman ragstone masonry, with yellow mortar like that of the projection. These lay on the line of the wall, but set at an angle to it, and the foundations of the northern pier had been cut through the flint and clay footings of the wall. There seems little doubt that the piers formed the central spine of a double gateway, and the projection part of its W. tower. The gate was apparently inserted after the building of the city wall.

R.C.H.M., p. 98.   *MS. notes by* Mr. A. H. OSWALD.

*See note at end of Gazetteer.

G9 *Newgate*

Portions of the four Roman walls of the N. guardroom were found in 1875, incorporated with the masonry of the mediaeval gate which projected further to the west. At the N.W. angle a double bonding-course of tiles remained. In 1903, a portion of the E. wall and the S.E. angle of the S. Roman guardroom were found. The plinth, which was of oolitic stone, was 6½ ft. below the pavement level, and rested on a foundation of puddled clay with fragments of ragstone, nearly 5 ft. deep. The plinth of the W. wall of the N. guardroom was examined in 1909, and found to be at the same depth, which is 4½ ft. higher than the plinth of the city wall. It has been suggested that this indicates that there had been a considerable rise in ground level, through the accumulation of rubbish and debris, between the time of the construction of the wall and this building of the gate, which must therefore be of later date. The recorded sections do not indicate such an accumulation of rubbish, and it is more likely that the difference in level simply means that the road surface was higher than the general level of the ground to the north and south.

The internal dimensions of the N. guardroom were 22 ft. by 15 ft., and the external 32 ft. by 30 ft. The width – 35 ft. – between

the guardrooms indicated that there was a double entrance. (*See Fig.* 11, *p.* 103, *and Pl.* 43.)
J.B.A.A., 1*st Series, XXXI, pp.* 76–80; *XXXII, pp.* 385–6.
R.C.H.M., pp. 98–9.   *Arch. LIX, pp.* 130*ff.*; *LXIII, pp.* 294 *f.*

G10 *Ludgate*
No Roman structural remains of this gate have been found. There were, however, Roman burials in the neighbourhood of Fleet Street, so it is likely that one of the Roman roads out of London passed through a gate at or near Ludgate. A Roman tomb-stone of a soldier of the II Augusta Legion, now in the Ashmolean Museum, was found in the rebuilding of St. Martin's Church, adjoining Ludgate, in 1669, and it has been suggested that this may have been a re-used stone incorporated in a later Roman gateway. (*See Pl.* 96.)
R.C.H.M., pp. 99, 173.   WREN: *Parentalia* (1750), *p.* 266.

Bastions

B1 *Wardrobe Tower, Tower of London*
The mediaeval tower incorporates the base of an earlier bastion, semi-circular in plan and apparently hollow. It consists of rubble masonry of stone and broken brick, and stands to a height of about 7 ft. (*See Pl.* 47.)
J.B.A.A., XXXVIII, p. 130.   *R.C.H.M., p.* 99.

B2 *Trinity Place,* 1852, 1882, *and* 1935
During excavations on the E. side of Trinity Place in 1852, a semi-circular bastion containing Roman architectural fragments and portions of tombstones was found. Among the latter was the first piece found of the tombstone of Classicianus the Procurator. (*See Pl.* 4.) A further portion of the bastion was destroyed in excavations for the Inner Circle Railway, 1882–5, and more sculptured stones were found. Finally in 1935, when the Trinity Place sub-station of the London Passenger Transport Board was being built, the remainder of the bastion, part of the N. side, standing four courses high, was exposed. In the lowest course, upside down, was a second portion of the inscription from the tomb of Classicianus, containing parts of the last three lines, including the title 'PROC. PROVINC. BRIT.' (*See Pl.* 5, *and Fig.* 4, *p.* 41.)
ROACH SMITH: *Illus. Rom. Lond., p.* 15.   *R.C.H.M., p.* 99.
Antiquaries' Journal, XVI (1936), *pp.* 1–7.   *Antiquary* (1885), *XI, p.* 33.

B3 *America Square, W. side (now part of Fenchurch Street Station)*, 1881
In widening the railway in 1880–1, a bastion, shown in Ogilby
and Morgan's survey of 1677, was destroyed. A drawing by
Henry Hodge in Guildhall Library shows that it was 21¾ ft. in
diameter and projected 14¾ ft. from the face of the wall. It stood
to a height of 1½ ft. above the excavation level, and was 'built
with rag, flint, chalk, brick, etc., grouted with grey gravelly
mortar like Thames ballast. The facing was of rag, flint and
limestone – all very smooth stone and random work'. In the core,
described as 'also of small material', were found two fragments
of shaped coping in oolite. A patch of pink mortar was found
extending about 2 ft. into the structure on each side of the bastion.
R.C.H.M., pp. 99–100, *and Pl.* 29.

B4 *Bastion 4, Crosswall*
This bastion is known only from Ogilby and Morgan's survey
of 1677.

B5 *Bastion 5, Jewry Street*
A bastion on the present site of the Sir John Cass College is
indicated on Ogilby and Morgan's survey of 1677. It is described
by Maitland in 1756 as a 'Roman tower about eight feet high
which supports a new building'.
W. MAITLAND: *History of London, I, p.* 31.   *R.C.H.M., p.* 100.

B6 *Bastion 6, Duke's Place E.*
This bastion is shown on Ogilby and Morgan's survey of 1677
and on the sixteenth century plan of Holy Trinity Priory. It is
said to have been 21 ft. high in the eighteenth century, and to
have had brick bonding-courses. The foundations were probably
seen in 1887.
W. MAITLAND: *History of London,* 1756, *I, p.* 31.   *Arch., LXIII,*
p. 340.   *J.B.A.A., 1st Series, XLIII, pp.* 203 *f.*   *R.C.H.M., p.* 100.

B7 *Duke Street, W.,* 1949
This bastion is shown on Ogilby and Morgan's map of 1677, and
was described by Woodward in 1707 (Letter to Hearne) as
'composed of stone with layers of brick interposed, after the
Roman manner'. An etching dated 1763 shows a semi-circular
tower of stone with four triple courses of brick. A small
portion of the N. side of the bastion was seen during building
excavations on the site of Nos. 23–7 Houndsditch in 1949. It
contained a re-used piece of worked limestone, probably a

portion of a coping stone. The rest of the bastion had evidently
been removed at an earlier date.
Observation by Mr. F. J. Collins *of the Architect's Department of the
L.C.C.*, 1949.   *R.C.H.M., p.* 100, *and Pl.* 28.   W. Maitland:
History of London, I, *p.* 31.

B8 *Bevis Marks, behind No.* 18, 1880
The base of a bastion was found during the rebuilding of No. 31
Houndsditch. It projected 18½ ft. from the face of the city wall.
Built into it were fragments of Roman architectural work, includ-
ing the base of a column, a shaft with trellis ornament, and an
inscribed stone. Red mortar was seen in some parts of the bastion.
A channel cut in solid stone,1½ ft. broad and 1¼ ft. deep, led from
the centre of the bastion to the ditch.
J.B.A.A., XXXVII, pp. 86–7; *XXXVIII, pp.* 132–5.   *R.C.H.M.,
p.* 100.

B9 *Goring Street*, 1884
The base of a bastion on the W. side of Goring Street was
uncovered and surveyed. It was 26 ft. wide and projected 15½ ft.,
standing on a foundation of flint and puddled clay surmounted
by a bed of chalk. The facing of the bastion consisted of coursed
ragstone, battering outwards towards the base and standing on a
projecting footing-course. 8½ ft. above the foundation was a
double course of bricks not carried through the wall. The filling
of the bastion contained lengths of stone coping, a cornice, a
fragment of an inscription, and a fragment of frieze carved with
running hares (now in Guildhall Museum).
Antiquaries' Journal, VII, pp. 518–20.   *R.C.H.M., p.* 100.

B10 *Camomile Street*, 1876
The remains of a semi-circular bastion, 20 ft. in diameter and
projecting 14 ft. 9 in. from the face of the city wall, were found
during building operations. Huge blocks of oolite and green
sandstone formed the nucleus of the structure, the rest of which
was of Kentish ragstone rubble with a facing of random courses
of the same material. Though later than the wall and separated
from it in places by a space filled in with rubble, there were signs
that the masonry had been toothed into the wall. The bastion
was solid to its surviving height of 10 ft., and contained much
re-used material, including sculptured figures of a soldier and a lion,

and the head of a large statue (now in Guildhall Museum). (*See Fig.* 7, *p.* 69, *and Plates* 93–5.)
J. E. PRICE: *On a Bastion of London Wall,* 1880. *R.C.H.M.,* pp. 100–3.

B11 *All Hallows Vestry,* 1905
The vestry of the church is built on the bastion, and the latter was revealed by excavation in 1905. Subsequently the whole of its external face was uncovered. Its diameter was 19 ft. and its projection 15 ft. It survived to a height of 8 ft., of which 3 ft. extended below the plinth of the city wall. The construction was of random rubble with white mortar resting on a plinth of re-used ashlar, which lay on a rectangular platform set in pink mortar, and also consisting of re-used ashlar. The northern edge of this overlay the southern edge of the original Roman ditch, which had been filled with chalk and stones at this point. (*See Fig.* 8, *p.* 71.)
Arch., LX, pp. 200ff.; *LXIII, pp.* 271ff. *R.C.H.M., pp.* 103–4.

B12 *Bastion 12, St. Giles' Churchyard*
This hollow corner bastion still survives, although only the upper portion (mediaeval and later) can be seen (*Pl.*46). Excavation about 1900 showed that it extended to a depth of 18 ft. below the present surface, and that the foundations and lower portion of the wall to a height of about 4 ft. were of different character from the rest, with mortar that might well have been Roman. Above this height the bastion contained much Roman material, such as pieces of tiles, but the mortar was of inferior quality and was probably of a later date. The possibility of a post-Roman origin for the western group of hollow bastions cannot be disregarded. (See notes on **B14**.)
London and Middlesex Arch. Soc. Trans., N.S., I, pp. 356–9.
R.C.H.M., p. 104.

B13 *Site of Barber Surgeons' Hall*
The seventeenth century courthouse of the Barber Surgeons' Company was built on this bastion, but was destroyed in 1864 and replaced by a warehouse, which in turn was destroyed by bombing in 1940. The semi-circular outline of the bastion, however, is preserved in the shape of the surviving cellar.
R.C.H.M., p. 104.

B14 *Windsor Court, Monkwell Street,* 1865 *and* 1948
This bastion, found in 1865, still survives, but the whole of the visible structure is mediaeval. It is built of flint and ragstone,

with narrow apertures – possibly mediaeval arrow-slits – filled with later brickwork. Excavation by Professor W. F. Grimes in 1948 showed that the lower masonry on the inside was of random rubble of Kentish ragstone, and the floor was a hard gravelly layer at the level of the offset in the city wall. It contained a coin of Constans, but lying on or just above its surface was an Anglo-Saxon pendant of ninth to tenth century date. There is some doubt therefore whether any part of the bastion is Roman, and it is possible that all of this western group of hollow bastions are of post-Roman origin. The junction of city wall and bastion showed that the latter was a later addition which had been built after the wall had been extensively refaced in a very similar style of masonry.

Illus. London News, 19 *August* 1865, *p.* 159 (*Engraving, p.* 161). *R.C.H.M., p.* 104.   *J.R.S., XXXIX* (1949), *p.* 107.

*B15 *Bastion* 15, *W. of Noble Street*, 1922 *and* 1949
During excavations on the site of Falcon House (formerly the site of the Castle and Falcon Hotel) part of the angle bastion was found in 1922. Its eastern corner, abutting on the city wall, was found in 1949, during excavations by the Roman and Mediaeval London Excavation Council. (*See Pl.* 35, *wall E.*)
J.R.S., XI, p. 220.   *R.C.H.M., p.* 104.
*See note at end of Gazetteer.

*B16 *Bastion* 16, *E. of King Edward Street*, 1887
The foundations of a hollow bastion, $5\frac{1}{4}$ ft. thick, and composed of Kentish ragstone with some chalk and a few fragments of old building material were found here. The internal measurements were $17\frac{1}{4}$ ft. by 16 ft. 'Some pieces of worked stone discovered in the foundations showed traces of Norman mouldings and of foliage of the Early English period'. The site is marked by the stairway projection at the N.W. corner of the G.P.O. site.
Arch., LII, p. 610.   *R.C.H.M., p.* 104.
*See note at end of Gazetteer.

*B17 *Bastion* 17, *General Post Office site, W. of King Edward Street* (*formerly E. end of Christ's Hospital*), 1908–9
Part of a solid bastion, about 26 ft. wide with a projection of 16 ft., was found here. It was built of random rubble, containing ragstone, flints, fragments of Roman tile, etc. It rested on undisturbed ground, with its foundations 7 ft. below the base of the plinth of the city wall.
Arch. LXIII, pp. 276 *ff.*   *R.C.H.M., p.* 104.
*See note at end of Gazetteer.

B18 *Bastion 18, General Post Office, N.W. part of the building (formerly site of Christ's Hospital)*, 1908–9

The remains of a hollow bastion were found near the middle of the Great Hall of Christ's Hospital. The wall was 5½ ft. thick, and the internal diameter was 13 ft. It was built upon soft soil, and the base of the structure lay at a depth of nearly 10 ft. below that of the city wall. It was without footings. The upper part of the bastion had evidently been destroyed when the Great Hall was built.

Arch., LXIII, p. 281.   *R.C.H.M., p.* 104.

B19 *Bastion 19, General Post Office Yard (formerly site of Christ's Hospital)*, 1907–9

This angle bastion is now preserved beneath the G.P.O. courtyard. It is hollow, with walls 7 ft. thick at the base, and has a projection of 26 ft. The masonry is ragstone set in white mortar, and the external face is carefully pointed and smoothed, while the inner face is irregular and unpointed. No re-used stones were found. The base is irregular, continuing to a maximum depth of 7 ft. below the level of the plinth of the city wall. The filling of the bastion below a depth of 10 ft. from the present surface contained only Roman objects (apart from the contents of a sump-hole of the sixteenth or seventeenth century).

Arch., LXIII, pp. 286–91.   *R.C.H.M., pp.* 104–6.

B20 and **21** *Bastions between Newgate and Ludgate*

Two bastions are shown in approximately these positions on the map by John Leake, engraved by Hollar in 1666, but nothing more is known of them.

R.C.H.M., p. 106.

*By the author's error, the line of the city wall between the south-west corner of the Roman fort and Bastion 18, with the associated gate and bastions, is shown from two to eight feet (¼ to 1mm. on the map) to the north of its correct position. The greatest error (six to eight feet) occurs between **W**49 and **W**53. At **W**54 the line as shown and the correct line converge, and **B**18 is practically in its correct position. **W**48 is shown about five feet to the north of its true position. It is correctly placed in relation to the corner turret of the fort (**31**), but the latter should be aligned with its central axis in a more southerly direction.

Bibliography

Publications and other sources of information cited or used in the preparation of this book, with the abbreviations employed in the text and references. The more important sources for the study of Roman London are marked *.

Ammianus Marcellinus: *Rerum Gestarum*, C. U. Clark's edition, Berlin, 1910.

Anthropological Review and Journal, The, London. (*Anthropological Review*.)

Antiquaries Journal, The (the Journal of the Society of Antiquaries of London), Oxford University Press. (*Ant. Journ.*)

Antiquary, The; a Magazine devoted to the Study of the Past, Elliot Stock, London, and J. W. Bouton, New York.

Antiquity, a Quarterly Review of Archaeology, Heffer, Cambridge.

Archaeologia, or Miscellaneous Tracts relating to Antiquity, the Society of Antiquaries of London. (*Arch.*)

Archaeologia Aeliana, the Society of Antiquaries of Newcastle upon Tyne.

Archaeologia Cambrensis, the Cambrian Archaeological Association.

Archaeological Journal, The, the Royal Archaeological Institute, London. (*Arch. Journ.*)

Archaeological Review, The; a Journal of Historic and Pre-historic Antiquities, David Nutt, London. (*Arch. Review*.)

Bell, W. G., Cottrill, F. and Spon, Charles: *London Wall Through Eighteen Centuries*, the Council for Tower Hill Improvement, London, 1937.

Birley, E. B.: *Report on recent Excavations in London; 1. the Midland Bank site, Princes Street, E.C.*, in *Ant. Journ.*, IX (1929), pp. 219–28.

Black, W. H.: *Observations on the Primitive Site, Extent, and Circumvallation of Roman London*, in *Archaeologia*, XL (1866), pp. 41–58.

*Bruce-Mitford, R. L. S. (ed.): *Recent Archaeological Excavations in Britain*, Routledge and Kegan Paul, London, 1956.

Builder, The; an Illustrated Weekly Magazine for the Architect, Engineer, Archaeologist, Constructor, and Artist, London.

Carson, R. A. G. and Kent, J. P. C.: *Constantinian Hoards and other Studies in the Later Roman Bronze Coinage*, in *Numismatic Chronicle*, 6th ser., XVI (1956), pp. 83–161.

City Sewers Plans: in the Record Office, Guildhall, Corporation of London.

Collingwood, R. G. and Myres, J. N. L.: *Roman Britain and the English Settlements*, 2nd edition, Oxford University Press, 1937.

Cook, N.: *The Old Wall of the City of London*, the Corporation of London, 1951.

Corder, P.: *The Reorganisation of the Defences of Romano-British Towns in the Fourth Century*, in *Arch. Journ.*, CXII (1955), pp. 20–42.

*Cottrill, F.: *A Bastion of the Town Wall of London, and the Sepulchral Monument of the Procurator Julius Classicianus*, in *Ant. Journ.*, XVI (1936), pp. 1–7.

Cottrill, F.: unpublished excavation notes and plans.

Cottrill, F.: see also Bell, W. G., Cottrill, F. and Spon, Charles.

Cumont, F.: *The Mysteries of Mithra*, translated by T. J. McCormack, Open Court Publishing Company, Chicago: Kegan Paul, Trench, Trubner and Co., London, 1910.

Dawe, D. and Oswald, A.: *11 Ironmonger Lane, the Story of a Site in the City of London*, Hutchinson, London, 1952.

Dio Cassius: *Roman History*.

*Dunning, G. C.: *Two Fires of Roman London*, in *Ant. Journ.*, XXV (1945), pp. 48–77.

Dunning, G. C.: unpublished field notes and plans.

Fitzstephen, William: *Descriptio Nobilissimae Civitatis Londoniae* (introduction to *Vita Sancti Thomae*), before 1183, quoted in Stow, J.: *A Survey of London*, Kingsford edition, Vol. II, pp. 219–29.

Fox, G. E.: *Notes on a recent discovery of part of the Roman Wall of London*, in *Archaeologia*, LII (1891), pp. 609–16.

Gentleman's Magazine, The, London. (*Gent. Mag.*)

Gillam, J. P. and MacIvor, I.: *The Temple of Mithras at Rudchester*, in *Archaeologia Aeliana*, 4th ser., XXXII, pp. 176–219.

Gough, anonymous letter to (from Jackson, J.), *Account of the discoveries in digging a Sewer in Lombard Street and Birchin Lane, 1786*, in *Archaeologia*, VIII (1787), pp. 116–32.

*Grimes, W. F.: *Excavations in the City of London*, in *Recent Archaeological Excavations in Britain*, edited by R. L. S. Bruce-Mitford, Routledge and Kegan Paul, London, 1956.

*Grimes, W. F.: annual summaries of the work of the Roman and Mediaeval London Excavation Council in the *Journal of Roman Studies*.

Guildhall Library Annual Reports. (*Guildhall Library Report*.)

Guildhall Museum: *Catalogue of the Collection of London Antiquities in the Guildhall Museum*, 2nd edition, 1908.

Guildhall Museum publications: *Discoveries on Walbrook, 1949–50; Finds in Roman London, 1949–52; Sculptures from the Temple of Mithras, Walbrook; Small Finds from Walbrook, 1954–1955*.

*Guildhall Museum: observations by Museum staff, recorded in Excavation Note-books (*G.M.*) or Excavations Register (*E.R.*).

Harben, H. A.: *A Dictionary of London; being notes topographical and historical relating to the streets and principal buildings in the City of London*, Herbert Jenkins, London, 1918.

Harden, D. B., ed.: *Dark Age Britain*, Studies presented to E. T. Leeds, Methuen and Co., London, 1956.

Haverfield, F.: *On two Marble Sculptures and a Mithraic Relief of the Roman Period found in London*, in *Archaeologia*, LX (1906), pp. 43–8.

Hawkes, C. F. C. and Hull, M. R.: *Camulodunum*, Report of the Research Committee of the Society of Antiquaries of London, No. 14, Oxford University Press, 1947.

Herbert, W.: *History of St. Michael, Crooked Lane*, London, 1831.

*Hodge, H.: Plans and drawings of Basilica, etc., in Guildhall Library.

Home, G.: *Roman London, A.D. 43–457*, Eyre and Spottiswoode, London, 1948.

Home, G.: article in *Morning Post*, 27 January 1927.

Hume, I. Noel: *A Roman Bath Building in Cheapside*, privately printed for Sun Life Assurance Society, London, 1956.

Hume, I. Noel: unpublished notes and plans in Guildhall Museum.

Illustrated London News, The. (*Illus. Lond. News*.)

Jackson, J.: see Gough, anonymous letter to.

Jahrbuch des Römisch-Germanischen Zentralmuseums, Mainz.

Journal of Roman Studies, The, containing annual summaries of finds in Roman Britain, the Society for the Promotion of Roman Studies, London. (*J.R.S.*)

Journal of the British Archaeological Association, The. (*J.B.A.A.*)

Kelsey, R.: *A Description of the Sewers of the City of London*, a MS. book in the charge of the City Engineer.

Kempe, A. J.: *Account of various Roman Antiquities discovered on the site of the Church of St. Michael, Crooked Lane, and in Eastcheap, in forming the northern approaches of the New London Bridge*, in *Archaeologia*, XXIV (1832), pp. 190–202.

Kenyon, K. M.: *Excavations in Southwark, 1945–1947*, Research Papers of the Surrey Archaeological Society, No. 5, 1959.

Knight, C.: *London*, London, 1875–7.

Knight, W., letter from: *Account of some Antiquities discovered in excavating for the foundations of London Bridge; and of the ancient Northern Embankment of the Thames in its neighbourhood*, in *Archaeologia*, XXV (1834), pp. 600–2.

*Lambert, F.: *Recent Roman Discoveries in London*, in *Archaeologia*, LXVI (1915), pp. 225–74.

*Lambert, F.: *Some Recent Excavations in London*, in *Archaeologia*, LXXI (1921), pp. 55–112.

Lane-Fox, Col. A. (afterwards General Pitt-Rivers): *A description of certain piles found near London Wall and Southwark, possibly the remains of pile buildings,* in *Anthropological Review,* V (1867), pp. lxxi ff.

Leland, J.: *Collectanea,* ed. Hearne, 1715.

Lethaby, W. R.: *Londinium, Architecture and the Crafts,* Duckworth and Co., London, 1923.

Lethbridge, T. C.: *The Anglo-Saxon Settlement in Eastern England,* in *Dark Age Britain.* See Harden, D. B., ed.

*London and Middlesex Archaeological Society's Transactions and Proceedings. (London and Middx. Arch. Soc. Trans.)

Maitland, W.: *The History and Survey of London from its Foundation to the Present Time,* London, 1756.

Mann, J. C.: *The Administration of Roman Britain,* in *Antiquity,* Vol. 35 (1961), pp. 316–20.

Margary, I. D.: *Roman Roads in Britain,* Vol. I, Phoenix House Ltd., London, 1955.

Marsden, P. R. V.: unpublished notes and plans in Guildhall Museum.

Merrifield, R.: *Coins from the Bed of the Walbrook and their Significance,* in *Ant. Journ.,* XLII (1962), pp. 38–52.

Merrifield, R.: *The Lime Street (1952) Hoard of Barbarous Radiates,* in *Numismatic Chronicle,* 6th Series, XV (1955), pp. 113–24.

Morgan, T.: *Romano-British Mosaic Pavements,* Whiting and Co., London, 1886. *(Rom. Brit. Mosaic Pavements.)*

Myres, J. N. L.: *Romano-Saxon Pottery,* in *Dark Age Britain.* See Harden, D. B., ed.

*Norman, P.: *Roman and later Remains found during the Excavations on the Site of Newgate Prison, 1903–1904,* in *Archaeologia,* LIX (1904), pp. 125–42.

*Norman, P. and Reader, F. W.: *Recent Discoveries in connexion with Roman London,* in *Archaeologia,* LX (1906), pp. 169–250.

*Norman, P. and Reader, F. W.: *Further Discoveries relating to Roman London, 1906–12,* in *Archaeologia,* LXIII (1912), pp. 257–344.

Numismatic Chronicle, the Royal Numismatic Society, London.

Old Lady of Threadneedle Street, The, (Bank of England Magazine).

Oswald, A. H.: unpublished notes and plans.

Oswald, A. H.: see also Dawe, D. and Oswald, A.

Oswald, Felix: see Pryce, T. Davies, and Oswald, F.

Pitt-Rivers, Lt.-Gen.: see Lane-Fox, Col. A.

*Price, J. E.: *A Description of the Roman Tessellated Pavement found in Bucklersbury; with Observations on Analogous Discoveries,* London, 1870.

*Price, J. E.: *On a Bastion of London Wall, or Excavations in Camomile Street, Bishopsgate,* London, 1880.

*Price, J. E.: *Roman Antiquities illustrated by Remains recently discovered on the Site of the National Safe Deposit Company's Premises, Mansion House, London*, London, 1873. (*Rom. Antiq. Nat. Safe Deposit Co's Premises.*)

Proceedings of the Society of Antiquaries, the Society of Antiquaries of London. (*Proc. Soc. Ant.*)

*Pryce, T. Davies, and Oswald, F.: *Roman London: Its initial occupation as evidenced by early types of Terra Sigillata*, in *Archaeologia*, LXXVIII (1928), pp. 73–110.

Reader, F. W.: see Norman, P. and Reader, F. W.

Revue Archéologique, Presses Universitaires de France, Paris.

Richmond, I. A.: *Roman Britain, The Pelican History of England I*, Penguin Books Inc., Baltimore, and Penguin Books Ltd., Harmondsworth, 2nd edition, 1963.

Riley, W. E., and Gomme, L.: *A Ship of the Roman Period discovered on the site of the New County Hall*, London County Council, 1912.

Rivet, A. L. F.: *Town and Country in Roman Britain*, Hutchinson University Library, 1958.

*Royal Commission on Historical Monuments (England): *An Inventory of the Historical Monuments in London, Vol. III. Roman London*, H.M. Stationery Office, 1928. (*R.C.H.M.*)

Smith, Charles Roach: *Catalogue of the Museum of London Antiquities*, printed by subscription, London, 1854.

*Smith, Charles Roach: *Illustrations of Roman London*, printed by subscription, and not published, London, 1859. (*Illus. Rom. Lond.*)

Smith, Charles Roach: *Observations on Roman Remains recently found in London*, in *Archaeologia*, XXIX (1842), pp. 145–66.

Smith, Charles Roach: *Further Observations on Roman Remains discovered in London*, ibid., pp. 267–74.

Smith, Charles Roach: *On some Roman Bronzes discovered in the bed of the Thames in January, 1837*, in *Archaeologia*, XXVIII (1840), pp. 38–46.

Smith, J. T.: *Antient Topography of London*, London, 1815.

Stanfield, J. A.: *Further examples of Claudian 'terra sigillata' in London*, in *Ant. Journ.*, X (1930), pp. 114–25.

Stow, John: *A Survey of London*, 1603, C. L. Kingsford ed., Oxford University Press, 1908. See also Strype, J.

Strype, J.: edition of Stow's *Survey of London*, 1755.

Suetonius Tranquillus, Gaius: *De Vita Caesarum—Divus Claudius.*

Tacitus, Cornelius: *Annals*, III, XIV.

Tacitus, Cornelius: *De Vita Agricolae.*

Tite, William: *a Descriptive Catalogue of the Antiquities found in the Excavations at the New Royal Exchange, preserved in the Museum of the Corporation of London, preceded by an Introduction containing an*

Account of their Discovery, with some Particulars and Suggestions relating to Roman London, printed for the use of the Members of the Corporation of the City of London, 1848. (*Tite, Cat. Antiq. Roy. Exch.*)

Tite, William: *Notes on the Discoveries of Roman Remains which have taken place at various times in London,* in Archaeologia, XXXIX (1863), pp. 491–502.

Toynbee, J. M. C.: *Art in Britain under the Romans,* Oxford University Press, 1964.

Toynbee, J. M. C.: *Art in Roman Britain,* Phaidon Press, London, 1962.

Toynbee, J. M. C.: *A Silver Casket and Strainer from the Walbrook Mithraeum in the City of London,* Leiden, 1963.

Tylor, A.: *New Points in the History of Roman Britain, as illustrated by discoveries at Warwick Square, in the City of London,* in Archaeologia, XLVIII (1884), pp. 221–48.

Viatores, The: *Roman Roads in the South-East Midlands,* Victor Gollancz, London, 1964.

Victoria History of London, The, Vol. I, Constable and Co., London, 1909. (*V.C.H. London.*)

Vitruvius Pollio: *De Architectura.*

Vulliamy, C. E.: *The Archaeology of Middlesex and London,* Methuen and Co., London, 1930.

Waddington, Q.: unpublished notes in Guildhall Museum.

Webster, G.: *The Roman Military Advance under Ostorius Scapula,* in Arch. Journ., CXV (1958), pp. 49–98.

*Wheeler, R. E. M.: Introduction to Report of Royal Commission on Historical Monuments on *Roman London.* (See Royal Commission on Historical Monuments.)

*Wheeler, R. E. M.: *London in Roman Times,* London Museum Catalogues: No. 3, 1930.

Wheeler, R. E. M.: *'Old England', Brentford,* in Antiquity, III (1929), pp. 20–32.

Wren, Christopher: *Parentalia, or Memoirs of the Family of the Wrens,* London, 1750.

Index

333

St. Peter's Alley, 254 (**221**)
St. Peter's upon Cornhill, 62, 78 n. 60, 252 (**215**)
St. Swithin's Church, 123, 271 (**267, 268**)
St. Swithin's House, Walbrook, 37–8, 270–1 (**263–6**), *Pl.* 15
St. Swithin's Lane, 271 (**266**)
St. Vedast House *see* Foster Lane
Samian pottery, 29, 37, 46, 89, 208 (**64, 65**), 211 (**75**), 242 (**179**), 252 (**214**), 259 (**232**), 269 (**262**), 277 (**285**), *Pl.* 118–19
Scotts Yard, 273 (**272, 273**)
Seething Lane, 143, 294 (**350**)
Selbourne House, Ironmonger Lane *see* Ironmonger Lane, No. 11
Serapis, head of, 62, *Pl.* 76
Sermon Lane, 213 (**81**)
Severus, Septimius, 50, 51, 52
Shelley House *see* Noble Street, No. 1
Shoe Lane, 95
silver box from temple of Mithras, 20, 27 n.29, 64, 163, *Pl.* 81–3
Silver Street, 99, 197 (**29**)
Sir John Cass College, 157, 303 (**W15, W16**), 321 (**B5**)
Skinner's Lane, 225 (**122**)
small finds from the Walbrook, 5, 93, 231 (**142**), 237 (**160**), 239 (**168**), *Pl.* 125–9, 131–40
Smith, C. Roach, 3, 4, 107–8, 110, 162
Smithfield, West, 95
Society of Antiquaries of London, 12, 15
Southwark, 22, 60, 82, 89, 116–17, 146, 163
spear-head, inscribed, 264 (**246**), *Pl.* 98
Stane Street, 117, 163
stili, 93, *Pl.* 105, 138
Stilicho, 67
"Stony Jack" (G. F. Lawrence), 9
Stow, John, 2
Strand Lane, "Roman bath" in, 164 n.4
streams, 87–9, 189 (**1**), 192 (**12, 13**), 204 (**50, 53**), 207 (**63**), 208 (**65**), 214 (**89**), 226–8 (**127, 128,**

130–2, **134**), 229 (**136**), 232–3 (**146, 147**), 245 (**192**), 256 (**226**), 278 (**287**), 303 (W16), 306 (W29), *Pl.* 18, 19. *See also* Walbrook, river
street plan, modern, 2, 26 n. 3
street plan, Roman, 13, 22, 39, 114, 116, 117–18, 120, 122–6, 128, 130. *See also* roads
Suetonius Tranquillus, 35
Suffolk Lane, 145–6, 275 (**278–80**)
Sun Life Assurance Society, Cheapside *see* Cheapside, Nos. 100–16

Tacitus, Cornelius, 36, 38
Temple Court, No. 11, Queen Victoria Street, 20, 160
Temple House *see* Cannon Street
temple of Mithras *see* Mithras, temple of
temples, 143–4, 260 (**235**)
temple to divinity of the Emperor, 44, 143, 276–7 (**284**)
terracing, 85, 220 (**109, 110**), 222 (**114**), 223 (**116**), *Pl.* 29
Thames, river, 1, 3, 29, 33, 49, 85, 269 (**262**)
Theodosius, 65–6
Theodosius I (the Great), 66–7, 79 n. 76
Threadneedle Street, 243 (**185**), *Pl.* 59; Nos. 28–9, 243 (**184**); No. 53 (site of French Protestant Church), 243 (**183**); No. 63 (formerly No. 62), 142, 243 (**182**)
Three Tuns, No. 36 Jewry Street, 157, 303 (**W17**)
Throgmorton Avenue, No. 2, 231 (**143**)
Throgmorton Street, 238 (**166**)
tiles, roofing, 132
tiles, stamped *see* bricks, stamped
"Times, The", office of, 316 (**W61**)
Toc H *see* Trinity Square, Nos. 40–1
Tokenhouse Yard, 237 (**159**), 238 (**165**)
tombs, 298 (**363**)
tombstones, 40, 41–2, 162, 320 (**G,10 B2**), *Pl.* 4–6, 96, 100